The Contemporary TORAH

A Gender-Sensitive Adaptation of the JPS Translation

Revising Editor
David E. S. Stein

Consulting Editors
Adele Berlin, Ellen Frankel, and Carol L. Meyers

2006 · 5766
THE JEWISH PUBLICATION SOCIETY
Philadelphia

NPJS translation © 1962, 1985, 1999
Exodus, Leviticus, Numbers, Deuteronomy adapted by URJ Press 2005 and used with permission
Genesis adapted by The Jewish Publication Society 2006

The Jewish Publication Society
2100 Arch Street
Philadelphia, PA 19103

www.jewishpub.org

Design and composition by David E. S. Stein
Manufactured in the United States of America

06 07 08 09 10   10 9 8 7 6 5 4 3 2 1

LIBRARY OF CONGRESS CATALOGING-IN-PUBLICATION DATA

Bible. O.T. Pentateuch. English. Stein. 2006
   The contemporary Torah : a gender-sensitive adaptation of the JPS translation : based on the 1962 JPS Torah translation and JPS Torah commentaries / revising editor, David E.S. Stein ; senior Bible consultant, Carol Meyers.
      p. cm.

ISBN-10: 0-8276-0796-2   ISBN-13: 978-0-8276-0796-5

I. Stein, David E. II. Meyers, Carol L. III. Bible. O.T. Pentateuch. English, Jewish Publication Society. 1962.

BS1223.S744 2006
222′.105208–dc22

                                                              2006040608

Contents

PREFACE

Translation is an abbreviated form of exegesis:
exegesis that does not have the space to explain
or justify itself.   —Adele Berlin

THE PRESENT TRANSLATION adapts the New Jewish Publication Society (NJPS) version only with respect to *social gender*.[1] To keep the presentation simple, this edition recasts the invaluable footnotes of the NJPS translation committee as endnotes; such notes are now called out in the translation via asterisks (*). As revising editor, I have added new endnotes that relate to social gender; such notes are called out via circules (°).[2]

THE NEED FOR A GENDER-SENSITIVE VERSION

My adaptation effort has followed the pioneering trail of the translation committee that produced NJPS. The driving force behind NJPS was the late Harry M. Orlinsky, who served as editor-in-chief of its first section, *The Torah*.[3] He stated with justifiable pride that NJPS was "the first translation of the Hebrew Bible that went behind all previous translations"—looking afresh at the original Hebrew text, in order to take full account of the tremendous advances in knowledge about the ancient Near East made possible by the modern study of the distant past. At the same time as it drew upon the findings of history and science, it took stock of those traditional rabbinic interpretations of the biblical text that accorded with the translators' plain-sense approach.

Orlinsky explained that NJPS relied rigorously on philology: "the meaning and nuance of every word and phrase and verse, in context, was considered anew and carefully before its equivalent in the idiom of the English language was decided upon." Its translators did not strive, as some do, to show how ambiguous the original text is, nor to convey how the text made meaning via rhetorical strategems. Rather, their aims were to convey the plain-sense meaning; to value clarity of expression; to employ idioms familiar to the contemporary audience; and to emphasize a religious message.

That distinctive set of characteristics has made NJPS the ideal basis for a gender-sensitive translation.

Inherent Strengths of NJPS

In 1969, Orlinsky authored another pioneering work, *Notes on the New Translation of the Torah* (1969)—"the first time that a committee responsible for an official translation of the Bible [had] attempted a public and systematic exposition. . . of its labors and reasoning." Shortly thereafter, he began to address a new topic in translation: gender. Lecturing widely, he would point out that the best-known Bible versions had too often rendered certain Hebrew nouns mechanically as referring to men—thus making women appear relatively invisible. For example, the Decalogue in the classic King James Version (KJV) of 1611 had God "visiting the iniquity of the fathers (*'avot*) upon the children" (Exod. 20:5) even though logic dictated—and other biblical passages indicated—that also in view were mothers and *their* sins. Orlinsky saw such customary renderings as misrepresenting the biblical text; and in his view, the solution lay in a contextual, idiomatic approach to translation—of which NJPS was the exemplar. (NJPS reads: "visiting the guilt of the parents upon the children.") He would reiterate that its philological approach has no inherent ideological bias, but rather "seeks to determine within the context and in the light of pertinent data elsewhere in the Bible and in related extra-biblical societies what the author meant to convey."

Where the Torah's language suggested a neutral sense, NJPS avoided misleadingly ascribing gender, not only by rendering inclusively some "male" nouns, but also by rendering masculine inflections and pronouns idiomatically rather than literally. Thus, for example, what KJV had rendered as "thou shalt not wrest the judgment of thy poor in *his* cause" appears in NJPS as "you shall not subvert the rights of your needy in *their* disputes" (Exod. 23:6).

In short, NJPS inadvertently led the way among contemporary translations in "gender-sensitive" rendering.

Limitations of NJPS

Despite its overall strengths, the gender ascriptions in NJPS can still be called into question on a number of counts. I will now discuss, as two distinct categories, how NJPS handled the biblical text's references to human beings and to divine beings.[4]

REFERENCES TO HUMAN BEINGS

Like every translation, NJPS contains some internal inconsistencies. For example, NJPS renders *'avot* in the same phrases and in similar contexts using terms with differing social-gender senses— NJPS reads "parents" in Exod. 20:5 (as noted above) yet "visiting the iniquity of *fathers* upon children" in Num. 14:18.

Meanwhile, at times the NJPS translators rendered in unduly male terms. For example, the Hebrew wording in Numbers 14 is ambiguous as to who is to be punished for brazen faithlessness: the men, or the people as a whole. Seeking the plain sense, the translators quite reasonably opted for the latter view (in contrast to some classic midrashic readings). Yet to render two Hebrew phrases that do not themselves specify gender, they employed English idioms at odds with their overall interpretation. We read that Moses urges an incensed God not to "slay the people to a *man*" (14:15), and that God then condemns a generation of Israelites to die in the wilderness "to the last *man*" (14:35).

Ironically, in some other cases NJPS reads neutrally where a *non-*inclusive rendering was actually called for. Three examples should suffice. First, NJPS could render *yeled* contextually as "lad, boy" (e.g., Gen. 4:23, 37:30); yet it unconventionally cast the plural *yeladim* as "children" in Gen. 32:23 even though in that context the term can refer only to Jacob's sons (not to his daughter, Dinah). Similarly, NJPS rendered the noun *'edah* five different ways in the Torah; yet its rendering states that Moses was instructed to take a census of the Israelite "community" (*'edah*, Num. 1:2) although ancient censuses counted men only. And unlike prior translations, NJPS renders *banim* as "children" in Lev. 10:13–15, although the topic is donations that are restricted to priests—i.e., Aaron's "sons."

The Need for a Gender-Sensitive Version   vii

When it comes to women's biological functions, NJPS sometimes echoes older translations by resorting to idioms that are hardly part of contemporary English. Such wording adds a touch of strangeness to the translation that is not part of the original text. For example, NJPS four times describes a pregnant woman as being "with child."

In a number of other instances, the NJPS translators appear to have based their rendering on an inaccurate understanding of social gender in the biblical setting. For example, where God referred to Abram's eventual death as going "to your *'avot*" (Gen. 15:15; cf. 47:30), NJPS seems to have relied on a modern scholarly opinion that the Israelites counted only their male forebears ("fathers") as kin. Yet that view appears to be based on an etymological fallacy, meanwhile ignoring ample circumstantial evidence that suggests ancient Israelites also viewed their deceased mother and even her forebears as kin.[5] The weight of the evidence argues for rendering *'avot* inclusively here as "ancestors" or the like.

Last but not least, the NJPS translators employed the standard English style of using male nouns and pronouns where a neutral sense was meant, which closely correlates with Hebrew grammatical structure. Unfortunately, this has proven ambiguous with regard to social gender: it can be difficult to tell whether "man," "kinsmen," "he," "his," and "him" connotes only male social gender or an inclusive meaning. In a sense-for-sense translation like NJPS, the standard style can confuse readers. The very nature of NJPS as contextually precise argues against readers' taking its male language as neutral; we would reasonably expect male terms to carry a male gender sense.

Contemporary readers make their way through a translation at a vast remove from the biblical setting. Many of us misconstrue that setting, perceiving the translated Bible as more male-oriented than the original audience probably perceived the Hebrew text to be. We imagine the Israelite past as having been so "patriarchal" that, for example, in the context of ritual animal sacrifices and male-only priests, some of us infer that women were not part of the scene. Thus when NJPS relates that if someone eats sacrificial meat while ritually impure, "that *person* shall be cut off from *his* kin" (Lev. 7:20b), we may take the word "his" not as gender neutral but as referring to a male—discounting "person" as if it were a falsely generic term. That is, we may well understand NJPS to mean "that *man* shall be cut off from *his* kin." In such ways the standard English style has put a stumbling block before readers.

REFERENCES TO DIVINE BEINGS

To refer to God, the Torah had used grammatically masculine language; as was typical of English translations, NJPS employed corresponding masculine terms in its rendering. Given that a Jewish translation would have reflected the standard belief that God *transcends* human gender categories, the translators presumably meant their masculine wording in a gender-neutral sense.[6]

The present adaptation remains a Jewish translation; that is, the publisher presumes that most of this book's readers will be seeking to reckon with the non-gendered God of (present-day) Judaism, which places the Torah at its center. And such readers have grounds for discontent with the NJPS God-language. Many are well aware that "lord" is a male title by common usage; for them, rendering God's personal name as "the LORD" can function like wearing male sunglasses to view the invisible deity: "I'm not sure what I'm seeing—but it appears to be masculine." Furthermore, the translation's masculine pronouns may conjure for them an image of a male deity, even though as a matter of logic or belief they would insist that God has no gender. In short, the NJPS style hinders their appreciation of the Torah text.

At the same time, many scholars of Israelite history now believe that our ancient text's masculine inflections and occasional male imagery refer to what everyone at the time understood to be a *male* god—which would have gone without saying. If so, then the most *historically accurate* way to render the Torah's God-language today would be in masculine terms. Such a view favors retaining the NJPS wording but construing it as truly male language.

Yet it can be argued that the Torah promoted to its original audience a deity "beyond gender." Its text never ascribes to God anatomical sex features or sexual activity, in contrast to some ancient Near Eastern literature about high gods. Only in poetry and other clearly figurative passages does the text depict God in male social status terms. It meanwhile cautions against taking

The Need for a Gender-Sensitive Version

such images too literally—stating that a male or female form mis-represents God (Deut. 4:16)—as if to say: the reality of God is be-yond such terms. Further, grammatically masculine language would have been the only way to refer to a *non*-gendered deity.[7] And con-trary to conventional wisdom, the text seems to be written as if the audience was expecting definite signals before ascribing gen-der. In short, the Torah's silence about God's gender may well be a meaningful one, even when viewed in its original setting.

Finally, although I suspect that few readers have considered the matter, the same question regarding the depiction of God's gender also applies to that of the Torah's other divine beings, namely angels. The NJPS translators appear to have presumed that in the ancient world all of God's divine agents were understood to be male, but there is reason to doubt that presumption.[8]

To mention shortcomings of NJPS is not to censure what remains as the Jewish translation of choice for those who value contex-tual precision and modern idiom. Rather, my point is that gender is such a complex and far-reaching cultural category that NJPS could not do it justice without a comprehensive and focused review of gender ascriptions both in the ancient text and in its translation.

I undertook such a review as the core of the present project. It showed me where to redress some NJPS oversights, how to take advantage of more recent scholarship, and where to reduce im-precision in NJPS's English style. I then proceeded to test (and hopefully prove) Orlinsky's 1991 assertion that "the English lan-guage has resources that allow a translator faithfully to translate ... biblical texts and be inclusive where the text is inclusive, and exclusive where the original is exclusive."

ADAPTATION METHODOLOGY

General Considerations

According to Professor Orlinsky, the charge presented to the orig-inal NJPS translators was "to render the Hebrew text as they be-lieved the original author of that text meant it to be understood" by the original audience. The present project took up the same challenge. (Of course, readers can never be sure about authorial intent, but we can make high-probability educated guesses in many cases—and narrow the range of possibilities in other instances.) The revising editor's task was also basically unchanged: to go back to the original Hebrew text and then stick to it as closely as possible while conveying its plain sense in idiomatic English.

I designed the adaptation effort to meet Orlinsky's twin goals of accuracy and clarity in the portrayal of social gender. I began with a comprehensive and scholarly analysis of the Torah's ascriptions of gender, taking nothing for granted. Often I and the consulting editors spent many hours (and sometimes days) in order to fully grasp the gender implications of a single Hebrew word—even a term that appeared only once or applied to the most minor of characters. Next came a review of how well NJPS conveyed the Torah's gender ascription in each passage. Where I found warrant to modify NJPS, I tried to employ the same rendering techniques as those that the NJPS translators had used as a matter of course.[9] Not for nothing have I quipped that this adaptation is "just like NJPS, only more so."

By now it should be clear that this adaptation is *not* a "gender-neutral" translation. On the contrary, it pays close attention to the nuances of social gender in the Torah. It reflects the depictions of an ancient text composed for an audience in which gender mattered a great deal. As revising editor I did not pass judgment on how Israelite society and the Torah constructed gender. My renderings neither commend nor condemn the ancient perception of the text. They take the text on its own terms, and they merely attempt to convey it accurately. (Where I know the social-gender sense to be disputed, I did sometimes note my interpretation.)

WHICH TEXT AND WHICH AUDIENCE?

This project has taken as the "text in question" the complete Torah that we have today, as preserved by the Tiberian Masoretes. With regard to establishing the text, I set aside the reconstructions of earlier source documents and of the text's historical development that have often preoccupied modern critical scholarship.[10] For at some point, the Torah's composer(s) promulgated the set of full five books as we know them, such that the audience would be inclined to make sense of a given passage by relating it to preceding passages and looking for coherence among them. The readers or listeners who were in the mind of the composer(s) at that point of "publication" are what I refer to as the "original audience."

My working definition of the text presumes that changes to the text have been inconsequential since the original audience encountered it. (Rarely does the range of disagreement among the Torah's Masoretic textual witnesses affect the meaning of a given verse.)

CONSTRUING AUTHORIAL INTENT

To this editor's eye, the Torah is a carefully crafted text. Presumably it was consciously formulated the way it is, rather than other conceivable ways. On that basis, I have assumed that what the text says *is* the intention of its composer(s). Careful examination of the text can then highlight the implicit word choices and thus point toward the intended message. This is what the scholar of exegesis Paul R. Noble has called "interpreting a text in relation to the milieu of its production."

At the same time, such weighing of the Torah's language is not enough by itself. Every communiqué also takes for granted a certain awareness among its audience: what "goes without saying" is at least as important as what is stated. Persuasive writing involves making judgments about how the target audience will construe a text (given what they will predictably bring to the act of reading) and then fashioning the text accordingly. Therefore, the composer(s) of the Torah surely had a mental image of the target audience that conditioned what and how much to say.

The very nature of texts thus prompted me to construct a mental model of the Torah's original audience—its worldview, assumptions, and concerns. What would they predictably *take as given*, especially with regard to gender? The closer that my mental model could match the one that the Torah's composer(s) had in mind while composing the text, the more accurate my perception of the original message would be.[11]

I reconstructed that long-ago mental model of the original audience by looking first of all to the Torah itself as a work of literature. Like all texts, the Torah includes many clues as to how it is intended to be read, and as to the social world that it presumes.[12] In addition, I drew upon the findings of scholarship in various fields: philology; archeology; Egyptology, Assyriology, and the study of other nearby ancient Near Eastern literatures, documents, and inscriptions; semantics and cognitive linguistics; social history; and social science—particularly the ethnography of present-day cultures with ecological and economic bases and kinship-oriented structures similar to those of ancient Israel. Comprehending the construction of gender in the mind of an ancient audience often required lengthy investigation into a wide variety of specific topics. Much of the information I found useful is of recent vintage—it had not been available to the NJPS translators.

With my model of the original audience in hand, I employed it to grasp why the text was written the way it was. Again, my aim was to think like the text's composer(s). I situated myself the way that an editor looks over an author's shoulder, critically assessing from a marketing-communications perspective a draft text's effect on its target audience.[13] In this way I determined what the finished text had meant to say.

Let me emphasize that the goal was *not* to establish how the Torah's actual audience historically construed the text. Whether anyone ever actually took the Torah as intended was the function of a broad range of factors beyond editorial control.

GENDER ASCRIPTION AND READING STRATEGY

All texts are ambiguous in many respects—including in their social-gender ascriptions.[14] Readers must necessarily employ some strategy for resolving that ambiguity as they strive to make sense of a text.

The Bible provides seven factors that its audience can take into account in order to construe social gender. Those factors are: inflection, status, role, anatomy, name, reflection, and outright designation. *Inflection* refers to distinctions in grammatical gender that correlate somewhat with social gender. *Status* means the referent's position in the social structure. *Role* refers to the expectations, rights, duties, and artifacts attached to a particular status. *Anatomy* refers to the physical characteristics associated with gender. *Name* is the character's name, including the "son of" or "daughter of" portion of a patronymic (or occasionally a matronymic). *Reflection* refers to how other characters treat the referent in question. And *outright designation* is when the narrator labels the referent in question as male or female.

Rarely, if ever, are all of those seven factors present in a single passage. The most definite ones are also the least common. The rest are not conclusive on their own. Given only incomplete data, the reader must usually infer the social gender via a kind of triangulation, combining the information from more than one factor. (A Hebrew-speaking audience usually reaches such a conclusion without conscious reflection.)

In determining the plain sense of the Torah, I presumed a first reading that proceeded from the start of the book—as opposed to re-reading in light of further information revealed only later in the text. However, I presumed that the audience would reliably withhold judgment about how to construe a noun at least until the end of the sentence in which it appeared, particularly if it was followed by a qualifying phrase. I also presumed that the audience would read for coherence, expecting a consistency of characterization as is typical of literature both ancient and modern.

LINGUISTIC AMBIGUITIES AND IMPERATIVES

The denizens of the ancient Near East characterized nearly all types of interpersonal relationships in terms of kinship. They regularly referred to someone unrelated by blood as "father" or "mother" or "brother" or "sister" or "son." They did not always use such terms with gender concord. For example, a king might describe himself as a "father and mother" to his subjects, or a hymn might refer to a god as a "mother," just as a goddess might be described with a male term. The book of Deuteronomy refers to a female Israelite slave explicitly as a "brother" (15:12). Such usages do not indicate that those kinship terms are common-gender nouns, but rather that they are being employed figuratively. Kinship terms had meaning aside from describing a blood relationship. In the Torah, the very high frequency of figurative usage of those terms leaves open the possibility that *any* biblical reference to a gendered kinship term (especially the "male" ones) might include those of the other gender.

One such instance of gender-inclusive usage of the kinship term *'aḥim*—literally "brothers"—occurs just after divine fire has consumed Aaron's two eldest sons. Moses speaks to Aaron and to the latter's surviving sons, instructing them not to mourn, because their priestly tasks takes priority. "But," says Moses, "your *'aḥim*, all the house of Israel, shall bewail the burning" (Lev. 10:6).[15] Now, the ancient Israelite audience would have reliably imagined that their ancestors, while camped all together in the wilderness, "bewailed" the priests' deaths via the involvement of women.[16] Thus in plain-sense terms, the text's composer(s) very likely intended *'aḥim* as gender inclusive.

In the text, not only kinship terms but also other "male" nouns often warrant scrutiny. In Hebrew, masculine grammatical gender is considered normative and thus takes priority when referring either to a definite mixed-gender group or to an indefinite person of unspecified gender (see, e.g., Exod. 21:21; Lev. 13:29–33; Num. 5:7–8; Deut. 13:7–11). A masculine-inflected verb can even refer to a feminine noun, which occurs most often if that verb precedes the noun. Similarly, status or role nouns, even when nominally male, are often used in such a way as to incorporate their female counterparts: the so-called male noun is also a generic term. Indeed, some grammarians prefer to describe it as *unmarked* for gender.

Because of the ambiguity of male nouns and masculine inflections, the original audience did not take them at face value. Therefore, we must now examine such language closely in order to determine precisely what it indicates with regard to social gender.

Ancient "inclusive" language cannot be dismissed as, say, a figment of a post-modern feminist imagination. Rather, it was part of the biblical ethos. This can be seen even in mundane conversation, as when the Bible's characters matter-of-factly refer to females using the grammatically masculine interrogative pronoun *mi* (Gen. 19:12; Job 38:29; Songs 3:6, 6:10, 8:5; Ruth 3:9, 16).

The same consideration applied when faced with wording that had morally binding force. In the book of Judges, the chieftain Jephthah makes an infamous vow to God that refers to its object in grammatically masculine terms. Even so, he and his daughter understand that his vow applies to *her* after she otherwise fulfills its conditions (Judg. 11:30–31, 34–40). It could hardly be true that the text's audience was expected to react by saying, "What a fool Jephthah was! He could have spared his daughter simply by claiming that he had only a *male* in mind when he made his vow." Rather, we can safely infer that the audience shared not only the biblical characters' sense of tragedy but also their understanding of the gender-inclusive sense of indefinite masculine language.

The Bible also expected Israelites to allow for "inclusive" language in the realm of civil law. The book of Jeremiah recounts how the king and Jerusalem's elite covenanted to free their male and female slaves (Jer. 34:8–16). Yet when the narrator quotes God's restatement of the relevant directive to Jeremiah, it reads: "each of you shall let his *brother* Hebrew go free who has been sold to you and has served you for six years—you must set *him* free" (Jer. 34:14, my translation; cf. Deut. 15:12). Grammatically speaking, the divine language is again decidedly masculine (even more so than my rendering reflects). But obviously Jeremiah is supposed to construe that language as gender-inclusive, as is the reader.

GENDER AND THE ORIGINAL AUDIENCE

In the ancient Near East, much of the course of a person's life was determined by facts of birth. One of those salient facts was biological sex characteristics, which prompted an assignment of gender. Gender distinctions helped to keep society running efficiently—predetermining who did what, and who answered to whom. Thus women possessed vital expertise that men seldom (if ever) grasped, while men held vital skills and knowledge that women seldom (if ever) learned. (In frontier rural areas where mere subsistence was the goal, such gender arrangements were probably seen as necessary for survival; in relatively more affluent areas, gender roles may have been more flexible.) Gender mattered in another way as well: as a factor in the definition of personal integrity and reputation. Prestige and influence—the regard of others—depended on social norms that differed by gender. So women and men each learned how to show themselves to be exemplars of their respective genders in somewhat distinct ways. Little wonder that when a baby was born, the first detail disclosed (as is the norm in America today) was whether it was a boy or a girl.[17]

The composer(s) of the Torah could rely upon the fact that as part of the act of reading—of making sense of the text—the original audience would apply their society's familiar gender categories to textual interpretation. That audience was practiced (already from childhood) in sorting out the social-gender sense of language as a matter of course, putting together various clues to the intended gender of a referent. Consider the tale in which a "messenger of יהוה" takes a position in the way of the seer Balaam as he traveled on his she-ass (Num. 22:22b). If the original audience read only that far and took the text on its own terms, then given certain conventions—of syntax, grammar, messenger protocol, and the nature of a divine being—they would have to say that this was not yet a definitively established character with a clear social gender. But by the next verse, when that messenger is further described as standing planted with a "drawn sword" in hand," the audience would reliably perceive the character as definitely male: a sword was an artifact that clearly signaled maleness, as a matter of social and literary convention.

Scholars dispute the date by which the Torah appears to have come together, although the range of disagreement is not great— a mere nine hundred years or so! Yet it turns out that one can draw robust conclusions about the text's gender ascriptions without having to fix a particular date within this period for the first promulgation of the Torah as a completed book. That's because the factors that would have most affected the original audience's gender perceptions of the biblical text remained quite stable over the period in question. Those factors include: more than three-quarters of the population lived in rural villages and engaged in agriculture; the basic social and economic unit was the corporate household, typically headed by a man; people conceived of their society in terms of extended patrilineages traced to a common ancestor; persons situated themselves in their community largely on the basis of kinship and gender roles; individuals derived their sense of identity from their ancestry, and they viewed the well-being of their corporate household as paramount; social order was maintained mainly by a balanced opposition between groups; the threat of war or marauders was always on the horizon, if not at hand, and "real men" knew how to handle a bow and a sword;

men featured not only in military endeavors but also in formal communal leadership; women made major contributions to the economy and to its management; women were highly visible in public communal settings of celebration or mourning; and women could acquire property (including slaves and land) via inheritance, dowry, or purchase.[18] The continuity and uniformity of that social world in these respects also makes it fairly safe to combine extant evidence from different centuries in order to draw conclusions about the construction of gender by the text's original audience.

GENDER AND THE PLAIN SENSE OF THE TEXT

The Bible speaks with many voices. Like great literature in general, it generates meaning not only through its straightforward statements but also via structural devices, motifs, word plays, and other allusive formulations that for attentive readers conjure up connections to many disparate things, such as other passages of the Bible. A plain-sense reading of the text focuses on the meaning of its words in their immediate context. Yet a given term can easily mean more than one thing in context. In a plain-sense translation, as a rule, only one meaning can appear at a time. So what happens in those cases if one meaning is gender neutral while the other is not—which gender sense prevails?

At such points, I defined my charge as deciding which sense the text's original audience would have perceived in the *foreground* of their mental image, as they encountered the word in that particular context. Then I sought to convey the foreground sense of the term. (Background meanings were then literally lost in translation.)

To the ancients, the foreground sense in some social situations would have been more *male* than in today's society. The Torah's original audience experienced as real and concrete their society's gendered social institutions: the male head of the corporate household; the patrilineal inheritance of land; male hegemony in the militia; men as clan elders and kings; etc. In the minds of the audience, textual allusions to such institutions probably conjured up an image of men carrying out their responsibilities as men.

For example, in one account of a communal ritual, God tells Moses to assemble the "whole Israelite *'edah*" and have them "lay their hands" upon the Levites, who are to be dedicated thereby to divine service (Num. 8:9–10). Although *'edah* often means "community," here practical logistical considerations confirm that the plain sense of *'edah* refers (as in some other passages) to a smaller body: the council of elders who customarily acts on behalf of the entire community. (The Hebrew word rendered as "whole" is often not used literally in the Torah.)

The text refers to that council by the broader term because its members are the community's acknowledged embodiment. Yet surely the text's composer(s) knew that the original audience was oriented by their everyday experience to the concrete reality of such an institution, which existed in their own villages and towns. If so, then the text's expansive wording was relying on the audience to place a leadership body in their mental foreground. Thus what appears at first glance to be a gender-inclusive phrase ("whole Israelite community") would probably have been perceived in terms of a body of men.

As translator, I wish to convey to the contemporary audience the implicit male image in the text, out of my commitment to give as precise a picture as possible of the social-gender sense. Therefore in that passage I replaced the NJPS rendering as "whole Israelite community" with "Israelite community leadership."

SOURCES CONSULTED

I enriched my direct encounter with the text by various means, looking most often to the following: the JPS publications *Notes on the New Translation of the Torah* and the *JPS Torah Commentary* series; rabbinic commentators who tended toward plain-sense readings of the text (Saadia, Rashi, Rashbam, Ibn Ezra, Ramban, Radak, Sforno, Benno Jacob); standard grammars and lexicons; feminist interpretations; other contemporary academic scholarship that sought a plain-sense reading of the text as it stands; and—particularly in the latter stages of the project—the products of translators who preceded me (for Genesis, for example: E. A. Speiser, Robert Alter, Stephen Mitchell, and the late Chaim Stern; the New Revised Standard Version; and others). Although these sources seldom addressed precisely the same questions that drove the present project, they often opened up possible readings that

I had not considered, or added to the arguments for or against a particular reading.

My interactions with the consulting editors were also happily fruitful. Carol L. Meyers (the Mary Grace Wilson Professor of Religion at Duke University in North Carolina) served as consulting editor for Genesis and Exodus; Adele Berlin (the Robert H. Smith Professor of Hebrew Bible at the University of Maryland in College Park) did so for Leviticus, Numbers, and Deuteronomy. They advocated the closest possible literal rendering. The third consulting editor was Ellen Frankel (editor-in-chief of The Jewish Publication Society), who meanwhile favored the most felicitous literary rendering. Both approaches complemented and balanced my own strong pull toward contextual precision.

References to Human Beings

PROCEDURE AND EXAMPLES

With regard to the Bible's human characters—the main focus of this project—my goal was to enable a contemporary audience to sit in on an ancient conversation between the Torah's composer(s) and its original audience.[19] The methodology that I used can be boiled down to two steps:

1. *Analyze the Torah's gender ascriptions.* Identify where social gender is at issue or otherwise in the foreground.
2. *Render into idiomatic English.* Map the text's ascriptions of gender onto a contemporary American view of gender.
   a. Where gender is at issue in the Hebrew text, make sure that it is rendered in gendered English; conversely, where gender is not at issue, make sure that the text is rendered in gender-neutral English.[20]
   b. Make sure that the gender ascription will not be misconstrued by the contemporary audience (which brings different gender assumptions to the reading than the ancient audience did).

A relatively simple example will serve to illustrate the procedure. In Gen. 13:7–8, both the narrator and Abram mention quarrels among *ro'im* (NJPS: "herdsmen"). Is social gender at issue—that is, in the foreground?

1. *Analysis.* Based on the following considerations, the text gives no indication that gender is germane.

   Grammar: A masculine plural noun nominally refers to boys or men but can include girls or women as well. The noun's referent is definite (designating specific groups).

   Semantics: The usage of this professional noun is literal rather than figurative.

   Gender roles: The text's ancient audience had no reason to view herding or quarreling as gender-restricted activities. In their society, women did some of both.

   Context: Gender is not at issue in this episode.

   Genre: For narrative, the audience is inclined to construe a noun as concretely as possible.

2. *Rendering.* This noun should be rendered in gender-inclusive terms. Although the NJPS "herdsmen" could have been meant as gender neutral, many readers today would not take it as such, or would at least pause to wonder. For clarity, I substitute a more clearly gender-neutral term. Hence, "herders."[21]

Other sample changes to NJPS as a result of the application of this procedure are shown in the table on page xxxi.

THE ROLE OF LITERARY GENRE

In the preceding narrative example, the genre did not affect the social-gender sense of the term in question. However, genre often does make a difference, as in *legal material*, which by its nature deals in generalizations. Students of law logically expect its rules to apply broadly and consistently unless the particulars of a situation make that case exceptional. Thus whenever men and women act in the same capacity doing something that the society does not mark as uniquely male or female, the rules should apply equally to both.

The Torah couches most of its laws in grammatically masculine indefinite terms. We saw earlier how the book of Jeremiah expected that prophet and the book's audience to construe such language as gender inclusive (Jer. 34:8–16). Further evidence comes from Mesopotamia, because many scholars have concluded that biblical law collections were part of a larger ancient Near Eastern legal tradition. In Mesopotamia, certain activities in which women occasionally participated in real life (such as creditor or slave owner) were treated in the laws only in male terms. Practically speaking, however, the masculine language regulated the situations of women as well as men. It thus appears that the Mesopotamians understood at least some of the masculine language of their laws in a gender-inclusive sense.

Some scholars hold that the male-oriented legal language indicates that the text's composer(s) had only men in view. It would be more accurate to say that the male language reflects the social hierarchy of the ancient Near East, in which the truly autonomous decision makers—those most capable of being held responsible for their actions—were heads of corporate households, who were typically men. Further, those householders would have been held responsible for many of the deeds of their household's members. To that extent, the applicable law is directed not to all men but only to *certain* men, those who have the requisite authority.

The real question, however, is how far the language can be extended given the nature of the case. In a society where women sometimes functioned in the capacities to which the laws refer, the audience would reliably tend to take the legal texts *juridically*. That is, they would construe those laws as if they must apply more broadly than merely to the typical case that a narrow reading might perceive. They would think about the women they knew— their newly married niece whose dowry included a slave, or their widowed sister who had begun to manage her late husband's estate on behalf of their minor son, or the prostitute in the next village who owned a troublesome ox—and expect that the text's civil and criminal laws applied equally to those situations. For that reason, I concluded that in a legal text, for a case in which gender was not at stake, the Torah's ancient audience was inclined to take male language in a neutral sense.

Another genre that affects how the original audience would have construed social gender is *genealogy*. The impact is best illustrated by example. In Gen. 22:24, the narrator states that Abraham is told that his brother Nahor has fathered offspring (a total of twelve), including four by a secondary wife: "And his concubine, whose name was Reumah, also bore [children]: Tebah, Gaham, Tahash, and Maacah." In the Hebrew text of this verse, is social gender at issue or otherwise in the foreground?

1. *Analysis.* Based on the following factors, the text does indicate that gender is germane: the original audience most likely
would have concluded that the first three children listed are
male, whereas the last one is female.

Grammar: In Hebrew, the form of a name does not always
correlate with social gender.[22] On the basis of these
names' form alone, the first three children mentioned in
our verse are probably (but not certainly) male; the fourth
child is probably (but not certainly) female.

Context: These four children are not otherwise referred to
by any noun, pronoun, inflection, or patronymic (*ben* or
bat) that would indicate social gender.

Familiarity and Convention: In the Bible, the name Maacah
is given to five or six other persons—all of whom are
women.[23] The reported societal prominence of some of
those women strongly suggests that the text's original audience was familiar with this name (apart from the Bible);
it also argues against Maacah's meanwhile having been in
Israelite practice a man's name as well.

Placement: Genesis discloses Nahor's progeny only after
Abraham has (by his own hand) nearly lost his only heir,
Isaac. Such literary placement does not in itself require
that all of Nahor's children be sons. If Abraham previously had a daughter he could have solved his heirship
problem through her;[24] but he has none, so the news of
his brother's twelve children (connoting a full comple-
ment) highlights the tenuousness of Abraham's situation
equally well regardless of their gender.

Genre: In a genealogy, the audience is inclined to construe
gender as germane, because lineages are normally stated
in terms of men. Thus names that appear to be male are
presumptively taken as such. However, biblical genealogies of Israelites do occasionally identify a lineage by a
woman's name—especially at the end of a list of seg-
ments.[25] This suggests that a female would come to mind
as a possibility at the end of the list in question.

Nahor's total of twelve offspring might well have
evoked for the original audience certain well-known tribal

confederations that were represented as descended from twelve *brothers*. If so, however, that audience most likely would have perceived as conspicuously *absent* the explicit mention here of "twelve sons" or the like, as well as a national designation such as *bene Nahor* ("sons of Nahor" or "Nahorites"; corresponding to "Ishmaelites" and "Israelites").26 Confederation is not the foreground sense here.

Names in biblical genealogies often represent ethnic groups or settled locales, and these names are no exception. In particular, the Bible twice mentions that the "Maacathites" lived in a territory that bordered that of the Israelite tribe of Manasseh (Deut. 3:14; Josh. 12:5). The Israelites did consider women to be the founders of towns in Manasseh's own territory;26 thus it would not be surprising if they understood Maacah, that neighboring people's eponymous ancestor, also to be a woman. Indeed, one of the many biblical women named Maacah was Manasseh's daughter or daughter-in-law. That high-level Israelite genealogical position seems to allude to the neighboring people—and to our Maacah (in Gen. 22).28

2. *Rendering*. Each child's gender in Gen. 22:24 as perceived by a contemporary reader of NJPS does not match the likely perception of an ancient reader of the Hebrew text. Rather, most contemporary readers would assume that all of the names are male. (In other words, like many other translations, NJPS obscured the presence of a woman here.) To give our readers an experience closer to that of the ancient audience, I have inserted some clarifying words and punctuation.29 Hence: ". . . also bore [sons]—Tebah, Gaham, and Tahash—and [a daughter,] Maacah."

THE ROLE OF PHILOLOGY

Often we found that a common noun's lexical domains significantly affected the social-gender sense in ways not recognized by NJPS or other English translations that we consulted. Of such words, the term *'ish* deserves special mention, because (together with its effective plural, *'anashim*) it is one of the most common nouns in biblical Hebrew—occurring about 570 times in the

Torah and 2200 times throughout the Bible. Lexicographers and grammarians customarily gloss *'ish* as "man," but the import of this assigned equivalence is often misunderstood: the word "man" in English has more than a dozen senses that correspond to the usage of *'ish* in the Bible, and only *one* of those senses is emphatically male. For most instances of *'ish* in the Torah, social gender is not at issue; while its use may correspond to that of "man" in English, the foreground sense is something other than "adult male."

NJPS recognized that *'ish* has a wide semantic range by rendering it variously according to context. In Genesis, for example, I count fourteen different renderings of the singular form alone. Still, in the majority of instances in that book, NJPS renders *'ish* as "man" (and *'anashim* as "men"). A gender-sensitive translation, however, warrants even more precision as to the contextual sense of *'ish*, because the audience for such a translation tends to expect clarity as to which gender is in view. To avoid giving the wrong impression, my adaptation restricts the use of "man" to mean "adult male," employing other words to cover the additional senses of *'ish* that traditionally are also rendered as "man."[30] This policy has turned out to be far-reaching: the present adaptation employs the words "man" or "men" only about a third as often as *The Torah* of NJPS. (See also the last section of the table on p. xxxi.)

That difference is not only dramatic but also revealing. It demonstrates that the Torah did not constantly emphasize social gender and maleness—as readers of NJPS (not to mention a more literal translation) might imagine. What the biblical text is attending to most often are matters of social roles, social station, and the like. While the Torah frequently refers to men, their social gender is supposed to be apparent from the topic or other wording; it usually goes without saying explicitly. The precise treatment of *'ish* is one way that the present translation reflects more accurately the degree of the text's attention (or inattention) to social gender, relative to other factors. It takes the text on its own terms. It serves to put gender in perspective.[31]

ACCOUNTING FOR UNCERTAINTY

I attempted to decide the social-gender sense based on the "preponderance of the evidence." Even so, a number of gray areas remained—usually because of contemporary ignorance about conditions in ancient Israel. In those cases I sometimes gave an alternative rendering in an endnote, similar to NJPS practice. Or, after making my best guess, I resorted to an endnote that is roughly equivalent to the phrase employed so forthrightly by the NJPS translators: "Meaning of Hebrew uncertain." One example is the divine instruction to *bene yisra'el* (NJPS "the Israelite people") to wear tassels on the "corners" of their garment (Num. 15:37–41). Given the text's vague wording, the lack of contextual gender-marked clues, and the lack of clear references to such practices among women either in the Bible or in extrabiblical literature or iconography, I remained at a loss to "predict" how the original audience would have ascribed a social-gender sense to this directive. So I retained the NJPS rendering and added an endnote: "Social-gender force here of Heb. *bene yisra'el* uncertain."

References to Divine Beings

THE TETRAGRAMMATON

To represent the Name (the four-letter "personal" name of God that is traditionally not pronounced as it is spelled), NJPS adopted a practice that has long been widespread: rendering the Name impersonally as "the LORD." That custom dates back more than two thousand years to the first translation of the Hebrew Bible— the ancient Jewish version in Greek called the Septuagint. (The audience for that translation lived in the polytheistic milieu of Hellenistic Egypt. The translation's producers apparently wanted to make an ideological point, emphasizing that their Deity was not merely one more named god among many. As a substitute name, *kyrios* ["Lord"] put this particular deity in the spotlight.) At the same time, however, some ancient Septuagint copyists employed another approach as well: they consistently inscribed the Name using Hebrew letters—in what was otherwise a Greek translation.

Meanwhile, in the land of Israel, some copyists of Hebrew manuscripts were employing a similar approach by writing the Name in a special way.[32] For the latter, they took to using the archaic Hebrew script that Jewish scribes had abandoned several hundred years earlier in favor of an alphabet used by Aramaic speakers.[33]

In the view of those scribes, not only could the Name not be translated into *another* language, it could not even be properly presented in the standard script in the *same* language!

In short, the Name has long been treated not like any ordinary Hebrew word but like something totally other. Such distinctive treatment appears to be a reflex of the monotheistic concept of God as unique and transcendent.

Ellen Frankel and I asked certain scholars, rabbis, and leaders for suggestions on how best to represent the Name in this translation. We received thoughtful input from two dozen respondents. Although we began by seeking an English rendering, we came to see that no rendering could do justice to the Name, neither as presented in the Bible nor as treated thereafter in Jewish lore. The Torah employs the Name primarily *as a name* (not an attribute, not as a declaration, and not in terms of etymology), which surely is how the original audience experienced it. All things considered, we decided to represent the Name untranslated, in (unvocalized) Hebrew letters.[34] This styling enables the word to function as a name, without limiting the conception of God to a single quality.

We invite those who read this translation aloud to pronounce the Name via whatever term that they customarily use for it.

GENDER IN REFERENCES TO GOD OR TO ANGELS

In the absence of contextual indications that gender was germane, I rendered the Torah's references to divine beings in gender-neutral terms. This policy is not meant to foreclose discussion about the force of the Hebrew wording. Rather, it provides better grounds for such a debate: a consistent experience of the text as noncommittal with regard to God's gender. And those who prefer to think that the deity of the Torah's composer(s) was "male" are still free to construe the neutral language in that way.

In practice, such a rendering meant recasting NJPS to avoid gendered pronouns for God. Usually I employed the kind of approaches illustrated by the examples in the table on the next page. Occasionally, a passive construction seemed a justifiable reflection of the Hebrew syntax, in which case I was careful to ensure that even without explicit mention the referent would still be clear from the context.

Adaptation Methodology

NJPS	THIS ADAPTATION
He said	[God] said
His people	God's people
His covenant	the Covenant
His laws that He enjoined upon you	the laws that were enjoined upon you
His voice	the divine voice[35]
the fear of Him	the fear of God
doing what displeased the LORD and vexing Him	doing what displeased and vexed יהוה

To remain true to the text's nuances, I did not employ neutral language throughout. Where God is called "lord," "father," and "king," the gendered nature of such status in the ancient Near East is germane. Rendering generically would alter the gist of the metaphor. Similarly, I recognized poetic license in passages of epic poetry that describe God as "warrior." There, too, masculine language is germane, for throughout the ancient Near East, warriors were understood to be male. In those cases, my rendering conveys the ancient perception via male language.[36]

SIGNIFICANCE

The present adaptation of *The Torah* is one of many useful translations. Other translation approaches—whether literary, midrashic, mystical, or historical—can be of value without having to agree.[37] The renderings herein will differ from some traditional rabbinic understandings, or from some contemporary feminist interpretations, or both. Such differences are to be expected especially if those approaches are not seeking the text's plain sense. Each way of reading the text can potentially serve as a jeweler's loupe for viewing one of the many facets of the brilliant-cut diamond that is the Torah.[38]

Those people who have been involved in this translation project, or with whom I—as an occasional teacher of Torah—have shared its approach, have come to it already in possession of a favored way of reading the text. Most if not all of us have been pleasantly surprised by how fascinating this particular approach has proven to be. It has opened up possibilities not previously imagined. And it has brought us closer to the text, to our ancestors, and to God. Speaking as a rabbi, I could hardly ask for more than that. Whether readers will be as captivated by the *results* of this approach remains to be seen. However, if those results stimulate in them even a few of the same bright-eyed questions, and even a bit of the open-ended encounter with the magic of Torah that I have experienced, I will consider this work to be a success.

ACKNOWLEDGMENTS

Happily, I am in the position to thank many people for their generous help in the production of this book. The present translation includes, extends, and substantially revises work performed on behalf of the Union for Reform Judaism and published in *The Torah: A Modern Commentary*, Revised Edition (URJ Press, 2005). I include here those who took part in that earlier effort.

I am grateful to the following persons:

Consulting editors for translation adaptation—the amazing team of Carol Meyers, Adele Berlin, and Ellen Frankel;

Scholars who kindly addressed my specific queries, as I sought to make sense of the text—Robert Alter, Marc Zvi Brettler, Joel S. Burnett, Ivan Caine, Marvin Chaney, David J. A. Clines, Miles B. Cohen, Alan Crown, Reinier de Blois, Carol Delaney, Nili Fox, Tikva Frymer-Kensky, Leland Giovanelli, Moshe Greenberg, Sam Greengus, Edward Greenstein, Mayer Gruber, Tamar Kamionkowski, Stephen Kaufman, Herb Levine, Meir Malul, Victor H. Matthews, Vivian Mayer, Samuel A. Meier, Bruce M. Metzger, Jacob Milgrom, Saul Olyan, Dale Patrick, Carolyn Pressler, Daniel Shevitz, Mark S. Smith, S. David Sperling, Naomi Steinberg, Bruce Waltke, Ray Westbrook, Timothy M. Willis; Ziony Zevit—and especially Carol Meyers and Susan Niditch, to whom I turned often;

Those who responded to our request for ideas on how best to represent the Tetragrammaton (and were not already mentioned)—Judith Antonelli, Yitz Greenberg, Frederick Greenspahn, Leonard Greenspoon, Joel M. Hoffman, Jonathan Keren Black, Harold Kushner, David L. Lieber, Goldie Milgram, Judith Plaskow, Sharon Ringe, Zalman Schachter-Shalomi, Drorah Setel, Marcia Cohn Spiegel, David A. Teutsch, and Arthur Waskow;

Librarians—Sally Nakanishi, Cheryl Stahl, and Yaffa Weisman at the Frances-Henry Library (HUC–JIR/LA); Haim Gottschalk and Paul Miller at the Ostrow Library (UJ); and Manel Frau at the Kaplan Library (RRC);

Copy editors and proofreaders—Emily Law and Reena Spicehandler.

Hara Person, the editor-in-chief of URJ Press, launched the earlier version of this adapted translation (together with then-publisher Kenneth Gesser) and served as a critical reader of its drafts.

My father, Peter K. Stein, while I was his student thirty years ago in measurement systems engineering, rigorously mapped out the pitfalls in any transmission of information—insights that continue to serve me in good stead as an editor.

The staff at JPS who nurtured this project include Janet Liss, Carol Hupping, Robin Norman, and Shannon MacDonald. Finally, the JPS Editor-in-Chief Ellen Frankel has remained a consistent champion of this project throughout the nearly three years that it has been underway.

This book is the beneficiary of the assiduousness and generosity of the aforementioned persons—and of still others. Even so, surely errors are to be found within, and the responsibility for those remains with me.

Finally, a word about the name of this book. We call this adapted translation *The Contemporary Torah* because it reflects contemporary interests about gendered language. Indeed, modern readers are keenly interested in how ancient audiences viewed social gender and how they verbally represented God. Meanwhile, scholars often refer to Bible translations via abbreviations—NJPS, OJPS, NRSV, KJV, etc. In keeping with this convention, we propose referring to this version of the JPS translation as CJPS, that is, the "Contemporary" JPS translation.

David E. S. Stein
Revising Editor
ראש חדש סיון הֹתשס״ו
May 28, 2006

Sample Social-Gender Changes to NJPS, by Problem Category

Gender not at issue—NJPS rendered in masculine terms

LOCALE	NJPS (EMPHASIS ADDED)	THE CONTEMPORARY TORAH
Gen. 42:11	we are honest *men*	we are honest people
Num. 14:35	they shall die to the last *man*	and so be finished off
Deut. 1:17	fear no *man*	fear no one
Deut. 12:8	every *man* as he pleases	each of us as we please

Gender at issue—NJPS rendered in neutral terms

LOCALE	NJPS (EMPHASIS ADDED)	THE CONTEMPORARY TORAH
Gen. 42:11	we are honest *men*	we are honest people
Exod. 21:2	a Hebrew *slave*	a male Hebrew slave
Num. 1:2	Israelite *community*	Israelite company [of fighters]
Num. 26:7	the *persons* enrolled	the men enrolled

Gender not at issue—NJPS unduly restricted gender roles

LOCALE	NJPS (EMPHASIS ADDED)	THE CONTEMPORARY TORAH
Exod. 21:7	a *man* sells *his* daughter	a parent sells a daughter
Deut. 23:16	turn over to *his* master	turn over to the master
Deut. 23:25	another *man's* vineyard	a fellow [Israelite]'s vineyard

NJPS English style that conveyed a neutral sense ambiguously

LOCALE	NJPS (EMPHASIS ADDED)	THE CONTEMPORARY TORAH
Exod. 8:13	*man* and beast	human and beast
Lev. 14:4	*him* who is to be cleansed	the one who is to be purified
Deut. 27:18	a blind person on *his* way	a blind person on the way

NJPS imprecision in rendering 'ish as "man"

LOCALE	NJPS (EMPHASIS ADDED)	THE CONTEMPORARY TORAH
Gen. 24:30	thus the *man* spoke to me	thus the emissary spoke to me
Exod. 4:10	a *man* of words	good with words
Num. 1:4	a *man* from each tribe	a representative from each tribe
Num. 13:3	all the *men*	all of them being notables
Num. 27:18	an inspired *man*	an inspired leader
Deut. 19:5	a *man* has two wives	a householder has two wives

NOTES

1. Begun in 1955, the NJPS translation of the Torah (that is, the Pentateuch) first appeared in 1962. The original translation committee then revised its work in 1967 ("second edition"), and again in 1985 when *The Torah* was incorporated into *Tanakh* (the full Hebrew Bible). Later, JPS issued a "third edition" in 1992 and a further revision as part of the *JPS Hebrew-English Tanakh* in 1999.

The present translation also incorporates a few minor punctuation and spelling corrections to NJPS.

For my working definition of *social gender*, see the Dictionary of Gender in the Torah (in the back of this book) under "gender."

2. For a list of the type of situations that warranted a note of either sort, see p. xxxviii. Some newly added notes respond not only to a prior *translation* but also (implicitly) to *interpretations* by contemporary scholars who have addressed gender issues.

3. Orlinsky was at the time a professor of Bible at the Hebrew Union College–Jewish Institute of Religion in New York. In addition to his leading role for *The Torah*, he served on the translation committee for other portions of NJPS, as well as for two Christian-sponsored translations, the Revised Standard Version and the New Revised Standard Version. For his quotations in this preface, see "A Jewish Scholar Looks at the Revised Standard Version and Its New Edition," *Religious Education* 85/2 (Spring 1990), pp. 211–221; "Introduction," *Notes on the New Translation of the Torah* (JPS, 1969), pp. 3–40; and "Male Oriented Language Originated by Bible Translators," in Harry M. Orlinsky and Robert G. Bratcher, *A History of Bible Translation and the North American Contribution* (Scholars Press, 1991) [for the Society of Biblical Literature], pp. 267–277.

4. The reason to distinguish between the two types of references is partly a matter of contemporary religious politics but even more a matter of differences in the applicable language itself. God-language is deployed to describe holistic aspects of reality and perceptions that elude the consciousness out of which "normal" language arises, the latter being a mode of thinking that is scarcity-based, reductionist, and causally oriented. Thus, for example, God-language does not operate with the same literalness as regular language; it is more metaphoric and paradoxical. I believe that the ancients understood the difference between the two types of language and had distinct ways of construing each type.

5. See the Dictionary under "predecessors."

6. A note on the copyright page of the 1999 *JPS Hebrew-English Tanakh* advises readers to understand the God-language as neutral.

7. The Bible employs the grammatical masculine whenever the referent is *indefinite*—that is, a generic individual—and social gender is not germane. God's unique nature provides an incentive to construe the

Torah's God-language as if God were indefinite. The Torah's deity can be seen as the ultimate "generic individual," a definite persona but with undefined gender. If so, this would justify construing grammatical gender differently for God than for human beings.

8. See the Dictionary under "messenger."

9. Typical gender-neutral rendering strategies included: casting a singular collective noun in the plural; using an equivalent English idiom that is not gendered; supplying nouns for clarity; and employing a demonstrative pronoun to convey the specificity of a possessive pronoun.

To avoid giving grammatical purists reason to complain, we refrained from using "they" as a common-gender singular pronoun, even though NJPS occasionally did so—like the KJV and the old (1917) JPS translation.

10. I did consider source-critical findings as indications of *literary* unities. From a literary perspective, the composer(s) of the text provided the original audience with a long and meandering document that expressed its messages in various registers (voices) and vocabularies. An audience attentive to literary nuance would be expected to read passages of *similar* register against each other first, before taking into account passages of *different* style.

11. A contemporary analogy may prove helpful: A DVD player, in order to show a movie from a digital video disc, needs to employ the same type of laser beam as was used to record the disc. In much the same way, I needed to employ an accurate picture of the ancient intended audience, to shine it on the text as an interrogating light so that its original meaning could again play before our eyes.

12. Textual clues are themselves somewhat ambiguous; compiling all the clues still leaves room for interpretation. But if text's features are like rocks in a watercourse and the meaning it contains is like the water flowing downstream, then the clues provide a topography that makes honest interpretation more likely to run in one direction than another.

Meanwhile, like any work of literature, the Bible was written partly to change the world around it. Like any recounting of past events, its portrayal was selective and intended to justify certain present or desired future conditions. Therefore, as many scholars have pointed out, we would be unwise today to accept its depictions uncritically as a mirror of ancient Israelite society. I have tried to be cautious in this regard by drawing where possible upon incidental details that do not seem to have ideological import in the passages where they appear, and by looking for corroborating nonbiblical evidence.

13. Such a working stance comes easily; most of my career has consisted of doing this as an editor for modern and contemporary authors.

14. To some extent a text's ambiguity is inherent in the nature of language. At the same time, multivalent wording, indirection, allusion, and withholding information are all vital parts of a writer's craft.

15. Here *'aḥim* is used figuratively—but poignantly so, because two of the addressees have just lost their literal brothers; and the bereft Aaron is being addressed by his own actual brother, Moses.

16. Women were the public face of mourning in ancient Israel, as reflected in the Bible (Exod. 33:4; Jer. 9:16–17, 19; 2 Chron. 35:25).

17. Gen. 35:17; 1 Sam. 4:20; Jer. 20:15; Job 3:3. I take the consistent biblical portrayal as an accurate depiction of its audience's attitude.

18. See the Dictionary for discussion of many of these factors.

19. The stated goal accords with the approach not only of the NJPS translators but also of the feminist scholar Phyllis Bird; see her "Translating Sexist Language as a Theological and Cultural Problem," *Union Seminary Quarterly Review* 42/1–2 (1988), p. 91.

20. For clarity, the present adaptation avoids using "he, his, him, himself" as gender-neutral (i.e., "generic") pronouns.

21. It's possible that a contemporary reader will presume that all ancient herders were men and still construe "herders" as if it were "herds-*men*." Practically speaking, however, the translation cannot make the point any clearer without calling undue attention to the issue.

22. See the Dictionary under "names."

23. They are: *Maacah* daughter of King Talmai of Geshur, whose husband is King David and whose son is Absalom (2 Sam. 3:3; 1 Chron. 3:2); *Maacah* daughter of Abishalom, whose husband is King Rehoboam and whose sons include King Abijam (1 Kings 15:2; 2 Chron. 11:20–22); *Maacah* daughter of Abishalom, whose son is King Asa son of Abijam (1 Kings 15:10); *Maacah*, a concubine and mother of four whose husband is Caleb (1 Chron. 2:48–49); and *Maacah*, the mother of ten whose husband was Jeiel of Gibeon (1 Chron. 9:35–37). For one additional *Maacah*, see note 28.

24. See the Dictionary under "inheritance."

25. See also the Dictionary under "genealogy."

26. Contrast the Torah's mention of "twelve chieftains" and "twelve sons" of Ishmael (17:20; 25:13–16) and of the "twelve sons" of Jacob (35:22b–36). Two of those passages come later in Genesis, so the original audience could not have made a direct comparison upon first encountering 22:24. I cite them, however, as evidence of a presumed conventional idiom for noting a tribal confederation where such exists.

27. Pre-exilic inscriptions (the "Samaria ostraca") several times mention two towns, Hoglah and Noah, whose names match two women who figure prominently in the biblical concern for lineages within Manasseh (see Num. 27:1–11; 36:1–12; Josh. 17:4–6; cf. 1 Chron. 7:14–18).

28. 1 Chron. 7:15–16; this Maacah was one of only two granddaughters of Jacob mentioned in the Bible, given that Manasseh was Joseph's son whom Jacob adopted as his own son (Gen. 48:5). Identifying this Maacah in 1 Chronicles 7 (Manasseh's daughter or daughter-in-law) with the one in Genesis 22 (Abraham's niece) is my own specula-

tion, based on geographic proximity and Occam's razor. One way to interpret both accounts historically is that the Manassites and the (Aramean) Maacathites intermarried and eventually assimilated.

29. What I am doing here as translator is tactically similar to what NJPS had done, presumably for good English idiom, by supplying the direct object "children" in this verse.

30. This tactic would not be suitable for all translation types; however, it accords well with the goal of contextual precision that characterizes NJPS. See further the Dictionary under 'ish.

31. Some of this translation's various precise renderings of 'ish (such as representative, delegate, candidate, commissioner, householder, authority, notable, leader, agent, emissary, envoy, deputy, laborer, subordinate, councillor, and more) may surprise readers who had not been fully aware of the wide semantic range of "man" in English. For that reason I have noted instances where 'ish is represented by a noun other than the well-accepted renderings as "person" or "man" or "husband." The endnotes contain more than a hundred such entries.

32. The manuscripts that I am referring to are among the collection commonly known as the Dead Sea Scrolls.

33. In the newer script—basically the same as is used today—the Name looked like יהוה, whereas in the old script it looked like 𐤉𐤄𐤅𐤄.

34. Our chosen styling of the Name happens to accord with the one selected earlier by the editorial board of *The Torah: A Women's Commentary*, sponsored by the Women of Reform Judaism and forthcoming in 2007 (URJ Press), which will incorporate a version of the present translation for four of the Torah's five books.

35. Except for one instance within poetry in Genesis, only in Deuteronomy did I render the possessive inflection as an adjective. For Deuteronomy it is a reflex of that book's distinctive style. With the adjective "divine" my intended meaning is that its noun's referent derives *from* the Divine, not that the referent is considered to *be* divine.

36. See the Dictionary under "male metaphors for God."

37. The idiomatic and the literary approaches to translation are particularly complementary. To get a feel for the register and the artistry of the Hebrew text, which the present translation is not designed to convey, readers would do well to consult alongside this one the renderings of Everett Fox (1995) or of Robert Alter (2004).

38. Cf. Midrash Numbers Rabbah § 13.15 (Land of Israel, ca. 400 C.E.): "There are seventy facets to the Torah."

Michael V. Fox, one of the JPS Bible commentators, makes a similar point via a more pragmatic metaphor, that of navigation: "Translation is a form of mapping. . . . There are different maps for different purposes, and recognizing this allows for a pluralistic approach to translation." Equally incisive, on the other hand, is religious studies professor Edwin M. Good's quip: "Only one translation always agrees with me: my own."

PREFACE
The Torah (1962)

THE JEWISH PUBLICATION SOCIETY OF AMERICA produced its
first translation of the Bible in 1917. It was quickly accepted
by English-speaking Jews the world over; it is still in use and will
no doubt continue to be widely favored. Nevertheless, the need for
a new translation has been obvious for years.

For one thing, it is possible—and therefore necessary—to im-
prove substantially on earlier versions in rendering both the shades
of meaning of words and expressions and the force of grammatical forms and constructions. This can be done partly with the help
of neglected insights of ancient and medieval Jewish scholarship,
and partly by utilizing the new knowledge of the ancient, as well
as of the more recent, Near East. For significant advances have
been made during the past half century in biblical archaeology and
in the recovery of the languages and civilizations of the peoples
among whom the Israelites lived and whose modes of living and
thinking they largely shared. In accuracy alone we believe this
translation has improved on the first JPS translation in literally
hundreds of passages.

Secondly, because the Bible is an eternal book, it must be made
intelligible to every generation. The King James Version, upon
which almost all English translations of the Bible have hitherto
been based, had an archaic flavor even for its readers in the year
1611, when it was first published. Moreover, it rendered the Hebrew to a considerable extent word for word rather than idiomatically, a procedure which nearly always results in quaintness or
awkwardness and not infrequently in obscurity. A translation
which is stilted where the original is natural, heavy where the original is graceful, or obscure where the original is perfectly intelligible, is the very opposite of faithful.

These were the primary reasons why the Trustees and the Publication Committee of the Jewish Publication Society decided to have
a new translation prepared. Dr. Harry M. Orlinsky, Professor of
Bible at the Hebrew Union College—Jewish Institute of Religion,

who had urged this undertaking upon the Society, was asked to serve as editor-in-chief. To serve with him as fellow editors, the Society invited two eminent scholars: Dr. H. L. Ginsberg, Professor of Bible at the Jewish Theological Seminary, and Dr. Ephraim A. Speiser, head of the Department of Semitic and Oriental Languages at the University of Pennsylvania. The Society further associated with them three learned rabbis familiar with the use of the Bible in the synagogue and home: Rabbis Max Arzt, Bernard J. Bamberger, and Harry Freedman, belonging to the three sections of organized Jewish religious life. Subsequently, Dr. Freedman left the United States to assume a rabbinic post in Australia; but, despite his inability to attend sessions, he has participated actively in the committee's work. Dr. Solomon Grayzel, editor of the Jewish Publication Society, served as secretary of the committee.

Messrs. Louis E. Levinthal, Sol Satinsky, Edwin Wolf, 2nd, and Lesser Zussman, by virtue of their positions in the Society, participated in the solution of the committee's problems.

The committee carried on its work through meetings and correspondence. Dr. Orlinsky prepared a draft translation which was circulated among the seven working members, each of whom made comments and suggested changes. These were in turn circulated among the members who then, at periodic meetings, arrived at decisions by majority vote.

While the committee profited much from the work of previous translators, the present rendering is not a revision, but essentially a new translation. A few of its characteristics may be noted. The committee undertook faithfully to follow the traditional (masoretic) text. There were certain points, however, at which footnotes appeared necessary: 1) where the committee had to admit that it did not understand a word or a passage; 2) where an alternative rendering was possible; 3) where an old rendering, no longer retained, was so well known that it would very likely be missed, in which case the traditional translation was given in the name of "others," usually as found in the Society's version of 1917; 4) where the understanding of a passage could be facilitated by reference to another passage elsewhere in the Bible; 5) where textual variants are to be found in some of the ancient manuscripts or versions of the Bible.

Obsolete words and phrases were avoided; and Hebrew idioms were translated, in so far as possible, by means of their normal English equivalents. For the second person singular, the modern "you" was used, even when referring to the Deity ("You"), rather than the archaic "thou" ("Thou"). A further obvious difference between this translation and most of the older ones may be noted in the rendering of the Hebrew particle *waw,* which is usually translated "and." The Hebrew Bible style demanded its frequent use. But in that style it had the force, not only of "and," but also of "however," "but," "yet," "when," and any number of such other words and particles, or of none at all that can be translated into English. Always to render it as "and" is to misrepresent the Hebrew rather than be faithful to it. Consequently, the committee translated the particle as the sense required, or left it untranslated.

The chapter and verse divisions found in the printed Bible are indispensable as a system of precise reference, but they do not always coincide with the organic divisions of the text. The chapter divisions, whose origin is neither ancient nor Jewish but medieval Christian, sometimes join or separate the wrong paragraphs, sentences, or even parts of sentences. The verse divisions, though considerably older and of Jewish origin, sometimes join together parts of different sentences or separate from each other parts of the same sentence. It is not surprising that Rav Saadia Gaon, the brilliant scholar who translated the Bible into Arabic in the tenth century, paid no attention to the chapter divisions, since they did not exist in his day. More noteworthy is the readiness with which he joined separate verses of the masoretic text (whose authority he did not question) into single sentences when the sense required it. Thus, in joining Gen. 7:24 and 8:1 into a single sentence, the present translation is merely following the example of Saadia. The attentive reader will discover other instances in which the translators have not hesitated to follow what they considered to be the logical units of meaning even when they do not coincide with the conventional chapters and verses. These, however, are marked and numbered throughout.

Neither the trustees of the Society nor the translators suspected that the task was of such magnitude as quickly became apparent.

It is, however, the hope of all those who have had a share in the work that the translation of the other two parts of the Holy Scriptures—the Prophets and the Writings—will be completed within a reasonable period of time and that the results of our labors will find favor with God and man.

The Jewish Publication Society of America
ערב ראש השנה הֹתשכ״ג
September 28, 1962

SCRIPTURAL READINGS

תורה

TORAH

The Five Books of Moses

בְּרֵאשִׁית

GENESIS

W HEN GOD BEGAN to create- heaven and earth—²the earth being unformed and void, with darkness over the surface of the deep and *-a wind from-* God sweeping over the water—³God said, "Let there be light"; and there was light. ⁴God saw that the light was good, and God separated the light from the darkness. ⁵God called the light Day and called the darkness Night. And there was evening and there was morning, *-a first day.-*

⁶God said, "Let there be an expanse in the midst of the water, that it may separate water from water." ⁷God made the expanse, and it separated the water which was below the expanse from the water which was above the expanse. And it was so. ⁸God called the expanse Sky. And there was evening and there was morning, a second day.

⁹God said, "Let the water below the sky be gathered into one area, that the dry land may appear." And it was so. ¹⁰God called the dry land Earth and called the gathering of waters Seas. And God saw that this was good. ¹¹And God said, "Let the earth sprout vegetation: seed-bearing plants, fruit trees of every kind on earth that bear fruit with the seed in it." And it was so. ¹²The earth brought forth vegetation: seed-bearing plants of every kind, and trees of every kind bearing fruit with the seed in it. And God saw that this was good. ¹³And there was evening and there was morning, a third day.

¹⁴God said, "Let there be lights in the expanse of the sky to separate day from night; they shall serve as signs for the set times—the days and the years; ¹⁵and they shall serve as lights in the expanse of the sky to shine upon the earth." And it was so. ¹⁶God made the two great lights, the greater light to dominate the day and the lesser light to dominate the night, and the stars. ¹⁷And God set them in the expanse of the sky to shine upon the earth, ¹⁸to dominate the day and the night, and to separate light from darkness. And God saw that this was good. ¹⁹And there was evening and there was morning, a fourth day.

²⁰God said, "Let the waters bring forth swarms of living creatures, and birds that fly above the earth across the expanse of the sky." ²¹God created the great sea monsters, and all the living creatures of every kind that creep, which the waters brought forth in swarms, and all the winged birds of every kind. And God saw that this was good. ²²God blessed them, saying, "Be fertile and increase, fill the waters in the seas, and let the birds increase on the earth." ²³And there was evening and there was morning, a fifth day.

²⁴God said, "Let the earth bring forth every kind of living creature: cattle, creeping things, and wild beasts of every kind." And it was so. ²⁵God made wild beasts of every kind and cattle of every kind, and all kinds of creeping things of the earth. And God saw that this was good. ²⁶And God said, "Let us make humankind in our image, after our likeness. They shall rule the fish of the sea, the birds of the sky, the cattle, the whole earth, and all the creeping things that creep on earth."

²⁷And God created humankind in the divine image,
creating it in the image of God—
creating them male and female.

²⁸God blessed them and God said to them, "Be fertile and increase, fill the earth and master it; and rule the fish of the sea, the birds of the sky, and all the living things that creep on earth."

²⁹God said, "See, I give you every seed-bearing plant that is upon all the earth, and every tree that has seed-bearing fruit; they shall be yours for food. ³⁰And to all the animals on land, to all the birds of the sky, and to everything that creeps on earth, in which there is the breath of life, [I give] all the green plants for food." And it was so. ³¹And God saw all that had been made, and found it very good. And there was evening and there was morning, the sixth day.

2 The heaven and the earth were finished, and all their array. ²On the seventh day God finished the work that had been undertaken: [God] ceased* on the seventh day from doing any of the work. ³And God blessed the seventh day and declared it holy—having ceased on it from all the work of creation that God had done. ⁴Such is the story of heaven and earth when they were created.

When God יהוה made earth and heaven—⁵when no °ˉshrub of the fieldˉ° was yet on earth and no °ˉgrasses of the fieldˉ° had yet sprouted, because God יהוה had not sent rain upon the earth and there were no human beings to till the soil, ⁶but a flow would well up from the ground and water the whole surface of the earth—⁷God יהוה formed °ˉthe Humanˉ° from the °ˉsoil's humus,ˉ° blowing into his nostrils the breath of life: the Human became a living being.

⁸God יהוה planted a garden in Eden, in the east, and placed there the Human who had been fashioned. ⁹And from the ground God יהוה caused to grow every tree that was pleasing to the sight and good for food, with the tree of life in the middle of the garden, and the tree of knowledge of good and bad.

¹⁰A river issues from Eden to water the garden, and it then divides and becomes four branches. ¹¹The name of the first is Pishon, the one that winds through the whole land of Havilah, where the gold is. (¹²The gold of that land is good; bdellium is there, and *ˉlapis lazuli.ˉ*) ¹³The name of the second river is Gihon, the one that winds through the whole land of Cush. ¹⁴The name of the third river is Tigris, the one that flows east of Asshur. And the fourth river is the Euphrates.

¹⁵God יהוה settled the Human in the garden of Eden, to till it and tend it. ¹⁶And God יהוה commanded the Human, saying, "Of every tree of the garden you are free to eat; ¹⁷but as for the tree of knowledge of good and bad, you must not eat of it; for as soon as you eat of it, you shall die."

¹⁸God יהוה said, "It is not good for the Human to be alone; I will make a fitting counterpart for him." ¹⁹And God יהוה formed out of the earth all the wild beasts and all the birds of the sky, and brought them to the Human to see what he would call them; and whatever the Human called each living creature, that would be its name. ²⁰And the Human gave names to all the cattle and to the birds of the sky and to all the wild beasts; but no fitting counterpart for a human being was found. ²¹So God יהוה cast a deep sleep upon the Human; and, while he slept, [God] took one of his sides° and closed up the flesh at that site. ²²And God יהוה fashioned the side that had been taken from the Human into a woman, bringing her to the Human.

²³Then the Human said,

> "This one at last
> Is bone of my bones
> And flesh of my flesh.
> This one shall be called Woman,°
> For from a Human° was she taken."

²⁴Hence a man° leaves his father and mother and clings to his wife,° so that they become one flesh.

²⁵The two of them were naked,* °‑the Human‑° and his wife, yet they felt no shame. **3** ¹Now the serpent was the shrewdest of all the wild beasts that God יהוה had made. It said to the woman, "Did God really say: You shall not eat of any tree of the garden?" ²The woman replied to the serpent, "We may eat of the fruit of the other trees of the garden. ³It is only about fruit of the tree in the middle of the garden that God said: 'You shall not eat of it or touch it, lest you die.'" ⁴And the serpent said to the woman, "You are not going to die, ⁵but God knows that as soon as you eat of it your eyes will be opened and you will be like *‑divine beings who know‑* good and bad." ⁶When the woman saw that the tree was good for eating and a delight to the eyes, and that the tree was desirable as a source of wisdom, she took of its fruit and ate. She also gave some to her husband, and he ate. ⁷Then the eyes of both of them were opened and they perceived that they were naked; and they sewed together fig leaves and made themselves loincloths.

⁸They heard the sound of God יהוה moving about in the garden at the breezy time of day; and the Human and his wife hid from God יהוה among the trees of the garden. ⁹God יהוה called out to the Human and said to him, "Where are you?" ¹⁰He replied, "I heard the sound of You in the garden, and I was afraid because I was naked, so I hid."

¹¹"Who told you that you were naked? Did you eat of the tree from which I had forbidden you to eat?"

¹²The Human said, "The woman You put at my side—she gave me of the tree, and I ate."

¹³And God יהוה said to the woman, "What is this you have done!" The woman replied, "The serpent duped me, and I ate."

¹⁴Then God יהוה said to the serpent,

> "Because you did this,
> More cursed shall you be
> Than all cattle
> And all the wild beasts:
> On your belly shall you crawl
> And dirt shall you eat
> All the days of your life.
> ¹⁵I will put enmity
> Between you and the woman,
> And between your offspring and hers;
> They shall strike at your head,
> And you shall strike at their heel."

¹⁶And to the woman [God] said,

> "I will greatly expand
> Your hard labor—and your pregnancies;
> In hardship shall you bear children.
> Yet your urge shall be for your husband,
> And he shall °rule over you.°"

¹⁷To Adam [God] said, "Because you did as your wife said and ate of the tree about which I commanded you, 'You shall not eat of it,'

> Cursed be the ground because of you;
> By hard labor shall you eat of it
> All the days of your life:
> ¹⁸Thorns and thistles shall it sprout for you.
> But your food shall be the grasses of the field;
> ¹⁹By the sweat of your brow
> Shall you get bread to eat,
> Until you return to the ground—
> For from it you were taken.
> For dust* you are,
> And to dust you shall return."

²⁰The Human named his wife Eve,* because she was the mother of all the living.* ²¹And God יהוה made garments of skins for Adam and his wife, and clothed them.

²²And God יהוה said, "Now that humankind has become like any of us, knowing good and bad, what if one should stretch out

a hand and take also from the tree of life and eat, and live forever!" 23So God יהוה banished humankind from the garden of Eden, to till the soil from which it was taken: 24it was driven out; and east of the garden of Eden were stationed the cherubim and the fiery ever-turning sword, to guard the way to the tree of life.

4 Now the Human knew* his wife Eve, and she conceived and bore Cain, saying, "I have created* a person° °·with the help of·° יהוה." 2She then bore his brother Abel. Abel became a keeper of sheep, and Cain became a tiller of the soil. 3In the course of time, Cain brought an offering to יהוה from the fruit of the soil; 4and Abel, for his part, brought the choicest of the firstlings of his flock. יהוה paid heed to Abel and his offering, 5but to Cain and his offering [God] paid no heed. Cain was much distressed and his face fell. 6And יהוה said to Cain,

"Why are you distressed,
And why is your face fallen?
7*Surely, if you do right,
There is uplift.
But if you do not do right
Sin couches at the door;
Its urge is toward you,
Yet you can be its master."

8Cain said to his brother Abel ...* and when they were in the field, Cain set upon his brother Abel and killed him. 9יהוה said to Cain, "Where is your brother Abel?" And he said, "I do not know. Am I my brother's keeper?"

10"What have you done? Hark, your brother's blood cries out to Me from the ground! 11Therefore, you shall be *·more cursed than the ground,* which opened its mouth to receive your brother's blood from your hand. 12If you till the soil, it shall no longer yield its strength to you. You shall become a ceaseless wanderer on earth."

13Cain said to יהוה, "My punishment is too great to bear! 14Since You have banished me this day from the soil, and I must avoid Your presence and become a restless wanderer on earth— anyone who meets me may kill me!" 15יהוה said to him, "I promise, if anyone kills Cain, sevenfold vengeance shall be exacted."

And יהוה put a mark on Cain, lest anyone who met him should kill him. 16Cain left the presence of יהוה and settled in the land of Nod, east of Eden.

17Cain knew his wife, and she conceived and bore Enoch. And he then founded a city, and named the city after his son Enoch. 18To Enoch was born Irad, and Irad begot Mehujael, and Mehujael* begot Methusael, and Methusael begot Lamech. 19Lamech took to himself two wives: the name of the one was Adah, and the name of the other was Zillah. 20Adah bore Jabal; he was the ancestor of those who dwell in tents and amidst herds. 21And the name of his brother was Jubal; he was the ancestor of all who play the lyre and the pipe. 22As for Zillah, she bore Tubal-cain, who forged all implements of copper and iron. And the sister of Tubal-cain was Naamah.

23And Lamech said to his wives,

> "Adah and Zillah, hear my voice;
> O wives of Lamech, give ear to my speech.
> I have slain a person for wounding me,
> And a lad for bruising me.
> 24If Cain is avenged sevenfold,
> Then Lamech seventy-sevenfold."

25Adam knew his wife again, and she bore a son and named him Seth, meaning, "God has *˙provided me with˙* another offspring in place of Abel," for Cain had killed him. 26And to Seth, in turn, a son was born, and he named him Enosh. It was then that יהוה began to be invoked by name.

5 This is the record of Adam's line.—When God created humankind, it was made in the likeness of God; 2male and female were they created. And when they were created, [God] blessed them and called them Humankind.°—3When Adam had lived 130 years, he begot a son in his likeness after his image, and he named him Seth. 4After the birth of Seth, Adam lived 800 years and begot sons and daughters. 5All the days that Adam lived came to 930 years; then he died.

6When Seth had lived 105 years, he begot Enosh. 7After the birth of Enosh, Seth lived 807 years and begot sons and daughters.

⁸All the days of Seth came to 912 years; then he died.

⁹When Enosh had lived 90 years, he begot Kenan. ¹⁰After the birth of Kenan, Enosh lived 815 years and begot sons and daughters. ¹¹All the days of Enosh came to 905 years; then he died.

¹²When Kenan had lived 70 years, he begot Mahalalel. ¹³After the birth of Mahalalel, Kenan lived 840 years and begot sons and daughters. ¹⁴All the days of Kenan came to 910 years; then he died.

¹⁵When Mahalalel had lived 65 years, he begot Jared. ¹⁶After the birth of Jared, Mahalalel lived 830 years and begot sons and daughters. ¹⁷All the days of Mahalalel came to 895 years; then he died.

¹⁸When Jared had lived 162 years, he begot Enoch. ¹⁹After the birth of Enoch, Jared lived 800 years and begot sons and daughters. ²⁰All the days of Jared came to 962 years; then he died.

²¹When Enoch had lived 65 years, he begot Methuselah. ²²After the birth of Methuselah, Enoch walked with God 300 years; and he begot sons and daughters. ²³All the days of Enoch came to 365 years. ²⁴Enoch walked with God; then he was no more, for God took him.

²⁵When Methuselah had lived 187 years, he begot Lamech. ²⁶After the birth of Lamech, Methuselah lived 782 years and begot sons and daughters. ²⁷All the days of Methuselah came to 969 years; then he died.

²⁸When Lamech had lived 182 years, he begot a son. ²⁹And he named him Noah, saying, "This one will provide us relief* from our work and from the toil of our hands, out of the very soil which יהוה placed under a curse." ³⁰After the birth of Noah, Lamech lived 595 years and begot sons and daughters. ³¹All the days of Lamech came to 777 years; then he died.

³²When Noah had lived 500 years, Noah begot Shem, Ham, and Japheth.

6 When humankind began to increase on earth and daughters were born to them, ²the [males among the] *⁻divine beings⁻* saw how pleasing the human women were and took wives from among those who delighted them.—³יהוה said, "My breath shall not abide* in humankind forever, since it too is flesh; let the days allowed them be one hundred and twenty years." —⁴It was then,

and later too, that the Nephilim appeared on earth—when divine beings cohabited with the human women, who bore them offspring. Such were the heroes of old, the renowned ones.

⁵יהוה saw how great was human wickedness on earth—how every plan devised by the human mind was nothing but evil all the time. ⁶And יהוה regretted having made humankind on earth. With a sorrowful heart, ⁷יהוה said, "I will blot out from the earth humankind whom I created—humans together with beasts, creeping things, and birds of the sky; for I regret that I made them." ⁸But Noah found favor with יהוה.

נֹחַ | NOAH

⁹This is the line of Noah.—Noah was a righteous personage;° he was blameless in his age; Noah walked with God.—¹⁰Noah begot three sons: Shem, Ham, and Japheth.

¹¹The earth became corrupt before God; the earth was filled with lawlessness. ¹²When God saw how corrupt the earth was, for all flesh had corrupted its ways on earth, ¹³God said to Noah, "I have decided to put an end to all flesh, for the earth is filled with lawlessness because of them: I am about to destroy them with the earth. ¹⁴Make yourself an ark of *gopher* wood; make it an ark with compartments, and cover it inside and out with pitch. ¹⁵This is how you shall make it: the length of the ark shall be three hundred cubits, its width fifty cubits, and its height thirty cubits. ¹⁶Make an opening for daylight in the ark, and *⁻terminate it within a cubit of the top.⁻* Put the entrance to the ark in its side; make it with bottom, second, and third decks.

¹⁷"For My part, I am about to bring the Flood—waters upon the earth—to destroy all flesh under the sky in which there is breath of life; everything on earth shall perish. ¹⁸But I will establish My covenant with you, and you shall enter the ark, with your sons, your wife, and your sons' wives. ¹⁹And of all that lives, of all flesh, you shall take two of each into the ark to keep alive with you; they shall be male and female. ²⁰From birds of every kind, cattle of every kind, every kind of creeping thing on earth, two of each shall come to you to stay alive. ²¹For your part, take of everything that is eaten and store it away, to serve as food for you and for them." ²²Noah did so; just as God commanded him, so he did.

7 Then יהוה said to Noah, "Go into the ark, with all your household, for you alone have I found righteous before Me in this generation. ²Of every pure animal you shall take seven pairs, males and their mates, and of every animal that is not pure, two, a male and its mate; ³of the birds of the sky also, seven pairs, male and female, to keep seed alive upon all the earth. ⁴For in seven days' time I will make it rain upon the earth, forty days and forty nights, and I will blot out from the earth all existence that I created." ⁵And Noah did just as יהוה commanded him.

⁶Noah was six hundred years old when the Flood came, waters upon the earth. ⁷Noah, with his sons, his wife, and his sons' wives, went into the ark because of the waters of the Flood. ⁸Of the pure animals, of the animals that are not pure, of the birds, and of everything that creeps on the ground, ⁹two of each, male and female, came to Noah into the ark, as God had commanded Noah. ¹⁰And on the seventh day the waters of the Flood came upon the earth.

¹¹In the six hundredth year of Noah's life, in the second month, on the seventeenth day of the month, on that day

All the fountains of the great deep burst apart,
And the floodgates of the sky broke open.

(¹²The rain fell on the earth forty days and forty nights.) ¹³That same day Noah and Noah's sons, Shem, Ham, and Japheth, went into the ark, with Noah's wife and the three wives of his sons— ¹⁴they and all beasts of every kind, all cattle of every kind, all creatures of every kind that creep on the earth, and all birds of every kind, every bird, every winged thing. ¹⁵They came to Noah into the ark, two each of all flesh in which there was breath of life. ¹⁶Thus they that entered comprised male and female of all flesh, as God had commanded him. And יהוה shut him in.

¹⁷The Flood continued forty days on the earth, and the waters increased and raised the ark so that it rose above the earth. ¹⁸The waters swelled and increased greatly upon the earth, and the ark drifted upon the waters. ¹⁹When the waters had swelled much more upon the earth, all the highest mountains everywhere under the sky were covered. ²⁰Fifteen cubits higher did the waters swell, as the mountains were covered. ²¹And all flesh that stirred on earth perished—birds, cattle, beasts, and all the things that swarmed upon the earth, and all humankind. ²²All in whose nostrils was the

merest breath of life, all that was on dry land, died. ²³All existence on earth was blotted out—humans, cattle, creeping things, and birds of the sky; they were blotted out from the earth. Only Noah was left, and those with him in the ark.

²⁴And when the waters had swelled on the earth one hundred and fifty days, **8** ¹God remembered Noah and all the beasts and all the cattle that were with him in the ark, and God caused a wind to blow across the earth, and the waters subsided. ²The fountains of the deep and the floodgates of the sky were stopped up, and the rain from the sky was held back; ³the waters then receded steadily from the earth. At the end of one hundred and fifty days the waters diminished, ⁴so that in the seventh month, on the seventeenth day of the month, the ark came to rest on the mountains of Ararat. ⁵The waters went on diminishing until the tenth month; in the tenth month, on the first of the month, the tops of the mountains became visible.

⁶At the end of forty days, Noah opened the window of the ark that he had made ⁷and sent out the raven; it went to and fro until the waters had dried up from the earth. ⁸Then he sent out the dove to see whether the waters had decreased from the surface of the ground. ⁹But the dove could not find a resting place for its foot, and returned to him to the ark, for there was water over all the earth. So putting out his hand, he took it into the ark with him. ¹⁰He waited another seven days, and again sent out the dove from the ark. ¹¹The dove came back to him toward evening, and there in its bill was a plucked-off olive leaf! Then Noah knew that the waters had decreased on the earth. ¹²He waited still another seven days and sent the dove forth; and it did not return to him any more.

¹³In the six hundred and first year, in the first month, on the first of the month, the waters began to dry from the earth; and when Noah removed the covering of the ark, he saw that the surface of the ground was drying. ¹⁴And in the second month, on the twenty-seventh day of the month, the earth was dry.

¹⁵God spoke to Noah, saying, ¹⁶"Come out of the ark, together with your wife, your sons, and your sons' wives. ¹⁷Bring out with you every living thing of all flesh that is with you: birds, animals, and everything that creeps on earth; and let them swarm on the

earth and be fertile and increase on earth." ¹⁸So Noah came out, together with his sons, his wife, and his sons' wives. ¹⁹Every animal, every creeping thing, and every bird, everything that stirs on earth came out of the ark by families.

²⁰Then Noah built an altar to יהוה and, taking of every pure animal and of every pure bird, he offered burnt offerings on the altar. ²¹יהוה smelled the pleasing odor, and יהוה resolved: "Never again will I doom the earth because of humankind, since the devisings of the human mind are evil from youth; nor will I ever again destroy every living being, as I have done.

> ²²So long as the earth endures,
> Seedtime and harvest,
> Cold and heat,
> Summer and winter,
> Day and night
> Shall not cease."

9 God blessed Noah and his sons, and said to them, "Be fertile and increase, and fill the earth. ²The fear and the dread of you shall be upon all the beasts of the earth and upon all the birds of the sky—everything with which the earth is astir—and upon all the fish of the sea; they are given into your hand. ³Every creature that lives shall be yours to eat; as with the green grasses, I give you all these. ⁴You must not, however, eat flesh with its life-blood in it. ⁵But for your own life-blood I will require a reckoning: I will require it of every beast; of humankind, too, will I require a reckoning for human life, of everyone for each other!

> ⁶Whoever sheds human blood,
> By human [hands] shall that one's blood be shed;
> For in the image of God
> Was humankind made.

⁷Be fertile, then, and increase; abound on the earth and increase on it."

⁸And God said to Noah and to his sons with him, ⁹"I now establish My covenant with you and your offspring to come, ¹⁰and with every living thing that is with you—birds, cattle, and every wild beast as well—all that have come out of the ark, every living thing on earth. ¹¹I will maintain My covenant with you: never again shall all flesh be cut off by the waters of a flood, and never again shall there be a flood to destroy the earth."

¹²God further said, "This is the sign that I set for the covenant between Me and you, and every living creature with you, for all ages to come. ¹³I have set My bow in the clouds, and it shall serve as a sign of the covenant between Me and the earth. ¹⁴When I bring clouds over the earth, and the bow appears in the clouds, ¹⁵I will remember My covenant between Me and you and every living creature among all flesh, so that the waters shall never again become a flood to destroy all flesh. ¹⁶When the bow is in the clouds, I will see it and remember the everlasting covenant between God and all living creatures, all flesh that is on earth. ¹⁷That," God said to Noah, "shall be the sign of the covenant that I have established between Me and all flesh that is on earth."

¹⁸The sons of Noah who came out of the ark were Shem, Ham, and Japheth—Ham being the father of Canaan. ¹⁹These three were the sons of Noah, and from these the whole world branched out.

²⁰Noah, the tiller of the soil, was the first to plant a vineyard. ²¹He drank of the wine and became drunk, and he uncovered himself within his tent. ²²Ham, the father of Canaan, saw his father's nakedness and told his two brothers outside. ²³But Shem and Japheth took a cloth, placed it against both their backs and, walking backward, they covered their father's nakedness; their faces were turned the other way, so that they did not see their father's nakedness. ²⁴When Noah woke up from his wine and learned what his youngest son had done to him, ²⁵he said,

> "Cursed be Canaan;
> The lowest of slaves
> Shall he be to his brothers."

²⁶And he said,

> "Blessed be יהוה,
> The God of Shem;
> Let Canaan be a slave to them.
> ²⁷May God enlarge* Japheth,
> And let him dwell in the tents of Shem;
> And let Canaan be a slave to them."

²⁸Noah lived after the Flood 350 years. ²⁹And all the days of Noah came to 950 years; then he died.

Noah

13

10 These are the lines of Shem, Ham, and Japheth, the sons of Noah: sons were born to them after the Flood.

²The descendants of Japheth: Gomer, Magog, Madai, Javan, Tubal, Meshech, and Tiras. ³The descendants of Gomer: Ashkenaz, Riphath, and Togarmah. ⁴The descendants of Javan: Elishah and Tarshish, the Kittim and the Dodanim.* ⁵From these the maritime nations branched out. [These are the descendants of Japheth]* by their lands—each with its language—their clans and their nations.

⁶The descendants of Ham: Cush, Mizraim, Put, and Canaan. ⁷The descendants of Cush: Seba, Havilah, Sabtah, Raamah, and Sabteca. The descendants of Raamah: Sheba and Dedan.

⁸Cush also begot Nimrod, who was the first mighty figure on earth. ⁹He was a mighty hunter by the grace of יהוה; hence the saying, "Like Nimrod a mighty hunter by the grace of יהוה." ¹⁰The mainstays of his kingdom were Babylon, Erech, Accad, *‑and Calneh‑* in the land of Shinar. ¹¹From that land Asshur went forth and built Nineveh, Rehoboth-ir, Calah, ¹²and Resen between Nineveh and Calah, that is the great city.

¹³And Mizraim begot the Ludim, the Anamim, the Lehabim, the Naphtuhim, ¹⁴the Pathrusim, the Casluhim, and the Caphtorim,* whence the Philistines came forth.

¹⁵Canaan begot Sidon, his first-born, and Heth; ¹⁶and the Jebusites, the Amorites, the Girgashites, ¹⁷the Hivites, the Arkites, the Sinites, ¹⁸the Arvadites, the Zemarites, and the Hamathites. Afterward the clans of the Canaanites spread out. (¹⁹The [original] Canaanite territory extended from Sidon as far as Gerar, near Gaza, and as far as Sodom, Gomorrah, Admah, and Zeboiim, near Lasha.) ²⁰These are the descendants of Ham, according to their clans and languages, by their lands and nations.

²¹Sons were also born to Shem, ancestor of all the descendants of Eber and older brother of Japheth. ²²The descendants of Shem: Elam, Asshur, Arpachshad, Lud, and Aram. ²³The descendants of Aram: Uz, Hul, Gether, and Mash. ²⁴Arpachshad begot Shelah, and Shelah begot Eber. ²⁵Two sons were born to Eber: the name of the first was Peleg, for in his days the earth was divided;* and the name of his brother was Joktan. ²⁶Joktan begot Almodad, Sheleph, Hazarmaveth, Jerah, ²⁷Hadoram, Uzal, Diklah, ²⁸Obal,

Abimael, Sheba, ²⁹Ophir, Havilah, and Jobab; all these were the descendants of Joktan. ³⁰Their settlements extended from Mesha as far as Sephar, the hill country to the east. ³¹These are the descendants of Shem according to their clans and languages, by their lands, according to their nations.

³²These are the groupings of Noah's descendants, according to their origins, by their nations; and from these the nations branched out over the earth after the Flood.

11 Everyone on earth had the same language and the same words. ²And as they migrated from the east, they came upon a valley in the land of Shinar and settled there. ³They said to one another, "Come, let us make bricks and burn them hard."— Brick served them as stone, and bitumen served them as mortar.— ⁴And they said, "Come, let us build us a city, and a tower with its top in the sky, to make a name for ourselves; else we shall be scattered all over the world." ⁵יהוה came down to look at the city and tower that humanity had built, ⁶and יהוה said, "If, as one people with one language for all, this is how they have begun to act, then nothing that they may propose to do will be out of their reach. ⁷Let us, then, go down and confound their speech there, so that they shall not understand one another's speech." ⁸Thus יהוה scattered them from there over the face of the whole earth; and they stopped building the city. ⁹That is why it was called Babel,* because there יהוה confounded* the speech of the whole earth; and from there יהוה scattered them over the face of the whole earth.

¹⁰This is the line of Shem. Shem was 100 years old when he begot Arpachshad, two years after the Flood. ¹¹*After the birth of ̄* Arpachshad, Shem lived 500 years and begot sons and daughters.

¹²When Arpachshad had lived 35 years, he begot Shelah. ¹³After the birth of Shelah, Arpachshad lived 403 years and begot sons and daughters.

¹⁴When Shelah had lived 30 years, he begot Eber. ¹⁵After the birth of Eber, Shelah lived 403 years and begot sons and daughters.

¹⁶When Eber had lived 34 years, he begot Peleg. ¹⁷After the birth of Peleg, Eber lived 430 years and begot sons and daughters.

¹⁸When Peleg had lived 30 years, he begot Reu. ¹⁹After the birth of Reu, Peleg lived 209 years and begot sons and daughters.

²⁰When Reu had lived 32 years, he begot Serug. ²¹After the birth of Serug, Reu lived 207 years and begot sons and daughters.

²²When Serug had lived 30 years, he begot Nahor. ²³After the birth of Nahor, Serug lived 200 years and begot sons and daughters.

²⁴When Nahor had lived 29 years, he begot Terah. ²⁵After the birth of Terah, Nahor lived 119 years and begot sons and daughters.

²⁶When Terah had lived 70 years, he begot Abram, Nahor, and Haran. ²⁷Now this is the line of Terah: Terah begot Abram, Nahor, and Haran; and Haran begot Lot. ²⁸Haran died in the lifetime of his father Terah, in his native land, Ur of the Chaldeans. ²⁹Abram and Nahor took wives for themselves, the name of Abram's wife being Sarai and that of Nahor's wife Milcah, the daughter of Haran, the father of Milcah and Iscah. ³⁰Now Sarai was barren, she had no child.

³¹Terah took his son Abram, his grandson Lot the son of Haran, and his daughter-in-law Sarai, the wife of his son Abram, and they set out together from Ur of the Chaldeans for the land of Canaan; but when they had come as far as Haran, they settled there. ³²The days of Terah came to 205 years; and Terah died in Haran.

לֶךְ לְךָ | LEKH LEKHA

12 יהוה said to Abram, "Go forth from your native land and from your father's house to the land that I will show you.

²I will make of you a great nation,
And I will bless you;
I will make your name great,
And you shall be *˙a blessing.˙*
³I will bless those who bless you
And curse the one who curses you;
And all the families of the earth
Shall bless themselves by you."

⁴Abram went forth as יהוה had commanded him, and Lot went with him. Abram was seventy-five years old when he left Haran. ⁵Abram took his wife Sarai and his brother's son Lot, and all the wealth that they had amassed, and the persons that they had

acquired in Haran; and they set out for the land of Canaan. When they arrived in the land of Canaan, ⁶Abram passed through the land as far as the site of Shechem, at the terebinth of Moreh. The Canaanites were then in the land.

⁷יהוה appeared to Abram and said, "I will assign this land to your offspring." And he built an altar there to יהוה who had appeared to him. ⁸From there he moved on to the hill country east of Bethel and pitched his tent, with Bethel on the west and Ai on the east; and he built there an altar to יהוה and invoked יהוה by name. ⁹Then Abram journeyed by stages toward the Negeb.

¹⁰There was a famine in the land, and Abram went down to Egypt to sojourn there, for the famine was severe in the land. ¹¹As he was about to enter Egypt, he said to his wife Sarai, "I* know what a beautiful woman you are. ¹²If the Egyptians see you, and think, 'She is his wife,' they will kill me and let you live. ¹³Please say that you are my sister, that it may go well with me because of you, and that I may remain alive thanks to you."

¹⁴When Abram entered Egypt, the Egyptians saw how very beautiful the woman was. ¹⁵Pharaoh's courtiers saw her and praised her to Pharaoh, and the woman was taken into Pharaoh's palace. ¹⁶And because of her, it went well with Abram; he acquired sheep, oxen, asses, male and female slaves, she-asses, and camels.

¹⁷But יהוה afflicted Pharaoh and his household with mighty plagues on account of Sarai, the wife of Abram. ¹⁸Pharaoh sent for Abram and said, "What is this you have done to me! Why did you not tell me that she was your wife? ¹⁹Why did you say, 'She is my sister,' so that I took her as my wife? Now, here is your wife; take her and begone!" ²⁰And Pharaoh put deputies° in charge of him, and they sent him off with his wife and all that he possessed.

13 From Egypt, Abram went up into the Negeb, with his wife and all that he possessed, together with Lot. ²Now Abram was very rich in cattle, silver, and gold. ³And he proceeded by stages from the Negeb as far as Bethel, to the place where his tent had been formerly, between Bethel and Ai, ⁴the site of the altar that he had built there at first; and there Abram invoked יהוה by name.

⁵Lot, who went with Abram, also had flocks and herds and

tents, 6so that the land could not support them staying together; for their possessions were so great that they could not remain together. 7And there was quarreling between the herders of Abram's cattle and those of Lot's cattle.—The Canaanites and Perizzites were then dwelling in the land.—8Abram said to Lot, "Let there be no strife between you and me, between my herders and yours, for we are kin. 9Is not the whole land before you? *˙Let us separate:˙* if you go north, I will go south; and if you go south, I will go north." 10Lot looked about him and saw how well watered was the whole plain of the Jordan, all of it—this was before יהוה had destroyed Sodom and Gomorrah—all the way to Zoar, like the garden of יהוה, like the land of Egypt. 11So Lot chose for himself the whole plain of the Jordan, and Lot journeyed eastward. Thus they parted from each other; 12Abram remained in the land of Canaan, while Lot settled in the cities of the Plain, pitching his tents near Sodom. 13Now the inhabitants of Sodom were very wicked sinners against יהוה.

14And יהוה said to Abram, after Lot had parted from him, "Raise your eyes and look out from where you are, to the north and south, to the east and west, 15for I give all the land that you see to you and your offspring forever. 16I will make your offspring as the dust of the earth, so that if one can count the dust of the earth, then your offspring too can be counted. 17Up, walk about the land, through its length and its breadth, for I give it to you." 18And Abram moved his tent, and came to dwell at the terebinths of Mamre, which are in Hebron; and he built an altar there to יהוה.

14 Now, when King Amraphel of Shinar, King Arioch of Ellasar, King Chedorlaomer of Elam, and King Tidal of Goiim 2made war on King Bera of Sodom, King Birsha of Gomorrah, King Shinab of Admah, King Shemeber of Zeboiim, and the king of Bela, which is Zoar, 3all the latter joined forces at the Valley of Siddim, now the *˙Dead Sea.˙* 4Twelve years they served Chedorlaomer, and in the thirteenth year they rebelled. 5In the fourteenth year Chedorlaomer and the kings who were with him came and defeated the Rephaim at Ashteroth-karnaim, the Zuzim at Ham, the Emim at Shaveh-kiriathaim, 6and the Horites in their hill country of Seir as far as El-paran, which is by the wilderness. [7]On their way back they came to En-mishpat, which is Kadesh, and subdued all the territory of the Amalekites, and also the Amorites who dwelt in Hazazon-tamar. [8]Then the king of Sodom, the king of Gomorrah, the king of Admah, the king of Zeboiim, and the king of Bela, which is Zoar, went forth and engaged them in battle in the Valley of Siddim: [9]King Chedorlaomer of Elam, King Tidal of Goiim, King Amraphel of Shinar, and King Arioch of Ellasar—four kings against those five.

[10]Now the Valley of Siddim was dotted with bitumen pits; and the kings of Sodom and Gomorrah, in their flight, threw themselves into them, while the rest escaped to the hill country. [11][The invaders] seized all the wealth of Sodom and Gomorrah and all their provisions, and went their way. [12]They also took Lot, the son of Abram's brother, and his possessions, and departed; for he had settled in Sodom.

[13]A fugitive brought the news to Abram the Hebrew, who was dwelling at the terebinths of Mamre the Amorite, kinsman of Eshkol and Aner, these being Abram's allies. [14]When Abram heard that his kinsman's [household] had been taken captive, he mustered his retainers,* born into his household, numbering three hundred and eighteen, and went in pursuit as far as Dan. [15]At night, he and his servants deployed against them and defeated them; and he pursued them as far as Hobah, which is north of Damascus. [16]He brought back all the possessions; he also brought back his kinsman Lot and his possessions, and the women and the rest of the people.

[17]When he returned from defeating Chedorlaomer and the kings with him, the king of Sodom came out to meet him in the Valley of Shaveh, which is the Valley of the King. [18]And King Melchizedek of Salem brought out bread and wine; he was a priest of *⁻God Most High.* [19]He blessed him, saying,

> "Blessed be Abram of God Most High,
> Creator of heaven and earth.
> [20]And blessed be God Most High,
> Who has delivered your foes into your hand."

And [Abram] gave him a tenth of everything.

[21]Then the king of Sodom said to Abram, "Give me the persons,

and take the possessions for yourself." ²²But Abram said to the king of Sodom, "I swear* to יהוה, God Most High, Creator of heaven and earth: ²³I will not take so much as a thread or a sandal strap of what is yours; you shall not say, 'It is I who made Abram rich.' ²⁴For me, nothing but what my servants have used up; as for the share of the notables° who went with me—Aner, Eshkol, and Mamre—let them take their share."

15 Some time later, the word of יהוה came to Abram in a vision:

"Fear not, Abram,
I am a shield to you;
Your reward shall be very great."

²But Abram said, "O °lord יהוה,° what can You give me, seeing that I shall die childless, *-and the one in charge of my household is Dammesek Eliezer!"-* ³Abram said further, "Since You have granted me no offspring, my steward will be my heir." ⁴The word of יהוה came to him in reply, "That one shall not be your heir; none but your very own issue shall be your heir." ⁵[Then in the vision, God] took him outside and said, "Look toward heaven and count the stars, if you are able to count them"—continuing, "So shall your offspring be." ⁶And he put his trust in יהוה, who reckoned it to his merit.

⁷Then [God] said to him, "I am יהוה who brought you out from Ur of the Chaldeans to assign this land to you as a possession." ⁸And he said, "O lord יהוה, how shall I know that I am to possess it?" ⁹Came the reply, "Bring Me a three-year-old heifer, a three-year-old she-goat, a three-year-old ram, a turtledove, and a young bird." ¹⁰He brought all these and cut them in two, placing each half opposite the other; but he did not cut up the bird. ¹¹Birds of prey came down upon the carcasses, and Abram drove them away. ¹²As the sun was about to set, a deep sleep fell upon Abram, and a great dark dread descended upon him. ¹³And [God] said to Abram, "Know well that your offspring shall be strangers in a land not theirs, and they shall be enslaved and oppressed four hundred years; ¹⁴but I will execute judgment on the nation they shall serve, and in the end they shall go free with great wealth.

¹⁵As for you,

> You shall go to your ancestors in peace;
> You shall be buried at a ripe old age.

¹⁶And they shall return here in the fourth generation, for the iniquity of the Amorites is not yet complete."

¹⁷When the sun set and it was very dark, there appeared a smoking oven, and a flaming torch which passed between those pieces. ¹⁸On that day יהוה made a covenant with Abram: "To your offspring I assign this land, from the river of Egypt to the great river, the river Euphrates—¹⁹the Kenites, the Kenizzites, the Kadmonites, ²⁰the Hittites, the Perizzites, the Rephaim, ²¹the Amorites, the Canaanites, the Girgashites, and the Jebusites."

16 Sarai, Abram's wife, had borne him no children. She had an Egyptian maidservant whose name was Hagar. ²And Sarai said to Abram, "Look, יהוה has kept me from bearing. Consort with my maid; perhaps I shall *have a child* through her." And Abram heeded Sarai's request. ³So Sarai, Abram's wife, took her maid, Hagar the Egyptian—after Abram had dwelt in the land of Canaan ten years—and gave her to her husband Abram as concubine. ⁴He cohabited with Hagar and she conceived; and when she saw that she had conceived, her mistress was lowered in her esteem. ⁵And Sarai said to Abram, "The wrong done me is your fault! I myself put my maid in your bosom; now that she sees that she is pregnant, I am lowered in her esteem. יהוה decide between you and me!" ⁶Abram said to Sarai, "Your maid is in your hands. Deal with her as you think right." Then Sarai treated her harshly, and she ran away from her.

⁷A messenger of יהוה found her by a spring of water in the wilderness, the spring on the road to Shur, ⁸and said, "Hagar, slave of Sarai, where have you come from, and where are you going?" And she said, "I am running away from my mistress Sarai."

⁹And the messenger of יהוה said to her, "Go back to your mistress, and submit to her harsh treatment." ¹⁰And the messenger of יהוה said to her,

> "I will greatly increase your offspring,
> And they shall be too many to count."

¹¹The messenger of יהוה said to her further,

"Behold, you are pregnant
And shall bear a son;
You shall call him Ishmael,*
For יהוה has paid heed to your suffering.
¹²He shall be a wild ass of a person;°
His hand against everyone,
And everyone's hand against him;
He shall dwell alongside of all his kin."

¹³And she called יהוה who spoke to her, "You Are El-roi,"* by which she meant, *"Have I not gone on seeing after my being seen!"* ¹⁴Therefore the well was called Beer-lahai-roi;* it is between Kadesh and Bered.—¹⁵Hagar bore a son to Abram, and Abram gave the son that Hagar bore him the name Ishmael. ¹⁶Abram was eighty-six years old when Hagar bore Ishmael to Abram.

17 When Abram was ninety-nine years old, יהוה appeared to Abram and said to him, "I am *El Shaddai.* Walk in My ways and be blameless. ²I will establish My covenant between Me and you, and I will make you exceedingly numerous."

³Abram threw himself on his face; and God spoke to him further, ⁴"As for Me, this is My covenant with you: You shall be the father of a multitude of nations. ⁵And you shall no longer be called Abram, but your name shall be Abraham,* for I make you the father of a multitude of nations. ⁶I will make you exceedingly fertile, and make nations of you; and kings shall come forth from you. ⁷I will maintain My covenant between Me and you, and your offspring to come, as an everlasting covenant throughout the ages, to be God to you and to your offspring to come. ⁸I assign the land you sojourn in to you and your offspring to come, all the land of Canaan, as an everlasting holding. I will be their God."

⁹God further said to Abraham, "As for you, you and your offspring to come throughout the ages shall keep My covenant. ¹⁰Such shall be the covenant between Me and you and your offspring to follow which you shall keep: every male among you shall be circumcised. ¹¹You shall circumcise the flesh of your foreskin, and that shall be the sign of the covenant between Me and you.

¹²And throughout the generations, every male among you shall be circumcised at the age of eight days. As for the homeborn slave and the one bought from an outsider who is not of your offspring, ¹³they must be circumcised, homeborn, and purchased alike. Thus shall My covenant be marked in your flesh as an everlasting pact. ¹⁴And if any male who is uncircumcised fails to circumcise the flesh of his foreskin, that person shall be cut off from kin; he has broken My covenant."

¹⁵And God said to Abraham, "As for your wife Sarai, you shall not call her Sarai, but her name shall be Sarah.* ¹⁶I will bless her; indeed, I will give you a son by her. I will bless her so that she shall give rise to nations; rulers of peoples shall issue from her." ¹⁷Abraham threw himself on his face and laughed, as he said to himself, "Can a child be born to a man a hundred years old, or can Sarah bear a child at ninety?" ¹⁸And Abraham said to God, "O that Ishmael might live by Your favor!" ¹⁹God said, "Nevertheless, Sarah your wife shall bear you a son, and you shall name him Isaac;* and I will maintain My covenant with him as an everlasting covenant for his offspring to come. ²⁰As for Ishmael, *I have heeded you.* I hereby bless him. I will make him fertile and exceedingly numerous. He shall be the father of twelve chieftains, and I will make of him a great nation. ²¹But My covenant I will maintain with Isaac, whom Sarah shall bear to you at this season next year." ²²Done speaking with him, God was gone from Abraham.

²³Then Abraham took his son Ishmael, and all his homeborn slaves and all those he had bought, every male in Abraham's household, and he circumcised the flesh of their foreskins on that very day, as God had spoken to him. ²⁴Abraham was ninety-nine years old when he circumcised the flesh of his foreskin, ²⁵and his son Ishmael was thirteen years old when he was circumcised in the flesh of his foreskin. ²⁶Thus Abraham and his son Ishmael were circumcised on that very day; ²⁷and all [men of] his household, his homeborn slaves and those that had been bought from outsiders, were circumcised with him.

וירא | VA-YERA'

18 יהוה appeared to him by the terebinths of Mamre; he was sitting at the entrance of the tent as the day grew hot.

²Looking up, he saw three [divine] envoys° standing near him. Perceiving this, he ran from the entrance of the tent to greet them and, bowing to the ground, ³he said, "*ᐧMy lords!ᐧ* If it please you, do not go on past your servant. ⁴Let a little water be brought; bathe your feet and recline under the tree. ⁵And let me fetch a morsel of bread that you may refresh yourselves; then go on— seeing that you have come your servant's way." They replied, "Do as you have said."

⁶Abraham hastened into the tent to Sarah, and said, "Quick, three *seah*s of choice flour! Knead and make cakes!" ⁷Then Abraham ran to the herd, took a calf, tender and choice, and gave it to a servant-boy, who hastened to prepare it. ⁸He took curds and milk and the calf that had been prepared and set these before them; and he waited on them under the tree as they ate.

⁹They said to him, "Where is your wife Sarah?" And he replied, "There, in the tent." ¹⁰Then one said, "I will return to you *ᐧnext year,ᐧ* and your wife Sarah shall have a son!" Sarah was listening at the entrance of the tent, which was behind him. ¹¹Now Abraham and Sarah were old, advanced in years; Sarah had stopped having °ᐧher periods.ᐧ° ¹²And Sarah laughed to herself, saying, "Now that °ᐧI've lost the ability,ᐧ° am I to have enjoyment—with my husband so old?" ¹³Then יהוה said to Abraham, "Why did Sarah laugh, saying, 'Shall I in truth bear a child, old as I am?' ¹⁴Is anything too wondrous for יהוה? I will return to you at the same season next year, and Sarah shall have a son." ¹⁵Sarah lied, saying, "I did not laugh," for she was frightened. Came the reply, "You did laugh."

¹⁶The envoys° set out from there and looked down toward Sodom, Abraham walking with them to see them off. ¹⁷Now יהוה had said, "Shall I hide from Abraham what I am about to do, ¹⁸since Abraham is to become a great and populous nation and all the nations of the earth are to bless themselves by him? ¹⁹For I have singled him out, that he may instruct his children and his posterity to keep the way of יהוה by doing what is just and right, in order that יהוה may bring about for Abraham what has been promised him." ²⁰Then יהוה said, "The outrage of Sodom and Gomorrah is so great, and their sin so grave! ²¹I will go down to see

whether they have acted altogether according to the outcry that has reached Me; if not, I will take note."

²²The envoys went on from there to Sodom, while Abraham remained standing before יהוה. ²³Abraham came forward and said, "Will You sweep away the innocent along with the guilty? ²⁴What if there should be fifty innocent within the city; will You then wipe out the place and not forgive it for the sake of the innocent fifty who are in it? ²⁵Far be it from You to do such a thing, to bring death upon the innocent as well as the guilty, so that innocent and guilty fare alike. Far be it from You! Shall not the Judge of all the earth deal justly?" ²⁶And יהוה answered, "If I find within the city of Sodom fifty innocent ones, I will forgive the whole place for their sake." ²⁷Abraham spoke up, saying, "Here I venture to speak to my lord, I who am but dust and ashes: ²⁸What if the fifty innocent should lack five? Will You destroy the whole city for want of the five?"

"I will not destroy if I find forty-five there."

²⁹But he spoke up again, and said, "What if forty should be found there?"

"I will not do it, for the sake of the forty."

³⁰And he said, "Let not my lord be angry if I go on: What if thirty should be found there?"

"I will not do it if I find thirty there."

³¹And he said, "I venture again to speak to my lord: What if twenty should be found there?"

"I will not destroy, for the sake of the twenty."

³²And he said, "Let not my lord be angry if I speak but this last time: What if ten should be found there?"

"I will not destroy, for the sake of the ten."

³³Having finished speaking to Abraham, יהוה departed; and Abraham returned to his place.

19 The two messengers arrived in Sodom in the evening, as Lot was sitting in the gate of Sodom. When Lot saw them, he rose to greet them and, bowing low with his face to the ground, ²he said, "Please, my lords, turn aside to your servant's house to spend the night, and bathe your feet; then you may be on your way early." But they said, "No, we will spend the night in

the square." ³But he urged them strongly, so they turned his way and entered his house. He prepared a feast for them and baked unleavened bread, and they ate.

⁴They had not yet lain down, when the °˗town council [and] the militia of Sodom,˗°—°˗insignificant and influential alike,˗° the whole assembly without exception—gathered about the house. ⁵And they shouted to Lot and said to him, "Where are the envoys° [of יהוה] who came to you tonight? Bring them out to us, that we may °˗be intimate with˗° them." ⁶So Lot went out to them to the entrance, shut the door behind him, ⁷and said, "I beg you, my friends, do not commit such a wrong. ⁸Look, I have two daughters° who have not known a man. Let me bring them out to you, and you may °˗do to them as you please;˗° but do not do anything to °˗these envoys,˗° since they have come under the shelter of my roof." ⁹But they said, "Stand back! The fellow," they said, "came here as an alien, and already he acts the ruler! Now we will deal worse with you than with them." And they pressed hard °˗against that householder˗°—against Lot—and moved forward to break the door. ¹⁰But the envoys stretched out their hands and pulled Lot into the house with them, and shut the door. ¹¹And the people° who were at the entrance of the house, °˗low and high alike,˗° they struck with blinding light, so that they were helpless to find the entrance.

¹²Then the envoys said to Lot, "Whom else have you here? Sons-in-law, your sons and daughters, or anyone else that you have in the city—bring them out of the place. ¹³For we are about to destroy this place; because the outcry against them before יהוה has become so great that יהוה has sent us to destroy it." ¹⁴So Lot went out and spoke to his sons-in-law, who had married his daughters, and said, "Up, get out of this place, for יהוה is about to destroy the city." But he seemed to his sons-in-law as one who jests.

¹⁵As dawn broke, the messengers urged Lot on, saying, "Up, take your wife and your two remaining daughters, lest you be swept away because of the iniquity of the city." ¹⁶Still he delayed. So the envoys seized his hand, and the hands of his wife and his two daughters—in יהוה's mercy on him—and brought him out and left him outside the city. ¹⁷When they had brought them outside,

one said, "Flee for your life! Do not look behind you, nor stop anywhere in the Plain; flee to the hills, lest you be swept away." ¹⁸But Lot said to them, "Oh no, my lord! ¹⁹You have been so gracious to your servant, and have already shown me so much kindness in order to save my life; but I cannot flee to the hills, lest the disaster overtake me and I die. ²⁰Look, that town there is near enough to flee to; it is such a little place! Let me flee there—it is such a little place—and let my life be saved." ²¹He replied, "Very well, I will grant you this favor too, and I will not annihilate the town of which you have spoken. ²²Hurry, flee there, for I cannot do anything until you arrive there." Hence the town came to be called Zoar.*

²³As the sun rose upon the earth and Lot entered Zoar, ²⁴יהוה rained upon Sodom and Gomorrah sulfurous fire from יהוה out of heaven—²⁵annihilating those cities and the entire Plain, and all the inhabitants of the cities and the vegetation of the ground. ²⁶Lot's* wife looked back,* and she thereupon turned into a pillar of salt.

²⁷Next morning, Abraham hurried to the place where he had stood before יהוה, ²⁸and, looking down toward Sodom and Gomorrah and all the land of the Plain, he saw the smoke of the land rising like the smoke of a kiln.

²⁹Thus it was that, when God destroyed the cities of the Plain and annihilated the cities where Lot dwelt, God was mindful of Abraham and removed Lot from the midst of the upheaval.

³⁰Lot went up from Zoar and settled in the hill country with his two daughters, for he was afraid to dwell in Zoar; and he and his two daughters lived in a cave. ³¹And the older one said to the younger, "Our father is old, and there is not a man on earth to consort with us in the way of all the world. ³²Come, let us make our father drink wine, and let us lie with him, that we may maintain life through our father." ³³That night they made their father drink wine, and the older one went in and lay with her father; he did not know when she lay down or when she rose. ³⁴The next day the older one said to the younger, "See, I lay with Father last night; let us make him drink wine tonight also, and you go and lie with him, that we may maintain life through our father." ³⁵That night also they made their father drink wine, and the younger one

went and lay with him; he did not know when she lay down or when she rose.

³⁶Thus the two daughters of Lot became pregnant by their father. ³⁷The older one bore a son and named him Moab;* he is the father of the Moabites of today. ³⁸And the younger also bore a son, and she called him Ben-ammi;* he is the father of the Ammonites of today.

20 Abraham journeyed from there to the region of the Negeb and settled between Kadesh and Shur. While he was sojourning in Gerar, ²Abraham said of Sarah his wife, "She is my sister." So King Abimelech of Gerar had Sarah brought to him. ³But God came to Abimelech in a dream by night and said to him, "You are to die because of the woman that you have taken, for she is a married woman." ⁴Now Abimelech had not approached her. He said, "O lord,° will You slay people even though innocent? ⁵He himself said to me, 'She is my sister!' And she also said, 'He is my brother.' When I did this, my heart was blameless and my hands were clean." ⁶And God said to him in the dream, "I knew that you did this with a blameless heart, and so I kept you from sinning against Me. That was why I did not let you touch her. ⁷Therefore, restore the wife of this householder°—since he is a prophet, he will intercede for you—to save your life. If you fail to restore her, know that you shall die, you and all that are yours."

⁸Early next morning, Abimelech called his servants and told them all that had happened. Those officials° were greatly frightened. ⁹Then Abimelech summoned Abraham and said to him, "What have you done to us? What wrong have I done that you should bring so great a guilt upon me and my kingdom? You have done to me things that ought not to be done. ¹⁰What, then," Abimelech demanded of Abraham, "was your purpose in doing this thing?" ¹¹"I thought," said Abraham, "surely there is no fear of God in this place, and they will kill me because of my wife. ¹²And besides, she is in truth my sister, my father's daughter though not my mother's; and she became my wife. ¹³So when God made me wander from my father's house, I said to her, 'Let this be the kindness that you shall do me: whatever place we come to, say there of me: He is my brother.'"

¹⁴Abimelech took sheep and oxen, and male and female slaves, and gave them to Abraham; and he restored his wife Sarah to him. ¹⁵And Abimelech said, "Here, my land is before you; settle wherever you please." ¹⁶And to Sarah he said, "I herewith give your brother a thousand pieces of silver; this will serve you as vindication* before all who are with you, and you are cleared before everyone." ¹⁷Abraham then prayed to God, and God healed Abimelech and his wife and his slave girls, so that they bore children; ¹⁸for יהוה had closed fast every womb of the household of Abimelech because of Sarah, the wife of Abraham.

21 יהוה took note of Sarah as promised, and יהוה did for Sarah what had been announced. ²Sarah conceived and bore a son to Abraham in his old age, at the set time of which God had spoken. ³Abraham gave his newborn son, whom Sarah had borne him, the name of Isaac. ⁴And when his son Isaac was eight days old, Abraham circumcised him, as God had commanded him. ⁵Now Abraham was a hundred years old when his son Isaac was born to him. ⁶Sarah said, "God has brought me laughter; everyone who hears will laugh with* me." ⁷And she added,

"Who would have said to Abraham
That Sarah would suckle children!
Yet I have borne a son in his old age."

⁸The child grew up and was weaned, and Abraham held a great feast on the day that Isaac was weaned.

⁹Sarah saw the son whom Hagar the Egyptian had borne to Abraham playing. ¹⁰She said to Abraham, "Cast out that slave-woman and her son, for the son of that slave shall not share in the inheritance with my son Isaac." ¹¹The matter distressed Abraham greatly, for it concerned a son of his. ¹²But God said to Abraham, "Do not be distressed over the boy or your slave; whatever Sarah tells you, do as she says, for it is through Isaac that offspring shall be continued* for you. ¹³As for the son of the slave-woman, I will make a nation of him, too, for he is your seed."

¹⁴Early next morning Abraham took some bread and a skin of water, and gave them to Hagar. He placed them over her shoulder, together with the child, and sent her away. And she wandered about in the wilderness of Beer-sheba. ¹⁵When the water was gone

from the skin, she left the child under one of the bushes, ¹⁶and went and sat down at a distance, a bowshot away; for she thought, "Let me not look on as the child dies." And sitting thus afar, she burst into tears.

¹⁷God heard the cry of the boy, and a messenger of God called to Hagar from heaven and said to her, "What troubles you, Hagar? Fear not, for God has heeded the cry of the boy where he is. ¹⁸Come, lift up the boy and hold him by the hand, for I will make a great nation of him." ¹⁹Then God opened her eyes and she saw a well of water. She went and filled the skin with water, and let the boy drink. ²⁰God was with the boy and he grew up; he dwelt in the wilderness and became skilled with a bow. ²¹He lived in the wilderness of Paran; and his mother got a wife for him from the land of Egypt.

²²At that time Abimelech and Phicol, chief of his troops, said to Abraham, "God is with you in everything that you do. ²³Therefore swear to me here by God that you will not deal falsely with me or with my kith and kin, but will deal with me and with the land in which you have sojourned as loyally as I have dealt with you." ²⁴And Abraham said, "I swear it."

²⁵Then Abraham reproached Abimelech for the well of water which the servants of Abimelech had seized. ²⁶But Abimelech said, "I do not know who did this; you did not tell me, nor have I heard of it until today." ²⁷Abraham took sheep and oxen and gave them to Abimelech, and the two of them made a pact. ²⁸Abraham then set seven ewes of the flock by themselves, ²⁹and Abimelech said to Abraham, "What mean these seven ewes which you have set apart?" ³⁰He replied, "You are to accept these seven ewes from me as proof that I dug this well." ³¹Hence that place was called Beer-sheba,* for there the two of them swore an oath. ³²When they had concluded the pact at Beer-sheba, Abimelech and Phicol, chief of his troops, departed and returned to the land of the Philistines. ³³[Abraham] planted a tamarisk at Beer-sheba, and invoked there the name of יהוה, the Everlasting God. ³⁴And Abraham resided in the land of the Philistines a long time.

22 Some time afterward, God put Abraham to the test, saying to him, "Abraham." He answered, "Here I am."

²"Take your son, your favored one, Isaac, whom you love, and go to the land of Moriah, and offer him there as a burnt offering on one of the heights that I will point out to you."

³So early next morning, Abraham saddled his ass and took with him two of his servants and his son Isaac. He split the wood for the burnt offering, and he set out for the place of which God had told him. ⁴On the third day Abraham looked up and saw the place from afar. ⁵Then Abraham said to his servants, "You stay here with the ass. The boy and I will go up there; we will worship and we will return to you."

⁶Abraham took the wood for the burnt offering and put it on his son Isaac. He himself took the firestone* and the knife; and the two walked off together. ⁷Then Isaac said to his father Abraham, "Father!" And he answered, "Yes, my son." And he said, "Here are the firestone and the wood; but where is the sheep for the burnt offering?" ⁸And Abraham said, "It is God who will see to the sheep for this burnt offering, my son." And the two of them walked on together.

⁹They arrived at the place of which God had told him. Abraham built an altar there; he laid out the wood; he bound his son Isaac; he laid him on the altar, on top of the wood. ¹⁰And Abraham picked up the knife to slay his son. ¹¹Then a messenger of יהוה called to him from heaven: "Abraham! Abraham!" And he answered, "Here I am."

¹²"Do not raise your hand against the boy, or do anything to him. For now I know that you fear God, since you have not withheld your son, your favored one, from Me."

¹³When Abraham looked up, his eye fell upon a*ram, caught in the thicket by its horns. So Abraham went and took the ram and offered it up as a burnt offering in place of his son. ¹⁴And Abraham named that site Adonai-yireh,* whence the present saying, *-"On the mount of יהוה there is vision."-*

¹⁵The messenger of יהוה called to Abraham a second time from heaven, ¹⁶and said, "By Myself I swear, יהוה declares: Because you have done this and have not withheld your son, your favored one, ¹⁷I will bestow My blessing upon you and make your descendants as numerous as the stars of heaven and the sands on the seashore; and your descendants shall seize the gates of their foes. ¹⁸All the

Va-yera'

nations of the earth shall bless themselves by your descendants, because you have obeyed My command." ¹⁹Abraham then returned to his servants, and they departed together for Beer-sheba; and Abraham stayed in Beer-sheba.

²⁰Some time later, Abraham was told, "Milcah too has borne sons to your brother Nahor: ²¹Uz the first-born, and Buz his brother, and Kemuel the father of Aram; ²²and Chesed, Hazo, Pildash, Jidlaph, and Bethuel"—²³Bethuel being the father of Rebekah. These eight Milcah bore to Nahor, Abraham's brother. ²⁴°And his concubine, whose name was Reumah, also bore [sons]— Tebah, Gaham, and Tahash—and [a daughter,] Maacah.

חַיֵּי שָׂרָה | ḤAYYEI SARAH

23 Sarah's lifetime—the span of Sarah's life—came to one hundred and twenty-seven years. ²Sarah died in Kiriath-arba—now Hebron—in the land of Canaan; and Abraham proceeded to mourn for Sarah and to bewail her. ³Then Abraham rose from beside his dead, and spoke to the Hittites, saying, ⁴"I am a resident alien among you; sell me a burial site among you, that I may remove my dead for burial." ⁵And the Hittites replied to Abraham, saying to him, ⁶"Hear us, my lord: you are the elect of God among us. Bury your dead in the choicest of our burial places; none of us will withhold his burial place from you for burying your dead." ⁷Thereupon Abraham bowed low to the °landowning citizens,° the Hittites, ⁸and he said to them, "If it is your wish that I remove my dead for burial, you must agree to intercede for me with Ephron son of Zohar. ⁹Let him sell me the cave of Machpelah that he owns, which is at the edge of his land. Let him sell it to me, at the full price, for a burial site in your midst."

¹⁰Ephron was present among the Hittites; so Ephron the Hittite answered Abraham in the hearing of the Hittites, °the assembly in his town's gate,° saying, ¹¹"No, my lord, hear me: I give you the field and I give you the cave that is in it; I give it to you in the presence of my people. Bury your dead." ¹²Then Abraham bowed low before the landowning citizens, ¹³and spoke to Ephron in the hearing of the landowning citizens, saying, "If only you would hear me out! Let me pay the price of the land; accept it from me, that I may bury my dead there." ¹⁴And Ephron replied to Abraham, saying to

him, ¹⁵"My lord, do hear me! A piece of land worth four hundred shekels of silver—what is that between you and me? Go and bury your dead." ¹⁶Abraham accepted Ephron's terms. Abraham paid out to Ephron the money that he had named in the hearing of the Hittites—four hundred shekels of silver at the going merchants' rate.

¹⁷So Ephron's land in Machpelah, near Mamre—the field with its cave and all the trees anywhere within the confines of that field—passed ¹⁸to Abraham as his possession, in the presence of the Hittites, of the assembly in his town's gate. ¹⁹And then Abraham buried his wife Sarah in the cave of the field of Machpelah, facing Mamre—now Hebron—in the land of Canaan. ²⁰Thus the field with its cave passed from the Hittites to Abraham, as a burial site.

24 Abraham was now old, advanced in years, and יהוה had blessed Abraham in all things. ²And Abraham said to the senior servant of his household, who had charge of all that he owned, "Put your hand under my thigh ³and I will make you swear by יהוה, the God of heaven and the God of the earth, that you will not take a wife for my son from the daughters of the Canaanites among whom I dwell, ⁴but will go to the land of my birth and get a wife for my son Isaac." ⁵And the servant said to him, "What if the woman does not consent to follow me to this land, shall I then take your son back to the land from which you came?" ⁶Abraham answered him, "On no account must you take my son back there! ⁷יהוה, the God of heaven—who took me from my father's house and from my native land, who promised me on oath, saying, 'I will assign this land to your offspring'—will send a messenger before you, and you will get a wife for my son from there. ⁸And if the woman does not consent to follow you, you shall then be clear of this oath to me; but do not take my son back there." ⁹So the servant put his hand under the thigh of his master Abraham and swore to him *⁻as bidden.⁻*

¹⁰Then the servant took ten of his master's camels and set out, taking with him all the bounty of his master; and he made his way to Aram-naharaim, to the city of Nahor. ¹¹He made the camels kneel down by the well outside the city, at evening time, the time

when women come out to draw water. ¹²And he said, "O יהוה, God of my master Abraham's [house], grant me good fortune this day, and deal graciously with my master Abraham: ¹³Here I stand by the spring as the daughters of the °‑town's householders‑° come out to draw water; ¹⁴let the maiden to whom I say, 'Please, lower your jar that I may drink,' and who replies, 'Drink, and I will also water your camels'—let her be the one whom You have decreed for Your servant Isaac. Thereby shall I know that You have dealt graciously with my master."

¹⁵He had scarcely finished speaking, when Rebekah, who was born to Bethuel, the son of Milcah the wife of Abraham's brother Nahor, came out with her jar on her shoulder. ¹⁶°‑The maiden was very beautiful—[and] a virgin, no man having known her.‑° She went down to the spring, filled her jar, and came up. ¹⁷The servant ran toward her and said, "Please, let me sip a little water from your jar." ¹⁸"Drink, my lord," she said, and she quickly lowered her jar upon her hand and let him drink. ¹⁹When she had let him drink his fill, she said, "I will also draw for your camels, until they finish drinking." ²⁰Quickly emptying her jar into the trough, she ran back to the well to draw, and she drew for all his camels.

²¹The emissary,° meanwhile, stood gazing at her, silently wondering whether יהוה had made his errand successful or not. ²²When the camels had finished drinking, the emissary took a gold nose-ring weighing a half-shekel,* and two gold bands for her arms, ten shekels in weight. ²³"Pray tell me," he said, "whose daughter are you? Is there room in your father's house for us to spend the night?" ²⁴She replied, "I am the daughter of Bethuel the son of Milcah, whom she bore to Nahor." ²⁵And she went on, "There is plenty of straw* and feed at home, and also room to spend the night." ²⁶The emissary bowed low in homage to יהוה ²⁷and said, "Blessed be יהוה, the God of my master Abraham's [house], who has not withheld steadfast faithfulness from my master. For I have been guided on my errand by יהוה, to the house of my master's kin."

²⁸The maiden ran and told all this to her mother's household. ²⁹Now Rebekah had a brother whose name was Laban. Laban ran out to the emissary at the spring—³⁰when he saw the nose-ring and the bands on his sister's arms, and when he heard his sister Rebekah say, "Thus the emissary spoke to me." He went up to the

emissary, who was still standing beside the camels at the spring. ³¹"Come in, O blessed of יהוה," he said, "why do you remain outside, when I have made ready the house and a place for the camels?" ³²So the emissary entered the house, and the camels were unloaded. The camels were given straw and feed, and water was brought to bathe his feet and the feet of the entourage° under him. ³³But when food was set before him, he said, "I will not eat until I have told my tale." He said, "Speak, then."

³⁴"I am Abraham's servant," he began. ³⁵"יהוה has greatly blessed my master, who has become rich—giving him sheep and cattle, silver and gold, male and female slaves, camels and asses. ³⁶And Sarah, my master's wife, bore my master a son in her old age, and he has assigned to him everything he owns. ³⁷Now my master made me swear, saying, 'You shall not get a wife for my son from the daughters of the Canaanites in whose land I dwell; ³⁸but you shall go to my father's house, to my kindred, and get a wife for my son.' ³⁹And I said to my master, 'What if the woman does not follow me?' ⁴⁰He replied to me, 'יהוה, whose ways I have followed, will send a messenger with you and make your errand successful; and you will get a wife for my son from my kindred, from my father's house. ⁴¹Thus only shall you be freed from my adjuration: if, when you come to my kindred, they refuse you—only then shall you be freed from my adjuration.'

⁴²"I came today to the spring, and I said: O יהוה, God of my master Abraham's [house], if You would indeed grant success to the errand on which I am engaged! ⁴³As I stand by the spring of water, let the young woman who comes out to draw and to whom I say, 'Please, let me drink a little water from your jar,' ⁴⁴and who answers, 'You may drink, and I will also draw for your camels'— let her be the wife whom יהוה has decreed for my master's son.' ⁴⁵I had scarcely finished praying in my heart, when Rebekah came out with her jar on her shoulder, and went down to the spring and drew. And I said to her, 'Please give me a drink.' ⁴⁶She quickly lowered her jar and said, 'Drink, and I will also water your camels.' So I drank, and she also watered the camels. ⁴⁷I inquired of her, 'Whose daughter are you?' And she said, 'The daughter of Bethuel, son of Nahor, whom Milcah bore to him.' And I put the ring on her nose and the bands on her arms. ⁴⁸Then I bowed low

in homage to יהוה and blessed יהוה, the God of my master Abraham's [house], who led me on the right way to get the daughter of my master's brother for his son. ⁴⁹And now, if you mean to treat my master with true kindness, tell me; and if not, tell me also, that I may turn right or left."

⁵⁰Then Laban and Bethuel answered, "The matter was decreed by יהוה; we cannot speak to you bad or good. ⁵¹Here is Rebekah before you; take her and go, and let her be a wife to your master's son, as יהוה has spoken." ⁵²When Abraham's servant heard their words, he bowed low to the ground before יהוה. ⁵³The servant brought out objects of silver and gold, and garments, and gave them to Rebekah; and he gave presents to her brother and her mother. ⁵⁴Then he and the entourage under him ate and drank, and they spent the night. When they arose next morning, he said, "Give me leave to go to my master." ⁵⁵But her brother and her mother said, "Let the maiden remain with us *˜some ten days;˜* then you may go." ⁵⁶He said to them, "Do not delay me, now that יהוה has made my errand successful. Give me leave that I may go to my master." ⁵⁷And they said, "Let us call the girl and ask for her reply." ⁵⁸They called Rebekah and said to her, "Will you go with this emissary°?" And she said, "I will." ⁵⁹So they sent off their sister Rebekah and her nurse along with Abraham's servant and his entourage. ⁶⁰And they blessed Rebekah and said to her,

"O sister!
May you grow
Into thousands of myriads;
May your descendants seize
The gates of their foes."

⁶¹Then Rebekah and her maids arose, mounted the camels, and followed the emissary. So the servant took Rebekah and went his way.

⁶²Isaac had just come back from the vicinity of Beer-lahai-roi, for he was settled in the region of the Negeb. ⁶³And Isaac went out walking* in the field toward evening and, looking up, he saw camels approaching. ⁶⁴Raising her eyes, Rebekah saw Isaac. She alighted from the camel ⁶⁵and said to the servant, "Who is that dignitary° walking in the field toward us?" And the servant said, "That is my master." So she took her veil and covered herself. ⁶⁶The servant told Isaac all the things that he had done. ⁶⁷Isaac

then brought her into the tent of his mother Sarah, and he took Rebekah as his wife. Isaac loved her, and thus found comfort after his mother's death.

25 Abraham took another wife, whose name was Keturah. ²She bore him Zimran, Jokshan, Medan, Midian, Ishbak, and Shuah. ³Jokshan begot Sheba and Dedan. The descendants of Dedan were the Asshurim, the Letushim, and the Leummim. ⁴The descendants of Midian were Ephah, Epher, Enoch,* Abida, and Eldaah. All these were descendants of Keturah. ⁵Abraham willed all that he owned to Isaac; ⁶but to Abraham's sons by concubines Abraham gave gifts while he was still living, and he sent them away from his son Isaac eastward, to the land of the East.

⁷This was the total span of Abraham's life: one hundred and seventy-five years. ⁸And Abraham breathed his last, dying at a good ripe age, old and contented; and he was gathered to his kin.° ⁹His sons Isaac and Ishmael buried him in the cave of Machpelah, in the field of Ephron son of Zohar the Hittite, facing Mamre, ¹⁰the field that Abraham had bought from the Hittites; there Abraham was buried, and Sarah his wife. ¹¹After the death of Abraham, God blessed his son Isaac. And Isaac settled near Beer-lahai-roi.

¹²This is the line of Ishmael, Abraham's son, whom Hagar the Egyptian, Sarah's slave, bore to Abraham. ¹³These are the names of the sons of Ishmael, by their names, in the order of their birth: Nebaioth, the first-born of Ishmael, Kedar, Adbeel, Mibsam, ¹⁴Mishma, Dumah, Massa, ¹⁵Hadad, Tema, Jetur, Naphish, and Kedmah. ¹⁶These are the sons of Ishmael and these are their names by their villages and by their encampments: twelve chieftains of as many tribes.—¹⁷These were the years of the life of Ishmael: one hundred and thirty-seven years; then he breathed his last and died, and was gathered to his kin.—¹⁸They dwelt from Havilah, by Shur, which is close to Egypt, all the way to Asshur; they camped alongside all their kin.

תּוֹלְדֹת | TOLEDOT

¹⁹This is the story of Isaac, son of Abraham. Abraham begot Isaac. ²⁰Isaac was forty years old when he took to wife Rebekah,

daughter of Bethuel the Aramean of Paddan-aram, sister of Laban the Aramean. ²¹Isaac pleaded with יהוה on behalf of his wife, because she was barren; and יהוה responded to his plea, and his wife Rebekah conceived. ²²But the children struggled in her womb, and she said, "If so, *"why do I exist?"-* She went to inquire of יהוה, ²³and יהוה answered her,

> "Two nations are in your womb,
> Two separate peoples shall issue from your body;
> One people shall be mightier than the other,
> And the older shall serve the younger."

²⁴When her time to give birth was at hand, there were twins in her womb. ²⁵The first one emerged red, like a hairy mantle all over; so they named him Esau.* ²⁶Then his brother emerged, holding on to the heel of Esau; so they named him Jacob.* Isaac was sixty years old when they were born.

²⁷When the boys grew up, Esau became a skillful hunter, the °¨wild sort;·° but Jacob became the °¨mild type,·° °¨raising livestock.·° ²⁸Isaac favored Esau because *¨he had a taste for game;* but Rebekah favored Jacob. ²⁹Once when Jacob was cooking a stew, Esau came in from the open, famished. ³⁰And Esau said to Jacob, "Give me some of that red stuff to gulp down, for I am famished"—which is why he was named Edom.* ³¹Jacob said, "First sell me your birthright." ³²And Esau said, "I am at the point of death, so of what use is my birthright to me?" ³³But Jacob said, "Swear to me first." So he swore to him, and sold his birthright to Jacob. ³⁴Jacob then gave Esau bread and lentil stew; he ate and drank, and he rose and went away. Thus did Esau spurn the birthright.

26 There was a famine in the land—aside from the previous famine that had occurred in the days of Abraham—and Isaac went to Abimelech, king of the Philistines, in Gerar. ²יהוה had appeared to him and said, "Do not go down to Egypt; stay in the land which I point out to you. ³Reside in this land, and I will be with you and bless you; I will assign all these lands to you and to your heirs, fulfilling the oath that I swore to your father Abraham. ⁴I will make your heirs as numerous as the stars of heaven, and assign to your heirs all these lands, so that all the nations of the earth shall bless themselves by your heirs—[5]inasmuch as Abraham obeyed Me and kept My charge: My commandments, My laws, and My teachings."

[6]So Isaac stayed in Gerar. [7]When the °local leaders° asked him about his wife, he said, "She is my sister," for he was afraid to say "my wife," thinking, "The local leaders might kill me on account of Rebekah, for she is beautiful." [8]When some time had passed, Abimelech king of the Philistines, looking out of the window, saw Isaac fondling his wife Rebekah. [9]Abimelech sent for Isaac and said, "So she is your wife! Why then did you say: 'She is my sister?'" Isaac said to him, "Because I thought I might lose my life on account of her." [10]Abimelech said, "What have you done to us! One of the men° might have lain with your wife, and you would have brought guilt upon us." [11]Abimelech then charged all the people, saying, "Anyone who molests this householder° or his wife shall be put to death."

[12]Isaac sowed in that land and reaped a hundredfold the same year. יהוה blessed the householder,° [13]and he grew richer and richer until he was very wealthy: [14]he acquired flocks and herds, and a large household, so that the Philistines envied him. [15]And the Philistines stopped up all the wells which his father's servants had dug in the days of his father Abraham, filling them with earth. [16]And Abimelech said to Isaac, "Go away from us, for you have become far too big for us."

[17]So Isaac departed from there and encamped in the wadi of Gerar, where he settled. [18]Isaac dug anew the wells which had been dug in the days of his father Abraham and which the Philistines had stopped up after Abraham's death; and he gave them the same names that his father had given them. [19]But when Isaac's servants, digging in the wadi, found there a well of spring water, [20]the herdsmen of Gerar quarreled with Isaac's herdsmen, saying, "The water is ours." He named that well Esek,* because they contended with him. [21]And when they dug another well, they disputed over that one also; so he named it Sitnah.* [22]He moved from there and dug yet another well, and they did not quarrel over it; so he called it Rehoboth, saying, "Now at last יהוה has granted us *ample space* to increase in the land."

[23]From there he went up to Beer-sheba. [24]That night יהוה

appeared to him and said, "I am the God of your father Abraham's [house]. Fear not, for I am with you, and I will bless you and increase your offspring for the sake of My servant Abraham." 25So he built an altar there and invoked יהוה by name. Isaac pitched his tent there and his servants started digging a well. 26And Abimelech came to him from Gerar, with Ahuzzath his councilor and Phicol chief of his troops. 27Isaac said to them, "Why have you come to me, seeing that you have been hostile to me and have driven me away from you?" 28And they said, "We now see plainly that יהוה has been with you, and we thought: Let there be a sworn treaty between our two parties, between you and us. Let us make a pact with you 29that you will not do us harm, just as we have not molested you but have always dealt kindly with you and sent you away in peace. From now on, be you blessed of יהוה!" 30Then he made for them a feast, and they ate and drank.

31Early in the morning, they exchanged oaths. Isaac then bade them farewell, and they departed from him in peace. 32That same day Isaac's servants came and told him about the well they had dug, and said to him, "We have found water!" 33He named it Shibah;* therefore the name of the city is Beer-sheba to this day.

34When Esau was forty years old, he took to wife Judith daughter of Beeri the Hittite, and Basemath daughter of Elon the Hittite; 35and they were a source of bitterness to Isaac and Rebekah.

27 When Isaac was old and his eyes were too dim to see, he called his older son Esau and said to him, "My son." He answered, "Here I am." 2And he said, "I am old now, and I do not know how soon I may die. 3Take your gear, your quiver and bow, and go out into the open and hunt me some game. 4Then prepare a dish for me such as I like, and bring it to me to eat, so that I may give you my innermost blessing before I die."

5Rebekah had been listening as Isaac spoke to his son Esau. When Esau had gone out into the open to hunt game to bring home, 6Rebekah said to her son Jacob, "I overheard your father speaking to your brother Esau, saying, 7'Bring me some game and prepare a dish for me to eat, that I may bless you, with יהוה's approval, before I die.' 8Now, my son, listen carefully as I instruct you. ⁹Go to the flock and fetch me two choice kids, and I will make of them a dish for your father, such as he likes. ¹⁰Then take it to your father to eat, in order that he may bless you before he dies." ¹¹Jacob answered his mother Rebekah, "But my brother Esau is the hairy type° and I am smooth-skinned. ¹²If my father touches me, I shall appear to him as a trickster and bring upon myself a curse, not a blessing." ¹³But his mother said to him, "Your curse, my son, be upon me! Just do as I say and go fetch them for me."

¹⁴He got them and brought them to his mother, and his mother prepared a dish such as his father liked. ¹⁵Rebekah then took the best clothes of her older son Esau, which were there° in the house, and had her younger son Jacob put them on; ¹⁶and she covered his hands and the hairless part of his neck with the skins of the kids. ¹⁷Then she put in the hands of her son Jacob the dish and the bread that she had prepared.

¹⁸He went to his father and said, "Father." And he said, "Yes, which of my sons are you?" ¹⁹Jacob said to his father, "I am Esau, your first-born; I have done as you told me. Pray sit up and eat of my game, that you may give me your innermost blessing." ²⁰Isaac said to his son, "How did you succeed so quickly, my son?" And he said, "Because your God יהוה granted me good fortune." ²¹Isaac said to Jacob, "Come closer that I may feel you, my son—whether you are really my son Esau or not." ²²So Jacob drew close to his father Isaac, who felt him and wondered. "The voice is the voice of Jacob, yet the hands are the hands of Esau." ²³He did not recognize him, because his hands were hairy like those of his brother Esau; and so he blessed him.

²⁴He asked, "Are you really my son Esau?" And when he said, "I am," ²⁵he said, "Serve me and let me eat of my son's game that I may give you my innermost blessing." So he served him and he ate, and he brought him wine and he drank. ²⁶Then his father Isaac said to him, "Come close and kiss me, my son"; ²⁷and he went up and kissed him. And he smelled his clothes and he blessed him, saying, "Ah, the smell of my son is like the smell of the fields that יהוה has blessed.

²⁸"May God give you
Of the dew of heaven and the fat of the earth,

Abundance of new grain and wine.
²⁹Let peoples serve you,
And nations bow to you;
Be master over your brothers,
And let your mother's sons bow to you.
Cursed be they who curse you,
Blessed they who bless you."

³⁰No sooner had Jacob left the presence of his father Isaac—after Isaac had finished blessing Jacob—than his brother Esau came back from his hunt. ³¹He too prepared a dish and brought it to his father. And he said to his father, "Let my father sit up and eat of his son's game, so that you may give me your innermost blessing." ³²His father Isaac said to him, "Who are you?" And he said, "I am your son, Esau, your first-born!" ³³Isaac was seized with very violent trembling. "Who was it then," he demanded, "that hunted game and brought it to me? Moreover, I ate of it before you came, and I blessed him; now he must remain blessed!" ³⁴When Esau heard his father's words, he burst into wild and bitter sobbing, and said to his father, "Bless me too, Father!" ³⁵But he answered, "Your brother came with guile and took away your blessing." ³⁶[Esau] said, "Was he, then, named Jacob that he might supplant* me these two times? First he took away my birthright and now he has taken away my blessing!" And he added, "Have you not reserved a blessing for me?" ³⁷Isaac answered, saying to Esau, "But I have made him master over you: I have given him all his brothers for servants, and sustained him with grain and wine. What, then, can I still do for you, my son?" ³⁸And Esau said to his father, "Have you but one blessing, Father? Bless me too, Father!" And Esau wept aloud. ³⁹And his father Isaac answered, saying to him,

"See, your abode shall *enjoy the fat of the earth
And-* the dew of heaven above.
⁴⁰Yet by your sword you shall live,
And you shall serve your brother;
But when you grow restive,
You shall break his yoke from your neck."

⁴¹Now Esau harbored a grudge against Jacob because of the blessing which his father had given him, and Esau said to himself, "Let but the mourning period of my father come, and I will kill

my brother Jacob." ⁴²When the words of her older son Esau were reported to Rebekah, she sent for her younger son Jacob and said to him, "Your brother Esau is consoling himself by planning to kill you. ⁴³Now, my son, listen to me. Flee at once to Haran, to my brother Laban. ⁴⁴Stay with him a while, until your brother's fury subsides—⁴⁵until your brother's anger against you subsides—and he forgets what you have done to him. Then I will fetch you from there. Let me not lose you both in one day!"

⁴⁶Rebekah said to Isaac, "I am disgusted with my life because of the Hittite women. If Jacob marries a Hittite woman like these, from among the native women, what good will life be to me?"

28 ¹So Isaac sent for Jacob and blessed him. He instructed him, saying, "You shall not take a wife from among the Canaanite women. ²Up, go to Paddan-aram, to the house of Bethuel, your mother's father, and take a wife there from among the daughters of Laban, your mother's brother. ³May *ᵃEl Shaddaiᵃ* bless you, make you fertile and numerous, so that you become an assembly of peoples. ⁴May you and your offspring be granted the blessing of Abraham, that you may possess the land where you are sojourning, which God assigned to Abraham."

⁵Then Isaac sent Jacob off, and he went to Paddan-aram, to Laban the son of Bethuel the Aramean, the brother of Rebekah, mother of Jacob and Esau.

⁶When Esau saw that Isaac had blessed Jacob and sent him off to Paddan-aram to take a wife from there, charging him, as he blessed him, "You shall not take a wife from among the Canaanite women," ⁷and that Jacob had obeyed his father and mother and gone to Paddan-aram, ⁸Esau realized that the Canaanite women displeased his father Isaac. ⁹So Esau went to Ishmael and took to wife, in addition to the wives he had, Mahalath the daughter of Ishmael son of Abraham, sister of Nebaioth.

ויצא | VA-YETSE'

¹⁰Jacob left Beer-sheba, and set out for Haran. ¹¹He came upon a certain place and stopped there for the night, for the sun had set. Taking one of the stones of that place, he put it under his head and lay down in that place. ¹²He had a dream; a stairway* was set

on the ground and its top reached to the sky, and messengers of God were going up and down on it. [13]And standing beside him was יהוה, who said, "I am יהוה, the God of your father Abraham's [house] and the God of Isaac's [house]: the ground on which you are lying I will assign to you and to your offspring. [14]Your descendants shall be as the dust of the earth; you shall spread out to the west and to the east, to the north and to the south. All the families of the earth shall bless themselves by you and your descendants. [15]Remember, I am with you: I will protect you wherever you go and will bring you back to this land. I will not leave you until I have done what I have promised you."

[16]Jacob awoke from his sleep and said, "Surely יהוה is present in this place, and I did not know it!" [17]Shaken, he said, "How awesome is this place! This is none other than the abode of God, and that is the gateway to heaven." [18]Early in the morning, Jacob took the stone that he had put under his head and set it up as a pillar and poured oil on the top of it. [19]He named that site Bethel;* but previously the name of the city had been Luz.

[20]Jacob then made a vow, saying, "If God remains with me, protecting me on this journey that I am making, and giving me bread to eat and clothing to wear, [21]and I return safe to my father's house—יהוה shall be my God. [22]And this stone, which I have set up as a pillar, shall be God's abode; and of all that You give me, I will set aside a tithe for You."

29 Jacob *-resumed his journey-* and came to the land of the Easterners. [2]There before his eyes was a well in the open. Three flocks of sheep were lying there beside it, for the flocks were watered from that well. The stone on the mouth of the well was large. [3]When all the flocks were gathered there, the stone would be rolled from the mouth of the well and the sheep watered; then the stone would be put back in its place on the mouth of the well.

[4]Jacob said to them, "My friends, where are you from?" And they said, "We are from Haran." [5]He said to them, "Do you know Laban the son of Nahor?" And they said, "Yes, we do." [6]He continued, "Is he well?" They answered, "Yes, he is; and there is his daughter Rachel, coming with the flock." [7]He said, "It is still broad daylight, too early to round up the animals; water the flock

and take them to pasture." ⁸But they said, "We cannot, until all the flocks are rounded up; then the stone is rolled off the mouth of the well and we water the sheep."

⁹While he was still speaking with them, Rachel came with her father's flock—for she was its shepherd. ¹⁰And when Jacob saw Rachel, the daughter of his uncle* Laban, and the flock of his uncle Laban, Jacob went up and rolled the stone off the mouth of the well, and watered the flock of his uncle Laban. ¹¹Then Jacob kissed Rachel, and broke into tears. ¹²Jacob told Rachel that he was her father's kinsman, that he was Rebekah's son; and she ran and told her father. ¹³On hearing the news of his sister's son Jacob, Laban ran to greet him; he embraced him and kissed him, and took him into his house. He told Laban all that had happened, ¹⁴and Laban said to him, "You are truly my bone and flesh."

When he had stayed with him a month's time, ¹⁵Laban said to Jacob, "Just because you are a kinsman, should you serve me for nothing? Tell me, what shall your wages be?" ¹⁶Now Laban had two daughters; the name of the older one was Leah, and the name of the younger was Rachel. ¹⁷Leah had weak eyes; Rachel was shapely and beautiful. ¹⁸Jacob loved Rachel; so he answered, "I will serve you seven years for your younger daughter Rachel." ¹⁹Laban said, "Better that I give her to you than that I should give her to an outsider. Stay with me." ²⁰So Jacob served seven years for Rachel and they seemed to him but a few days because of his love for her.

²¹Then Jacob said to Laban, "Give me my wife, for my time is fulfilled, that I may cohabit with her." ²²And Laban gathered all the °‑people of the place‑° and made a feast. ²³When evening came, he took his daughter Leah and brought her to him; and he cohabited with her.—²⁴Laban had given his maidservant Zilpah to his daughter Leah as her maid.—²⁵When morning came, there was Leah! So he said to Laban, "What is this you have done to me? I was in your service for Rachel! Why did you deceive me?" ²⁶Laban said, "It is not the practice in our place to marry off the younger before the older. ²⁷Wait until the bridal week of this one is over and we will give you that one too, provided you serve me another seven years." ²⁸Jacob did so; he waited out the bridal week of the one, and then he gave him his daughter Rachel as

wife.—²⁹Laban had given his maidservant Bilhah to his daughter Rachel as her maid.—³⁰And Jacob cohabited with Rachel also; indeed, he loved Rachel more than Leah. And he served him another seven years.

³¹Seeing that Leah was unloved, יהוה opened her womb; but Rachel was barren. ³²Leah conceived and bore a son, and named him Reuben;* for she declared, "It means: 'יהוה *-has seen-* my affliction'; it also means: 'Now my husband *-will love me.'"-* ³³She conceived again and bore a son, and declared, "This is because יהוה heard* that I was unloved and has given me this one also"; so she named him Simeon. ³⁴Again she conceived and bore a son and declared, "This time my husband *-will become attached-* to me, for I have borne him three sons." Therefore he was named Levi. ³⁵She conceived again and bore a son, and declared, "This time *-I will praise-* יהוה." Therefore she named him Judah. Then she stopped bearing.

30 When Rachel saw that she had borne Jacob no children, she became envious of her sister; and Rachel said to Jacob, "Give me children, or I shall die." ²Jacob was incensed at Rachel, and said, "Can I take the place of God, who has denied you fruit of the womb?" ³She said, "Here is my maid Bilhah. Consort with her, that she may bear on my knees and that through her I too may have children." ⁴So she gave him her maid Bilhah as concubine, and Jacob cohabited with her. ⁵Bilhah conceived and bore Jacob a son. ⁶And Rachel said, "God *-has vindicated me;-* indeed, [God] has heeded my plea and given me a son." Therefore she named him Dan. ⁷Rachel's maid Bilhah conceived again and bore Jacob a second son. ⁸And Rachel said, "*-A fateful contest I waged-* with my sister; yes, and I have prevailed." So she named him Naphtali.

⁹When Leah saw that she had stopped bearing children, she took her maid Zilpah and gave her to Jacob as concubine. ¹⁰And when Leah's maid Zilpah bore Jacob a son, ¹¹Leah said, *-"What luck!"-* So she named him Gad. ¹²When Leah's maid Zilpah bore Jacob a second son, ¹³Leah declared, *-"What fortune!"-* meaning, "Women will deem me fortunate." So she named him Asher.

¹⁴Once, at the time of the wheat harvest, Reuben came upon some mandrakes in the field and brought them to his mother

Leah. Rachel said to Leah, "Please give me some of your son's mandrakes." ¹⁵But she said to her, "Was it not enough for you to take away my husband, that you would also take my son's mandrakes?" Rachel replied, "I promise, he shall lie with you tonight, in return for your son's mandrakes." ¹⁶When Jacob came home from the field in the evening, Leah went out to meet him and said, "You are to sleep with me, for I have hired you with my son's mandrakes." And he lay with her that night. ¹⁷God heeded Leah, and she conceived and bore him a fifth son. ¹⁸And Leah said, "God has given me *⁻my reward⁻* for having given my maid to my husband." So she named him Issachar. ¹⁹When Leah conceived again and bore Jacob a sixth son, ²⁰Leah said, "God *⁻has given me a choice gift;⁻* this time my husband *⁻will exalt me,⁻* for I have borne him six sons." So she named him Zebulun. ²¹Last, she bore him a daughter, and named her Dinah.

²²Now God remembered Rachel; God heeded her and opened her womb. ²³She conceived and bore a son, and said, "God *⁻has taken away⁻* my disgrace." ²⁴So she named him Joseph, which is to say, "May יהוה add* another son for me."

²⁵After Rachel had borne Joseph, Jacob said to Laban, "Give me leave to go back to my own homeland. ²⁶Give me my wives and my children, for whom I have served you, that I may go; for well you know what services I have rendered you." ²⁷But Laban said to him, *⁻"If you will indulge me,⁻* I have learned by divination that יהוה has blessed me on your account." ²⁸And he continued, "Name the wages due from me, and I will pay you." ²⁹But he said, "You know well how I have served you and how your livestock has fared with me. ³⁰For the little you had before I came has grown to much, since יהוה has blessed you wherever I turned. And now, when shall I make provision for my own household?" ³¹He said, "What shall I pay you?" And Jacob said, "Pay me nothing! If you will do this thing for me, I will again pasture and keep your flocks: ³²let me pass through your whole flock today, removing from there every speckled and spotted animal—every dark-colored sheep and every spotted and speckled goat. Such shall be my wages. ³³In the future when you go over my wages, let my honesty toward you testify for me: if there are among my goats any

that are not speckled or spotted or any sheep that are not dark-colored, they got there by theft." 34And Laban said, "Very well, let it be as you say."

35But that same day he removed the streaked and spotted he-goats and all the speckled and spotted she-goats—every one that had white on it—and all the dark-colored sheep, and left them in the charge of his sons. 36And he put a distance of three days' journey between himself and Jacob, while Jacob was pasturing the rest of Laban's flock.

37Jacob then got fresh shoots of poplar, and of almond and plane, and peeled white stripes in them, laying bare the white of the shoots. 38The rods that he had peeled he set up in front of the goats* in the troughs, the water receptacles, that the goats came to drink from. Their mating occurred when they came to drink, 39and since the goats mated by the rods, the goats brought forth streaked, speckled, and spotted young. 40But Jacob dealt separately with the sheep; he made these animals face the streaked or wholly dark-colored animals in Laban's flock. And so he produced special flocks for himself, which he did not put with Laban's flocks. 41Moreover, when the sturdier* animals were mating, Jacob would place the rods in the troughs, in full view of the animals, so that they mated by the rods; 42but with the feebler* animals he would not place them there. Thus the *feeble ones* went to Laban and the sturdy to Jacob. 43So as a householder° he grew exceedingly prosperous, and came to own large flocks, maidservants and menservants, camels and asses.

31 Now he heard the things that Laban's sons were saying: "Jacob has taken all that was our father's, and from that which was our father's he has built up all this wealth." 2Jacob also saw that Laban's manner toward him was not as it had been in the past. 3Then יהוה said to Jacob, "Return to your ancestors' land—where you were born—and I will be with you." 4Jacob had Rachel and Leah called to the field, where his flock was, 5and said to them, "I see that your father's manner toward me is not as it has been in the past. But the God of my father's [house] has been with me. 6As you know, I have served your father with all my might; 7but your father has cheated me, changing my wages *time and again.˙* God, however, would not let him do me harm. ⁸If he said thus, 'The speckled shall be your wages,' then all the flocks would drop speckled young; and if he said thus, 'The streaked shall be your wages,' then all the flocks would drop streaked young. ⁹God has taken away your father's livestock and given it to me.

¹⁰"Once, at the mating time of the flocks, *˙I had a dream in which I saw˙* that the he-goats mating with the flock were streaked, speckled, and mottled. ¹¹And in the dream a messenger of God said to me, 'Jacob!' 'Here,' I answered. ¹²And the messenger said, 'Note well that all the he-goats which are mating with the flock are streaked, speckled, and mottled; for I have noted all that Laban has been doing to you. ¹³I am the God of Bethel, where you anointed a pillar and where you made a vow to Me. Now, arise and leave this land and return to your native land.'"

¹⁴Then Rachel and Leah answered him, saying, "Have we still a share in the inheritance of our father's house? ¹⁵Surely, he regards us as outsiders, now that he has sold us and has used up our purchase price. ¹⁶Truly, all the wealth that God has taken away from our father belongs to us and to our children. Now then, do just as God has told you."

¹⁷Thereupon Jacob put his children and wives on camels; ¹⁸and he drove off all his livestock and all the wealth that he had amassed, the livestock in his possession that he had acquired in Paddan-aram, to go to his father Isaac in the land of Canaan.

¹⁹Meanwhile Laban had gone to shear his sheep, and Rachel stole her father's household idols. ²⁰Jacob *˙kept Laban the Aramean in the dark,˙* not telling him that he was fleeing, ²¹and fled with all that he had. Soon he was across the Euphrates and heading toward the hill country of Gilead.

²²On the third day, Laban was told that Jacob had fled. ²³So he took his kinsmen with him and pursued him a distance of seven days, catching up with him in the hill country of Gilead. ²⁴But God appeared to Laban the Aramean in a dream by night and said to him, "Beware of attempting anything with Jacob, good or bad."

²⁵Laban overtook Jacob. Jacob had pitched his tent on the Height, and Laban with his kinsmen encamped in the hill country of Gilead. ²⁶And Laban said to Jacob, "What did you mean by keeping me in the dark and carrying off my daughters like captives

of the sword? 27Why did you flee in secrecy and mislead me and not tell me? I would have sent you off with festive music, with timbrel and lyre. 28You did not even let me kiss my °ˉsons and daughtersˉ° good-by! It was a foolish thing for you to do. 29I have it in my power to do you harm; but the God of your father's [house] said to me last night, 'Beware of attempting anything with Jacob, good or bad.' 30Very well, you had to leave because you were longing for your father's house; but why did you steal my gods?"

31Jacob answered Laban, saying, "I was afraid because I thought you would take your daughters from me by force. 32But anyone with whom you find your gods shall not remain alive! In the presence of our kin, point out what I have of yours and take it." Jacob, of course, did not know that Rachel had stolen them.

33So Laban went into Jacob's tent and Leah's tent and the tents of the two maidservants; but he did not find them. Leaving Leah's tent, he entered Rachel's tent. 34Rachel, meanwhile, had taken the idols and placed them in the camel cushion and sat on them; and Laban rummaged through the tent without finding them. 35For she said to her father, "Let not my lord take it amiss that I cannot rise before you, for I am in a womanly way." Thus he searched, but could not find the household idols.

36Now Jacob became incensed and took up his grievance with Laban. Jacob spoke up and said to Laban, "What is my crime, what is my guilt that you should pursue me? 37You rummaged through all my things; what have you found of all your household objects? Set it here, before my kin and yours, and let them decide between us two.

38"These twenty years I have spent in your service, your ewes and she-goats never miscarried, nor did I feast on rams from your flock. 39That which was torn by beasts I never brought to you; I myself made good the loss; you exacted it of me, whether snatched by day or snatched by night. 40Often,* scorching heat ravaged me by day and frost by night; and sleep fled from my eyes. 41Of the twenty years that I spent in your household, I served you fourteen years for your two daughters, and six years for your flocks; and you changed my wages *ˉtime and again.ˉ* 42Had not the God of my father's [house]—the God of Abraham and the Fear* of

Isaac—been with me, you would have sent me away empty-handed. But it was my plight and the toil of my hands that God took notice of—and gave judgment on last night."

⁴³Then Laban spoke up and said to Jacob, "The daughters are my daughters, the children are my children, and the flocks are my flocks; all that you see is mine. Yet what can I do now about my daughters or the children they have borne? ⁴⁴Come, then, let us make a pact, you and I, that there may be a witness between you and me." ⁴⁵Thereupon Jacob took a stone and set it up as a pillar. ⁴⁶And Jacob said to his kinsmen, "Gather stones." So they took stones and made a mound; and they partook of a meal there by the mound. ⁴⁷Laban named it Yegar-sahadutha,* but Jacob named it Gal-ed.* ⁴⁸And Laban declared, "This mound is a witness between you and me this day." That is why it was named Gal-ed; ⁴⁹and [it was called] Mizpah, because he said, "May יהוה watch* between you and me, when we are out of sight of each other. ⁵⁰If you ill-treat my daughters or take other wives besides my daughters—though no one else° be about, remember, it is God who will be witness between you and me."

⁵¹And Laban said to Jacob, "Here is this mound and here the pillar which I have set up between you and me: ⁵²this mound shall be witness and this pillar shall be witness that I am not to cross to you past this mound, and that you are not to cross to me past this mound and this pillar, with hostile intent. ⁵³May the God of Abraham's [house] and the god of Nahor's [house]"—their ancestral deities—"judge between us." And Jacob swore by the Fear* of his father Isaac's [house]. ⁵⁴Jacob then offered up a sacrifice on the Height, and invited his kinsmen to partake of the meal. After the meal, they spent the night on the Height.

32 Early in the morning, Laban kissed his °sons and daughters° and bade them good-by; then Laban left on his journey homeward. ²Jacob went on his way, and messengers of God encountered him. ³When he saw them, Jacob said, "This is God's camp." So he named that place Mahanaim.*

וישלח | VA-YISHLAH

⁴Jacob sent messengers ahead to his brother Esau in the land of Seir, the country of Edom, ⁵and instructed them as follows, *-"Thus

shall you say, 'To my lord Esau, thus says your servant Jacob:⸰* I stayed with Laban and remained until now; ⁶I have acquired cattle, asses, sheep, and male and female slaves; and I send this message to my lord in the hope of gaining your favor.'" ⁷The messengers returned to Jacob, saying, "We came to your brother Esau; he himself is coming to meet you, and his retinue° numbers four hundred." ⁸Jacob was greatly frightened; in his anxiety, he divided the people with him, and the flocks and herds and camels, into two camps, ⁹thinking, "If Esau comes to the one camp and attacks it, the other camp may yet escape."

¹⁰Then Jacob said, "O God of my father Abraham's [house] and God of my father Isaac's [house], O יהוה, who said to me, 'Return to your native land and I will deal bountifully with you'! ¹¹I am unworthy of all the kindness that You have so steadfastly shown Your servant: with my staff alone I crossed this Jordan, and now I have become two camps. ¹²Deliver me, I pray, from the hand of my brother, from the hand of Esau; else, I fear, he may come and strike me down, mothers and children alike. ¹³Yet You have said, 'I will deal bountifully with you and make your offspring as the sands of the sea, which are too numerous to count.'"

¹⁴After spending the night there, he selected from what was at hand these presents for his brother Esau: ¹⁵200 she-goats and 20 he-goats; 200 ewes and 20 rams; ¹⁶30 milch camels with their colts; 40 cows and 10 bulls; 20 she-asses and 10 he-asses. ¹⁷These he put in the charge of his servants, drove by drove, and he told his servants, "Go on ahead, and keep a distance between droves." ¹⁸He instructed the one in front as follows, "When my brother Esau meets you and asks you, 'Who's your master? Where are you going? And whose [animals] are these ahead of you?' ¹⁹you shall answer, 'Your servant Jacob's; they are a gift sent to my lord Esau; and [Jacob] himself is right behind us.'" ²⁰He gave similar instructions to the second one, and the third, and all the others who followed the droves, namely, "Thus and so shall you say to Esau when you reach him. ²¹And you shall add, 'And your servant Jacob himself is right behind us.'" For he reasoned, "If I propitiate him with presents in advance, and then face him, perhaps he will show me favor." ²²And so the gift went on ahead, while he remained in camp that night.

²³That same night he arose, and taking his two wives, his two maidservants, and his eleven sons,° he crossed the ford of the Jabbok. ²⁴After taking them across the stream, he sent across all his possessions. ²⁵Jacob was left alone. And a figure° wrestled with him until the break of dawn. ²⁶When he saw that he had not prevailed against him, he wrenched Jacob's hip at its socket, so that the socket of his hip was strained as he wrestled with him. ²⁷Then he said, "Let me go, for dawn is breaking." But he answered, "I will not let you go, unless you bless me." ²⁸Said the other, "What is your name?" He replied, "Jacob." ²⁹Said he, "Your name shall no longer be Jacob, but Israel, for you have striven* with *⁻beings divine and human,⁻* and have prevailed." ³⁰Jacob asked, "Pray tell me your name." But he said, "You must not ask my name!" And he took leave of him there. ³¹So Jacob named the place Peniel,* meaning, "I have seen a divine being face to face, yet my life has been preserved." ³²The sun rose upon him as he passed Penuel, limping on his hip. ³³That is why the children of Israel to this day do not eat the thigh muscle that is on the socket of the hip, since Jacob's hip socket was wrenched at the thigh muscle.

33 Looking up, Jacob saw Esau coming, with a retinue° of four hundred. He divided the children° among Leah, Rachel, and the two maids, ²putting the maids and their children first, Leah and her children next, and Rachel and Joseph last. ³He himself went on ahead and bowed low to the ground seven times until he was near his brother. ⁴Esau ran to greet him. He embraced him and, falling on his neck, he kissed him; and they wept. ⁵Looking about, he saw the women and the children. "Who," he asked, "are these with you?" He answered, "The children with whom God has favored your servant." ⁶Then the maids, with their children, came forward and bowed low; ⁷next Leah, with her children, came forward and bowed low; and last, Joseph and Rachel came forward and bowed low. ⁸And he asked, "What do you mean by all this company which I have met?" He answered, "To gain my lord's favor." ⁹Esau said, "I have enough, my brother; let what you have remain yours." ¹⁰But Jacob said, "No, I pray you; if you would do me this favor, accept from me this gift; for to see your face is like seeing the face of God, and you have received me favorably. ¹¹Please accept my present which has been brought to you, for God has favored me and I have plenty." And when he urged him, he accepted.

¹²And [Esau] said, "Let us start on our journey, and I will proceed at your pace." ¹³But he said to him, "My lord knows that the children are frail and that the flocks and herds, which are nursing, are a care to me; if they are driven hard a single day, all the flocks will die. ¹⁴Let my lord go on ahead of his servant, while I travel slowly, at the pace of the cattle before me and at the pace of the children, until I come to my lord in Seir."

¹⁵Then Esau said, "Let me assign to you some of the people who are with me." But he said, "Oh no, my lord is too kind to me!" ¹⁶So Esau started back that day on his way to Seir. ¹⁷But Jacob journeyed on to Succoth, and built a house for himself and made stalls for his cattle; that is why the place was called Succoth.*

¹⁸Jacob arrived safe in the city of Shechem which is in the land of Canaan—having come thus from Paddan-aram—and he encamped before the city. ¹⁹The parcel of land where he pitched his tent he purchased from the kin of Hamor, Shechem's father, for a hundred *kesitah*s.* ²⁰He set up an altar there, and called it El-elohe-yisrael.*

34 Now Dinah, the daughter whom Leah had borne to Jacob, went out to visit the daughters of the land. ²Shechem son of Hamor the Hivite, chief of the country, saw her, and took her and lay with her °ʾand disgraced her.ʾ° ³Being strongly drawn to Dinah daughter of Jacob, and in love with the maiden, he spoke to the maiden tenderly. ⁴So Shechem said to his father Hamor, "Get me this girl as a wife."

⁵Jacob heard that he had defiled his daughter Dinah; but since his sons were in the field with his cattle, Jacob kept silent until they came home. ⁶Then Shechem's father Hamor came out to Jacob to speak to him. ⁷Meanwhile Jacob's sons, having heard the news, came in from the field. As the representatives° [of Jacob's house], they were distressed and very angry, because he had committed an outrage in Israel by lying with Jacob's daughter—a thing not to be done.

⁸And Hamor spoke with them, saying, "My son Shechem longs for your daughter. Please give her to him in marriage. ⁹Intermarry with us: give your daughters to us, and take our daughters for yourselves: ¹⁰You will dwell among us, and the land will be open before you; settle, move about, and acquire holdings in it." ¹¹Then Shechem said to her father and brothers, "Do me this favor, and I will pay whatever you tell me. ¹²Ask of me a bride-price ever so high, as well as gifts, and I will pay what you tell me; only give me the maiden for a wife."

¹³Jacob's sons answered Shechem and his father Hamor—speaking with guile because he had defiled their sister Dinah—¹⁴and said to them, "We cannot do this thing, to give our sister to someone uncircumcised, for that is a disgrace among us. ¹⁵Only on this condition will we agree with you; that you will become like us in that every male among you is circumcised. ¹⁶Then we will give our daughters to you and take your daughters to ourselves; and we will dwell among you and become as one kindred. ¹⁷But if you will not listen to us and become circumcised, we will take our daughter and go."

¹⁸Their words pleased Hamor and Hamor's son Shechem. ¹⁹And the youth lost no time in doing the thing, for he wanted Jacob's daughter. Now he was the most respected in his father's house. ²⁰So Hamor and his son Shechem went to the *⁻public place⁻* of their town and spoke to °⁻their town council,⁻° saying, ²¹"These people° are our friends; let them settle in the land and move about in it, for the land is large enough for them; we will take their daughters to ourselves as wives and give our daughters to them. ²²But only on this condition will their representatives° agree with us to dwell among us and be as one kindred: that all our males become circumcised as they are circumcised. ²³Their cattle and substance and all their beasts will be ours, if we only agree to their terms, so that they will settle among us." ²⁴°⁻All his fellow townsmen⁻° heeded Hamor and his son Shechem, and all males, °⁻all his fellow townsmen,⁻° were circumcised.

²⁵On the third day, when they were in pain, Simeon and Levi, two of Jacob's sons, brothers of Dinah, took each his sword, came upon the city unmolested, and slew all the males. ²⁶They put

Hamor and his son Shechem to the sword, took Dinah out of Shechem's house, and went away. 27The other sons of Jacob came upon the slain and plundered the town, because their sister had been defiled. 28They seized their flocks and herds and asses, all that was inside the town and outside; 29all their wealth, all their children, and their wives, all that was in the houses, they took as captives and booty.

30Jacob said to Simeon and Levi, "You have brought trouble on me, making me odious among the inhabitants of the land, the Canaanites and the Perizzites; my fighters° are few in number, so that if they unite against me and attack me, I and my house will be destroyed." 31But they answered, "Should our sister be treated like a whore?"

35 God said to Jacob, "Arise, go up to Bethel and remain there; and build an altar there to the God who appeared to you when you were fleeing from your brother Esau." 2So Jacob said to his household and to all who were with him, "Rid yourselves of the alien gods in your midst, purify yourselves, and change your clothes. 3Come, let us go up to Bethel, and I will build an altar there to the God who answered me when I was in distress and who has been with me wherever I have gone." 4They gave to Jacob all the alien gods that they had, and the rings that were in their ears, and Jacob buried them under the terebinth that was near Shechem. 5As they set out, a terror from God fell on the cities round about, so that they did not pursue the sons of Jacob.

6Thus Jacob came to Luz—that is, Bethel—in the land of Canaan, he and all the people who were with him. 7There he built an altar and named the site El-bethel,* for it was there that God had been revealed to him when he was fleeing from his brother.

8Deborah, Rebekah's nurse, died, and was buried under the oak below Bethel; so it was named Allon-bacuth.*

9God appeared again to Jacob on his arrival from Paddan-aram. God blessed him, 10saying to him,

"You whose name is Jacob,
You shall be called Jacob no more,
But Israel shall be your name."
Thus he was named Israel.

¹¹And God said to him,
"I am *˙El Shaddai.˙*
Be fertile and increase;
A nation, yea an assembly of nations,
Shall descend from you.
Kings shall issue from your loins.
¹²The land that I assigned to Abraham and Isaac
I assign to you;
And to your offspring to come
Will I assign the land."

¹³God parted from him at the spot where [God] had spoken to him; ¹⁴and Jacob set up a pillar at the site where [God] had spoken to him, a pillar of stone, and he offered a libation on it and poured oil upon it. ¹⁵Jacob gave the site, where God had spoken to him, the name of Bethel.

¹⁶They set out from Bethel; but when they were still some distance short of Ephrath, Rachel was in childbirth, and she had hard labor. ¹⁷When her labor was at its hardest, the midwife said to her, "Have no fear, for it is another boy for you." ¹⁸But as she breathed her last—for she was dying—she named him Ben-oni;* but his father called him Benjamin.* ¹⁹Thus Rachel died. She was buried on the road to Ephrath—now Bethlehem. ²⁰Over her grave Jacob set up a pillar; it is the pillar at Rachel's grave to this day. ²¹Israel journeyed on, and pitched his tent beyond Migdal-eder.

²²While Israel stayed in that land, Reuben went and lay with Bilhah, his father's concubine; and Israel found out.

Now the sons of Jacob were twelve in number. ²³The sons of Leah: Reuben—Jacob's first-born—Simeon, Levi, Judah, Issachar, and Zebulun. ²⁴The sons of Rachel: Joseph and Benjamin. ²⁵The sons of Bilhah, Rachel's maid: Dan and Naphtali. ²⁶And the sons of Zilpah, Leah's maid: Gad and Asher. These are the sons of Jacob who were born to him in Paddan-aram.

²⁷And Jacob came to his father Isaac at Mamre, at Kiriath-arba—now Hebron—where Abraham and Isaac had sojourned. ²⁸Isaac was a hundred and eighty years old ²⁹when he breathed his last and died. He* was gathered to his kin° in ripe old age; and he was buried by his sons Esau and Jacob.

36 This is the line of Esau—that is, Edom. ²Esau took his wives from among the Canaanite women—Adah daughter of Elon the Hittite, and Oholibamah daughter of Anah daughter of Zibeon the Hivite*—³and also Basemath daughter of Ishmael and sister of Nebaioth. ⁴Adah bore to Esau Eliphaz; Basemath bore Reuel; ⁵and Oholibamah bore Jeush, Jalam, and Korah. Those were the sons of Esau, who were born to him in the land of Canaan.

⁶Esau took his wives, his sons and daughters, and all the members of his household, his cattle and all his livestock, and all the property that he had acquired in the land of Canaan, and went to another land because of his brother Jacob. ⁷For their possessions were too many for them to dwell together, and the land where they sojourned could not support them because of their livestock. ⁸So Esau settled in the hill country of Seir—Esau being Edom.

⁹This, then, is the line of Esau, the ancestor of the Edomites, in the hill country of Seir.

¹⁰These are the names of Esau's sons: Eliphaz, the son of Esau's wife Adah; Reuel, the son of Esau's wife Basemath. ¹¹The sons of Eliphaz were Teman, Omar, Zepho, Gatam, and Kenaz. ¹²Timna was a concubine of Esau's son Eliphaz; she bore Amalek to Eliphaz. Those were the descendants of Esau's wife Adah. ¹³And these were the sons of Reuel: Nahath, Zerah, Shammah, and Mizzah. Those were the descendants of Esau's wife Basemath. ¹⁴And these were the sons of Esau's wife Oholibamah, daughter of Anah daughter of Zibeon: she bore to Esau Jeush, Jalam, and Korah.

¹⁵These are the clans of the sons of Esau. The descendants of Esau's first-born Eliphaz: the clans Teman, Omar, Zepho, Kenaz, ¹⁶Korah, Gatam, and Amalek; these are the clans of Eliphaz in the land of Edom. Those are the descendants of Adah. ¹⁷And these are the descendants of Esau's son Reuel: the clans Nahath, Zerah, Shammah, and Mizzah; these are the clans of Reuel in the land of Edom. Those are the descendants of Esau's wife Basemath. ¹⁸And these are the descendants of Esau's wife Oholibamah: the clans Jeush, Jalam, and Korah; these are the clans of Esau's wife Oholibamah, the daughter of Anah. ¹⁹Those were the sons of Esau—that is, Edom—and those are their clans.

²⁰These were the sons of Seir the Horite, who were settled in the

land: Lotan, Shobal, Zibeon, Anah, 21Dishon, Ezer, and Dishan. Those are the clans of the Horites, the descendants of Seir, in the land of Edom.

22The sons of Lotan were Hori and Hemam; and Lotan's sister was Timna. 23The sons of Shobal were these: Alvan, Manahath, Ebal, Shepho, and Onam. 24The sons of Zibeon were these: Aiah* and Anah—that was the Anah who discovered the *‑hot springs‑* in the wilderness while pasturing the asses of his father Zibeon. 25The children of Anah were these: Dishon and Anah's daughter Oholibamah. 26The sons of Dishon* were these: Hemdan, Eshban, Ithran, and Cheran. 27The sons of Ezer were these: Bilhan, Zaavan, and Akan. 28And the sons of Dishan were these: Uz and Aran.

29These are the clans of the Horites: the clans Lotan, Shobal, Zibeon, Anah, 30Dishon, Ezer, and Dishan. Those are the clans of the Horites, clan by clan, in the land of Seir.

31These are the kings who reigned in the land of Edom before any king reigned over the Israelites. 32Bela son of Beor reigned in Edom, and the name of his city was Dinhabah. 33When Bela died, Jobab son of Zerah, from Bozrah, succeeded him as king. 34When Jobab died, Husham of the land of the Temanites succeeded him as king. 35When Husham died, Hadad son of Bedad, who defeated the Midianites in the country of Moab, succeeded him as king; the name of his city was Avith. 36When Hadad died, Samlah of Masrekah succeeded him as king. 37When Samlah died, Saul* of Rehoboth-on-the-river succeeded him as king. 38When Saul died, Baal-hanan son of Achbor succeeded him as king. 39And when Baal-hanan son of Achbor died, Hadar succeeded him as king; the name of his city was Pau, and his wife's name was Mehetabel daughter of Matred daughter of Me-zahab.

40These are the names of the clans of Esau, each with its families and locality, name by name: the clans Timna, Alvah, Jetheth, 41Oholibamah, Elah, Pinon, 42Kenaz, Teman, Mibzar, 43Magdiel, and Iram. Those are the clans of Edom—that is, of Esau, father of the Edomites—by their settlements in the land which they hold.

וישב | VA-YESHEV

37 Now Jacob was settled in the land where his father had sojourned, the land of Canaan. 2This, then, is the line of Jacob:

At seventeen years of age, Joseph tended the flocks with his brothers, as a helper to the sons of his father's wives Bilhah and Zilpah. And Joseph brought bad reports of them to their father. ³Now Israel loved Joseph best of all his sons—he was his °child of old age;° and he had made him an *⁻ornamented tunic.⁻* ⁴And when his brothers saw that their father loved him more than any of his brothers, they hated him so that they could not speak a friendly word to him.

⁵Once Joseph had a dream which he told to his brothers; and they hated him even more. ⁶He said to them, "Hear this dream which I have dreamed: ⁷There we were binding sheaves in the field, when suddenly my sheaf stood up and remained upright; then your sheaves gathered around and bowed low to my sheaf." ⁸His brothers answered, "Do you mean to reign over us? Do you mean to rule over us?" And they hated him even more for his talk about his dreams.

⁹He dreamed another dream and told it to his brothers, saying, "Look, I have had another dream: And this time, the sun, the moon, and eleven stars were bowing down to me." ¹⁰And when he told it to his father and brothers, his father berated him. "What," he said to him, "is this dream you have dreamed? Are we to come, I and your mother and your brothers, and bow low to you to the ground?" ¹¹So his brothers were wrought up at him, and his father kept the matter in mind.

¹²One time, when his brothers had gone to pasture their father's flock at Shechem, ¹³Israel said to Joseph, "Your brothers are pasturing at Shechem. Come, I will send you to them." He answered, "I am ready." ¹⁴And he said to him, "Go and see how your brothers are and how the flocks are faring, and bring me back word." So he sent him from the valley of Hebron.

When he reached Shechem, ¹⁵°someone came upon him° wandering in the fields. The man° asked him, "What are you looking for?" ¹⁶He answered, "I am looking for my brothers. Could you tell me where they are pasturing?" ¹⁷The man° said, "They have gone from here, for I heard them say: Let us go to Dothan." So Joseph followed his brothers and found them at Dothan.

¹⁸They saw him from afar, and before he came close to them they conspired to kill him. ¹⁹They said to one another, "Here

comes that dreamer! ²⁰Come now, let us kill him and throw him into one of the pits; and we can say, 'A savage beast devoured him.' We shall see what comes of his dreams!" ²¹But when Reuben heard it, he tried to save him from them. He said, "Let us not take his life." ²²And Reuben went on, "Shed no blood! Cast him into that pit out in the wilderness, but do not touch him yourselves"— intending to save him from them and restore him to his father. ²³When Joseph came up to his brothers, they stripped Joseph of his tunic, the ornamented tunic that he was wearing, ²⁴and took him and cast him into the pit. The pit was empty; there was no water in it.

²⁵Then they sat down to a meal. Looking up, they saw a caravan of Ishmaelites coming from Gilead, their camels bearing gum, balm, and ladanum to be taken to Egypt. ²⁶Then Judah said to his brothers, "What do we gain by killing our brother and covering up his blood? ²⁷Come, let us sell him to the Ishmaelites, but let us not do away with him ourselves. After all, he is our brother, our own flesh." His brothers agreed. ²⁸When Midianite traders passed by, they pulled Joseph up out of the pit. They sold Joseph for twenty pieces of silver to the Ishmaelites, who brought Joseph to Egypt.

²⁹When Reuben returned to the pit and saw that Joseph was not in the pit, he rent his clothes. ³⁰Returning to his brothers, he said, "The boy is gone! Now, what am I to do?" ³¹Then they took Joseph's tunic, slaughtered a kid, and dipped the tunic in the blood. ³²They had the ornamented tunic taken to their father, and they said, "We found this. Please examine it; is it your son's tunic or not?" ³³He recognized it, and said, "My son's tunic! A savage beast devoured him! Joseph was torn by a beast!" ³⁴Jacob rent his clothes, put sackcloth on his loins, and observed mourning for his son many days. ³⁵All his sons and daughters sought to comfort him; but he refused to be comforted, saying, "No, I will go down mourning to my son in Sheol." Thus his father bewailed him.

³⁶The Midianites,* meanwhile, sold him in Egypt to Potiphar, a courtier of Pharaoh and his °chief prefect.°

38 About that time Judah left his brothers and camped near a prominent° Adullamite whose name was Hirah. ²There

Judah saw the daughter of a prominent Canaanite whose name was Shua, and he took her [into his household as wife] and cohabited with her. ³She conceived and bore a son, and he named him Er. ⁴She conceived again and bore a son, and named him Onan. ⁵Once again she bore a son, and named him Shelah; he was at Chezib when she bore him.

⁶Judah got a wife for Er his first-born; her name was Tamar. ⁷But Er, Judah's first-born, was displeasing to יהוה, and יהוה took his life. ⁸Then Judah said to Onan, "Join with your brother's wife and do your duty* by her as a brother-in-law, and provide offspring for your brother." ⁹But Onan, knowing that the offspring would not count as his, let [the semen] *⁻go to waste⁻* whenever he joined with his brother's wife, so as not to provide offspring for his brother. ¹⁰What he did was displeasing to יהוה, who took his life also. ¹¹Then Judah said to his daughter-in-law Tamar, "Stay as a widow in your father's house until my son Shelah grows up"—for he thought, "He too might die like his brothers." So Tamar went to live in her father's house.

¹²A long time afterward, Shua's daughter, the wife of Judah, died. When *⁻his period of mourning was over,⁻* Judah went up to Timnah to his sheepshearers, together with his friend Hirah the Adullamite. ¹³And Tamar was told, "Your father-in-law is coming up to Timnah for the sheepshearing." ¹⁴So she took off her widow's garb, covered her face with a veil, and, wrapping herself up, sat down at the entrance to Enaim,* which is on the road to Timnah; for she saw that Shelah was grown up, yet she had not been given to him as wife. ¹⁵When Judah saw her, he took her for a harlot; for she had covered her face. ¹⁶So he turned aside to her by the road and said, "Here, let me sleep with you"—for he did not know that she was his daughter-in-law. "What," she asked, "will you pay for sleeping with me?" ¹⁷He replied, "I will send a kid from my flock." But she said, "You must leave a pledge until you have sent it." ¹⁸And he said, "What pledge shall I give you?" She replied, "Your seal and cord, and the staff which you carry." So he gave them to her and slept with her, and she conceived by him. ¹⁹Then she went on her way. She took off her veil and again put on her widow's garb.

²⁰Judah sent the kid by his friend the Adullamite, to redeem

the pledge from the woman; but he could not find her. ²¹He in-quired of the °-council of that locale,-° "Where is the prostitute,° the one at Enaim, by the road?" But they said, "There has been no prostitute here." ²²So he returned to Judah and said, "I could not find her; moreover, the °local council-° said: There has been no prostitute here." ²³Judah said, "Let her keep them, lest we be-come a laughingstock. I did send her this kid, but you did not find her."

²⁴About three months later, Judah was told, "Your daughter-in-law Tamar has played the harlot; in fact, she is pregnant from harlotry." "Bring her out,°" said Judah. "She should be burned!" ²⁵As she was being brought out, she sent this message to her father-in-law, "I am pregnant by the dignitary° to whom these belong." And she added, "Examine these: whose seal and cord and staff are these?" ²⁶Judah recognized them, and said, "She is more in the right than I, inasmuch as I did not give her to my son Shelah." And he was not intimate with her again.

²⁷When the time came for her to give birth, there were twins in her womb! ²⁸While she was in labor, one of them put out a hand, and the midwife tied a crimson thread on that hand, to signify: This one came out first. ²⁹But just then it drew back its hand, and out came its brother; and she said, "What a breach* you have made for yourself!" So he was named Perez. ³⁰Afterward his brother came out, on whose hand was the crimson thread; he was named Zerah.*

39 When Joseph was taken down to Egypt, Potiphar, a courtier of Pharaoh and his °chief prefect-°—an Egyp-tian official°—bought him from the Ishmaelites who had brought him there. ²יהוה was with Joseph, and he proved °highly capable;-° and he stayed in the house of his Egyptian master. ³And when his master saw that יהוה was with him and that יהוה lent success to everything he undertook, ⁴he took a liking to Joseph. He made him his personal attendant and put him in charge of his house-hold, placing in his hands all that he owned. ⁵And from the time that the Egyptian put him in charge of his household and of all that he owned, יהוה blessed his house for Joseph's sake, so that the blessing of יהוה was upon everything that he owned, in the house and outside. ⁶He left all that he had in Joseph's hands and, with him there, he paid attention to nothing save the food that he ate. Now Joseph was well built and handsome.

⁷After a time, his master's wife cast her eyes upon Joseph and said, "Lie with me." ⁸But he refused. He said to his master's wife, "Look, with me here, my master gives no thought to anything in this house, and all that he owns he has placed in my hands. ⁹He wields no more authority in this house than I, and he has withheld nothing from me except yourself, since you are his wife. How then could I do this most wicked thing, and sin before God?" ¹⁰And much as she coaxed Joseph day after day, he did not yield to her request to lie beside her, to be with her.

¹¹One such day, he came into the house to do his work. None of the household being there inside, ¹²she caught hold of him by his garment and said, "Lie with me!" But he left his garment in her hand and got away and fled outside. ¹³When she saw that he had left it in her hand and had fled outside, ¹⁴she called out to her servants and said to them, "Look, he had to bring us °a Hebrew⁻ ° to dally with us! This one came to lie with me; but I screamed loud. ¹⁵And when he heard me screaming at the top of my voice, he left his garment with me and got away and fled outside." ¹⁶She kept his garment beside her, until his master came home. ¹⁷Then she told him the same story, saying, "The Hebrew slave whom you brought into our house came to me to dally with me; ¹⁸but when I screamed at the top of my voice, he left his garment with me and fled outside."

¹⁹When his master heard the story that his wife told him, namely, "Thus and so your slave did to me," he was furious. ²⁰So Joseph's master had him put in prison, where the king's prisoners were confined. But even while he was there in prison, ²¹יהוה was with Joseph—extending kindness to him and disposing the chief jailer favorably toward him. ²²The chief jailer put in Joseph's charge all the prisoners who were in that prison, and he was the one to carry out everything that was done there. ²³The chief jailer did not supervise anything that was in Joseph's* charge, because יהוה was with him, and whatever he did יהוה made successful.

40 Some time later, the cupbearer and the baker of the king of Egypt gave offense to their lord the king of Egypt. ²Pharaoh was angry with his two courtiers, the chief cupbearer and the chief baker, ³and put them in custody, in the house of the °chief prefect,⁻° in the same prison house where Joseph was confined. ⁴The chief prefect assigned Joseph to them, and he attended them.

When they had been in custody for some time, ⁵both of them—the cupbearer and the baker of the king of Egypt, who were confined in the prison—dreamed in the same night, each his own dream and each dream with its own meaning. ⁶When Joseph came to them in the morning, he saw that they were distraught. ⁷He asked Pharaoh's courtiers, who were with him in custody in his master's house, saying, "Why do you appear downcast today?" ⁸And they said to him, "We had dreams, and there is no one to interpret them." So Joseph said to them, "Surely God can interpret! Tell me [your dreams]."

⁹Then the chief cupbearer told his dream to Joseph. He said to him, "In my dream, there was a vine in front of me. ¹⁰On the vine were three branches. It had barely budded, when out came its blossoms and its clusters ripened into grapes. ¹¹Pharaoh's cup was in my hand, and I took the grapes, pressed them into Pharaoh's cup, and placed the cup in Pharaoh's hand." ¹²Joseph said to him, "This is its interpretation: The three branches are three days. ¹³In three days Pharaoh will *⁻pardon you⁻* and restore you to your post; you will place Pharaoh's cup in his hand, as was your custom formerly when you were his cupbearer. ¹⁴But think of me when all is well with you again, and do me the kindness of mentioning me to Pharaoh, so as to free me from this place. ¹⁵For in truth, I was kidnapped from the land of the Hebrews; nor have I done anything here that they should have put me in the dungeon."

¹⁶When the chief baker saw how favorably he had interpreted, he said to Joseph, "In my dream, similarly, there were three *⁻openwork baskets⁻* on my head. ¹⁷In the uppermost basket were all kinds of food for Pharaoh that a baker prepares; and the birds were eating it out of the basket above my head." ¹⁸Joseph answered, "This is its interpretation: The three baskets are three days. ¹⁹In three days Pharaoh will lift off your head and impale you upon a pole; and the birds will pick off your flesh."

²⁰On the third day—his birthday—Pharaoh made a banquet for all his officials, and he *⁻singled out⁻* his chief cupbearer and his chief baker from among his officials. ²¹He restored the chief cupbearer to his cupbearing, and he placed the cup in Pharaoh's hand; ²²but the chief baker he impaled—just as Joseph had interpreted to them.

²³Yet the chief cupbearer did not think of Joseph; he forgot him.

מִקֵּץ ‌| MIKKETS

41 After two years' time, Pharaoh dreamed that he was standing by the Nile, ²when out of the Nile there came up seven cows, handsome and sturdy, and they grazed in the reed grass. ³But presently, seven other cows came up from the Nile close behind them, ugly and gaunt, and stood beside the cows on the bank of the Nile; ⁴and the ugly gaunt cows ate up the seven handsome sturdy cows. And Pharaoh awoke.

⁵He fell asleep and dreamed a second time: Seven ears of grain, solid and healthy, grew on a single stalk. ⁶But close behind them sprouted seven ears, thin and scorched by the east wind. ⁷And the thin ears swallowed up the seven solid and full ears. Then Pharaoh awoke: it was a dream!

⁸Next morning, his spirit was agitated, and he sent for all the magician-priests of Egypt, and all its sages; and Pharaoh told them his dreams, but none could interpret them for Pharaoh.

⁹The chief cupbearer then spoke up and said to Pharaoh, "I must make mention today of my offenses. ¹⁰Once Pharaoh was angry with his servants, and placed me in custody in the house of the °⁻chief prefect,⁻° together with the chief baker. ¹¹We had dreams the same night, he and I, each of us a dream with a meaning of its own. ¹²A Hebrew youth was there with us, a servant of the chief prefect; and when we told him our dreams, he interpreted them for us, telling each of the meaning of his dream. ¹³And as he interpreted for us, so it came to pass: I was restored to my post, and the other was impaled."

¹⁴Thereupon Pharaoh sent for Joseph, and he was rushed from the dungeon. He had his hair cut and changed his clothes, and he appeared before Pharaoh. ¹⁵And Pharaoh said to Joseph, "I have had a dream, but no one can interpret it. Now I have heard it said of you

that for you to hear a dream is to tell its meaning." [16]Joseph answered Pharaoh, saying, "Not I! God will see to Pharaoh's welfare."

[17]Then Pharaoh said to Joseph, "In my dream, I was standing on the bank of the Nile, [18]when out of the Nile came up seven sturdy and well-formed cows and grazed in the reed grass. [19]Presently there followed them seven other cows, scrawny, ill-formed, and emaciated—never had I seen their likes for ugliness in all the land of Egypt! [20]And the seven lean and ugly cows ate up the first seven cows, the sturdy ones; [21]but when they had consumed them, one could not tell that they had consumed them, for they looked just as bad as before. And I awoke. [22]In my other dream, I saw seven ears of grain, full and healthy, growing on a single stalk; [23]but right behind them sprouted seven ears, shriveled, thin, and scorched by the east wind. [24]And the thin ears swallowed the seven healthy ears. I have told my magician-priests, but none has an explanation for me."

[25]And Joseph said to Pharaoh, "Pharaoh's dreams are one and the same: Pharaoh has been told what God is about to do. [26]The seven healthy cows are seven years, and the seven healthy ears are seven years; it is the same dream. [27]The seven lean and ugly cows that followed are seven years, as are also the seven empty ears scorched by the east wind; they are seven years of famine. [28]It is just as I have told Pharaoh: Pharaoh has been shown what God is about to do. [29]Immediately ahead are seven years of great abundance in all the land of Egypt. [30]After them will come seven years of famine, and all the abundance in the land of Egypt will be forgotten. As the land is ravaged by famine, [31]no trace of the abundance will be left in the land because of the famine thereafter, for it will be very severe. [32]As for Pharaoh having had the same dream twice, it means that the matter has been determined by God, and that God will soon carry it out.

[33]"Accordingly, let Pharaoh °⁻select an official who's discerning and wise,⁻° and set him over the land of Egypt. [34]And let Pharaoh take steps to appoint overseers over the land, and organize* the land of Egypt in the seven years of plenty. [35]Let all the food of these good years that are coming be gathered, and let the grain be collected under Pharaoh's authority as food to be stored in the cities. [36]Let that food be a reserve for the land for the seven years

Mikkets

of famine which will come upon the land of Egypt, so that the land may not perish in the famine."

37The plan pleased Pharaoh and all his courtiers. 38And Pharaoh said to his courtiers, "°Could we find an [existing] official like him—one in whom is the spirit of God?-°" 39So Pharaoh said to Joseph, "Since God has made all this known to you, there is none so discerning and wise as you. 40You shall be in charge of my court, and by your command shall all my people *-be directed;-* only with respect to the throne shall I be superior to you." 41Pharaoh further said to Joseph, "See, I put you in charge of all the land of Egypt." 42And removing his signet ring from his hand, Pharaoh put it on Joseph's hand; and he had him dressed in robes of fine linen, and put a gold chain about his neck. 43He had him ride in the chariot of his second-in-command, and they cried before him, "Abrek!"* Thus he placed him over all the land of Egypt.

44Pharaoh said to Joseph, "I am Pharaoh; yet without you, no one shall lift up hand or foot in all the land of Egypt." 45Pharaoh then gave Joseph the name Zaphenath-paneah;* and he gave him for a wife Asenath daughter of Poti-phera, priest of On. Thus Joseph emerged in charge of the land of Egypt.—46Joseph was thirty years old when he entered the service of Pharaoh king of Egypt.—Leaving Pharaoh's presence, Joseph traveled through all the land of Egypt.

47During the seven years of plenty, the land produced in abundance. 48And he gathered all the grain of *-the seven years that the land of Egypt was enjoying,-* and stored the grain in the cities; he put in each city the grain of the fields around it. 49So Joseph collected produce in very large quantity, like the sands of the sea, until he ceased to measure it, for it could not be measured.

50Before the years of famine came, Joseph became the father of two sons, whom Asenath daughter of Poti-phera, priest of On, bore to him. 51Joseph named the first-born Manasseh, meaning, "God *-has made me forget-* completely my hardship and my parental home." 52And the second he named Ephraim, meaning, "God *-has made me fertile-* in the land of my affliction."

53The seven years of abundance that the land of Egypt enjoyed came to an end, 54and the seven years of famine set in, just as Joseph had foretold. There was famine in all lands, but throughout the land of Egypt there was bread. ⁵⁵And when all the land of Egypt felt the hunger, the people cried out to Pharaoh for bread; and Pharaoh said to all the Egyptians, "Go to Joseph; whatever he tells you, you shall do."—⁵⁶Accordingly, when the famine became severe in the land of Egypt, Joseph laid open all that was within, and rationed out grain to the Egyptians. The famine, however, spread over the whole world. ⁵⁷So all the world came to Joseph in Egypt to procure rations, for the famine had become severe throughout the world.

42 When Jacob saw that there were food rations to be had in Egypt, he* said to his sons, "Why do you keep looking at one another? ²Now I hear," he went on, "that there are rations to be had in Egypt. Go down and procure rations for us there, that we may live and not die." ³So ten of Joseph's brothers went down to get grain rations in Egypt; ⁴for Jacob did not send Joseph's brother Benjamin with his brothers, since he feared that he might meet with disaster. ⁵Thus the sons of Israel were among those who came to procure rations, for the famine extended to the land of Canaan.

⁶Now Joseph was the vizier of the land; it was he who dispensed rations to all the people of the land. And Joseph's brothers came and bowed low to him, with their faces to the ground. ⁷When Joseph saw his brothers, he recognized them; but he acted like a stranger toward them and spoke harshly to them. He asked them, "Where do you come from?" And they said, "From the land of Canaan, to procure food." ⁸For though Joseph recognized his brothers, they did not recognize him. ⁹Recalling the dreams that he had dreamed about them, Joseph said to them, "You are spies, you have come to see the land in its nakedness." ¹⁰But they said to him, "No, my lord! Truly, your servants have come to procure food. ¹¹We are all of us °members of the same household;° we are honest people; your servants have never been spies!" ¹²And he said to them, "No, you have come to see the land in its nakedness!" ¹³And they replied, "We your servants were twelve brothers, sons of a certain householder° in the land of Canaan; the youngest, however, is now with our father, and one is no more." ¹⁴But Joseph said to them, "It is just as I have told you: You are spies!

Mikkets 69

¹⁵By this you shall be put to the test: unless your youngest brother comes here, by Pharaoh, you shall not depart from this place! ¹⁶Let one of you go and bring your brother, while the rest of you remain confined, that your words may be put to the test whether there is truth in you. Else, by Pharaoh, you are nothing but spies!" ¹⁷And he confined them in the guardhouse for three days.

¹⁸On the third day Joseph said to them, "Do this and you shall live, for I fear God. ¹⁹If you are 'honest people,' let one of you brothers be held in your place of detention, while the rest of you go and take home rations for your starving households; ²⁰but you must bring me your youngest brother, that your words may be verified and that you may not die." And they did accordingly. ²¹They said to one another, "Alas, we are being punished on account of our brother, because we looked on at his anguish, yet paid no heed as he pleaded with us. That is why this distress has come upon us." ²²Then Reuben spoke up and said to them, "Did I not tell you, 'Do no wrong to the boy'? But you paid no heed. Now comes the reckoning for his blood." ²³They did not know that Joseph understood, for there was an interpreter between him and them. ²⁴He turned away from them and wept. But he came back to them and spoke to them; and he took Simeon from among them and had him bound before their eyes. ²⁵Then Joseph gave orders to fill their bags with grain, return each one's money to his sack, and give them provisions for the journey; and this was done for them. ²⁶So they loaded their asses with the rations and departed from there.

²⁷As one of them was opening his sack to give feed to his ass at the night encampment, he saw his money right there at the mouth of his bag. ²⁸And he said to his brothers, "My money has been returned! It is here in my bag!" Their hearts sank; and, trembling, they turned to one another, saying, "What is this that God has done to us?"

²⁹When they came to their father Jacob in the land of Canaan, they told him all that had befallen them, saying, ³⁰"The official° who is lord of the land spoke harshly to us and accused us of spying on the land. ³¹We said to him, 'We are honest people; we have never been spies! ³²There were twelve of us brothers, sons by the same father; but one is no more, and the youngest is now with our

father in the land of Canaan.' ³³But the official who is lord of the land said to us, 'By this I shall know that you are "honest people": leave one of your brothers with me, and take something for your starving households and be off. ³⁴And bring your youngest brother to me, that I may know that you are not spies but honest people. I will then restore your brother to you, and you shall be free to move about in the land.'"

³⁵As they were emptying their sacks, there, in each one's sack, was his money-bag! When they and their father saw their money-bags, they were dismayed. ³⁶Their father Jacob said to them, "It is always me that you bereave: Joseph is no more and Simeon is no more, and now you would take away Benjamin. These things always happen to me!" ³⁷Then Reuben said to his father, "You may kill my two sons if I do not bring him back to you. Put him in my care, and I will return him to you." ³⁸But he said, "My son must not go down with you, for his brother is dead and he alone is left. If he meets with disaster on the journey you are taking, you will send my white head down to Sheol in grief."

43 But the famine in the land was severe. ²And when they had eaten up the rations which they had brought from Egypt, their father said to them, "Go again and procure some food for us." ³But Judah said to him, "The official° warned us, *-'Do not let me see your faces-* unless your brother is with you.' ⁴If you will let our brother go with us, we will go down and procure food for you; ⁵but if you will not let him go, we will not go down, for that official said to us, *-'Do not let me see your faces-* unless your brother is with you.'" ⁶And Israel said, "Why did you serve me so ill as to tell the official that you had another brother?" ⁷They replied, "But the official kept asking about us and our family, saying, 'Is your father still living? Have you another brother?' And we answered him accordingly. How were we to know that he would say, 'Bring your brother here'?"

⁸Then Judah said to his father Israel, "Send the boy in my care, and let us be on our way, that we may live and not die—you and we and our children. ⁹I myself will be surety for him; you may hold me responsible: if I do not bring him back to you and set him before you, I shall stand guilty before you forever. ¹⁰For we could have been there and back twice if we had not dawdled."

¹¹Then their father Israel said to them, "If it must be so, do this: take some of the choice products of the land in your baggage, and carry them down as a gift for the official—some balm and some honey, gum, ladanum, pistachio nuts, and almonds. ¹²And take with you double the money, carrying back with you the money that was replaced in the mouths of your bags; perhaps it was a mistake. ¹³Take your brother too; and go back at once to that official. ¹⁴And may El Shaddai dispose that official to mercy toward you, that he may release to you your other brother, as well as Benjamin. As for me, if I am to be bereaved, I shall be bereaved."

¹⁵So the emissaries° took that gift, and they took with them double the money, as well as Benjamin. They made their way down to Egypt, where they presented themselves to Joseph. ¹⁶When Joseph saw Benjamin with them, he said to his house steward, "Take the emissaries into the house; slaughter and prepare an animal, for those emissaries will dine with me at noon." ¹⁷The steward° did as Joseph said, and he brought those emissaries into Joseph's house. ¹⁸But the emissaries were frightened at being brought into Joseph's house. "It must be," they thought, "because of the money replaced in our bags the first time that we have been brought inside, as a pretext to attack us and seize us as slaves, with our pack animals." ¹⁹So they went up to Joseph's house steward and spoke to him at the entrance of the house. ²⁰"If you please, my lord," they said, "we came down once before to procure food. ²¹But when we arrived at the night encampment and opened our bags, there was each one's money in the mouth of his bag, our money *⁻in full.⁻* So we have brought it back with us. ²²And we have brought down with us other money to procure food. We do not know who put the money in our bags." ²³He replied, "All is well with you; do not be afraid. Your God, the God of your father, must have put treasure in your bags for you. I got your payment." And he brought out Simeon to them.

²⁴Then the steward brought the emissaries into Joseph's house; he gave them water to bathe their feet, and he provided feed for their asses. ²⁵They laid out their gifts to await Joseph's arrival at noon, for they had heard that they were to dine there.

²⁶When Joseph came home, they presented to him the gifts that they had brought with them into the house, bowing low before

him to the ground. ²⁷He greeted them, and he said, "How is your aged father of whom you spoke? Is he still in good health?" ²⁸They replied, "It is well with your servant our father; he is still in good health." And they bowed and made obeisance.

²⁹Looking about, he saw his brother Benjamin, his mother's son, and asked, "Is this your youngest brother of whom you spoke to me?" And he went on, "May God be gracious to you, my boy." ³⁰With that, Joseph hurried out, for he was overcome with feeling toward his brother and was on the verge of tears; he went into a room and wept there. ³¹Then he washed his face, reappeared, and—now in control of himself—gave the order, "Serve the meal." ³²They served him by himself, and them by themselves, and the Egyptians who ate with him by themselves; for the Egyptians could not dine with the Hebrews, since that would be abhorrent to the Egyptians. ³³As they were seated by his direction, from the oldest in the order of his seniority to the youngest in the order of his youth, the emissaries looked at one another in astonishment. ³⁴Portions were served them from his table; but Benjamin's portion was several* times that of anyone else. And they drank their fill with him.

44 Then he instructed his house steward as follows, "Fill these emissaries' bags with food, as much as they can carry, and put each one's money in the mouth of his bag. ²Put my silver goblet in the mouth of the bag of the youngest one, together with his money for the rations." And he did as Joseph told him.

³With the first light of morning, the emissaries were sent off with their pack animals. ⁴They had just left the city and had not gone far, when Joseph said to his house steward, "Up, go after those emissaries! And when you overtake them, say to them, 'Why did you repay good with evil? ⁵It is the very one from which my master drinks and which he uses for divination. It was a wicked thing for you to do!'"

⁶He overtook them and spoke those words to them. ⁷And they said to him, "Why does my lord say such things? Far be it from your servants to do anything of the kind! ⁸Here we brought back to you from the land of Canaan the money that we found in the mouths of our bags. How then could we have stolen any silver or gold from your master's house! ⁹Whichever of your servants it is

found with shall die; the rest of us, moreover, shall become slaves to my lord." ¹⁰He replied, "Although what you are proposing is right, only the one with whom it is found shall be my slave; but the rest of you shall go free."

¹¹So each one hastened to lower his bag to the ground, and each one opened his bag. ¹²He searched, beginning with the oldest and ending with the youngest; and the goblet turned up in Benjamin's bag. ¹³At this they rent their clothes. Each reloaded his pack animal, and they returned to the city.

¹⁴When Judah and his brothers reentered the house of Joseph, who was still there, they threw themselves on the ground before him. ¹⁵Joseph said to them, "What is this deed that you have done? Do you not know that °⁻someone in my position⁻° practices divination?" ¹⁶Judah replied, "What can we say to my lord? How can we plead, how can we prove our innocence? God has uncovered the crime of your servants. Here we are, then, slaves of my lord, the rest of us as much as he in whose possession the goblet was found." ¹⁷But he replied, "Far be it from me to act thus! Only the one in whose possession the goblet was found shall be my slave; the rest of you go back in peace to your father."

וַיִּגַּשׁ | VA-YIGGASH

¹⁸Then Judah went up to him and said, "Please, my lord, let your servant appeal to my lord, and do not be impatient with your servant, you who are the equal of Pharaoh. ¹⁹My lord asked his servants, 'Have you a father or another brother?' ²⁰We told my lord, 'We have an old father, and there is a child of his old age, the youngest; his full brother is dead, so that he alone is left of his mother, and his father dotes on him.' ²¹Then you said to your servants, 'Bring him down to me, that I may set eyes on him.' ²²We said to my lord, 'The boy cannot leave his father; if he were to leave him, his father would die.' ²³But you said to your servants, 'Unless your youngest brother comes down with you, do not let me see your faces.' ²⁴When we came back to your servant my father, we reported my lord's words to him.

²⁵"Later our father said, 'Go back and procure some food for us.' ²⁶We answered, 'We cannot go down; only if our youngest brother is with us can we go down, for we may not *⁻show our

faces to the official°-* unless our youngest brother is with us.'
²⁷Your servant my father said to us, 'As you know, my wife bore
me two sons. ²⁸But one is gone from me, and I said: Alas, he was
torn by a beast! And I have not seen him since. ²⁹If you take this
one from me, too, and he meets with disaster, you will send my
white head down to Sheol in sorrow.'

³⁰"Now, if I come to your servant my father and the boy is not
with us—since his own life is so bound up with his—³¹when he
sees that the boy is not with us, he will die, and your servants will
send the white head of your servant our father down to Sheol in
grief. ³²Now your servant has pledged himself for the boy to my
father, saying, 'If I do not bring him back to you, I shall stand
guilty before my father forever.' ³³Therefore, please let your servant remain as a slave to my lord instead of the boy, and let the
boy go back with his brothers. ³⁴For how can I go back to my father unless the boy is with me? Let me not be witness to the woe
that would overtake my father!"

45

Joseph could no longer control himself before all his
attendants, and he cried out, "Have all of the staff° withdraw from me!" So none of the staff° was about when Joseph made
himself known to his brothers. ²His sobs were so loud that the
Egyptians could hear, and so the news reached Pharaoh's palace.

³Joseph said to his brothers, "I am Joseph. Is my father still
well?" But his brothers could not answer him, so dumfounded
were they on account of him.

⁴Then Joseph said to his brothers, "Come forward to me." And
when they came forward, he said, "I am your brother Joseph, he
whom you sold into Egypt. ⁵Now, do not be distressed or re-
proach yourselves because you sold me hither; it was to save life
that God sent me ahead of you. ⁶It is now two years that there has
been famine in the land, and there are still five years to come in
which there shall be no yield from tilling. ⁷God has sent me ahead
of you to ensure your survival on earth, and to save your lives in
an extraordinary deliverance. ⁸So, it was not you who sent me
here, but God—who has made me a °-father to Pharaoh,-° lord of
all his household, and ruler over the whole land of Egypt.

⁹"Now, hurry back to my father and say to him: Thus says your
son Joseph, 'God has made me lord of all Egypt; come down to

Va-yiggash

me without delay. [10]You will dwell in the region of Goshen, where you will be near me—you and your children and your grandchildren, your flocks and herds, and all that is yours. [11]There I will provide for you—for there are yet five years of famine to come—that you and your household and all that is yours may not suffer want.' [12]You can see for yourselves, and my brother Benjamin for himself, that it is indeed I who am speaking to you. [13]And you must tell my father everything about my high station in Egypt and all that you have seen; and bring my father here with all speed."

[14]With that he embraced* his brother Benjamin around the neck and wept, and Benjamin wept on his neck. [15]He kissed all his brothers and wept upon them; only then were his brothers able to talk to him.

[16]The news reached Pharaoh's palace: "Joseph's brothers have come." Pharaoh and his courtiers were pleased. [17]And Pharaoh said to Joseph, "Say to your brothers, 'Do as follows: load up your beasts and go at once to the land of Canaan. [18]Take your father and your households and come to me; I will give you the best of the land of Egypt and you shall live off the fat of the land.' [19]And you are bidden [to add], 'Do as follows: take from the land of Egypt wagons for your children and your wives, and bring your father here. [20]And never mind your belongings, for the best of all the land of Egypt shall be yours.'"

[21]The sons of Israel did so; Joseph gave them wagons as Pharaoh had commanded, and he supplied them with provisions for the journey. [22]To each of them, moreover, he gave a change of clothing; but to Benjamin he gave three hundred pieces of silver and several* changes of clothing. [23]And to his father he sent the following: ten he-asses laden with the best things of Egypt, and ten she-asses laden with grain, bread, and provisions for his father on the journey. [24]As he sent his brothers off on their way, he told them, "Do not be quarrelsome on the way."

[25]They went up from Egypt and came to their father Jacob in the land of Canaan. [26]And they told him, "Joseph is still alive; yes, he is ruler over the whole land of Egypt." His heart went numb, for he did not believe them. [27]But when they recounted all that Joseph had said to them, and when he saw the wagons that Joseph had sent to transport him, the spirit of their father Jacob revived.

²⁸"Enough!" said Israel. "My son Joseph is still alive! I must go and see him before I die."

46 So Israel set out with all that was his, and he came to Beer-sheba, where he offered sacrifices to the God of his father Isaac. ²God called to Israel in a vision by night: "Jacob! Jacob!" He answered, "Here."

³"I am God, the God of your father. Fear not to go down to Egypt, for I will make you there into a great nation. ⁴I Myself will go down with you to Egypt, and I Myself will also bring you back; and Joseph's hand shall close your eyes."

⁵So Jacob set out from Beer-sheba. The sons of Israel put their father Jacob and their children and their wives in the wagons that Pharaoh had sent to transport him; ⁶and they took along their livestock and the wealth that they had amassed in the land of Canaan. Thus Jacob and all his offspring with him came to Egypt: ⁷he brought with him to Egypt his sons and grandsons, his daughters° and granddaughters—all his offspring.

⁸These are the names of the Israelites, Jacob and his descendants, who came to Egypt.

Jacob's first-born Reuben; ⁹Reuben's sons: Enoch,* Pallu, Hezron, and Carmi. ¹⁰Simeon's sons: Jemuel, Jamin, Ohad, Jachin, Zohar, and Saul* the son of a Canaanite woman. ¹¹Levi's sons: Gershon, Kohath, and Merari. ¹²Judah's sons: Er, Onan, Shelah, Perez, and Zerah—but Er and Onan had died in the land of Canaan; and Perez's sons were Hezron and Hamul. ¹³Issachar's sons: Tola, Puvah, Iob, and Shimron. ¹⁴Zebulun's sons: Sered, Elon, and Jahleel. ¹⁵Those were the sons whom Leah bore to Jacob in Paddan-aram, in addition to his daughter Dinah. Persons in all, male and female: 33.*

¹⁶Gad's sons: Ziphion, Haggi, Shuni, Ezbon, Eri, Arodi, and Areli. ¹⁷Asher's sons: Imnah, Ishvah, Ishvi, and Beriah, and their sister Serah. Beriah's sons: Heber and Malchiel. ¹⁸These were the descendants of Zilpah, whom Laban had given to his daughter Leah. These she bore to Jacob—16 persons.

¹⁹The sons of Jacob's wife Rachel were Joseph and Benjamin. ²⁰To Joseph were born in the land of Egypt Manasseh and Ephraim, whom Asenath daughter of Poti-phera priest of On bore to him. ²¹Benjamin's sons: Bela, Becher, Ashbel, Gera, Naaman,

Ehi, Rosh, Muppim, Huppim, and Ard. ²²These were the descendants of Rachel who were born to Jacob—14 persons in all.

²³Dan's son:* Hushim. ²⁴Naphtali's sons: Jahzeel, Guni, Jezer, and Shillem. ²⁵These were the descendants of Bilhah, whom Laban had given to his daughter Rachel. These she bore to Jacob—7 persons in all.

²⁶All the persons belonging to Jacob *⁻who came to Egypt*—his own issue, aside from the wives of Jacob's sons—all these persons numbered 66. ²⁷And Joseph's sons who were born to him in Egypt were two in number. Thus the total of Jacob's household who came to Egypt was *⁻seventy persons.⁻*

²⁸He had sent Judah ahead of him to Joseph, to point the way before him to Goshen. So when they came to the region of Goshen, ²⁹Joseph ordered* his chariot and went to Goshen to meet his father Israel; he presented himself to him and, embracing him around the neck, he wept on his neck a good while. ³⁰Then Israel said to Joseph, "Now I can die, having seen for myself that you are still alive."

³¹Then Joseph said to his brothers and to his father's household, "I will go up and tell the news to Pharaoh, and say to him, 'My brothers and my father's household, who were in the land of Canaan, have come to me. ³²These householders° are shepherds; they have always been breeders of livestock, and they have brought with them their flocks and herds and all that is theirs.' ³³So when Pharaoh summons you and asks, 'What is your occupation?' ³⁴you shall answer, 'Your servants have been breeders of livestock from the start until now, both we and our fathers'—so that you may stay in the region of Goshen. For all shepherds are abhorrent to Egyptians."

47 Then Joseph came and reported to Pharaoh, saying, "My father and my brothers, with their flocks and herds and all that is theirs, have come from the land of Canaan and are now in the region of Goshen." ²And having selected from among his brothers *⁻a few*⁻ representatives,° he presented them to Pharaoh. ³Pharaoh said to his brothers, "What is your occupation?" They answered Pharaoh, "We your servants are shepherds, as were also our fathers. ⁴We have come," they told Pharaoh, "to sojourn in this land, for there is no pasture for your servants' flocks, the famine being severe in the land of Canaan. Pray, then, let your servants stay in the region of Goshen." ⁵Then Pharaoh said to Joseph, "As regards your father and your brothers who have come to you, ⁶the land of Egypt is open before you: settle your father and your brothers in the best part of the land; let them stay in the region of Goshen. And if you know any °capable administrators⁻° among them, put them in charge of my livestock."

⁷Joseph then brought his father Jacob and presented him to Pharaoh; and Jacob greeted Pharaoh. ⁸Pharaoh asked Jacob, "How many are the years of your life?" ⁹And Jacob answered Pharaoh, "The years of my sojourn [on earth] are one hundred and thirty. Few and hard have been the years of my life, nor do they come up to the life spans of my ancestors° during their sojourns." ¹⁰Then Jacob bade Pharaoh farewell, and left Pharaoh's presence.

¹¹So Joseph settled his father and his brothers, giving them holdings in the choicest part of the land of Egypt, in the region of Rameses, as Pharaoh had commanded. ¹²Joseph sustained his father, and his brothers, and all his father's household with bread, down to the little ones.

¹³Now there was no bread in all the world, for the famine was very severe; both the land of Egypt and the land of Canaan languished because of the famine. ¹⁴Joseph gathered in all the money that was to be found in the land of Egypt and in the land of Canaan, as payment for the rations that were being procured, and Joseph brought the money into Pharaoh's palace. ¹⁵And when the money gave out in the land of Egypt and in the land of Canaan, all the Egyptians came to Joseph and said, "Give us bread, lest we die before your very eyes; for the money is gone!" ¹⁶And Joseph said, "Bring your livestock, and I will sell to you against your livestock, if the money is gone." ¹⁷So they brought their livestock to Joseph, and Joseph gave them bread in exchange for the horses, for the stocks of sheep and cattle, and the asses; thus he provided them with bread that year in exchange for all their livestock. ¹⁸And when that year was ended, they came to him the next year and said to him, "We cannot hide from my lord that, with all the money and animal stocks consigned

to my lord, nothing is left at my lord's disposal save our persons and our farmland. ¹⁹Let us not perish before your eyes, both we and our land. Take us and our land in exchange for bread, and we with our land will be serfs to Pharaoh; provide the seed, that we may live and not die, and that the land may not become a waste."

²⁰So Joseph gained possession of all the farm land of Egypt for Pharaoh, all the Egyptians having sold their fields because the famine was too much for them; thus the land passed over to Pharaoh. ²¹And he removed the population *ʾtown by town,ʾ* from one end of Egypt's border to the other. ²²Only the land of the priests he did not take over, for the priests had an allotment from Pharaoh, and they lived off the allotment which Pharaoh had made to them; therefore they did not sell their land.

²³Then Joseph said to the people, "Whereas I have this day acquired you and your land for Pharaoh, here is seed for you to sow the land. ²⁴And when harvest comes, you shall give one-fifth to Pharaoh, and four-fifths shall be yours as seed for the fields and as food for you and those in your households, and as nourishment for your children." ²⁵And they said, "You have saved our lives! We are grateful to my lord, and we shall be serfs to Pharaoh." ²⁶And Joseph made it into a land law in Egypt, which is still valid, that a fifth should be Pharaoh's; only the land of the priests did not become Pharaoh's.

²⁷Thus Israel settled in the country of Egypt, in the region of Goshen; they acquired holdings in it, and were fertile and increased greatly.

ויחי | VA-YEHI

²⁸Jacob lived seventeen years in the land of Egypt, so that the span of Jacob's life came to one hundred and forty-seven years. ²⁹And when the time approached for Israel to die, he summoned his son Joseph and said to him, "Do me this favor, place your hand under my thigh as a pledge of your steadfast loyalty: please do not bury me in Egypt. ³⁰When I lie down with my ancestors,° take me up from Egypt and bury me in their burial-place." He replied, "I will do as you have spoken." ³¹And he said, "Swear to me." And he swore to him. Then Israel bowed at the head of the bed.

48 Some time afterward, Joseph was told, "Your father is ill." So he took with him his two sons, Manasseh and Ephraim. ²When Jacob was told, "Your son Joseph has come to see you," Israel summoned his strength and sat up in bed.

³And Jacob said to Joseph, "El Shaddai, who appeared to me at Luz in the land of Canaan, blessed me—⁴and said to me, 'I will make you fertile and numerous, making of you a community of peoples; and I will assign this land to your offspring to come for an everlasting possession.' ⁵Now, your two sons, who were born to you in the land of Egypt before I came to you in Egypt, shall be mine; Ephraim and Manasseh shall be mine no less than Reuben and Simeon. ⁶But progeny born to you after them shall be yours; they shall be recorded instead* of their brothers in their inheritance. ⁷I [do this because], when I was returning from Paddan, Rachel died, to my sorrow, while I was journeying in the land of Canaan, when still some distance short of Ephrath; and I buried her there on the road to Ephrath"—now Bethlehem.

⁸Noticing Joseph's sons, Israel asked, "Who are these?" ⁹And Joseph said to his father, "They are my sons, whom God has given me here." "Bring them up to me," he said, "that I may bless them." ¹⁰Now Israel's eyes were dim with age; he could not see. So [Joseph] brought them close to him, and he kissed them and embraced them. ¹¹And Israel said to Joseph, "I never expected to see you again, and here God has let me see your children as well."

¹²Joseph then removed them from his knees, and bowed low with his face to the ground. ¹³Joseph took the two of them, Ephraim with his right hand—to Israel's left—and Manasseh with his left hand—to Israel's right—and brought them close to him. ¹⁴But Israel stretched out his right hand and laid it on Ephraim's head, though he was the younger, and his left hand on Manasseh's head—thus crossing his hands—although Manasseh was the firstborn. ¹⁵And he blessed Joseph, saying,

> "The God in whose ways my fathers Abraham and Isaac walked,
> The God who has been my shepherd from my birth to this day—
> ¹⁶The Messenger who has redeemed me from all harm—

Bless the lads.
In them may my name be recalled,
And the names of my fathers Abraham and Isaac,
And may they be teeming multitudes upon the earth."

17When Joseph saw that his father was placing his right hand on Ephraim's head, he thought it wrong; so he took hold of his father's hand to move it from Ephraim's head to Manasseh's. 18"Not so, Father," Joseph said to his father, "for the other is the first-born; place your right hand on his head." 19But his father objected, saying, "I know, my son, I know. He too shall become a people, and he too shall be great. Yet his younger brother shall be greater than he, and his offspring shall be plentiful enough for nations." 20So he blessed them that day, saying, "By you shall Israel invoke blessings, saying: God make you like Ephraim and Manasseh." Thus he put Ephraim before Manasseh.

21Then Israel said to Joseph, "I am about to die; but God will be with you and bring you back to the land of your ancestors. 22And now, I assign to you one portion* more than to your brothers, which I wrested from the Amorites with my sword and bow."

49 And Jacob called his sons and said, "Come together that I may tell you what is to befall you in days to come. 2Assemble and hearken, O sons of Jacob;
Hearken to Israel your father:

3Reuben, you are my first-born,
My might and first fruit of my vigor,
Exceeding in rank
And exceeding in honor.
4Unstable as water, you shall excel no longer;
For when you mounted your father's bed,
You brought disgrace—my couch he mounted!

5Simeon and Levi are a pair;
Their weapons are tools of lawlessness.
6Let not my person be included in their council,
Let not my being be counted in their assembly.
For when angry they °⁻slay a man,⁻°
And when pleased they °⁻maim an ox.⁻°
7Cursed be their anger so fierce,

               Va-yeḥi

And their wrath so relentless.
I will divide them in Jacob,
Scatter them in Israel.

8You, O Judah, your brothers shall praise;
Your hand shall be on the nape of your foes;
Your father's sons shall bow low to you.
9Judah is a lion's whelp;
On prey, my son, have you grown.
He crouches, lies down like a lion,
Like °⁻a lioness⁻°—who dare rouse him?
10The scepter shall not depart from Judah,
Nor the ruler's staff from between his feet;
⁻So that tribute shall come to him⁻
And the homage of peoples be his.

11He tethers his ass to a vine,
His ass's foal to a choice vine;
He washes his garment in wine,
His robe in blood of grapes.
12*⁻His eyes are darker than wine;
His teeth are whiter than milk.⁻*

13Zebulun shall dwell by the seashore;
He shall be a haven for ships,
And his flank shall rest on Sidon.

14Issachar is a strong-boned ass,
Crouching among the sheepfolds.
15When he saw how good was security,
And how pleasant was the country,
He bent his shoulder to the burden,
And became a toiling serf.

16Dan shall govern his people,
As one of the tribes of Israel.
17Dan shall be a serpent by the road,
A viper by the path,
That bites the horse's heels
So that his rider is thrown backward.

¹⁸I wait for Your deliverance, O יהוה!

¹⁹Gad shall be raided by raiders,
But he shall raid at their heels.

²⁰Asher's bread shall be rich,
And he shall yield royal dainties.

²¹Naphtali is a hind let loose,
Which yields lovely fawns.

²²*-Joseph is a wild ass,
A wild ass by a spring
—Wild colts on a hillside.-*

²³Archers bitterly assailed him;
They shot at him and harried him.
²⁴Yet his bow stayed taut,
And *-his arms-* were made firm
By the hands of the Mighty One of Jacob—
There, the Shepherd, the Rock of Israel—
²⁵The God of your father's [house], who helps you,
And Shaddai who blesses you
With blessings of heaven above,
Blessings of the deep that couches below,
Blessings of the breast and womb.
²⁶*-The blessings of your father
Surpass the blessings of my ancestors,
To the utmost bounds of the eternal hills.-*
May they rest on the head of Joseph,
On the brow of the elect of his brothers.

²⁷Benjamin is a ravenous wolf;
In the morning he consumes the foe,*
And in the evening he divides the spoil."

²⁸All these were the tribes of Israel, twelve in number, and this is what their father said to them as he bade them farewell, addressing to each a parting word appropriate to him.

²⁹Then he instructed them, saying to them, "I am about to be gathered to my kin. Bury me with my ancestors° in the cave which is in the field of Ephron the Hittite, ³⁰the cave which is in the field

of Machpelah, facing Mamre, in the land of Canaan, the field that Abraham bought from Ephron the Hittite for a burial site— 31there Abraham and his wife Sarah were buried; there Isaac and his wife Rebekah were buried; and there I buried Leah—32the field and the cave in it, bought from the Hittites." 33When Jacob finished his instructions to his sons, he drew his feet into the bed and, breathing his last, he was gathered to his kin.°

50 Joseph flung himself upon his father's face and wept over him and kissed him. 2Then Joseph ordered the physicians in his service to embalm his father, and the physicians embalmed Israel. 3It required forty days, for such is the full period of embalming. The Egyptians bewailed him seventy days; 4and when the wailing period was over, Joseph spoke to Pharaoh's court, saying, "Do me this favor, and lay this appeal before Pharaoh: 5'My father made me swear, saying, "I am about to die. Be sure to bury me in the grave which I made ready for myself in the land of Canaan." Now, therefore, let me go up and bury my father; then I shall return.'" 6And Pharaoh said, "Go up and bury your father, as he made you promise on oath."

7So Joseph went up to bury his father; and with him went up all the officials of Pharaoh, the senior members of his court, and all of Egypt's dignitaries, 8together with all of Joseph's household, his brothers, and his father's household; only their children, their flocks, and their herds were left in the region of Goshen. 9Chariots, too, and horsemen went up with him; it was a very large troop.

10When they came to Goren* ha-Atad, which is beyond the Jordan, they held there a very great and solemn lamentation; and he observed a mourning period of seven days for his father. 11And when the Canaanite inhabitants of the land saw the mourning at Goren ha-Atad, they said, "This is a solemn mourning on the part of the Egyptians." That is why it was named Abel-mizraim,* which is beyond the Jordan. 12Thus his sons did for him as he had instructed them. 13His sons carried him to the land of Canaan, and buried him in the cave of the field of Machpelah, the field near Mamre, which Abraham had bought for a burial site from Ephron the Hittite. 14After burying his father, Joseph returned to Egypt, he and his brothers and all who had gone up with him to bury his father.

Va-yeḥi

¹⁵When Joseph's brothers saw that their father was dead, they said, "What if Joseph still bears a grudge against us and pays us back for all the wrong that we did him!" ¹⁶So they sent this message to Joseph, "Before his death your father left this instruction: ¹⁷So shall you say to Joseph, 'Forgive, I urge you, the offense and guilt of your brothers who treated you so harshly.' Therefore, please forgive the offense of the servants of the God of your father." And Joseph was in tears as they spoke to him.

¹⁸His brothers went to him themselves, flung themselves before him, and said, "We are prepared to be your slaves." ¹⁹But Joseph said to them, "Have no fear! Am I a substitute for God? ²⁰Besides, although you intended me harm, God intended it for good, so as to bring about the present result—the survival of many people. ²¹And so, fear not. I will sustain you and your dependents.°" Thus he reassured them, speaking kindly to them.

²²So Joseph and his father's household remained in Egypt. Joseph lived one hundred and ten years. ²³Joseph lived to see children of the third generation of Ephraim; the children of Machir son of Manasseh were likewise born upon Joseph's knees. ²⁴At length, Joseph said to his brothers, "I am about to die. God will surely take notice of you and bring you up from this land to the land promised on oath to Abraham, to Isaac, and to Jacob." ²⁵So Joseph made the sons of Israel swear, saying, "When God has taken notice of you, you shall carry up my bones from here."

²⁶Joseph died at the age of one hundred and ten years; and he was embalmed and placed in a coffin in Egypt.

חֲזַק

שְׁמוֹת
EXODUS

1 These are the names of the sons of Israel who came to Egypt with Jacob, each coming with his household: ²Reuben, Simeon, Levi, and Judah; ³Issachar, Zebulun, and Benjamin; ⁴Dan and Naphtali, Gad and Asher. ⁵The total number of persons that were of Jacob's issue came to seventy, Joseph being already in Egypt. ⁶Joseph died, and all his brothers, and all that generation. ⁷But the Israelites were fertile and prolific; they multiplied and increased very greatly, so that the land was filled with them.

⁸A new king arose over Egypt who did not know Joseph. ⁹And he said to his people, "Look, the Israelite people are much too numerous for us. ¹⁰Let us deal shrewdly with them, so that they may not increase; otherwise in the event of war they may join our enemies in fighting against us and *⁻rise from the ground."⁻*

¹¹So they set taskmasters over them to oppress them with forced labor; and they built *⁻garrison cities⁻* for Pharaoh: Pithom and Rameses. ¹²But the more they were oppressed, the more they increased and spread out, so that the [Egyptians] came to dread the Israelites.

¹³The Egyptians ruthlessly imposed upon the Israelites ¹⁴*⁻the various labors that they made them perform. Ruthlessly⁻* they made life bitter for them with harsh labor at mortar and bricks and with all sorts of tasks in the field.

¹⁵The king of Egypt spoke to the Hebrew midwives, one of whom was named Shiphrah and the other Puah, ¹⁶saying, "When you deliver the Hebrew women, look at the birthstool:* if it is a boy, kill him; if it is a girl, let her live." ¹⁷The midwives, fearing God, did not do as the king of Egypt had told them; they let the boys live. ¹⁸So the king of Egypt summoned the midwives and said to them, "Why have you done this thing, letting the boys live?" ¹⁹The midwives said to Pharaoh, "Because the Hebrew women are not like the Egyptian women: they are vigorous. Before the midwife can come to them, they have given birth." ²⁰And God dealt

well with the midwives; and the people multiplied and increased greatly. ²¹And [God] established households* for the midwives, because they feared God. ²²Then Pharaoh charged all his people, saying, "Every boy that is born you shall throw into the Nile, but let every girl live."

2 A certain member° of the house of Levi went and took [into his household as his wife] a woman of Levi. ²The woman conceived and bore a son; and when she saw how beautiful he was, she hid him for three months. ³When she could hide him no longer, she got a wicker basket for him and caulked it with bitumen and pitch. She put the child into it and placed it among the reeds by the bank of the Nile. ⁴And his sister stationed herself at a distance, to learn what would befall him.

⁵The daughter of Pharaoh came down to bathe in the Nile, while her maidens walked along the Nile. She spied the basket among the reeds and sent her slave girl to fetch it. ⁶When she opened it, she saw that it was a child, a boy crying. She took pity on it and said, "This must be a Hebrew child." ⁷Then his sister said to Pharaoh's daughter, "Shall I go and get you a Hebrew nurse to suckle the child for you?" ⁸And Pharaoh's daughter answered, "Yes." So the girl went and called the child's mother. ⁹And Pharaoh's daughter said to her, "Take this child and nurse it for me, and I will pay your wages." So the woman took the child and nursed it. ¹⁰When the child grew up, she brought him to Pharaoh's daughter, who made him her son. She named him Moses,* explaining, "I drew him out of the water."

¹¹Some time after that, when Moses had grown up, he went out to his kinsfolk and witnessed their labors. He saw an Egyptian beating a Hebrew, one of his kinsmen. ¹²He turned this way and that and, seeing no one about, he struck down the Egyptian and hid him in the sand. ¹³When he went out the next day, he found two Hebrews fighting; so he said to the offender, "Why do you strike your fellow?" ¹⁴He retorted, "Who made you chief and ruler over us? Do you mean to kill me as you killed the Egyptian?" Moses was frightened, and thought: Then the matter is known! ¹⁵When Pharaoh learned of the matter, he sought to kill Moses;

but Moses fled from Pharaoh. He arrived* in the land of Midian, and sat down beside a well.

¹⁶Now the priest of Midian had seven daughters. They came to draw water, and filled the troughs to water their father's flock; ¹⁷but shepherds came and drove them off. Moses rose to their defense, and he watered their flock. ¹⁸When they returned to their father Reuel, he said, "How is it that you have come back so soon today?" ¹⁹They answered, "An Egyptian° rescued us from the shepherds; he even drew water for us and watered the flock." ²⁰He said to his daughters, "Where is he then? Why did you leave the [Egyptian]?° Ask him in to break bread." ²¹Moses consented to stay °in that household,° and [Reuel] gave Moses his daughter Zipporah as wife. ²²She bore a son whom he named Gershom,* for he said, "I have been a stranger in a foreign land."

²³A long time after that, the king of Egypt died. The Israelites were groaning under the bondage and cried out; and their cry for help from the bondage rose up to God. ²⁴God heard their moaning, and God remembered the covenant with Abraham and Isaac and Jacob. ²⁵God looked upon the Israelites, and God took notice of them.

3 Now Moses, tending the flock of his father-in-law Jethro, the priest of Midian, drove the flock into the wilderness, and came to Horeb, the mountain of God. ²A messenger of יהוה appeared to him in a blazing fire out of a bush. He gazed, and there was a bush all aflame, yet the bush was not consumed. ³Moses said, "I must turn aside to look at this marvelous sight; why doesn't the bush burn up?" ⁴When יהוה saw that he had turned aside to look, God called to him out of the bush: "Moses! Moses!" He answered, "Here I am." ⁵And [God] said, "Do not come closer! Remove your sandals from your feet, for the place on which you stand is holy ground!" ⁶and continued, "I am the God of your father's [house]—the God of Abraham, the God of Isaac, and the God of Jacob." And Moses hid his face, for he was afraid to look at God.

⁷And יהוה continued, "I have marked well the plight of My people in Egypt and have heeded their outcry because of their

taskmasters; yes, I am mindful of their sufferings. ⁸I have come down to rescue them from the Egyptians and to bring them out of that land to a good and spacious land, a land flowing with milk and honey, the region of the Canaanites, the Hittites, the Amorites, the Perizzites, the Hivites, and the Jebusites. ⁹Now the cry of the Israelites has reached Me; moreover, I have seen how the Egyptians oppress them. ¹⁰Come, therefore, I will send you to Pharaoh, and you shall free My people, the Israelites, from Egypt."

¹¹But Moses said to God, "Who am I that I should go to Pharaoh and free the Israelites from Egypt?" ¹²And [God] said, "I will be with you; that shall be your sign that it was I who sent you. And when you have freed the people from Egypt, you shall worship God at this mountain."

¹³Moses said to God, "When I come to the Israelites and say to them, 'The God of your ancestors has sent me to you,' and they ask me, 'What is his name?' what shall I say to them?" ¹⁴And God said to Moses, *-"Ehyeh-Asher-Ehyeh,"-* continuing, "Thus shall you say to the Israelites, 'Ehyeh* sent me to you.'" ¹⁵And God said further to Moses, "Thus shall you speak to the Israelites: יהוה, the God of your ancestors—the God of Abraham, the God of Isaac, and the God of Jacob—has sent me to you:

This shall be My name forever,

This My appellation for all eternity.

¹⁶"Go and assemble the elders of Israel and say to them: יהוה,* the God of your ancestors—the God of Abraham, Isaac, and Jacob—has appeared to me and said, 'I have taken note of you and of what is being done to you in Egypt, ¹⁷and I have declared: I will take you out of the misery of Egypt to the land of the Canaanites, the Hittites, the Amorites, the Perizzites, the Hivites, and the Jebusites, to a land flowing with milk and honey.' ¹⁸They will listen to you; then you shall go with the elders of Israel to the king of Egypt and you shall say to him, 'יהוה, the God of the Hebrews, became manifest to us. Now therefore, let us go a distance of three days into the wilderness to sacrifice to our God יהוה.' ¹⁹Yet I know that the king of Egypt will let you go only because of a greater might. ²⁰So I will stretch out My hand and smite Egypt with various wonders which I will work upon them; after that he shall let you go. ²¹And I will dispose the Egyptians favor-

ably toward this people, so that when you go, you will not go away empty-handed. ²²Each woman shall borrow from her neighbor and the lodger in her house objects of silver and gold, and clothing, and you shall put these on your sons and daughters, thus stripping the Egyptians."

4 But Moses spoke up and said, "What if they do not believe me and do not listen to me, but say: יהוה did not appear to you?" ²יהוה said to him, "What is that in your hand?" And he replied, "A rod." ³[God] said, "Cast it on the ground." He cast it on the ground and it became a snake; and Moses recoiled from it. ⁴Then יהוה said to Moses, "Put out your hand and grasp it by the tail"—he put out his hand and seized it, and it became a rod in his hand—⁵"that they may believe that יהוה, the God of their ancestors, the God of Abraham, the God of Isaac, and the God of Jacob, did appear to you."

⁶יהוה said to him further, "Put your hand into your bosom." He put his hand into his bosom; and when he took it out, his hand was encrusted with snowy scales!* ⁷And [God] said, "Put your hand back into your bosom."—He put his hand back into his bosom; and when he took it out of his bosom, there it was again like the rest of his body.—⁸"And if they do not believe you or pay heed to the first sign, they will believe the second. ⁹And if they are not convinced by both these signs and still do not heed you, take some water from the Nile and pour it on the dry ground, and it—the water that you take from the Nile—will turn to blood on the dry ground."

¹⁰But Moses said to יהוה, "Please, O my lord, I have never been °good with words,° either in times past or now that You have spoken to Your servant; I am slow of speech and slow of tongue." ¹¹And יהוה said to him, "Who gives humans speech? Who makes them dumb or deaf, seeing or blind? Is it not I, יהוה? ¹²Now go, and I will be with you as you speak and will instruct you what to say." ¹³But he said, "Please, O my lord, *make someone else Your agent."* ¹⁴יהוה became angry with Moses and said, "There is your brother Aaron the Levite. He, I know, speaks readily. Even now he is setting out to meet you, and he will be happy to see you. ¹⁵You shall speak to him and put the words in his mouth—I will be with you and with him as you speak, and tell both of you what to do—¹⁶and he shall speak for you to the people. Thus he shall

Shemot

91

serve as your spokesman, with you *-playing the role of God-* to him, [17]and take with you this rod, with which you shall perform the signs."

[18]Moses went back to his father-in-law Jether* and said to him, "Let me go back to my kinsfolk in Egypt and see *-how they are faring."-* And Jethro said to Moses, "Go in peace."

[19]יהוה said to Moses in Midian, "Go back to Egypt, for all the authorities° who sought to kill you are dead." [20]So Moses took his wife and sons, mounted them on an ass, and went back to the land of Egypt; and Moses took the rod of God with him.

[21]And יהוה said to Moses, "When you return to Egypt, see that you perform before Pharaoh all the marvels that I have put within your power. I, however, will stiffen his heart so that he will not let the people go. [22]Then you shall say to Pharaoh, 'Thus says יהוה: Israel is My first-born son. [23]I have said to you, "Let My son go, that he may worship Me," yet you refuse to let him go. Now I will slay your first-born son.'"

[24]At a night encampment on the way, יהוה encountered him and sought to kill him. *-[25]So Zipporah took a flint and cut off her son's foreskin, and touched his legs with it, saying, "You are truly a bridegroom of blood to me!" [26]And when [God] let him alone, she added, "A bridegroom of blood because of the circumcision."-*

[27]יהוה said to Aaron, "Go to meet Moses in the wilderness." He went and met him at the mountain of God, and he kissed him. [28]Moses told Aaron about all the things that יהוה had committed to him and all the signs about which he had been instructed. [29]Then Moses and Aaron went and assembled all the elders of the Israelites. [30]Aaron repeated all the words that יהוה had spoken to Moses, and he performed the signs in the sight of the people, [31]and the people were convinced. When they heard that יהוה had taken note of the Israelites and that [God] had seen their plight, they bowed low in homage.

5   Afterward Moses and Aaron went and said to Pharaoh, "Thus says יהוה, the God of Israel: Let My people go that they may celebrate a festival for Me in the wilderness." [2]But Pharaoh said, "Who is יהוה that I should heed him and let Israel go?

I do not know יהוה, nor will I let Israel go." 3They answered, "The God of the Hebrews has become manifest to us. Let us go, we pray, a distance of three days into the wilderness to sacrifice to our God יהוה, lest [God] strike us with pestilence or sword." 4But the king of Egypt said to them, "Moses and Aaron, why do you distract the people from their tasks? Get to your labors!" 5And Pharaoh continued, "*The people of the land are already so numerous,* and you would have them cease *from their labors!"-*

6That same day Pharaoh charged the taskmasters and overseers of the people, saying, 7"You shall no longer provide the people with straw for making bricks as heretofore; let them go and gather straw for themselves. 8But impose upon them the same quota of bricks as they have been making heretofore; do not reduce it, for they are shirkers; that is why they cry, 'Let us go and sacrifice to our God!' 9Let heavier work be laid upon the laborers;° let them keep at it and not pay attention to deceitful promises."

10So the taskmasters and overseers of the people went out and said to the people, "Thus says Pharaoh: I will not give you any straw. 11You must go and get the straw yourselves wherever you can find it; but there shall be no decrease whatever in your work." 12Then the people scattered throughout the land of Egypt to gather stubble for straw. 13And the taskmasters pressed them, saying, "You must complete the same work assignment each day as when you had straw." 14And the overseers of the Israelites, whom Pharaoh's taskmasters had set over them, were beaten. "Why," they were asked, "did you not complete the prescribed amount of bricks, either yesterday or today, as you did before?"

15Then the overseers of the Israelites came to Pharaoh and cried: "Why do you deal thus with your servants? 16No straw is issued to your servants, yet they demand of us: Make bricks! Thus your servants are being beaten, when the fault is with your own people." 17He replied, "You are shirkers, shirkers! That is why you say, 'Let us go and sacrifice to יהוה.' 18Be off now to your work! No straw shall be issued to you, but you must produce your quota of bricks!"

19Now the overseers of the Israelites found themselves in trouble because of the order, "You must not reduce your daily quantity of bricks." 20As they left Pharaoh's presence, they came upon Moses and Aaron standing in their path, 21and they said to them, "May

יהוה look upon you and punish you for making us loathsome to Pharaoh and his courtiers—putting a sword in their hands to slay us." ²²Then Moses returned to יהוה and said, "O my lord, why did You bring harm upon this people? Why did You send me? ²³Ever since I came to Pharaoh to speak in Your name, he has dealt worse with this people; and still You have not delivered Your people."

6 Then יהוה said to Moses, "You shall soon see what I will do to Pharaoh: he shall let them go because of a greater might; indeed, because of a greater might he shall drive them from his land."

וָאֵרָא | VA-'ERA'

²God spoke to Moses and said to him, "I am יהוה. ³I appeared to Abraham, Isaac, and Jacob as El Shaddai, but I did not make Myself known to them by My name יהוה. ⁴I also established My covenant with them, to give them the land of Canaan, the land in which they lived as sojourners. ⁵I have now heard the moaning of the Israelites because the Egyptians are holding them in bondage, and I have remembered My covenant. ⁶Say, therefore, to the Israelite people: I am יהוה. I will free you from the labors of the Egyptians and deliver you from their bondage. I will redeem you with an outstretched arm and through extraordinary chastisements. ⁷And I will take you to be My people, and I will be your God. And you shall know that I, יהוה, am your God who freed you from the labors of the Egyptians. ⁸I will bring you into the land which I swore* to give to Abraham, Isaac, and Jacob, and I will give it to you for a possession, I יהוה." ⁹But when Moses told this to the Israelites, they would not listen to Moses, their spirits crushed by cruel bondage.

¹⁰יהוה spoke to Moses, saying, ¹¹"Go and tell Pharaoh king of Egypt to let the Israelites depart from his land." ¹²But Moses appealed to יהוה, saying, "The Israelites would not listen to me; how then should Pharaoh heed me, me—who gets tongue-tied!" ¹³So יהוה spoke to both Moses and Aaron in regard to the Israelites and Pharaoh king of Egypt, instructing them to deliver the Israelites from the land of Egypt.

¹⁴The following are the heads of their respective clans.

The sons of Reuben, Israel's first-born: Enoch* and Pallu, Hezron and Carmi; those are the families of Reuben. ¹⁵The sons of Simeon: Jemuel, Jamin, Ohad, Jachin, Zohar, and Saul* the son of a Canaanite woman; those are the families of Simeon. ¹⁶These are the names of Levi's sons by their lineage: Gershon, Kohath, and Merari; and the span of Levi's life was 137 years. ¹⁷The sons of Gershon: Libni and Shimei, by their families. ¹⁸The sons of Kohath: Amram, Izhar, Hebron, and Uzziel; and the span of Kohath's life was 133 years. ¹⁹The sons of Merari: Mahli and Mushi. These are the families of the Levites by their lineage.

²⁰Amram took into his [household] as wife his father's sister Jochebed, and she bore him Aaron and Moses; and the span of Amram's life was 137 years. ²¹The sons of Izhar: Korah, Nepheg, and Zichri. ²²The sons of Uzziel: Mishael, Elzaphan, and Sithri. ²³Aaron took into his [household] as wife Elisheba, daughter of Amminadab and sister of Nahshon, and she bore him Nadab and Abihu, Eleazar and Ithamar. ²⁴The sons of Korah: Assir, Elkanah, and Abiasaph. Those are the families of the Korahites. ²⁵And Aaron's son Eleazar took into his [household] as wife one of Putiel's daughters, and she bore him Phinehas. Those are the heads of the ancestral houses of the Levites by their families.

²⁶It is the same Aaron and Moses to whom יהוה said, "Bring forth the Israelites from the land of Egypt, troop by troop." ²⁷It was they who spoke to Pharaoh king of Egypt to free the Israelites from the Egyptians; these are the same Moses and Aaron. ²⁸For when יהוה spoke to Moses in the land of Egypt ²⁹and יהוה said to Moses, "I am יהוה; speak to Pharaoh king of Egypt all that I will tell you," ³⁰Moses appealed to יהוה, saying, "See, I °get tongue-tied;˚° how then should Pharaoh heed me!"

7 יהוה replied to Moses, "See, I place you in the role of God to Pharaoh, with your brother Aaron as your prophet.* ²You shall repeat all that I command you, and your brother Aaron shall speak to Pharaoh to let the Israelites depart from his land. ³But I will harden Pharaoh's heart, that I may multiply My signs and marvels in the land of Egypt. ⁴When Pharaoh does not heed you, I will lay My hand upon Egypt and deliver My ranks, My people the Israelites, from the land of Egypt with extraordinary chastisements. ⁵And the Egyptians shall know that I am יהוה, when I

stretch out My hand over Egypt and bring out the Israelites from their midst." ⁶This Moses and Aaron did; as יהוה commanded them, so they did. ⁷Moses was eighty years old and Aaron eighty-three, when they made their demand on Pharaoh.

⁸יהוה said to Moses and Aaron, ⁹"When Pharaoh speaks to you and says, 'Produce your marvel,' you shall say to Aaron, 'Take your rod and cast it down before Pharaoh.' It shall turn into a serpent." ¹⁰So Moses and Aaron came before Pharaoh and did just as יהוה had commanded: Aaron cast down his rod in the presence of Pharaoh and his courtiers, and it turned into a serpent. ¹¹Then Pharaoh, for his part, summoned the sages and the sorcerers; and the Egyptian magician-priests, in turn, did the same with their spells: ¹²each cast down his rod, and they turned into serpents. But Aaron's rod swallowed their rods. ¹³Yet Pharaoh's heart stiffened and he did not heed them, as יהוה had said.

¹⁴And יהוה said to Moses, "Pharaoh is stubborn; he refuses to let the people go. ¹⁵Go to Pharaoh in the morning, as he is coming out to the water, and station yourself before him at the edge of the Nile, taking with you the rod that turned into a snake. ¹⁶And say to him, 'יהוה, the God of the Hebrews, sent me to you to say, "Let My people go that they may worship Me in the wilderness." But you have paid no heed until now. ¹⁷Thus says יהוה, "By this you shall know that I am יהוה." See, I shall strike the water in the Nile with the rod that is in my hand, and it will be turned into blood; ¹⁸and the fish in the Nile will die. The Nile will stink so that the Egyptians will find it impossible to drink the water of the Nile.'"

¹⁹And יהוה said to Moses, "Say to Aaron: Take your rod and hold out your arm over the waters of Egypt—its rivers, its canals, its ponds, all its bodies of water—that they may turn to blood; there shall be blood throughout the land of Egypt, even in vessels of wood and stone." ²⁰Moses and Aaron did just as יהוה commanded: he lifted up the rod and struck the water in the Nile in the sight of Pharaoh and his courtiers, and all the water in the Nile was turned into blood ²¹and the fish in the Nile died. The Nile stank so that the Egyptians could not drink water from the Nile; and there was blood throughout the land of Egypt. ²²But when the Egyptian magician-priests did the same with their spells, Pharaoh's heart

stiffened and he did not heed them—as יהוה had spoken. ²³Pharaoh turned and went into his palace, paying no regard even to this. ²⁴And all the Egyptians had to dig round about the Nile for drinking water, because they could not drink the water of the Nile.

²⁵When seven days had passed after יהוה struck the Nile, ²⁶*יהוה said to Moses, "Go to Pharaoh and say to him, 'Thus says יהוה: Let My people go that they may worship Me. ²⁷If you refuse to let them go, then I will plague your whole country with frogs. ²⁸The Nile shall swarm with frogs, and they shall come up and enter your palace, your bedchamber and your bed, the houses of your courtiers and your people, and your ovens and your kneading bowls. ²⁹The frogs shall come up on you and on your people and on all your courtiers.'"

8 And יהוה said to Moses, "Say to Aaron: Hold out your arm with the rod over the rivers, the canals, and the ponds, and bring up the frogs on the land of Egypt." ²Aaron held out his arm over the waters of Egypt, and the frogs came up and covered the land of Egypt. ³But the magician-priests did the same with their spells, and brought frogs upon the land of Egypt.

⁴Then Pharaoh summoned Moses and Aaron and said, "Plead with יהוה to remove the frogs from me and my people, and I will let the people go to sacrifice to יהוה." ⁵And Moses said to Pharaoh, "You may have this triumph over me: for what time shall I plead in behalf of you and your courtiers and your people, that the frogs be cut off from you and your houses, to remain only in the Nile?" ⁶"For tomorrow," he replied. And [Moses] said, "As you say—that you may know that there is none like our God יהוה; ⁷the frogs shall retreat from you and your courtiers and your people; they shall remain only in the Nile." ⁸Then Moses and Aaron left Pharaoh's presence, and Moses cried out to יהוה in the matter of the frogs which had been inflicted upon Pharaoh. ⁹And יהוה did as Moses asked; the frogs died out in the houses, the courtyards, and the fields. ¹⁰And they piled them up in heaps, till the land stank. ¹¹But when Pharaoh saw that there was relief, he became stubborn and would not heed them, as יהוה had spoken.

¹²Then יהוה said to Moses, "Say to Aaron: Hold out your rod and strike the dust of the earth, and it shall turn to lice throughout the land of Egypt." ¹³And they did so. Aaron held out his arm

with the rod and struck the dust of the earth, and vermin came upon human and beast; all the dust of the earth turned to lice throughout the land of Egypt. ¹⁴The magician-priests did the like with their spells to produce lice, but they could not. The vermin remained upon human and beast; ¹⁵and the magician-priests said to Pharaoh, "This is the finger of God!" But Pharaoh's heart stiffened and he would not heed them, as יהוה had spoken.

¹⁶And יהוה said to Moses, "Early in the morning present yourself to Pharaoh, as he is coming out to the water, and say to him, 'Thus says יהוה: Let My people go that they may worship Me. ¹⁷For if you do not let My people go, I will let loose *swarms of insects* against you and your courtiers and your people and your houses; the houses of the Egyptians, and the very ground they stand on, shall be filled with swarms of insects. ¹⁸But on that day I will set apart the region of Goshen, where My people dwell, so that no swarms of insects shall be there, that you may know that I יהוה am in the midst of the land. ¹⁹And I will make a distinction* between My people and your people. Tomorrow this sign shall come to pass.'" ²⁰And יהוה did so. Heavy swarms of insects invaded Pharaoh's palace and the houses of his courtiers; throughout the country of Egypt the land was ruined because of the swarms of insects.

²¹Then Pharaoh summoned Moses and Aaron and said, "Go and sacrifice to your God within the land." ²²But Moses replied, "It would not be right to do this, for what we sacrifice to our God יהוה is untouchable to the Egyptians. If we sacrifice that which is untouchable to the Egyptians before their very eyes, will they not stone us! ²³So we must go a distance of three days into the wilderness and sacrifice to יהוה as our God may command us." ²⁴Pharaoh said, "I will let you go to sacrifice to your God יהוה in the wilderness; but do not go very far. Plead, then, for me." ²⁵And Moses said, "When I leave your presence, I will plead with יהוה that the swarms of insects depart tomorrow from Pharaoh and his courtiers and his people; but let not Pharaoh again act deceitfully, not letting the people go to sacrifice to יהוה."

²⁶So Moses left Pharaoh's presence and pleaded with יהוה. ²⁷And יהוה did as Moses asked—removing the swarms of insects from Pharaoh, from his courtiers, and from his people; not one re-

mained. ²⁸But Pharaoh became stubborn this time also, and would not let the people go.

9 יהוה said to Moses, "Go to Pharaoh and say to him, 'Thus says יהוה, the God of the Hebrews: Let My people go to worship Me. ²For if you refuse to let them go, and continue to hold them, ³then the hand of יהוה will strike your livestock in the fields—the horses, the asses, the camels, the cattle, and the sheep— with a very severe pestilence. ⁴But יהוה will make a distinction between the livestock of Israel and the livestock of the Egyptians, so that nothing shall die of all that belongs to the Israelites. ⁵יהוה has fixed the time: tomorrow יהוה will do this thing in the land.' " ⁶And יהוה did so the next day: all the livestock of the Egyptians died, but of the livestock of the Israelites not a beast died. ⁷When Pharaoh inquired, he found that not a head of the livestock of Israel had died; yet Pharaoh remained stubborn, and he would not let the people go.

⁸Then יהוה said to Moses and Aaron, "Each of you take handfuls of soot from the kiln, and let Moses throw it toward the sky in the sight of Pharaoh. ⁹It shall become a fine dust all over the land of Egypt, and cause an inflammation breaking out in boils on human and beast throughout the land of Egypt." ¹⁰So they took soot of the kiln and appeared before Pharaoh; Moses threw it toward the sky, and it caused an inflammation breaking out in boils on human and beast. ¹¹The magician-priests were unable to confront Moses because of the inflammation, for the inflammation afflicted the magician-priests as well as all the other Egyptians. ¹²But יהוה stiffened the heart of Pharaoh, and he would not heed them, just as יהוה had told Moses.

¹³יהוה said to Moses, "Early in the morning present yourself to Pharaoh and say to him, 'Thus says יהוה, the God of the Hebrews: Let My people go to worship Me. ¹⁴For this time I will send all My plagues upon your person, and your courtiers, and your people, in order that you may know that there is none like Me in all the world. ¹⁵I could have stretched forth My hand and stricken you and your people with pestilence, and you would have been effaced from the earth. ¹⁶Nevertheless I have spared you for this purpose: in order to show you My power, and in order that My fame may resound throughout the world. ¹⁷Yet you continue to

thwart* My people, and do not let them go! ¹⁸This time tomorrow I will rain down a very heavy hail, such as has not been in Egypt from the day it was founded until now. ¹⁹Therefore, order your livestock and everything you have in the open brought under shelter; every human and beast that is found outside, not having been brought indoors, shall perish when the hail comes down upon them!'" ²⁰Those among Pharaoh's courtiers who feared יהוה's word brought their slaves and livestock indoors to safety; ²¹but those who paid no regard to the word of יהוה left their slaves and livestock in the open.

²²יהוה said to Moses, "Hold out your arm toward the sky that hail may fall on all the land of Egypt, upon human and beast and all the grasses of the field in the land of Egypt." ²³So Moses held out his rod toward the sky, and יהוה sent thunder and hail, and fire streamed down to the ground, as יהוה rained down hail upon the land of Egypt. ²⁴The hail was very heavy—fire flashing in the midst of the hail—such as had not fallen on the land of Egypt since it had become a nation. ²⁵Throughout the land of Egypt the hail struck down all that were in the open, both human and beast; the hail also struck down all the grasses of the field and shattered all the trees of the field. ²⁶Only in the region of Goshen, where the Israelites were, there was no hail.

²⁷Thereupon Pharaoh sent for Moses and Aaron and said to them, "I stand guilty this time. יהוה is in the right, and I and my people are in the wrong. ²⁸Plead with יהוה that there may be an end of God's thunder and of hail. I will let you go; you need stay no longer." ²⁹Moses said to him, "As I go out of the city, I shall spread out my hands to יהוה; the thunder will cease and the hail will fall no more, so that you may know that the earth is יהוה's. ³⁰But I know that you and your courtiers do not yet fear God יהוה."—³¹Now the flax and barley were ruined, for the barley was in the ear and the flax was in bud; ³²but the wheat and the emmer* were not hurt, for they ripen late.—³³Leaving Pharaoh, Moses went outside the city and spread out his hands to יהוה: the thunder and the hail ceased, and no rain came pouring down upon the earth. ³⁴But when Pharaoh saw that the rain and the hail and the thunder had ceased, he became stubborn and reverted to his guilty ways, as did his courtiers. ³⁵So Pharaoh's

heart stiffened and he would not let the Israelites go, just as יהוה had foretold through Moses.

בּא | BO'

10 Then יהוה said to Moses, "Go to Pharaoh. For I have hardened his heart and the hearts of his courtiers, in order that I may display these My signs among them, ²and that you may recount in the hearing of your children and of your children's children how I made a mockery of the Egyptians and how I displayed My signs among them—in order that you may know that I am יהוה." ³So Moses and Aaron went to Pharaoh and said to him, "Thus says יהוה, the God of the Hebrews, 'How long will you refuse to humble yourself before Me? Let My people go that they may worship Me. ⁴For if you refuse to let My people go, tomorrow I will bring locusts on your territory. ⁵They shall cover the surface of the land, so that no one will be able to see the land. They shall devour the surviving remnant that was left to you after the hail; and they shall eat away all your trees that grow in the field. ⁶Moreover, they shall fill your palaces and the houses of all your courtiers and of all the Egyptians—something that neither your fathers nor fathers' fathers have seen from the day they appeared on earth to this day.'" With that he turned and left Pharaoh's presence.

⁷Pharaoh's courtiers said to him, "How long shall this one be a snare to us? Let their notables° go to worship their God יהוה! Are you not yet aware that Egypt is lost?" ⁸So Moses and Aaron were brought back to Pharaoh and he said to them, "Go, worship your God יהוה! Who are the ones to go?" ⁹Moses replied, "We will all go—°regardless of social station°—we will go with our sons and daughters, our flocks and herds; for we must observe יהוה's festival." ¹⁰But he said to them, "יהוה be with you—the same as I mean to let your dependents go with you! Clearly, you are bent on mischief. ¹¹No! You menfolk go and worship יהוה, since that is what you want." And they were expelled from Pharaoh's presence.

¹²Then יהוה said to Moses, "Hold out your arm over the land of Egypt for the locusts, that they may come upon the land of Egypt and eat up all the grasses in the land, whatever the hail has left." ¹³So Moses held out his rod over the land of Egypt, and יהוה

drove an east wind over the land all that day and all night; and when morning came, the east wind had brought the locusts. [14]Locusts invaded all the land of Egypt and settled within all the territory of Egypt in a thick mass; never before had there been so many, nor will there ever be so many again. [15]They hid all the land from view, and the land was darkened; and they ate up all the grasses of the field and all the fruit of the trees which the hail had left, so that nothing green was left, of tree or grass of the field, in all the land of Egypt.

[16]Pharaoh hurriedly summoned Moses and Aaron and said, "I stand guilty before your God יהוה and before you. [17]Forgive my offense just this once, and plead with your God יהוה that this death but be removed from me." [18]So he left Pharaoh's presence and pleaded with יהוה. [19]יהוה caused a shift to a very strong west wind, which lifted the locusts and hurled them into the *⁻Sea of Reeds;⁻* not a single locust remained in all the territory of Egypt. [20]But יהוה stiffened Pharaoh's heart, and he would not let the Israelites go.

[21]Then יהוה said to Moses, "Hold out your arm toward the sky that there may be darkness upon the land of Egypt, a darkness that can be touched." [22]Moses held out his arm toward the sky and thick darkness descended upon all the land of Egypt for three days. [23]People could not see one another, and for three days no one could move about; but all the Israelites enjoyed light in their dwellings.

[24]Pharaoh then summoned Moses and said, "Go, worship יהוה! Only your flocks and your herds shall be left behind; even your dependents may go with you." [25]But Moses said, "You yourself must provide us with sacrifices and burnt offerings to offer up to our God יהוה; [26]our own livestock, too, shall go along with us—not a hoof shall remain behind: for we must select from it for the worship of our God יהוה; and we shall not know with what we are to worship יהוה until we arrive there." [27]But יהוה stiffened Pharaoh's heart and he would not agree to let them go. [28]Pharaoh said to him, "Be gone from me! Take care not to see me again, for the moment you look upon my face you shall die." [29]And Moses replied, "You have spoken rightly. I shall not see your face again!"

11 And יהוה said to Moses, "I will bring but one more plague upon Pharaoh and upon Egypt; after that he shall let you go from here; indeed, when he lets you go, he will drive you out of here one and all. ²Tell the people to borrow, each man from his neighbor and each woman from hers, objects of silver and gold." ³יהוה disposed the Egyptians favorably toward the people. Moreover, °ʾtheir leaderʾ° Moses was much esteemed in the land of Egypt, among Pharaoh's courtiers and among the people.

⁴Moses said, "Thus says יהוה: Toward midnight I will go forth among the Egyptians, ⁵and every [male] first-born in the land of Egypt shall die, from the first-born of Pharaoh who sits on his throne to the first-born of the slave girl who is behind the millstones; and all the first-born of the cattle. ⁶And there shall be a loud cry in all the land of Egypt, such as has never been or will ever be again; ⁷but not a dog shall snarl* at any of the Israelites, at human or beast—in order that you may know that יהוה makes a distinction between Egypt and Israel.

⁸"Then all these courtiers of yours shall come down to me and bow low to me, saying, 'Depart, you and all the people who follow you!' After that I will depart." And he left Pharaoh's presence in hot anger.

⁹Now יהוה had said to Moses, "Pharaoh will not heed you, in order that My marvels may be multiplied in the land of Egypt." ¹⁰Moses and Aaron had performed all these marvels before Pharaoh, but יהוה had stiffened the heart of Pharaoh so that he would not let the Israelites go from his land.

12 יהוה said to Moses and Aaron in the land of Egypt: ²This month shall mark for you the beginning of the months; it shall be the first of the months of the year for you. ³Speak to the °ʾwhole community of Israelʾ° and say that on the tenth of this month each of them shall take a lamb* to a family, a lamb to a household. ⁴But if the household is too small for a lamb, let it share one with a neighbor who dwells nearby, in proportion to the number of persons: you shall contribute for the lamb according to what each household will eat. ⁵Your lamb shall be without blemish, a yearling male; you may take it from the sheep or from the goats. ⁶You shall keep watch over it until the fourteenth day of this month; and all the assembled congregation of the Israelites shall slaughter it at twilight. ⁷They shall take some of the blood and put it on the two doorposts and the lintel of the houses in which they are to eat it. ⁸They shall eat the flesh that same night; they shall eat it roasted over the fire, with unleavened bread and with bitter herbs. ⁹Do not eat any of it raw, or cooked in any way with water, but roasted—head, legs, and entrails—over the fire. ¹⁰You shall not leave any of it over until morning; if any of it is left until morning, you shall burn it.

¹¹This is how you shall eat it: your loins girded, your sandals on your feet, and your staff in your hand; and you shall eat it hurriedly: it is a *⁻passover offering⁻* to יהוה. ¹²For that night I will go through the land of Egypt and strike down every [male] first-born in the land of Egypt, both human and beast; and I will mete out punishments to all the gods of Egypt, I יהוה. ¹³And the blood on the houses where you are staying shall be a sign for you: when I see the blood I will pass over you, so that no plague will destroy you when I strike the land of Egypt.

¹⁴This day shall be to you one of remembrance: you shall celebrate it as a festival to יהוה throughout the ages; you shall celebrate it as an institution for all time. ¹⁵Seven days you shall eat unleavened bread; on the very first day you shall remove leaven from your houses, for whoever eats leavened bread from the first day to the seventh day, that person shall be cut off from Israel.

¹⁶You shall celebrate a sacred occasion on the first day, and a sacred occasion on the seventh day; no work at all shall be done on them; only what every person is to eat, that alone may be prepared for you. ¹⁷You shall observe the [Feast of] Unleavened Bread, for on this very day I brought your ranks out of the land of Egypt; you shall observe this day throughout the ages as an institution for all time. ¹⁸In the first month, from the fourteenth day of the month at evening, you shall eat unleavened bread until the twenty-first day of the month at evening. ¹⁹No leaven shall be found in your houses for seven days. For whoever eats what is leavened, that person—whether a stranger or a citizen of the country—shall be cut off from the community of Israel. ²⁰You shall eat nothing leavened; in all your settlements you shall eat unleavened bread.

21Moses then summoned all the elders of Israel and said to them, "Go, pick out lambs for your families, and slaughter the passover offering. 22Take a bunch of hyssop, dip it in the blood that is in the basin, and apply some of the blood that is in the basin to the lintel and to the two doorposts. None of you shall go outside the door of your house until morning. 23For יהוה, when going through to smite the Egyptians, will see the blood on the lintel and the two doorposts, and יהוה will *‑pass over‑* the door and not let the Destroyer enter and smite your home.

24"You shall observe this as an institution for all time, for you and for your descendants. 25And when you enter the land that יהוה will give you, as promised, you shall observe this rite. 26And when your children ask you, 'What do you mean by this rite?' 27you shall say, 'It is the passover sacrifice to יהוה, who passed over the houses of the Israelites in Egypt when smiting the Egyptians, but saved our houses.'"

The people then bowed low in homage. 28And the Israelites went and did so; just as יהוה had commanded Moses and Aaron, so they did.

29In the middle of the night יהוה struck down all the [male] first-born in the land of Egypt, from the first-born of Pharaoh who sat on the throne to the first-born of the captive who was in the dungeon, and all the first-born of the cattle. 30And Pharaoh arose in the night, with all his courtiers and all the Egyptians— because there was a loud cry in Egypt; for there was no house where there was not someone dead. 31He summoned Moses and Aaron in the night and said, "Up, depart from among my people, you and the Israelites with you! Go, worship יהוה as you said! 32Take also your flocks and your herds, as you said, and begone! And may you bring a blessing upon me also!"

33The Egyptians urged the people on, impatient to have them leave the country, for they said, "We shall all be dead." 34So the people took their dough before it was leavened, their kneading bowls wrapped in their cloaks upon their shoulders. 35The Israelites had done Moses' bidding and borrowed from the Egyptians objects of silver and gold, and clothing. 36And יהוה had disposed the Egyptians favorably toward the people, and they let them have their request; thus they stripped the Egyptians.

37The Israelites journeyed from Rameses to Succoth, about six hundred thousand men on foot, aside from dependents. 38Moreover, a mixed multitude went up with them, and very much livestock, both flocks and herds. 39And they baked unleavened cakes of the dough that they had taken out of Egypt, for it was not leavened, since they had been driven out of Egypt and could not delay; nor had they prepared any provisions for themselves.

40The length of time that the Israelites lived in Egypt was four hundred and thirty years; 41at the end of the four hundred and thirtieth year, to the very day, all the ranks of יהוה departed from the land of Egypt. 42That was for יהוה a night of vigil to bring them out of the land of Egypt; that same night is יהוה's, one of vigil for all the children of Israel throughout the ages.

43יהוה said to Moses and Aaron: This is the law of the passover offering: No foreigner shall eat of it. 44But any householder's° purchased male slave may eat of it once he has been circumcised. 45No bound or hired laborer shall eat of it. 46It shall be eaten in one house: you shall not take any of the flesh outside the house; nor shall you break a bone of it. 47The whole community of Israel shall offer it. 48If a male stranger who dwells with you would offer the passover to יהוה, all his males must be circumcised; then he shall be admitted to offer it; he shall then be as a citizen of the country. But no uncircumcised man may eat of it. 49There shall be one law for the citizen and for the stranger who dwells among you.

50And all the Israelites did so; as יהוה had commanded Moses and Aaron, so they did.

51That very day יהוה freed the Israelites from the land of Egypt, troop by troop.

13 יהוה spoke further to Moses, saying, 2"Consecrate to Me every male first-born; human and beast, the first [male] issue of every womb among the Israelites is Mine."

3And Moses said to the people,

"Remember this day, on which you went free from Egypt, the house of bondage, how יהוה freed you from it with a mighty hand: no leavened bread shall be eaten. 4You go free on this day, *–in the

Bo'

month·* of Abib. 5So, when יהוה has brought you into the land of the Canaanites, the Hittites, the Amorites, the Hivites, and the Jebusites, which was sworn to your fathers to be given you, a land flowing with milk and honey, you shall observe in this month the following practice:

6"Seven days you shall eat unleavened bread, and on the seventh day there shall be a festival of יהוה. 7Throughout the seven days unleavened bread shall be eaten; no leavened bread shall be found with you, and no leaven shall be found in all your territory. 8And you shall explain to your child on that day, 'It is because of what יהוה did for me when I went free from Egypt.'

9"And this shall serve you as a sign on your hand and as a reminder *·on your forehead·*—in order that the Teaching of יהוה may be in your mouth—that with a mighty hand יהוה freed you from Egypt. 10You shall keep this institution at its set time from year to year.

11"And when יהוה has brought you into the land of the Canaanites, as [God] swore to you and to your fathers, and has given it to you, 12you shall set apart for יהוה every first issue of the womb: every male firstling that your cattle drop shall be יהוה's. 13But every firstling ass you shall redeem with a sheep; if you do not redeem it, you must break its neck. And you must redeem every male first-born among your children. 14And when, in time to come, a child of yours asks you, saying, 'What does this mean?' you shall reply, 'It was with a mighty hand that יהוה brought us out from Egypt, the house of bondage. 15When Pharaoh stubbornly refused to let us go, יהוה slew every [male] first-born in the land of Egypt, the first-born of both human and beast. Therefore I sacrifice to יהוה every first male issue of the womb, but redeem every male first-born among my children.'

16"And so it shall be as a sign upon your hand and as a symbol* on your forehead that with a mighty hand יהוה freed us from Egypt."

בשלח | BE-SHALLAḤ

17Now when Pharaoh let the people go, God did not lead them by way of the land of the Philistines, although it was nearer; for God said, "The people may have a change of heart when they see war, and return to Egypt." ¹⁸So God led the people round about, by way of the wilderness at the Sea of Reeds.

Now the Israelites went up armed* out of the land of Egypt. ¹⁹And Moses took with him the bones of Joseph, who had exacted an oath from the children of Israel, saying, "God will be sure to take notice of you: then you shall carry up my bones from here with you."

²⁰They set out from Succoth, and encamped at Etham, at the edge of the wilderness. ²¹יהוה went before them in a pillar of cloud by day, to guide them along the way, and in a pillar of fire by night, to give them light, that they might travel day and night. ²²The pillar of cloud by day and the pillar of fire by night did not depart from before the people.

14 יהוה said to Moses: ²Tell the Israelites to turn back and encamp before Pi-hahiroth, between Migdol and the sea, before Baal-zephon; you shall encamp facing it, by the sea. ³Pharaoh will say of the Israelites, "They are astray in the land; the wilderness has closed in on them." ⁴Then I will stiffen Pharaoh's heart and he will pursue them, that I may gain glory through Pharaoh and all his host; and the Egyptians shall know that I am יהוה.

And they did so.

⁵When the king of Egypt was told that the people had fled, Pharaoh and his courtiers had a change of heart about the people and said, "What is this we have done, releasing Israel from our service?" ⁶He ordered* his chariot and took his force with him; ⁷he took six hundred of his picked chariots, and the rest of the chariots of Egypt, with officers* in all of them. ⁸יהוה stiffened the heart of Pharaoh king of Egypt, and he gave chase to the Israelites. As the Israelites were departing defiantly,* ⁹the Egyptians gave chase to them, and all the chariot horses of Pharaoh, his riders, and his warriors overtook them encamped by the sea, near Pi-hahiroth, before Baal-zephon.

¹⁰As Pharaoh drew near, the Israelites caught sight of the Egyptians advancing upon them. Greatly frightened, the Israelites cried out to יהוה. ¹¹And they said to Moses, "Was it for want of graves in Egypt that you brought us to die in the wilderness? What have you done to us, taking us out of Egypt? ¹²Is this not the very thing we told you in Egypt, saying, 'Let us be, and we will serve the Egyp-

tians, for it is better for us to serve the Egyptians than to die in the wilderness'?" 13But Moses said to the people, "Have no fear! Stand by, and witness the deliverance which יהוה will work for you today; for the Egyptians whom you see today you will never see again. 14יהוה will battle for you; you hold your peace!"

15Then יהוה said to Moses, "Why do you cry out to Me? Tell the Israelites to go forward. 16And you lift up your rod and hold out your arm over the sea and split it, so that the Israelites may march into the sea on dry ground. 17And I will stiffen the hearts of the Egyptians so that they go in after them; and I will gain glory through Pharaoh and all his warriors, his chariots, and his riders. 18Let the Egyptians know that I am יהוה, when I gain glory through Pharaoh, his chariots, and his riders."

19The messenger of God, who had been going ahead of the Israelite army, now moved and followed behind them; and the pillar of cloud shifted from in front of them and took up a place behind them, 20and it came between the army of the Egyptians and the army of Israel. Thus there was the cloud with the darkness, *⁻and it cast a spell upon* the night, so that the one could not come near the other all through the night.

21Then Moses held out his arm over the sea and יהוה drove back the sea with a strong east wind all that night, and turned the sea into dry ground. The waters were split, 22and the Israelites went into the sea on dry ground, the waters forming a wall for them on their right and on their left. 23The Egyptians came in pursuit after them into the sea, all of Pharaoh's horses, chariots, and riders. 24At the morning watch, יהוה looked down upon the Egyptian army from a pillar of fire and cloud, and threw the Egyptian army into panic. 25[God] locked* the wheels of their chariots so that they moved forward with difficulty. And the Egyptians said, "Let us flee from the Israelites, for יהוה is fighting for them against Egypt."

26Then יהוה said to Moses, "Hold out your arm over the sea, that the waters may come back upon the Egyptians and upon their chariots and upon their riders." 27Moses held out his arm over the sea, and at daybreak the sea returned to its normal state, and the Egyptians fled at its approach. But יהוה hurled the Egyptians into the sea. 28The waters turned back and covered the chariots and the riders—Pharaoh's entire army that followed them into the sea; not one of them remained. ²⁹But the Israelites had marched through the sea on dry ground, the waters forming a wall for them on their right and on their left.

³⁰Thus יהוה delivered Israel that day from the Egyptians. Israel saw the Egyptians dead on the shore of the sea. ³¹And when Israel saw the wondrous power which יהוה had wielded against the Egyptians, the people feared יהוה; they had faith in יהוה and in God's servant Moses.

15 Then Moses and the Israelites sang this song to יהוה. They said:
I will sing to יהוה, for He° has triumphed gloriously;
Horse and driver He has hurled into the sea.
²יהוה* is my strength and might;*
He is become my deliverance.
This is my God and I will enshrine* Him;
The God of my ancestors, and I will exalt Him.
³יהוה, the Warrior—
יהוה is His name!
⁴Pharaoh's chariots and his army
He has cast into the sea;
And the pick of his officers
Are drowned in the Sea of Reeds.
⁵The deeps covered them;
They went down into the depths like a stone.
⁶Your right hand, יהוה, glorious in power,
Your right hand, יהוה, shatters the foe!
⁷In Your great triumph You break Your opponents;
You send forth Your fury, it consumes them like straw.
⁸At the blast of Your nostrils the waters piled up,
The floods stood straight like a wall;
The deeps froze in the heart of the sea.
⁹The foe said,
"I will pursue, I will overtake,
I will divide the spoil;
My desire shall have its fill of them.
I will bare my sword—

My hand shall subdue them."
¹⁰You made Your wind blow, the sea covered them;
They sank like lead in the majestic waters.

¹¹Who is like You, יהוה, among the celestials;*
Who is like You, majestic in holiness,
Awesome in splendor, working wonders!
¹²You put out Your right hand,
The earth swallowed them.
¹³In Your love You lead the people You redeemed;
In Your strength You guide them to Your holy abode.
¹⁴The peoples hear, they tremble;
Agony grips the dwellers in Philistia.
¹⁵Now are the clans of Edom dismayed;
The tribes of Moab—trembling grips them;
All the dwellers in Canaan are aghast.
¹⁶Terror and dread descend upon them;
Through the might of Your arm they are still as stone—
Till Your people cross over, יהוה,
Till Your people cross whom You have ransomed.

¹⁷You will bring them and plant them in Your own
    mountain,
The place You made to dwell in, יהוה,
The sanctuary, יהוה, which Your hands established.
¹⁸יהוה will reign for ever and ever!

¹⁹For the horses of Pharaoh, with his chariots and riders, went into the sea; and יהוה turned back on them the waters of the sea; but the Israelites marched on dry ground in the midst of the sea.

²⁰Then Miriam the prophet, Aaron's sister, picked up a hand-drum,° and all the women went out after her in dance with hand-drums. ²¹And Miriam chanted for them:

Sing to יהוה, for He° has triumphed gloriously;
Horse and driver He has hurled into the sea.

²²Then Moses caused Israel to set out from the Sea of Reeds. They went on into the wilderness of Shur; they traveled three days

in the wilderness and found no water. ²³They came to Marah, but they could not drink the water of Marah because it was bitter; that is why it was named Marah.* ²⁴And the people grumbled against Moses, saying, "What shall we drink?" ²⁵So he cried out to יהוה, and יהוה showed him a piece of wood; he threw it into the water and the water became sweet.

There [God] made for them a fixed rule; there they were put to the test. ²⁶[God] said, "If you will heed your God יהוה diligently, doing what is upright in God's sight, giving ear to God's commandments and keeping all God's laws, then I will not bring upon you any of the diseases that I brought upon the Egyptians, for I יהוה am your healer."

²⁷And they came to Elim, where there were twelve springs of water and seventy palm trees; and they encamped there beside the water.

16 Setting out from Elim, the whole Israelite community came to the wilderness of Sin, which is between Elim and Sinai, on the fifteenth day of the second month after their departure from the land of Egypt. ²In the wilderness, the whole Israelite community grumbled against Moses and Aaron. ³The Israelites said to them, "If only we had died by the hand of יהוה in the land of Egypt, when we sat by the fleshpots, when we ate our fill of bread! For you have brought us out into this wilderness to starve this whole congregation to death."

⁴And יהוה said to Moses, "I will rain down bread for you from the sky, and the people shall go out and gather each day that day's portion—that I may thus test them, to see whether they will follow My instructions or not. ⁵But on the sixth day, when they apportion what they have brought in, it shall prove to be double the amount they gather each day." ⁶So Moses and Aaron said to all the Israelites, "By evening you shall know it was יהוה who brought you out from the land of Egypt; ⁷and in the morning you shall behold the Presence* of יהוה, because [God] has heard your grumblings against יהוה. For who are we that you should grumble against us? ⁸Since it is יהוה," Moses continued, "who will give you flesh to eat in the evening and bread in the morning to the full—because יהוה has heard the grumblings you utter—what is our part? Your grumbling is against יהוה, not against us!"

⁹Then Moses said to Aaron, "Say to the whole Israelite community: Advance toward יהוה, who has heard your grumbling." ¹⁰And as Aaron spoke to the whole Israelite community, they turned toward the wilderness, and there, in a cloud, appeared the Presence of יהוה.

¹¹יהוה spoke to Moses: ¹²"I have heard the grumbling of the Israelites. Speak to them and say: By evening you shall eat flesh, and in the morning you shall have your fill of bread; and you shall know that I יהוה am your God."

¹³In the evening quail appeared and covered the camp; in the morning there was a fall of dew about the camp. ¹⁴When the fall of dew lifted, there, over the surface of the wilderness, lay a fine and flaky substance, as fine as frost on the ground. ¹⁵When the Israelites saw it, they said to one another, *⁻"What is it?"⁻*—for they did not know what it was. And Moses said to them, "That is the bread which יהוה has given you to eat. ¹⁶This is what יהוה has commanded: Gather as much of it as each of you requires to eat, an *omer* to a person for as many of you as there are; you shall each fetch for those in your tent."

¹⁷The Israelites did so, some gathering much, some little. ¹⁸But when they measured it by the *omer*, anyone who had gathered much had no excess, and anyone who had gathered little had no deficiency: they had gathered as much as they needed to eat. ¹⁹And Moses said to them, "Let no one leave any of it over until morning." ²⁰But they paid no attention to Moses; °some of them⁻° left of it until morning, and it became infested with maggots and stank. And Moses was angry with them.

²¹So they gathered it every morning, as much as each one needed to eat; for when the sun grew hot, it would melt. ²²On the sixth day they gathered double the amount of food, two *omer*s for each; and when all the chieftains of the community came and told Moses, ²³he said to them, "This is what יהוה meant: Tomorrow is a day of rest, a holy sabbath of יהוה. Bake what you would bake and boil what you would boil; and all that is left put aside to be kept until morning." ²⁴So they put it aside until morning, as Moses had ordered; and it did not turn foul, and there were no maggots in it. ²⁵Then Moses said, "Eat it today, for today is a sabbath of יהוה; you will not find it today on the plain. ²⁶Six days

Be-shallaḥ

you shall gather it; on the seventh day, the sabbath, there will be none."

²⁷Yet some of the people went out on the seventh day to gather, but they found nothing. ²⁸And יהוה said to Moses, "How long will you all refuse to obey My commandments and My teachings? ²⁹Mark that it is יהוה who, having given you the sabbath, therefore gives you two days' food on the sixth day. Let everyone remain in place: let no one leave the vicinity on the seventh day." ³⁰So the people remained inactive on the seventh day.

³¹The house of Israel named it manna;* it was like coriander seed, white, and it tasted like wafers* in honey. ³²Moses said, "This is what יהוה has commanded: Let one *omer* of it be kept throughout the ages, in order that they may see the bread that I fed you in the wilderness when I brought you out from the land of Egypt." ³³And Moses said to Aaron, "Take a jar, put one *omer* of manna in it, and place it before יהוה, to be kept throughout the ages." ³⁴As יהוה had commanded Moses, Aaron placed it before the Pact,* to be kept. ³⁵And the Israelites ate manna forty years, until they came to a settled land; they ate the manna until they came to the border of the land of Canaan. ³⁶The *omer* is a tenth of an *ephah*.

17 From the wilderness of Sin the whole Israelite community continued by stages as יהוה would command. They encamped at Rephidim, and there was no water for the people to drink. ²The people quarreled with Moses. "Give us water to drink," they said; and Moses replied to them, "Why do you quarrel with me? Why do you try יהוה?" ³But the people thirsted there for water; and the people grumbled against Moses and said, "Why did you bring us up from Egypt, to kill us and our children and livestock with thirst?" ⁴Moses cried out to יהוה, saying, "What shall I do with this people? Before long they will be stoning me!" ⁵Then יהוה said to Moses, "Pass before the people; take with you some of the elders of Israel, and take along the rod with which you struck the Nile, and set out. ⁶I will be standing there before you on the rock at Horeb. Strike the rock and water will issue from it, and the people will drink." And Moses did so in the sight of the elders of Israel. ⁷The place was named Massah* and Meribah,*

because the Israelites quarreled and because they tried יהוה, say-ing, "Is יהוה present among us or not?"

8Amalek came and fought with Israel at Rephidim. 9Moses said to Joshua, "Pick °-some troops-° for us, and go out and do battle with Amalek. Tomorrow I will station myself on the top of the hill, with the rod of God in my hand." 10Joshua did as Moses told him and fought with Amalek, while Moses, Aaron, and Hur went up to the top of the hill. 11Then, whenever Moses held up his hand, Israel prevailed; but whenever he let down his hand, Amalek prevailed. 12But Moses' hands grew heavy; so they took a stone and put it under him and he sat on it, while Aaron and Hur, one on each side, supported his hands; thus his hands remained steady until the sun set. 13And Joshua overwhelmed *-the people of Amalek-* with the sword.

14Then יהוה said to Moses, "Inscribe this in a document as a reminder, and read it aloud to Joshua: I will utterly blot out the memory of Amalek from under heaven!" 15And Moses built an altar and named it Adonai-nissi.* 16He said, "It means, 'Hand upon the throne* of יהוה!' יהוה will be at war with Amalek throughout the ages."

יתרו | YITRO

18 Jethro priest of Midian, Moses' father-in-law, heard all that God had done for Moses and for Israel, God's peo-ple, how יהוה had brought Israel out from Egypt. 2So Jethro, Moses' father-in-law, took Zipporah, Moses' wife, after she had been sent home, 3and her two sons—of whom one was named Gershom, that is to say, "I have been a stranger* in a foreign land"; 4and the other was named Eliezer,* meaning, "My ances-tors' God was my help, delivering me from the sword of Pha-raoh." 5Jethro, Moses' father-in-law, brought Moses' sons and wife to him in the wilderness, where he was encamped at the mountain of God. 6He sent word to Moses, "I, your father-in-law Jethro, am coming to you, with your wife and her two sons." 7Moses went out to meet his father-in-law; he bowed low and kissed him; each asked after the other's welfare, and they went into the tent.

⁸Moses then recounted to his father-in-law everything that יהוה had done to Pharaoh and to the Egyptians for Israel's sake, all the hardships that had befallen them on the way, and how יהוה had delivered them. ⁹And Jethro rejoiced over all the kindness that יהוה had shown Israel when delivering them from the Egyptians. ¹⁰"Blessed be יהוה," Jethro said, "who delivered you from the Egyptians and from Pharaoh, and who delivered the people from under the hand of the Egyptians. ¹¹Now I know that יהוה is greater than all gods, *⁻yes, by the result of their very schemes against [the people]."⁻* ¹²And Jethro, Moses' father-in-law, brought a burnt offering and sacrifices for God; and Aaron came with all the elders of Israel to partake of the meal before God with Moses' father-in-law.

¹³Next day, Moses sat as magistrate among the people, while the people stood about Moses from morning until evening. ¹⁴But when Moses' father-in-law saw how much he had to do for the people, he said, "What is this thing that you are doing to the people? Why do you act* alone, while all the people stand about you from morning until evening?" ¹⁵Moses replied to his father-in-law, "It is because the people come to me to inquire of God. ¹⁶When they have a dispute, it comes before me, and I decide between one person and another, and I make known the laws and teachings of God."

¹⁷But Moses' father-in-law said to him, "The thing you are doing is not right; ¹⁸you will surely wear yourself out, and these people as well. For the task is too heavy for you; you cannot do it alone. ¹⁹Now listen to me. I will give you counsel, and God be with you! You represent the people before God: you bring the disputes before God, ²⁰and enjoin upon them the laws and the teachings, and make known to them the way they are to go and the practices they are to follow. ²¹You shall also seek out, from among all the people, capable individuals° who fear God—trustworthy ones° who spurn ill-gotten gain. Set these over them as chiefs of thousands, hundreds, fifties, and tens, and ²²let them judge the people at all times. Have them bring every major dispute to you, but let them decide every minor dispute themselves. Make it easier for yourself by letting them share the burden with you. ²³If you

do this—and God so commands you—you will be able to bear up; and all these people too will go home unwearied."

24Moses heeded his father-in-law and did just as he had said. 25Moses chose capable individuals out of all Israel, and appointed them heads over the people—chiefs of thousands, hundreds, fifties, and tens; 26and they judged the people at all times: the difficult matters they would bring to Moses, and all the minor matters they would decide themselves. 27Then Moses bade his father-in-law farewell, and he went his way to his own land.

19 On the third new moon after the Israelites had gone forth from the land of Egypt, on that very day, they entered the wilderness of Sinai. 2Having journeyed from Rephidim, they entered the wilderness of Sinai and encamped in the wilderness. Israel encamped there in front of the mountain, 3and Moses went up to God. יהוה called to him from the mountain, saying, "Thus shall you say to the house of Jacob and declare to the children of Israel: 4"You have seen what I did to the Egyptians, how I bore you on eagles' wings and brought you to Me. 5Now then, if you will obey Me faithfully and keep My covenant, you shall be My treasured possession among all the peoples. Indeed, all the earth is Mine, 6but you shall be to Me a kingdom of priests and a holy nation.' These are the words that you shall speak to the children of Israel."

7Moses came and summoned the elders of the people and put before them all that יהוה had commanded him. 8All the people answered as one, saying, "All that יהוה has spoken we will do!" And Moses brought back the people's words to יהוה. 9And יהוה said to Moses, "I will come to you in a thick cloud, in order that the people may hear when I speak with you and so trust you ever after." Then Moses reported the people's words to יהוה, 10and יהוה said to Moses, "Go to the people and warn them to stay pure* today and tomorrow. Let them wash their clothes. 11Let them be ready for the third day; for on the third day יהוה will come down, in the sight of all the people, on Mount Sinai. 12You shall set bounds for the people round about, saying, 'Beware of going up the mountain or touching the border of it. Whoever touches the mountain shall be put to death 13without being touched—

Yitro   117 by being either stoned or shot; beast or person, a trespasser shall not live.' When the ram's horn *⁻sounds a long blast,⁻* they may go up on the mountain."

¹⁴Moses came down from the mountain to the people and warned the people to stay pure, and they washed their clothes. ¹⁵And he said to the people, "Be ready for the third day: [the men among]° you should not go near a woman."

¹⁶On the third day, as morning dawned, there was thunder, and lightning, and a dense cloud upon the mountain, and a very loud blast of the horn; and all the people who were in the camp trembled. ¹⁷Moses led the people out of the camp toward God, and they took their places at the foot of the mountain.

¹⁸Now Mount Sinai was all in smoke, for יהוה had come down upon it in fire; the smoke rose like the smoke of a kiln, and *⁻the whole mountain⁻* trembled violently. ¹⁹The blare of the horn grew louder and louder. As Moses spoke, God answered him in thunder. ²⁰יהוה came down upon Mount Sinai, on the top of the mountain, and יהוה called Moses to the top of the mountain and Moses went up. ²¹יהוה said to Moses, "Go down, warn the people not to break through to יהוה to gaze, lest many of them perish. ²²The priests also, who come near יהוה, must stay pure, lest יהוה break out against them." ²³But Moses said to יהוה, "The people cannot come up to Mount Sinai, for You warned us saying, 'Set bounds about the mountain and sanctify it.'" ²⁴So יהוה said to him, "Go down, and come back together with Aaron; but let not the priests or the people break through to come up to יהוה, lest [God] break out against them." ²⁵And Moses went down to the people and spoke to them.

20 God spoke all these words,* saying: ²I יהוה am your God who brought you out of the land of Egypt, the house of bondage: ³You° shall have no other gods besides Me.

⁴You shall not make for yourself a sculptured image, or any likeness of what is in the heavens above, or on the earth below, or in the waters under the earth. ⁵You shall not bow down to them

or serve them. For I your God יהוה am an impassioned God, visiting the guilt of the parents upon the children, upon the third and upon the fourth generations of those who reject Me, ⁶but showing kindness to the thousandth generation of those who love Me and keep My commandments.

⁷You shall not *⁻swear falsely by⁻* the name of your God יהוה; for יהוה will not clear one who swears falsely by God's name.

⁸Remember the sabbath day and keep it holy. ⁹Six days you shall labor and do all your work, ¹⁰but the seventh day is a sabbath of your God יהוה: you shall not do any work—you, your son or daughter, your male or female slave, or your cattle, or the stranger who is within your settlements. ¹¹For in six days יהוה made heaven and earth and sea—and all that is in them—and then rested on the seventh day; therefore יהוה blessed the sabbath day and hallowed it.

¹²Honor your father and your mother, that you may long endure on the land that your God יהוה is assigning to you.

¹³You shall not murder. You shall not commit adultery. You shall not steal. You shall not bear false witness against your neighbor.

¹⁴You shall not covet your neighbor's house:° you shall not covet your neighbor's wife,° nor male or female slave, nor ox or ass, nor anything that is your neighbor's.

¹⁵All the people witnessed the thunder and lightning, the blare of the horn and the mountain smoking; and when the people saw it, they fell back and stood at a distance. ¹⁶"You speak to us," they said to Moses, "and we will obey; but let not God speak to us, lest we die." ¹⁷Moses answered the people, "Be not afraid; for God has come only in order to test you, and in order that the fear of God may be ever with you, so that you do not go astray." ¹⁸So the people remained at a distance, while Moses approached the thick cloud where God was.

¹⁹יהוה said to Moses:

Thus shall you say to the Israelites: You yourselves saw that I spoke to you from the very heavens: ²⁰With Me, therefore, you shall not make any gods of silver, nor shall you make for yourselves any gods of gold. ²¹Make for Me an altar of earth and sacrifice on it your burnt offerings and your *⁻sacrifices of well-being,⁻* your sheep and your oxen; in every place where I cause My name to be mentioned I will come to you and bless you. ²²And if you make for Me an altar of stones, do not build it of hewn stones; for by wielding your tool upon them you have profaned them. ²³Do not ascend My altar by steps, that your nakedness may not be exposed upon it.

מִשְׁפָּטִים | MISHPATIM

21 These are the rules that you shall set before them:

²When you acquire a Hebrew slave, that person shall serve six years—and shall go free in the seventh year, without payment. ³If [a male slave] came single, he shall leave single; if he had a wife, his wife shall leave with him. ⁴If his master gave him a wife, and she has borne him children, the wife and her children shall belong to the master, and he shall leave alone. ⁵But if the slave declares, "I love my master, and my wife and children: I do not wish to go free," ⁶his master shall take him *⁻before God.⁻* He shall be brought to the door or the doorpost, and his master shall pierce his ear with an awl; and he shall then remain his master's slave for life.

⁷When a parent° sells a daughter as a slave, she shall not go free as male slaves do. ⁸If she proves to be displeasing to her (male) master, who designated her for himself, he must let her be redeemed; he shall not have the right to sell her to outsiders, since he broke faith with her. ⁹And if the master designated her for a son, he shall deal with her as is the practice with free maidens. ¹⁰If he takes another [into the household as his wife], he must not withhold from this one her food, her clothing, or her *⁻conjugal rights.⁻* ¹¹If he fails her in these three ways, she shall go free, without payment.

¹²One who fatally strikes another person shall be put to death. ¹³If [a male killer]° did not do it by design, but it came about by an act of God, I will assign you a place to which he can flee.

¹⁴When a person schemes against another and kills through treachery, you shall take that person from My very altar to be put to death.

¹⁵One who strikes one's father or mother shall be put to death.

¹⁶One who kidnaps a person—whether having sold or still holding the victim—shall be put to death.

¹⁷One who insults* one's father or mother shall be put to death.

¹⁸When individuals quarrel and one strikes the other with stone or fist, and the victim does not die but has to take to bed: ¹⁹if that victim then gets up and walks outdoors upon a staff, the assailant shall go unpunished—except for paying for the idleness and the cure.

²⁰When a person [who is a slave owner] strikes a slave, male or female, with a rod, who dies *ᐧthere and then,ᐧ* it must be avenged. ²¹But if the victim survives a day or two, it is not to be avenged, since the one is the other's property.

²²When individuals fight, and one of them pushes a pregnant woman and a miscarriage results, but no other damage ensues, *ᐧthe one responsibleᐧ* shall be fined according as the woman's husband may exact, the payment to be based *ᐧon reckoning.ᐧ* ²³But if other damage ensues, the penalty shall be life for life, ²⁴eye for eye, tooth for tooth, hand for hand, foot for foot, ²⁵burn for burn, wound for wound, bruise for bruise.

²⁶When a person [who is a slave owner] strikes the eye of a slave, male or female, and destroys it, that person shall let the slave go free on account of the eye. ²⁷If the owner knocks out the tooth of a slave, male or female, that person shall let the slave go free on account of the tooth.

²⁸When an ox gores a man or a woman to death, the ox shall be stoned and its flesh shall not be eaten, but the owner of the ox is not to be punished. ²⁹If, however, that ox has been in the habit of goring, and its owner, though warned, has failed to guard it, and it kills a man or a woman—the ox shall be stoned and its owner, too, shall be put to death. ³⁰If ransom is imposed, the owner must pay whatever is imposed to redeem the owner's own life. ³¹So, too, if it gores a minor, male or female, [its owner] shall be dealt with according to the same rule. ³²But if the ox gores a slave, male or female, [its owner] shall pay thirty shekels of silver to the master, and the ox shall be stoned.

³³When a person opens a pit, or digs a pit and does not cover it, and an ox or an ass falls into it, ³⁴the one responsible for the

pit must make restitution—paying the price to the owner, but keeping the dead animal.

35When a person's ox injures a neighbor's ox and it dies, they shall sell the live ox and divide its price; they shall also divide the dead animal. 36If, however, it is known that the ox was in the habit of goring, and its owner has failed to guard it, that person must restore ox for ox, but shall keep the dead animal.

37*When a person steals an ox or a sheep, and slaughters it or sells it, that person shall pay five oxen for the ox, and four sheep for the sheep.— **22** 1If the thief is seized while tunneling* and beaten to death, there is no bloodguilt in that case. 2If the sun had already risen, there is bloodguilt in that case.—The thief must make restitution, and if lacking the means, shall be sold for the theft. 3But if what was stolen—whether ox or ass or sheep—is found alive and in hand, that person shall pay double.

4When a person who owns livestock lets it loose to graze in another's land, and so allows a field or a vineyard to be grazed bare, restitution must be made for the impairment* of that field or vineyard.

5When a fire is started and spreads to thorns, so that stacked, standing, or growing* grain is consumed, the one who started the fire must make restitution.

6When a person gives money or goods to another for safekeeping, and they are stolen from that other person's house: if caught, the thief shall pay double; 7if the thief is not caught, the owner of the house shall depose *-before God-* and deny laying hands on the other's property. (8In all charges of misappropriation—pertaining to an ox, an ass, a sheep, a garment, or any other loss, whereof one party alleges, "This is it"—the case of both parties shall come before God: the one whom God declares guilty shall pay double to the other.)

9When a person gives to another an ass, an ox, a sheep or any other animal to guard, and it dies or is injured or is carried off, with no witness about, 10an oath before יהוה shall decide between the two of them that the one has not laid hands on the property of the other; the owner must acquiesce, and no restitution shall be made. 11But if [the animal] was stolen from the guardian, restitution shall be made to its owner. ¹²If it was torn by beasts, the guardian shall bring it as evidence—not needing to replace what has been torn by beasts.

¹³When a person borrows [an animal] from another and it dies or is injured, its owner not being with it, that person must make restitution. ¹⁴If its owner was with it, no restitution need be made; but if it was hired, that payment is due.

¹⁵If a man seduces a virgin for whom the bride-price has not been paid,* and lies with her, he must make her his wife by payment of a bride-price. ¹⁶If her father refuses to give her to him, he must still weigh out silver in accordance with the bride-price for virgins.

¹⁷You shall not tolerate* a sorceress.

¹⁸Whoever lies with a beast shall be put to death.

¹⁹Whoever sacrifices to a god other than יהוה alone shall be proscribed.*

²⁰You shall not wrong or oppress a stranger, for you were strangers in the land of Egypt.

²¹You [communal leaders]° shall not ill-treat any widow or orphan. ²²If you do mistreat them, I will heed their outcry as soon as they cry out to Me, ²³and My anger shall blaze forth and I will put you to the sword, and your own wives shall become widows and your children orphans.

²⁴If you lend money to My people, to the poor among you, do not act toward them as a creditor; exact no interest from them. ²⁵If you take your neighbor's garment in pledge, you must return it before the sun sets; ²⁶it is the only available clothing—it is what covers the skin. In what else shall [your neighbor] sleep? Therefore, if that person cries out to Me, I will pay heed, for I am compassionate.

²⁷You shall not revile God, nor put a curse upon a chieftain among your people.

²⁸You shall not *⁻put off the skimming of the first yield of your vats.⁻* You shall give Me the male first-born among your children. ²⁹You shall do the same with your cattle and your flocks: seven days it* shall remain with its mother; on the eighth day you shall give it to Me.

³⁰You shall be holy people to Me: you must not eat flesh torn by beasts in the field; you shall cast it to the dogs.

Mishpatim   123

23 You must not carry false rumors; you shall not join hands with the guilty to act as a malicious witness: [2]You shall neither side with the mighty* to do wrong—you shall not give perverse testimony in a dispute so as to pervert it in favor of the mighty—[3]nor shall you show deference to a poor person in a dispute.

[4]When you encounter your enemy's ox or ass wandering, you must take it back.

[5]When you see the ass of your enemy lying under its burden and would refrain from raising* it, you must nevertheless help raise it.

[6]You shall not subvert the rights of your needy in their disputes. [7]Keep far from a false charge; do not bring death on those who are innocent and in the right, for I will not acquit the wrongdoer. [8]Do not take bribes, for bribes blind the clear-sighted and upset the pleas of those who are in the right.

[9]You shall not oppress a stranger, for you know the feelings of the stranger, having yourselves been strangers in the land of Egypt.

[10]Six years you shall sow your land and gather in its yield; [11]but in the seventh you shall let it rest and lie fallow. Let the needy among your people eat of it, and what they leave let the wild beasts eat. You shall do the same with your vineyards and your olive groves.

[12]Six days you shall do your work, but on the seventh day you shall cease from labor, in order that your ox and your ass may rest, and that your home-born slave and the stranger may be refreshed.

[13]Be on guard concerning all that I have told you. Make no mention of the names of other gods; they shall not be heard on your lips.

[14]Three times a year you shall hold a festival for Me: [15]You shall observe the Feast of Unleavened Bread—eating unleavened bread for seven days as I have commanded you—at the set time *̄in the month¯* of Abib, for in it you went forth from Egypt; and none shall appear before Me empty-handed; [16]and the Feast of the Harvest, of the first fruits of your work, of what you sow in the field; and the Feast of Ingathering at the end of the year, when you gather in the results of your work from the field. [17]Three times a year all your males shall appear before the Sovereign, יהוה.

¹⁸You shall not offer the blood of My sacrifice with anything leavened; and the fat of My festal offering shall not be left lying until morning.

¹⁹The choice first fruits of your soil you shall bring to the house of your God יהוה.

You shall not boil a kid in its mother's milk.

²⁰I am sending a messenger before you to guard you on the way and to bring you to the place that I have made ready. ²¹Pay heed to him and obey him. Do not defy him, for he will not pardon your offenses, since My Name is in him; ²²but if you obey him and do all that I say, I will be an enemy to your enemies and a foe to your foes.

²³When My messenger goes before you and brings you to the Amorites, the Hittites, the Perizzites, the Canaanites, the Hivites, and the Jebusites, and I annihilate them, ²⁴you shall not bow down to their gods in worship or follow their practices, but shall tear them down and smash their pillars to bits. ²⁵You shall serve your God יהוה, who will bless your bread and your water. And I will remove sickness from your midst. ²⁶No woman in your land shall miscarry or be barren. I will let you enjoy the full count of your days.

²⁷I will send forth My terror before you, and I will throw into panic all the people among whom you come, and I will make all your enemies turn tail* before you. ²⁸I will send a plague* ahead of you, and it shall drive out before you the Hivites, the Canaanites, and the Hittites. ²⁹I will not drive them out before you in a single year, lest the land become desolate and the wild beasts multiply to your hurt. ³⁰I will drive them out before you little by little, until you have increased and possess the land. ³¹I will set your borders from the Sea of Reeds to the Sea of Philistia, and from the wilderness to the Euphrates; for I will deliver the inhabitants of the land into your hands, and you will drive them out before you. ³²You shall make no covenant with them and their gods. ³³They shall not remain in your land, lest they cause you to sin against Me; for you will serve their gods—and it will prove a snare to you.

24 Then [God] said to Moses, "Come up to יהוה, with Aaron, Nadab and Abihu, and seventy elders of Israel, and bow low from afar. ²Moses alone shall come near יהוה; but the others shall not come near, nor shall the people come up with him.”

³Moses went and repeated to the people all the commands of יהוה and all the rules; and all the people answered with one voice, saying, “All the things that יהוה has commanded we will do!” ⁴Moses then wrote down all the commands of יהוה.

Early in the morning, he set up an altar at the foot of the mountain, with twelve pillars for the twelve tribes of Israel. ⁵He designated °ˉsome assistantsˉ° among the Israelites, and they offered burnt offerings and sacrificed bulls as offerings of well-being to יהוה. ⁶Moses took one part of the blood and put it in basins, and the other part of the blood he dashed against the altar. ⁷Then he took the record of the covenant and read it aloud to the people. And they said, “All that יהוה has spoken *ˉwe will faithfully do!”ˉ * ⁸Moses took the blood and dashed it on the people and said, “This is the blood of the covenant that יהוה now makes with you concerning all these commands.”

⁹Then Moses and Aaron, Nadab and Abihu, and seventy elders of Israel ascended; ¹⁰and they saw the God of Israel—under whose feet was the likeness of a pavement of sapphire, like the very sky for purity. ¹¹Yet [God] did not raise a hand against the leaders* of the Israelites; they beheld God, and they ate and drank.

¹²יהוה said to Moses, “Come up to Me on the mountain and wait there, and I will give you the stone tablets with the teachings and commandments which I have inscribed to instruct them.” ¹³So Moses and his attendant Joshua arose, and Moses ascended the mountain of God. ¹⁴To the elders he had said, “Wait here for us until we return to you. You have Aaron and Hur with you; let anyone who has a legal matter approach them.”

¹⁵When Moses had ascended the mountain, the cloud covered the mountain. ¹⁶The Presence of יהוה abode on Mount Sinai, and the cloud hid it for six days. On the seventh day [God] called to Moses from the midst of the cloud. ¹⁷Now the Presence of יהוה appeared in the sight of the Israelites as a consuming fire on the top of the mountain. ¹⁸Moses went inside the cloud and ascended the mountain; and Moses remained on the mountain forty days and forty nights.

תרומה | TERUMAH

25 יהוה spoke to Moses, saying: [2]Tell the Israelite people to bring Me gifts; you shall accept gifts for Me from every person whose heart is so moved. [3]And these are the gifts that you shall accept from them: gold, silver, and copper; [4]blue, purple, and crimson yarns, fine linen, goats' hair; [5]*tanned ram skins,* dolphin* skins, and acacia wood; [6]oil for lighting, spices for the anointing oil and for the aromatic incense; [7]*lapis lazuli* and other stones for setting, for the ephod and for the breastpiece. [8]And let them make Me a sanctuary that I may dwell among them. [9]Exactly as I show you—the pattern of the Tabernacle and the pattern of all its furnishings—so shall you make it.

[10]They shall make an ark of acacia wood, two and a half cubits long, a cubit and a half wide, and a cubit and a half high. [11]Overlay it with pure gold—overlay it inside and out—and make upon it a gold molding round about. [12]Cast four gold rings for it, to be attached to its four feet, two rings on one of its side walls and two on the other. [13]Make poles of acacia wood and overlay them with gold; [14]then insert the poles into the rings on the side walls of the ark, for carrying the ark. [15]The poles shall remain in the rings of the ark: they shall not be removed from it. [16]And deposit in the Ark [the tablets of] the Pact which I will give you.

[17]You shall make a cover of pure gold, two and a half cubits long and a cubit and a half wide. [18]Make two cherubim of gold—make them of hammered work—at the two ends of the cover. [19]Make one cherub at one end and the other cherub at the other end; of one piece with the cover shall you make the cherubim at its two ends. [20]The cherubim shall have their wings spread out above, shielding the cover with their wings. They shall confront each other, the faces of the cherubim being turned toward the cover. [21]Place the cover on top of the Ark, after depositing inside the Ark the Pact that I will give you. [22]There I will meet with you, and I will impart to you—from above the cover, from between the two cherubim that are on top of the Ark of the Pact—all that I will command you concerning the Israelite people.

[23]You shall make a table of acacia wood, two cubits long, one cubit wide, and a cubit and a half high. [24]Overlay it with pure

gold, and make a gold molding around it. ²⁵Make a rim of a hand's breadth around it, and make a gold molding for its rim round about. ²⁶Make four gold rings for it, and attach the rings to the four corners at its four legs. ²⁷The rings shall be next to the rim, as holders for poles to carry the table. ²⁸Make the poles of acacia wood, and overlay them with gold; by these the table shall be carried. ²⁹Make its bowls, ladles, jars and jugs with which to offer libations; make them of pure gold. ³⁰And on the table you shall set the bread of display, to be before Me always.

³¹You shall make a lampstand of pure gold; the lampstand shall be made of hammered work; its base and its shaft, its cups, calyxes, and petals shall be of one piece. ³²Six branches shall issue from its sides; three branches from one side of the lampstand and three branches from the other side of the lampstand. ³³On one branch there shall be three cups shaped like almond-blossoms, each with calyx and petals, and on the next branch there shall be three cups shaped like almond-blossoms, each with calyx and petals; so for all six branches issuing from the lampstand. ³⁴And on the lampstand itself there shall be four cups shaped like almond-blossoms, each with calyx and petals: ³⁵a calyx, of one piece with it, under a pair of branches; and a calyx, of one piece with it, under the second pair of branches, and a calyx, of one piece with it, under the last pair of branches; so for all six branches issuing from the lampstand. ³⁶Their calyxes and their stems shall be of one piece with it, the whole of it a single hammered piece of pure gold. ³⁷Make its seven lamps—the lamps shall be so mounted as to give the light on its front side—³⁸and its tongs and fire pans of pure gold. ³⁹It shall be made, with all these furnishings, out of a talent of pure gold. ⁴⁰Note well, and follow the patterns for them that are being shown you on the mountain.

26 As for the tabernacle,* make it of ten strips of cloth; make these of fine twisted linen, of blue, purple, and crimson yarns, with a design of cherubim worked into them. ²The length of each cloth shall be twenty-eight cubits, and the width of each cloth shall be four cubits, all the cloths to have the same measurements. ³Five of the cloths shall be joined to one another, and the other five cloths shall be joined to one another. ⁴Make loops of blue wool on the edge of the outermost cloth of the one set; and do likewise on the edge of the outermost cloth of the other set: [5]make fifty loops on the one cloth, and fifty loops on the edge of the end cloth of the other set, the loops to be opposite one another. [6]And make fifty gold clasps, and couple the cloths to one another with the clasps, so that the Tabernacle becomes one whole.

[7]You shall then make cloths of goats' hair for a tent over the Tabernacle; make the cloths eleven in number. [8]The length of each cloth shall be thirty cubits, and the width of each cloth shall be four cubits, the eleven cloths to have the same measurements. [9]Join five of the cloths by themselves, and the other six cloths by themselves; and fold over the sixth cloth at the front of the tent. [10]Make fifty loops on the edge of the outermost cloth of the one set, and fifty loops on the edge of the cloth of the other set. [11]Make fifty copper clasps, and fit the clasps into the loops, and couple the tent together so that it becomes one whole. [12]As for the overlapping excess of the cloths of the tent, the extra half-cloth shall overlap the back of the Tabernacle, [13]while the extra cubit at either end of each length of tent cloth shall hang down to the bottom of the two sides of the Tabernacle and cover it. [14]And make for the tent a covering of tanned ram skins, and a covering of dolphin skins above.

[15]You shall make the planks for the Tabernacle of acacia wood, upright. [16]The length of each plank shall be ten cubits and the width of each plank a cubit and a half. [17]Each plank shall have two tenons, parallel* to each other; do the same with all the planks of the Tabernacle. [18]Of the planks of the Tabernacle, make twenty planks on the south* side: [19]making forty silver sockets under the twenty planks, two sockets under the one plank for its two tenons and two sockets under each following plank for its two tenons; [20]and for the other side wall of the Tabernacle, on the north side, twenty planks, [21]with their forty silver sockets, two sockets under the one plank and two sockets under each following plank. [22]And for the rear of the Tabernacle, to the west, make six planks; [23]and make two planks for the corners of the Tabernacle at the rear. [24]*They shall match at the bottom, and terminate alike at the top inside one ring;* thus shall it be with both of them: they shall form the two corners. [25]Thus there shall be

eight planks with their sockets of silver: sixteen sockets, two sockets under the first plank, and two sockets under each of the other planks.

²⁶You shall make bars of acacia wood: five for the planks of the one side wall of the Tabernacle, ²⁷five bars for the planks of the other side wall of the Tabernacle, and five bars for the planks of the wall of the Tabernacle at the rear to the west. ²⁸The center bar halfway up the planks shall run from end to end. ²⁹Overlay the planks with gold, and make their rings of gold, as holders for the bars; and overlay the bars with gold. ³⁰Then set up the Tabernacle according to the manner of it that you were shown on the mountain.

³¹You shall make a curtain of blue, purple, and crimson yarns, and fine twisted linen; it shall have a design of cherubim worked into it. ³²Hang it upon four posts of acacia wood overlaid with gold and having hooks of gold, [set] in four sockets of silver. ³³Hang the curtain under the clasps, and carry the Ark of the Pact there, behind the curtain, so that the curtain shall serve you as a partition between the Holy and the Holy of Holies. ³⁴Place the cover upon the Ark of the Pact in the Holy of Holies. ³⁵Place the table outside the curtain, and the lampstand by the south wall of the Tabernacle opposite the table, which is to be placed by the north wall.

³⁶You shall make a screen for the entrance of the Tent, of blue, purple, and crimson yarns, and fine twisted linen, done in embroidery. ³⁷Make five posts of acacia wood for the screen and overlay them with gold—their hooks being of gold—and cast for them five sockets of copper.

27 You shall make the altar of acacia wood, five cubits long and five cubits wide—the altar is to be square—and three cubits high. ²Make its horns on the four corners, the horns to be of one piece with it; and overlay it with copper. ³Make the pails for removing its ashes, as well as its scrapers, basins, flesh hooks, and fire pans—make all its utensils of copper. ⁴Make for it a grating of meshwork in copper; and on the mesh make four copper rings at its four corners. ⁵Set the mesh below, under the ledge of the altar, so that it extends to the middle of the altar. ⁶And make poles for the altar, poles of acacia wood, and overlay them with copper. ⁷The poles shall be inserted into the rings, so that the poles remain on the two sides of the altar when it is carried. ⁸Make it hollow, of boards. As you were shown on the mountain, so shall they be made.

⁹You shall make the enclosure of the Tabernacle:
On the *⁻south side,* a hundred cubits of hangings of fine twisted linen for the length of the enclosure on that side—¹⁰with its twenty posts and their twenty sockets of copper, the hooks and bands of the posts to be of silver.

¹¹Again a hundred cubits of hangings for its length along the north side—with its twenty posts and their twenty sockets of copper, the hooks and bands of the posts to be of silver.

¹²For the width of the enclosure, on the west side, fifty cubits of hangings, with their ten posts and their ten sockets.

¹³For the width of the enclosure on the front, or east side, fifty cubits: ¹⁴fifteen cubits of hangings on the one flank, with their three posts and their three sockets; ¹⁵fifteen cubits of hangings on the other flank, with their three posts and their three sockets; ¹⁶and for the gate of the enclosure, a screen of twenty cubits, of blue, purple, and crimson yarns, and fine twisted linen, done in embroidery, with their four posts and their four sockets.

¹⁷All the posts round the enclosure shall be banded with silver and their hooks shall be of silver; their sockets shall be of copper.

¹⁸The length of the enclosure shall be a hundred cubits, and the width fifty throughout; and the height five cubits—[with hangings] of fine twisted linen. The sockets shall be of copper: ¹⁹all the utensils of the Tabernacle,* for all its service, as well as all its pegs and all the pegs of the court, shall be of copper.

תצוה | TETSAVVEH

²⁰You shall further instruct the Israelites to bring you clear oil of beaten olives for lighting, for kindling lamps regularly. ²¹Aaron and his sons shall set them up in the Tent of Meeting, outside the curtain which is over [the Ark of] the Pact, [to burn] from evening to morning before יהוה. It shall be a due from the Israelites for all time, throughout the ages.

28 You shall bring forward your brother Aaron, with his sons, from among the Israelites, to serve Me as priests: Aaron, Nadab and Abihu, Eleazar and Ithamar, the sons of Aaron. ²Make sacral vestments for your brother Aaron, for dignity and adornment. ³Next you shall instruct all who are *⁻skillful, whom I have endowed with the gift of skill,* to make Aaron's vestments, for consecrating him to serve Me as priest. ⁴These are the vestments they are to make: a breastpiece, an ephod, a robe, a fringed* tunic, a headdress, and a sash. They shall make those sacral vestments for your brother Aaron and his sons, for priestly service to Me; ⁵they, therefore, shall receive the gold, the blue, purple, and crimson yarns, and the fine linen.

⁶They shall make the ephod of gold, of blue, purple, and crimson yarns, and of fine twisted linen, worked into designs. ⁷It shall have two shoulder-pieces attached; they shall be attached at its two ends. ⁸And the decorated band that is upon it shall be made like it, of one piece with it: of gold, of blue, purple, and crimson yarns, and of fine twisted linen. ⁹Then take two lazuli stones and engrave on them the names of the sons of Israel: ¹⁰six of their names on the one stone, and the names of the remaining six on the other stone, in the order of their birth. ¹¹On the two stones you shall make seal engravings—the work of a lapidary—of the names of the sons of Israel. Having bordered them with frames of gold, ¹²attach the two stones to the shoulder-pieces of the ephod, as stones for remembrance of the Israelite people, whose names Aaron shall carry upon his two shoulder-pieces for remembrance before יהוה.

¹³Then make frames of gold ¹⁴and two chains of pure gold; braid these like corded work, and fasten the corded chains to the frames.

¹⁵You shall make a breastpiece of decision,* worked into a design; make it in the style of the ephod: make it of gold, of blue, purple, and crimson yarns, and of fine twisted linen. ¹⁶It shall be square and doubled, a span in length and a span in width. ¹⁷Set in it mounted stones, in four rows of stones. The first row shall be a row of *⁻carnelian, chrysolite, and emerald; ¹⁸the second row: a turquoise, a sapphire, and an amethyst; ¹⁹the third row: a jacinth, an agate, and a crystal; ²⁰and the fourth row: a beryl, a lapis

lazuli, and a jasper.̠* They shall be framed with gold in their mountings. 21The stones shall correspond [in number] to the names of the sons of Israel: twelve, corresponding to their names. They shall be engraved like seals, each with its name, for the twelve tribes.

22On the breastpiece make braided chains of corded work in pure gold. 23Make two rings of gold on the breastpiece, and fasten the two rings at the two ends of the breastpiece, 24attaching the two golden cords to the two rings at the ends of the breastpiece. 25Then fasten the two ends of the cords to the two frames, which you shall attach to the shoulder-pieces of the ephod, at the front. 26Make two rings of gold and attach them to the two ends of the breastpiece, at its inner edge, which faces the ephod. 27And make two other rings of gold and fasten them on the front of the ephod, low on the two shoulder-pieces, close to its seam above the decorated band. 28The breastpiece shall be held in place by a cord of blue from its rings to the rings of the ephod, so that the breastpiece rests on the decorated band and does not come loose from the ephod. 29Aaron shall carry the names of the sons of Israel on the breastpiece of decision over his heart, when he enters the sanctuary, for remembrance before יהוה at all times. 30Inside the breastpiece of decision you shall place the *̠Urim and Thummim,̠* so that they are over Aaron's heart when he comes before יהוה. Thus Aaron shall carry the instrument of decision for the Israelites over his heart before יהוה at all times.

31You shall make the robe of the ephod *̠of pure blue.̠* 32The opening for the head shall be in the middle of it; the opening shall have a binding of woven work round about—it shall be like the opening of a coat of mail—so that it does not tear. 33On its hem make pomegranates of blue, purple, and crimson yarns, all around the hem, with bells of gold between them all around: 34a golden bell and a pomegranate, a golden bell and a pomegranate, all around the hem of the robe. 35Aaron shall wear it while officiating, so that the sound of it is heard when he comes into the sanctuary before יהוה and when he goes out—that he may not die.

36You shall make a frontlet of pure gold and engrave on it the seal inscription: "Holy to יהוה." 37Suspend it on a cord of blue, so that it may remain on the headdress; it shall remain on the front of the headdress. ³⁸It shall be on Aaron's forehead, that Aaron may take away any sin arising from the holy things that the Israelites consecrate, from any of their sacred donations; it shall be on his forehead at all times, to win acceptance for them before יהוה.

³⁹You shall make the fringed tunic of fine linen.

You shall make the headdress of fine linen.

You shall make the sash of embroidered work.

⁴⁰And for Aaron's sons also you shall make tunics, and make sashes for them, and make turbans for them, for dignity and adornment. ⁴¹Put these on your brother Aaron and on his sons as well; anoint them, *⁻and ordain them⁻* and consecrate them to serve Me as priests.

⁴²You shall also make for them linen breeches to cover their nakedness; they shall extend from the hips to the thighs. ⁴³They shall be worn by Aaron and his sons when they enter the Tent of Meeting or when they approach the altar to officiate in the sanctuary, so that they do not incur punishment and die. It shall be a law for all time for him and for his offspring to come.

29 This is what you shall do to them in consecrating them to serve Me as priests: Take a young bull of the herd and two rams without blemish; ²also unleavened bread, unleavened cakes with oil mixed in, and unleavened wafers spread with oil—make these of choice wheat flour. ³Place these in one basket and present them in the basket, along with the bull and the two rams. ⁴Lead Aaron and his sons up to the entrance of the Tent of Meeting, and wash them with water. ⁵Then take the vestments, and clothe Aaron with the tunic, the robe of the ephod, the ephod, and the breastpiece, and gird him with the decorated band of the ephod. ⁶Put the headdress on his head, and place the holy diadem upon the headdress. ⁷Take the anointing oil and pour it on his head and anoint him. ⁸Then bring his sons forward; clothe them with tunics ⁹and wind turbans upon them. And gird both Aaron and his sons with sashes. And so they shall have priesthood as their right for all time.

You shall then ordain Aaron and his sons. ¹⁰Lead the bull up to the front of the Tent of Meeting, and let Aaron and his sons lay their hands upon the head of the bull. ¹¹Slaughter the bull before

יהוה, at the entrance of the Tent of Meeting, ¹²and take some of the bull's blood and put it on the horns of the altar with your finger; then pour out the rest of the blood at the base of the altar. ¹³Take all the fat that covers the entrails, the protuberance on the liver, and the two kidneys with the fat on them, and turn them into smoke upon the altar. ¹⁴The rest of the flesh of the bull, its hide, and its dung shall be put to the fire outside the camp; it is a *-sin offering.-*

¹⁵Next take the one ram, and let Aaron and his sons lay their hands upon the ram's head. ¹⁶Slaughter the ram, and take its blood and dash it against all sides of the altar. ¹⁷Cut up the ram into sections, wash its entrails and legs, and put them with its quarters and its head. ¹⁸Turn all of the ram into smoke upon the altar. It is a burnt offering to יהוה, a pleasing odor, an offering by fire to יהוה.

¹⁹Then take the other ram, and let Aaron and his sons lay their hands upon the ram's head. ²⁰Slaughter the ram, and take some of its blood and put it on the ridge* of Aaron's right ear and on the ridges of his sons' right ears, and on the thumbs of their right hands, and on the big toes of their right feet; and dash the rest of the blood against every side of the altar round about. ²¹Take some of the blood that is on the altar and some of the anointing oil and sprinkle upon Aaron and his vestments, and also upon his sons and his sons' vestments. Thus shall he and his vestments be holy, as well as his sons and his sons' vestments.

²²You shall take from the ram the fat parts—the broad tail, the fat that covers the entrails, the protuberance on the liver, the two kidneys with the fat on them—and the right thigh; for this is a ram of ordination. ²³Add one flat loaf of bread, one cake of oil bread, and one wafer, from the basket of unleavened bread that is before יהוה. ²⁴Place all these on the palms of Aaron and his sons, and offer them as an elevation offering before יהוה. ²⁵Take them from their hands and turn them into smoke upon the altar with the burnt offering, as a pleasing odor before יהוה; it is an offering by fire to יהוה.

²⁶Then take the breast of Aaron's ram of ordination and offer it as an elevation offering before יהוה; it shall be your portion. ²⁷You shall consecrate the breast that was offered as an elevation offering

and the thigh that was offered as a gift offering from the ram of ordination—from that which was Aaron's and from that which was his sons'—²⁸and those parts shall be a due for all time from the Israelites to Aaron and his descendants. For they are a gift; and so shall they be a gift from the Israelites, their gift to יהוה out of their sacrifices of well-being.

²⁹The sacral vestments of Aaron shall pass on to his sons after him, for them to be anointed and ordained in. ³⁰He among his sons who becomes priest in his stead, who enters the Tent of Meeting to officiate within the sanctuary, shall wear them seven days.

³¹You shall take the ram of ordination and boil its flesh in the sacred precinct; ³²and Aaron and his sons shall eat the flesh of the ram, and the bread that is in the basket, at the entrance of the Tent of Meeting. ³³These things shall be eaten only by those for whom expiation was made with them when they were ordained and consecrated; they may not be eaten by a lay person, for they are holy. ³⁴And if any of the flesh of ordination, or any of the bread, is left until morning, you shall put what is left to the fire; it shall not be eaten, for it is holy.

³⁵Thus you shall do to Aaron and his sons, just as I have commanded you. You shall ordain them through seven days, ³⁶and each day you shall prepare a bull as a sin offering for expiation; you shall purge the altar by performing purification upon it, and you shall anoint it to consecrate it. ³⁷Seven days you shall perform purification for the altar to consecrate it, and the altar shall become most holy; whatever touches the altar shall become consecrated.

³⁸Now this is what you shall offer upon the altar: two yearling lambs each day, regularly. ³⁹You shall offer the one lamb in the morning, and you shall offer the other lamb at twilight. ⁴⁰There shall be a tenth of a measure of choice flour with a quarter of a *hin* of beaten oil mixed in, and a libation of a quarter *hin* of wine for one lamb; ⁴¹and you shall offer the other lamb at twilight, repeating with it the meal offering of the morning with its libation—an offering by fire for a pleasing odor to יהוה, ⁴²a regular burnt offering throughout the generations, at the entrance of the Tent of Meeting before יהוה.

For there I will meet with you, and there I will speak with you,

43and there I will meet with the Israelites, and it shall be sanctified by My Presence. 44I will sanctify the Tent of Meeting and the altar, and I will consecrate Aaron and his sons to serve Me as priests. 45I will abide among the Israelites, and I will be their God. 46And they shall know that I יהוה am their God, who brought them out from the land of Egypt that I might abide among them— I, their God יהוה.

30

You shall make an altar for burning incense; make it of acacia wood. 2It shall be a cubit long and a cubit wide— it shall be square—and two cubits high, its horns of one piece with it. 3Overlay it with pure gold: its top, its sides round about, and its horns; and make a gold molding for it round about. 4And make two gold rings for it under its molding; make them on its two side walls, on opposite*sides. They shall serve as holders for poles with which to carry it. 5Make the poles of acacia wood, and overlay them with gold.

6Place it in front of the curtain that is over the Ark of the Pact— in front of the cover that is over the Pact—where I will meet with you. 7On it Aaron shall burn aromatic incense: he shall burn it every morning when he tends the lamps, 8and Aaron shall burn it at twilight when he lights the lamps—a regular incense offering before יהוה throughout the ages. 9You shall not offer alien incense on it, or a burnt offering or a meal offering; neither shall you pour a libation on it. 10Once a year Aaron shall perform purification upon its horns with blood of the sin offering of purification; purification shall be performed upon it once a year throughout the ages. It is most holy to יהוה.

כי תשׂא | KI TISSA'

11יהוה spoke to Moses, saying: 12When you take a census of the Israelite men according to their army enrollment, each shall pay יהוה a ransom for himself on being enrolled, that no plague may come upon them through their being enrolled. 13This is what every-one who is entered in the records shall pay: a half-shekel by the sanctuary weight—twenty gerahs to the shekel—a half-shekel as an offering to יהוה. 14Everyone who is entered in the records, from the age of twenty years up, shall give יהוה's offering: 15the rich shall not pay more and the poor shall not pay less than half a shekel when giving יהוה's offering as expiation for your persons. [16]You shall take the expiation money from the Israelites and assign it to the service of the Tent of Meeting; it shall serve the Israelites as a reminder before יהוה, as expiation for your persons.

[17]יהוה spoke to Moses, saying: [18]Make a laver of copper and a stand of copper for it, for washing; and place it between the Tent of Meeting and the altar. Put water in it, [19]and let Aaron and his sons wash their hands and feet [in water drawn] from it. [20]When they enter the Tent of Meeting they shall wash with water, that they may not die; or when they approach the altar to serve, to turn into smoke an offering by fire to יהוה, [21]they shall wash their hands and feet, that they may not die. It shall be a law for all time for them—for him and his offspring—throughout the ages.

[22]יהוה spoke to Moses, saying: [23]Next take choice spices: five hundred weight of solidified* myrrh, half as much—two hundred and fifty—of fragrant cinnamon, two hundred and fifty of aromatic cane, [24]five hundred—by the sanctuary weight—of cassia, and a *hin* of olive oil. [25]Make of this a sacred anointing oil, a compound of ingredients expertly blended, to serve as sacred anointing oil. [26]With it anoint the Tent of Meeting, the Ark of the Pact, [27]the table and all its utensils, the lampstand and all its fittings, the altar of incense, [28]the altar of burnt offering and all its utensils, and the laver and its stand. [29]Thus you shall consecrate them so that they may be most holy; whatever touches them shall be consecrated. [30]You shall also anoint Aaron and his sons, consecrating them to serve Me as priests.

[31]And speak to the Israelite people, as follows: This shall be an anointing oil sacred to Me throughout the ages. [32]It must not be rubbed on any person's body, and you must not make anything like it in the same proportions; it is sacred, to be held sacred by you. [33]Whoever compounds its like, or puts any of it on a lay person, shall be cut off from kin.

[34]And יהוה said to Moses: Take the herbs stacte, onycha, and galbanum—these herbs together with pure frankincense; let there be an equal part of each. [35]Make them into incense, a compound

expertly blended, refined, pure, sacred. ³⁶Beat some of it into powder, and put some before the Pact in the Tent of Meeting, where
I will meet with you; it shall be most holy to you. ³⁷But when you
make this incense, you must not make any in the same proportions for yourselves; it shall be held by you sacred to יהוה. ³⁸Who-
ever makes any like it, to smell of it, shall be cut off from kin.

31

יהוה spoke to Moses: ²See, I have singled out by name
Bezalel son of Uri son of Hur, of the tribe of Judah. ³I
have endowed him with a divine spirit of skill, ability, and knowledge in every kind of craft; ⁴to make designs for work in gold,
silver, and copper, ⁵to cut stones for setting and to carve wood—
to work in every kind of craft. ⁶Moreover, I have assigned to him
Oholiab son of Ahisamach, of the tribe of Dan; and I have also
granted skill to all who are skillful, that they may make everything
that I have commanded you: ⁷the Tent of Meeting, the Ark for the
Pact and the cover upon it, and all the furnishings of the Tent; ⁸the
table and its utensils, the *⁻pure lampstand⁻* and all its fittings, and
the altar of incense; ⁹the altar of burnt offering and all its utensils,
and the laver and its stand; ¹⁰the service* vestments, the sacral vestments of Aaron the priest and the vestments of his sons, for their
service as priests; ¹¹as well as the anointing oil and the aromatic
incense for the sanctuary. Just as I have commanded you, they
shall do.

¹²And יהוה said to Moses: ¹³Speak to the Israelite people and
say: Nevertheless, you must keep My sabbaths, for this is a sign
between Me and you throughout the ages, that you may know
that I יהוה have consecrated you. ¹⁴You shall keep the sabbath, for
it is holy for you. One who profanes it shall be put to death: whoever does work on it, that person shall be cut off from among kin.
¹⁵Six days may work be done, but on the seventh day there shall
be a sabbath of complete rest, holy to יהוה; whoever does work
on the sabbath day shall be put to death. ¹⁶The Israelite people
shall keep the sabbath, observing the sabbath throughout the ages
as a covenant for all time: ¹⁷it shall be a sign for all time between
Me and the people of Israel. For in six days יהוה made heaven and
earth, and on the seventh day [God] ceased from work and was
refreshed.

Ki Tissa'

¹⁸Upon finishing speaking with him on Mount Sinai, [God] gave Moses the two tablets of the Pact, stone tablets inscribed with the finger of God.

32 When the people saw that Moses was so long in coming down from the mountain, the people gathered against Aaron and said to him, "Come, make us a god who shall go before us, for that fellow Moses—the leader° who brought us from the land of Egypt—we do not know what has happened to him." ²Aaron said to them, "[You men,] take off the gold rings that are on the ears of your wives, your sons, and your daughters, and bring them to me." ³And all the people took off the gold rings that were in their ears and brought them to Aaron. ⁴This he took from them and *‑cast in a mold,‑* and made it into a molten calf. And they exclaimed, "*‑This is your god,‑* O Israel, who brought you out of the land of Egypt!" ⁵When Aaron saw this, he built an altar before it; and Aaron announced: "Tomorrow shall be a festival of יהוה!" ⁶Early next day, the people offered up burnt offerings and brought sacrifices of well-being; they sat down to eat and drink, and then rose to dance.

⁷יהוה spoke to Moses, "Hurry down, for your people, whom you brought out of the land of Egypt, have acted basely. ⁸They have been quick to turn aside from the way that I enjoined upon them. They have made themselves a molten calf and bowed low to it and sacrificed to it, saying: 'This is your god, O Israel, who brought you out of the land of Egypt!'"

⁹יהוה further said to Moses, "I see that this is a stiffnecked people. ¹⁰Now, let Me be, that My anger may blaze forth against them and that I may destroy them, and make of you a great nation." ¹¹But Moses implored his God יהוה, saying, "Let not Your anger, יהוה, blaze forth against Your people, whom You delivered from the land of Egypt with great power and with a mighty hand. ¹²Let not the Egyptians say, 'It was with evil intent that he delivered them, only to kill them off in the mountains and annihilate them from the face of the earth.' Turn from Your blazing anger, and renounce the plan to punish Your people. ¹³Remember Your servants, Abraham, Isaac, and Israel, how You swore to them by Your Self and said to them: I will make your offspring as numer-

ous as the stars of heaven, and I will give to your offspring this whole land of which I spoke, to possess forever." [14]And יהוה renounced the punishment planned for God's people.

[15]Thereupon Moses turned and went down from the mountain bearing the two tablets of the Pact, tablets inscribed on both their surfaces: they were inscribed on the one side and on the other. [16]The tablets were God's work, and the writing was God's writing, incised upon the tablets. [17]When Joshua heard the sound of the people in its boisterousness, he said to Moses, "There is a cry of war in the camp." [18]But he answered,

"It is not the sound of the tune of triumph,
Or the sound of the tune of defeat;
It is the sound of song that I hear!"

[19]As soon as Moses came near the camp and saw the calf and the dancing, he became enraged; and he hurled the tablets from his hands and shattered them at the foot of the mountain. [20]He took the calf that they had made and burned it; he ground it to powder and strewed it upon the water and so made the Israelites drink it.

[21]Moses said to Aaron, "What did this people do to you that you have brought such great sin upon them?" [22]Aaron said, "Let not my lord be enraged. You know that this people is bent on evil. [23]They said to me, 'Make us a god to lead us; for that fellow Moses—the leader who brought us from the land of Egypt—we do not know what has happened to him.' [24]So I said to them, 'Whoever has gold, take it off!' They gave it to me and I hurled it into the fire and out came this calf!"

[25]Moses saw that the people were out of control—since Aaron had let them get out of control—so that they were *⁻a menace⁻* to any who might oppose them. [26]Moses stood up in the gate of the camp and said, "Whoever is for יהוה, come here!" And all the men of Levi rallied to him. [27]He said to them, "Thus says יהוה, the God of Israel: Each of you put sword on thigh, go back and forth from gate to gate throughout the camp, and slay sibling, neighbor, and kin." [28]The men of Levi did as Moses had bidden; and some three thousand of the people fell that day. [29]And Moses said, "*⁻Dedicate yourselves⁻* to יהוה this day—for each of you has been against blood relations—that [God] may bestow a blessing upon you today."

³⁰The next day Moses said to the people, "You have been guilty of a great sin. Yet I will now go up to יהוה; perhaps I may win forgiveness for your sin." ³¹Moses went back to יהוה and said, "Alas, this people is guilty of a great sin in making for themselves a god of gold. ³²Now, if You will forgive their sin [well and good]; but if not, erase me from the record which You have written!" ³³But יהוה said to Moses, "Only one who has sinned against Me will I erase from My record. ³⁴Go now, lead the people where I told you. See, My messenger shall go before you. But when I make an accounting, I will bring them to account for their sins."

³⁵Then יהוה sent a plague upon the people, *⁻for what they did with the calf that Aaron made.⁻*

33 Then יהוה said to Moses, "Set out from here, you and the people that you have brought up from the land of Egypt, to the land of which I swore to Abraham, Isaac, and Jacob, saying, 'To your offspring will I give it'—²I will send a messenger before you, and I will drive out the Canaanites, the Amorites, the Hittites, the Perizzites, the Hivites, and the Jebusites—³a land flowing with milk and honey. But I will not go in your midst, since you are a stiffnecked people, lest I destroy you on the way."

⁴When the people heard this harsh word, they went into mourning, and none put on finery.

⁵יהוה said to Moses, "Say to the Israelite people, 'You are a stiffnecked people. If I were to go in your midst for one moment, I would destroy you. Now, then, leave off your finery, and I will consider what to do to you.'" ⁶So the Israelites remained stripped of the finery from Mount Horeb on.

⁷Now Moses would take the Tent and pitch it outside the camp, at some distance from the camp. It was called the Tent of Meeting, and whoever sought יהוה would go out to the Tent of Meeting that was outside the camp. ⁸Whenever Moses went out to the Tent, all the people would rise and stand, at the entrance of each tent, and gaze after Moses until he had entered the Tent. ⁹And when Moses entered the Tent, the pillar of cloud would descend and stand at the entrance of the Tent, while [God] spoke with Moses. ¹⁰When all the people saw the pillar of cloud poised at the

Ki Tissa'

entrance of the Tent, all the people would rise and bow low, at the entrance of each tent. ¹¹יהוה would speak to Moses face to face, as one person speaks to another. And he would then return to the camp; but his attendant, Joshua son of Nun, °[serving as] deputy,° would not stir out of the Tent.

¹²Moses said to יהוה, "See, You say to me, 'Lead this people forward,' but You have not made known to me whom You will send with me. Further, You have said, 'I have singled you out by name, and you have, indeed, gained My favor.' ¹³Now, if I have truly gained Your favor, pray let me know Your ways, that I may know You and continue in Your favor. Consider, too, that this nation is Your people." ¹⁴And [God] said, "*I will go in the lead and will* lighten your burden." ¹⁵And he replied, "Unless You go in the lead, do not make us leave this place. ¹⁶For how shall it be known that Your people have gained Your favor unless You go with us, so that we may be distinguished, Your people and I, from every people on the face of the earth?"

¹⁷And יהוה said to Moses, "I will also do this thing that you have asked; for you have truly gained My favor and I have singled you out by name." ¹⁸He said, "Oh, let me behold Your Presence!" ¹⁹And [God] answered, "I will make all My goodness pass before you, and I will proclaim before you the name יהוה, *and the grace that I grant and the compassion that I show,"* ²⁰continuing, "But you cannot see My face, for a human being may not see Me and live." ²¹And יהוה said, "See, there is a place near Me. Station yourself on the rock ²²and, as My Presence passes by, I will put you in a cleft of the rock and shield you with My hand until I have passed by. ²³Then I will take My hand away and you will see My back; but My face must not be seen."

34 יהוה said to Moses: "Carve two tablets of stone like the first, and I will inscribe upon the tablets the words that were on the first tablets, which you shattered. ²Be ready by morning, and in the morning come up to Mount Sinai and present yourself there to Me, on the top of the mountain. ³No one else shall come up with you, and no one else shall be seen anywhere on the mountain; neither shall the flocks and the herds graze at the foot of this mountain."

⁴So Moses carved two tablets of stone, like the first, and early in the morning he went up on Mount Sinai, as יהוה had commanded him, taking the two stone tablets with him. ⁵יהוה came down in a cloud—and stood with him there, proclaiming the name יהוה. ⁶יהוה passed before him *⁻and proclaimed: "יהוה! יהוה!⁻* a God compassionate and gracious, slow to anger, abounding in kindness and faithfulness, ⁷extending kindness to the thousandth genera-tion, forgiving iniquity, transgression, and sin—yet not remitting all punishment, but visiting the iniquity of parents upon children and children's children, upon the third and fourth generations."

⁸Moses hastened to bow low to the ground in homage, ⁹and said, "If I have gained Your favor, O my lord, pray, let my lord go in our midst, even though this is a stiffnecked people. Pardon our iniquity and our sin, and take us for Your own!"

¹⁰[God] said: I hereby make a covenant. Before all your people I will work such wonders as have not been wrought on all the earth or in any nation; and all the people *⁻who are with you⁻* shall see how awesome are יהוה's deeds which I will perform for you. ¹¹Mark well what I command you this day. I will drive out before you the Amorites, the Canaanites, the Hittites, the Periz-zites, the Hivites, and the Jebusites. ¹²Beware of making a cove-nant with the inhabitants of the land against which you are ad-vancing, lest they be a snare in your midst. ¹³No, you must tear down their altars, smash their pillars, and cut down their sacred posts; ¹⁴for you must not worship any other god, because יהוה, whose name is Impassioned, is an impassioned God. ¹⁵You must not make a covenant with the inhabitants of the land, for they will lust after their gods and sacrifice to their gods and invite you, and you will eat of their sacrifices. ¹⁶And when you take [wives into your households] from among their daughters for your sons, their daughters will lust after their gods and will cause your sons to lust after their gods.

¹⁷You shall not make molten gods for yourselves.

¹⁸You shall observe the Feast of Unleavened Bread—eating un-leavened bread for seven days, as I have commanded you—at the set time *⁻of the month⁻* of Abib, for in the month of Abib you went forth from Egypt.

¹⁹Every first issue of the womb is Mine, from all your livestock

that drop a male* as firstling, whether cattle or sheep. ²⁰But the firstling of an ass you shall redeem with a sheep; if you do not redeem it, you must break its neck. And you must redeem every male first-born among your children.

None shall appear before Me empty-handed.

²¹Six days you shall work, but on the seventh day you shall cease from labor; you shall cease from labor even at plowing time and harvest time.

²²You shall observe the Feast of Weeks, of the first fruits of the wheat harvest; and the Feast of Ingathering at the turn of the year. ²³Three times a year all your males shall appear before the Sovereign יהוה, the God of Israel. ²⁴I will drive out nations from your path and enlarge your territory; no one will covet your land when you go up to appear before your God יהוה three times a year.

²⁵You shall not offer the blood of My sacrifice with anything leavened; and the sacrifice of the Feast of Passover shall not be left lying until morning.

²⁶The choice first fruits of your soil you shall bring to the house of your God יהוה.

You shall not boil a kid in its mother's milk.

²⁷And יהוה said to Moses: Write down these commandments, for in accordance with these commandments I make a covenant with you and with Israel.

²⁸And he was there with יהוה forty days and forty nights; he ate no bread and drank no water; and he wrote down on the tablets the terms of the covenant, the Ten Commandments.

²⁹So Moses came down from Mount Sinai. And as Moses came down from the mountain bearing the two tablets of the Pact, Moses was not aware that the skin of his face was radiant, since he had spoken with God. ³⁰Aaron and all the Israelites saw that the skin of Moses' face was radiant; and they shrank from coming near him. ³¹But Moses called to them, and Aaron and all the chieftains in the assembly returned to him, and Moses spoke to them. ³²Afterward all the Israelites came near, and he instructed them concerning all that יהוה had imparted to him on Mount Sinai. ³³And when Moses had finished speaking with them, he put a veil over his face.

³⁴Whenever Moses went in before יהוה to converse, he would leave the veil off until he came out; and when he came out and told the Israelites what he had been commanded, ³⁵the Israelites would see how radiant the skin of Moses' face was. Moses would then put the veil back over his face until he went in to speak with God.

וַיַּקְהֵל | VA-YAKHEL

35 Moses then convoked the whole Israelite community and said to them:

These are the things that יהוה has commanded you to do: ²On six days work may be done, but on the seventh day you shall have a sabbath of complete rest, holy to יהוה; whoever does any work on it shall be put to death. ³You shall kindle no fire throughout your settlements on the sabbath day.

⁴Moses said further to the whole community of Israelites:

This is what יהוה has commanded: ⁵Take from among you gifts to יהוה; everyone whose heart is so moved shall bring them—gifts for יהוה: gold, silver, and copper; *⁶blue, purple, and crimson yarns, fine linen, and goats' hair; ⁷tanned ram skins, dolphin skins, and acacia wood; ⁸oil for lighting, spices for the anointing oil and for the aromatic incense; ⁹lapis lazuli and other stones for setting, for the ephod and the breastpiece.

¹⁰And let all among you who are skilled come and make all that יהוה has commanded: ¹¹the Tabernacle, its tent and its covering, its clasps and its planks, its bars, its posts, and its sockets; ¹²the ark and its poles, the cover, and the curtain for the screen; ¹³the table, and its poles and all its utensils; and the bread of display; ¹⁴the lampstand for lighting, its furnishings and its lamps, and the oil for lighting; ¹⁵the altar of incense and its poles; the anointing oil and the aromatic incense; and the entrance screen for the entrance of the Tabernacle; ¹⁶the altar of burnt offering, its copper grating, its poles, and all its furnishings; the laver and its stand; ¹⁷the hangings of the enclosure, its posts and its sockets, and the screen for the gate of the court; ¹⁸the pegs for the Tabernacle, the pegs for the enclosure, and their cords; ¹⁹the service vestments for officiating in the sanctuary, the sacral vestments of Aaron the priest and the vestments of his sons for priestly service.

²⁰So the whole community of the Israelites left Moses' presence. ²¹And everyone who excelled in ability and everyone whose spirit was moved came, bringing to יהוה an offering for the work of the Tent of Meeting and for all its service and for the sacral vestments. ²²Men and women, all whose hearts moved them, all who would make an elevation offering of gold to יהוה, came bringing brooches, earrings, rings, and pendants*—gold objects of all kinds. ²³And everyone who possessed blue, purple, and crimson yarns, fine linen, goats' hair, tanned ram skins, and dolphin skins, brought them; ²⁴everyone who would make gifts of silver or copper brought them as gifts for יהוה; and everyone who possessed acacia wood for any work of the service brought that. ²⁵And all the skilled women spun with their own hands, and brought what they had spun, in blue, purple, and crimson yarns, and in fine linen. ²⁶And all the women who excelled in that skill spun the goats' hair. ²⁷And the chieftains brought lapis lazuli and other stones for setting, for the ephod and for the breastpiece; ²⁸and spices and oil for lighting, for the anointing oil, and for the aromatic incense. ²⁹Thus the Israelites, all the men and women whose hearts moved them to bring anything for the work that יהוה, through Moses, had commanded to be done, brought it as a freewill offering to יהוה.

³⁰And Moses said to the Israelites: See, יהוה has singled out by name Bezalel, son of Uri son of Hur, of the tribe of Judah, ³¹endowing him with a divine spirit of skill, ability, and knowledge in every kind of craft, ³²and *⁻inspiring him⁻* to make designs for work in gold, silver, and copper, ³³to cut stones for setting and to carve wood—to work in every kind of designer's craft—³⁴and to give directions. He and Oholiab son of Ahisamach of the tribe of Dan ³⁵have been endowed with the skill to do any work—of the carver, the designer, the embroiderer in blue, purple, crimson yarns, and in fine linen, and of the weaver—as workers in all crafts and as makers of designs. **36** ¹Let, then, Bezalel and Oholiab and all the skilled per- sons whom יהוה has endowed with skill and ability to perform expertly all the tasks connected with the service of the sanctuary carry out all that יהוה has commanded.

²Moses then called Bezalel and Oholiab, and every skilled person whom יהוה had endowed with skill, everyone who excelled in

ability, to undertake the task and carry it out. ³They took over from Moses all the gifts that the Israelites had brought, to carry out the tasks connected with the service of the sanctuary. But when these continued to bring freewill offerings to him morning after morning, ⁴all the artisans who were engaged in the tasks of the sanctuary came, from the task upon which each one was engaged, ⁵and said to Moses, "The people are bringing more than is needed for the tasks entailed in the work that יהוה has commanded to be done." ⁶Moses thereupon had this proclamation made throughout the camp: "Let no man or woman make further effort toward gifts for the sanctuary!" So the people stopped bringing: ⁷their efforts had been more than enough for all the tasks to be done.

⁸Then all the skilled among those engaged in the work made the Tabernacle of ten strips of cloth, which they made of fine twisted linen, blue, purple, and crimson yarns; into these they worked a design of cherubim. ⁹The length of each cloth was twenty-eight cubits, and the width of each cloth was four cubits, all cloths having the same measurements. ¹⁰They joined five of the cloths to one another, and they joined the other five cloths to one another. ¹¹They made loops of blue wool on the edge of the outermost cloth of the one set, and did the same on the edge of the outermost cloth of the other set: ¹²they made fifty loops on the one cloth, and they made fifty loops on the edge of the end cloth of the other set, the loops being opposite one another. ¹³And they made fifty gold clasps and coupled the units* to one another with the clasps, so that the Tabernacle became one whole.

¹⁴They made cloths of goats' hair for a tent over the Tabernacle; they made the cloths eleven in number. ¹⁵The length of each cloth was thirty cubits, and the width of each cloth was four cubits, the eleven cloths having the same measurements. ¹⁶They joined five of the cloths by themselves, and the other six cloths by themselves. ¹⁷They made fifty loops on the edge of the outermost cloth of the one set, and they made fifty loops on the edge of the end cloth of the other set. ¹⁸They made fifty copper clasps to couple the Tent together so that it might become one whole. ¹⁹And they made a covering of tanned ram skins for the tent, and a covering of dolphin skins above.

²⁰They made the planks for the Tabernacle of acacia wood, upright. ²¹The length of each plank was ten cubits, the width of each plank a cubit and a half. ²²Each plank had two tenons, parallel* to each other; they did the same with all the planks of the Tabernacle. ²³Of the planks of the Tabernacle, they made twenty planks for the *⁻south side,⁻* ²⁴making forty silver sockets under the twenty planks, two sockets under one plank for its two tenons and two sockets under each following plank for its two tenons; ²⁵and for the other side wall of the Tabernacle, the north side, twenty planks, ²⁶with their forty silver sockets, two sockets under one plank and two sockets under each following plank. ²⁷And for the rear of the Tabernacle, to the west, they made six planks; ²⁸and they made two planks for the corners of the Tabernacle at the rear. ²⁹*⁻They matched at the bottom, but terminated as one at the top into one ring;⁻* they did so with both of them at the two corners. ³⁰Thus there were eight planks with their sockets of silver: sixteen sockets, two under each plank.

³¹They made bars of acacia wood, five for the planks of the one side wall of the Tabernacle, ³²five bars for the planks of the other side wall of the Tabernacle, and five bars for the planks of the wall of the Tabernacle at the rear, to the west; ³³they made the center bar to run, halfway up the planks, from end to end. ³⁴They overlaid the planks with gold, and made their rings of gold, as holders for the bars; and they overlaid the bars with gold.

³⁵They made the curtain of blue, purple, and crimson yarns, and fine twisted linen, working into it a design of cherubim. ³⁶They made for it four posts of acacia wood and overlaid them with gold, with their hooks of gold; and they cast for them four silver sockets.

³⁷They made the screen for the entrance of the Tent, of blue, purple, and crimson yarns, and fine twisted linen, done in embroidery; ³⁸and five posts for it with their hooks. They overlaid their tops and their bands with gold; but the five sockets were of copper.

37 Bezalel made the ark of acacia wood, two and a half cubits long, a cubit and a half wide, and a cubit and a half high. ²He overlaid it with pure gold, inside and out; and he made a gold molding for it round about. ³He cast four gold rings for it, for its four feet: two rings on one of its side walls and two rings on the other. ⁴He made poles of acacia wood, overlaid them with gold, ⁵and inserted the poles into the rings on the side walls of the ark for carrying the ark.

⁶He made a cover of pure gold, two and a half cubits long and a cubit and a half wide. ⁷He made two cherubim of gold; he made them of hammered work, at the two ends of the cover: ⁸one cherub at one end and the other cherub at the other end; he made the cherubim of one piece with the cover, at its two ends. ⁹The cherubim had their wings spread out above, shielding the cover with their wings. They faced each other; the faces of the cherubim were turned toward the cover.

¹⁰He made the table of acacia wood, two cubits long, one cubit wide, and a cubit and a half high; ¹¹he overlaid it with pure gold and made a gold molding around it. ¹²He made a rim of a hand's breadth around it and made a gold molding for its rim round about. ¹³He cast four gold rings for it and attached the rings to the four corners at its four legs. ¹⁴The rings were next to the rim, as holders for the poles to carry the table. ¹⁵He made the poles of acacia wood for carrying the table, and overlaid them with gold. ¹⁶The utensils that were to be upon the table—its bowls, ladles, jugs, and jars with which to offer libations—he made of pure gold.

¹⁷He made the lampstand of pure gold. He made the lampstand—its base and its shaft—of hammered work; its cups, calyxes, and petals were of one piece with it. ¹⁸Six branches issued from its sides: three branches from one side of the lampstand, and three branches from the other side of the lampstand. ¹⁹There were three cups shaped like almond-blossoms, each with calyx and petals, on one branch; and there were three cups shaped like almond-blossoms, each with calyx and petals, on the next branch; so for all six branches issuing from the lampstand. ²⁰On the lampstand itself there were four cups shaped like almond-blossoms, each with calyx and petals: ²¹a calyx, of one piece with it, under a pair of branches; and a calyx, of one piece with it, under the second pair of branches; and a calyx, of one piece with it, under the last pair of branches; so for all six branches issuing from it. ²²Their calyxes and their stems were of one piece with it, the whole of it a single hammered piece of pure gold. ²³He made its seven lamps, its

tongs, and its fire pans of pure gold. ²⁴He made it and all its furnishings out of a talent of pure gold.

²⁵He made the incense altar of acacia wood, a cubit long and a cubit wide—square—and two cubits high; its horns were of one piece with it. ²⁶He overlaid it with pure gold: its top, its sides round about, and its horns; and he made a gold molding for it round about. ²⁷He made two gold rings for it under its molding, on its two walls—on opposite sides—as holders for the poles with which to carry it. ²⁸He made the poles of acacia wood, and overlaid them with gold. ²⁹He prepared the sacred anointing oil and the pure aromatic incense, expertly blended.

38 He made the altar for burnt offering of acacia wood, five cubits long and five cubits wide—square—and three cubits high. ²He made horns for it on its four corners, the horns being of one piece with it; and he overlaid it with copper. ³He made all the utensils of the altar—the pails, the scrapers, the basins, the flesh hooks, and the fire pans; he made all these utensils of copper. ⁴He made for the altar a grating of meshwork in copper, extending below, under its ledge, to its middle. ⁵He cast four rings, at the four corners of the copper grating, as holders for the poles. ⁶He made the poles of acacia wood and overlaid them with copper; ⁷and he inserted the poles into the rings on the side walls of the altar, to carry it by them. He made it hollow, of boards.

⁸He made the laver of copper and its stand of copper, from the mirrors of the *⁻women who performed tasks⁻* at the entrance of the Tent of Meeting.

⁹He made the enclosure:

On the south* side, a hundred cubits of hangings of fine twisted linen for the enclosure—¹⁰with their twenty posts and their twenty sockets of copper, the hooks and bands of the posts being silver.

¹¹On the north side, a hundred cubits—with their twenty posts and their twenty sockets of copper, the hooks and bands of the posts being silver.

¹²On the west side, fifty cubits of hangings—with their ten posts and their ten sockets, the hooks and bands of the posts being silver.

¹³And on the front side, to the east, fifty cubits: ¹⁴fifteen cubits of hangings on the one flank, with their three posts and their three sockets, ¹⁵and fifteen cubits of hangings on the other flank—on

each side of the gate of the enclosure*—with their three posts and their three sockets.

16All the hangings around the enclosure were of fine twisted linen. 17The sockets for the posts were of copper, the hooks and bands of the posts were of silver, the overlay of their tops was of silver; all the posts of the enclosure were banded with silver.— 18The screen of the gate of the enclosure, done in embroidery, was of blue, purple, and crimson yarns, and fine twisted linen. It was twenty cubits long. *Its height—or width—was five cubits, like that of* the hangings of the enclosure. 19The posts were four; their four sockets were of copper, their hooks of silver; and the overlay of their tops was of silver, as were also their bands.— 20All the pegs of the Tabernacle and of the enclosure round about were of copper.

פְּקוּדֵי | PEKUDEI

21These are the records of the Tabernacle, the Tabernacle of the Pact, which were drawn up at Moses' bidding—the work of the Levites under the direction of Ithamar son of Aaron the priest. 22Now Bezalel, son of Uri son of Hur, of the tribe of Judah, had made all that יהוה had commanded Moses; 23at his side was Oholiab son of Ahisamach, of the tribe of Dan, carver and designer, and embroiderer in blue, purple, and crimson yarns and in fine linen.

24All the gold that was used for the work, in all the work of the sanctuary—the elevation offering of gold—came to 29 talents* and 730 shekels by the sanctuary weight. 25The silver of those of the community who were recorded came to 100 talents and 1,775 shekels by the sanctuary weight: 26a half-shekel* a head, half a shekel by the sanctuary weight, for each one who was entered in the records, from the age of twenty years up, 603,550 men. 27The 100 talents of silver were for casting the sockets of the sanctuary and the sockets for the curtain, 100 sockets to the 100 talents, a talent a socket. 28And of the 1,775 shekels he made hooks for the posts, overlay for their tops, and bands around them.

29The copper from the elevation offering came to 70 talents and 2,400 shekels. 30Of it he made the sockets for the entrance of the Tent of Meeting; the copper altar and its copper grating and all the utensils of the altar; 31the sockets of the enclosure round about and the sockets of the gate of the enclosure; and all the pegs of the Tabernacle and all the pegs of the enclosure round about.

39 Of the blue, purple, and crimson yarns they also* made the service vestments for officiating in the sanctuary; they made Aaron's sacral vestments—as יהוה had commanded Moses.

²The ephod was made* of gold, blue, purple, and crimson yarns, and fine twisted linen. ³They hammered out sheets of gold and cut threads to be worked into designs among the blue, the purple, and the crimson yarns, and the fine linen. ⁴They made for it attaching shoulder-pieces; they were attached at its two ends. ⁵The decorated band that was upon it was made like it, of one piece with it; of gold, blue, purple, and crimson yarns, and fine twisted linen— as יהוה had commanded Moses.

⁶They bordered the lazuli stones with frames of gold, engraved with seal engravings of the names of the sons of Israel. ⁷They were set on the shoulder-pieces of the ephod, as stones of remembrance for the Israelites—as יהוה had commanded Moses.

⁸The breastpiece was made in the style of the ephod: of gold, blue, purple, and crimson yarns, and fine twisted linen. ⁹It was square; they made the breastpiece doubled—a span in length and a span in width, doubled. ¹⁰They set in it four rows of stones. The first row was a row of *⁻carnelian, chrysolite, and emerald; ¹¹the second row: a turquoise, a sapphire, and an amethyst; ¹²the third row: a jacinth, an agate, and a crystal; ¹³and the fourth row: a beryl, a lapis lazuli, and a jasper.⁻* They were encircled in their mountings with frames of gold. ¹⁴The stones corresponded [in number] to the names of the sons of Israel: twelve, corresponding to their names; engraved like seals, each with its name, for the twelve tribes.

¹⁵On the breastpiece they made braided chains of corded work in pure gold. ¹⁶They made two frames of gold and two rings of gold, and fastened the two rings at the two ends of the breastpiece, ¹⁷attaching the two golden cords to the two rings at the ends of the breastpiece. ¹⁸They then fastened the two ends of the cords to the two frames, attaching them to the shoulder-pieces of the ephod, at the front. ¹⁹They made two rings of gold and attached them to the two ends of the breastpiece, at its inner edge,

which faced the ephod. ²⁰They made two other rings of gold and fastened them on the front of the ephod, low on the two shoulder-pieces, close to its seam above the decorated band. ²¹The breastpiece was held in place by a cord of blue from its rings to the rings of the ephod, so that the breastpiece rested on the decorated band and did not come loose from the ephod—as יהוה had commanded Moses.

²²The robe for the ephod was made of woven work, *⁻of pure blue.⁻* ²³The opening of the robe, in the middle of it, was like the opening of a coat of mail, with a binding around the opening, so that it would not tear. ²⁴On the hem of the robe they made pomegranates of blue, purple, and crimson yarns, twisted. ²⁵They also made bells of pure gold, and attached the bells between the pomegranates, all around the hem of the robe, between the pomegranates: ²⁶a bell and a pomegranate, a bell and a pomegranate, all around the hem of the robe for officiating in—as יהוה had commanded Moses.

²⁷They made the tunics of fine linen, of woven work, for Aaron and his sons; ²⁸and the headdress of fine linen, and the decorated turbans of fine linen, and the linen breeches of fine twisted linen; ²⁹and sashes of fine twisted linen, blue, purple, and crimson yarns, done in embroidery—as יהוה had commanded Moses.

³⁰They made the frontlet for the holy diadem of pure gold, and incised upon it the seal inscription: "Holy to יהוה." ³¹They attached to it a cord of blue to fix it upon the headdress above—as יהוה had commanded Moses.

³²Thus was completed all the work of the Tabernacle of the Tent of Meeting. The Israelites did so; just as יהוה had commanded Moses, so they did.

³³Then they brought the Tabernacle to Moses, with the Tent and all its furnishings: its clasps, its planks, its bars, its posts, and its sockets; ³⁴the covering of tanned ram skins, the covering of dolphin skins, and the curtain for the screen; ³⁵the Ark of the Pact and its poles, and the cover; ³⁶the table and all its utensils, and the bread of display; ³⁷the *⁻pure lampstand,⁻* its lamps—lamps in due order—and all its fittings, and the oil for lighting; ³⁸the altar of gold, the oil for anointing, the aromatic incense, and the screen for the entrance of the Tent; ³⁹the copper altar with its copper grating, its poles and all its utensils, and the laver and its stand; ⁴⁰the

hangings of the enclosure, its posts and its sockets, the screen for the gate of the enclosure, its cords and its pegs—all the furnishings for the service of the Tabernacle, the Tent of Meeting; ⁴¹the service vestments for officiating in the sanctuary, the sacral vestments of Aaron the priest, and the vestments of his sons for priestly service. ⁴²Just as יהוה had commanded Moses, so the Israelites had done all the work. ⁴³And when Moses saw that they had performed all the tasks—as יהוה had commanded, so they had done—Moses blessed them.

40 And יהוה spoke to Moses, saying:
²On the first day of the first month you shall set up the Tabernacle of the Tent of Meeting. ³Place there the Ark of the Pact, and screen off the ark with the curtain. ⁴Bring in the table and lay out its due setting; bring in the lampstand and light its lamps; ⁵and place the gold altar of incense before the Ark of the Pact. Then put up the screen for the entrance of the Tabernacle.

⁶You shall place the altar of burnt offering before the entrance of the Tabernacle of the Tent of Meeting. ⁷Place the laver between the Tent of Meeting and the altar, and put water in it. ⁸Set up the enclosure round about, and put in place the screen for the gate of the enclosure.

⁹You shall take the anointing oil and anoint the Tabernacle and all that is in it to consecrate it and all its furnishings, so that it shall be holy. ¹⁰Then anoint the altar of burnt offering and all its utensils to consecrate the altar, so that the altar shall be most holy. ¹¹And anoint the laver and its stand to consecrate it.

¹²You shall bring Aaron and his sons forward to the entrance of the Tent of Meeting and wash them with the water. ¹³Put the sacral vestments on Aaron, and anoint him and consecrate him, that he may serve Me as priest. ¹⁴Then bring his sons forward, put tunics on them, ¹⁵and anoint them as you have anointed their father, that they may serve Me as priests. This their anointing shall serve them for everlasting priesthood throughout the ages.

¹⁶This Moses did; just as יהוה had commanded him, so he did.

¹⁷In the first month of the second year, on the first of the month, the Tabernacle was set up. ¹⁸Moses set up the Tabernacle, placing

its sockets, setting up its planks, inserting its bars, and erecting its posts. ¹⁹He spread the tent over the Tabernacle, placing the covering of the tent on top of it—just as יהוה had commanded Moses.

²⁰He took the Pact and placed it in the ark; he fixed the poles to the ark, placed the cover on top of the ark, ²¹and brought the ark inside the Tabernacle. Then he put up the curtain for screening, and screened off the Ark of the Pact—just as יהוה had commanded Moses.

²²He placed the table in the Tent of Meeting, outside the curtain, on the north side of the Tabernacle. ²³Upon it he laid out the setting of bread before יהוה—as יהוה had commanded Moses. ²⁴He placed the lampstand in the Tent of Meeting opposite the table, on the south side of the Tabernacle. ²⁵And he lit the lamps before יהוה—as יהוה had commanded Moses. ²⁶He placed the altar of gold in the Tent of Meeting, before the curtain. ²⁷On it he burned aromatic incense—as יהוה had commanded Moses.

²⁸Then he put up the screen for the entrance of the Tabernacle. ²⁹At the entrance of the Tabernacle of the Tent of Meeting he placed the altar of burnt offering. On it he offered up the burnt offering and the meal offering—as יהוה had commanded Moses. ³⁰He placed the laver between the Tent of Meeting and the altar, and put water in it for washing. ³¹From it Moses and Aaron and his sons would wash their hands and feet; ³²they washed when they entered the Tent of Meeting and when they approached the altar—as יהוה had commanded Moses. ³³And he set up the enclosure around the Tabernacle and the altar, and put up the screen for the gate of the enclosure.

When Moses had finished the work, ³⁴the cloud covered the Tent of Meeting, and the Presence of יהוה filled the Tabernacle. ³⁵Moses could not enter the Tent of Meeting, because the cloud had settled upon it and the Presence of יהוה filled the Tabernacle. ³⁶When the cloud lifted from the Tabernacle, the Israelites would set out, on their various journeys; ³⁷but if the cloud did not lift, they would not set out until such time as it did lift. ³⁸For over the Tabernacle a cloud of יהוה rested by day, and fire would appear *⁻in it⁻* by night, in the view of all the house of Israel throughout their journeys.

חזק

וַיִּקְרָא
LEVITICUS

1 יהוה called to Moses and spoke to him from the Tent of Meeting, saying: ²Speak to the Israelite people, and say to them:

When any of you presents an offering of cattle to יהוה: You shall choose your offering from the herd or from the flock.

³If your° offering is a burnt offering from the herd, you shall make your offering a male without blemish. You shall bring it to the entrance of the Tent of Meeting, for acceptance in your behalf before יהוה. ⁴You shall lay a hand upon the head of the burnt offering, that it may be acceptable in your behalf, in expiation for you. ⁵The bull shall be slaughtered before יהוה; and Aaron's sons, the priests, shall offer the blood, dashing the blood against all sides of the altar which is at the entrance of the Tent of Meeting. ⁶The burnt offering shall be flayed and cut up into sections. ⁷The sons of Aaron the priest shall put fire on the altar and lay out wood upon the fire; ⁸and Aaron's sons, the priests, shall lay out the sections, with the head and the suet, on the wood that is on the fire upon the altar. ⁹Its entrails and legs shall be washed with water, and the priest shall turn the whole into smoke on the altar as a burnt offering, an offering by fire of pleasing odor to יהוה.

¹⁰If your° offering for a burnt offering is from the flock, of sheep or of goats, you shall make your offering a male without blemish. ¹¹It shall be slaughtered before יהוה on the north side of the altar, and Aaron's sons, the priests, shall dash its blood against all sides of the altar. ¹²When it has been cut up into sections, the priest shall lay them out, with the head and the suet, on the wood that is on the fire upon the altar. ¹³The entrails and the legs shall be washed with water; the priest shall offer up and turn the whole into smoke on the altar. It is a burnt offering, an offering by fire, of pleasing odor to יהוה.

¹⁴If your° offering to יהוה is a burnt offering of birds, you shall choose your offering from turtledoves or pigeons. ¹⁵The priest

shall bring it to the altar, pinch off its head, and turn it into smoke on the altar; and its blood shall be drained out against the side of the altar. ¹⁶He shall remove its crop with its contents,* and cast it into the place of the ashes, at the east side of the altar. ¹⁷The priest shall tear it open by its wings, without severing it, and turn it into smoke on the altar, upon the wood that is on the fire. It is a burnt offering, an offering by fire, of pleasing odor to יהוה.

2 When a person presents an offering of meal to יהוה: The offering shall be of choice flour; the offerer shall pour oil upon it, lay frankincense on it, ²and present it to Aaron's sons, the priests. The priest shall scoop out of it a handful of its choice flour and oil, as well as all of its frankincense; and this token portion he shall turn into smoke on the altar, as an offering by fire, of pleasing odor to יהוה. ³And the remainder of the meal offering shall be for Aaron and his sons, a most holy portion from יהוה's offerings by fire.

⁴When you present an offering of meal baked in the oven, [it shall be of] choice flour: unleavened cakes with oil mixed in, or unleavened wafers spread with oil.

⁵If your offering is a meal offering on a griddle, it shall be of choice flour with oil mixed in, unleavened. ⁶Break it into bits and pour oil on it; it is a meal offering.

⁷If your offering is a meal offering in a pan, it shall be made of choice flour in oil.

⁸When you present to יהוה a meal offering that is made in any of these ways, it shall be brought to the priest who shall take it up to the altar. ⁹The priest shall remove the token portion from the meal offering and turn it into smoke on the altar as an offering by fire, of pleasing odor to יהוה. ¹⁰And the remainder of the meal offering shall be for Aaron and his sons, a most holy portion from יהוה's offerings by fire.

¹¹No meal offering that you offer to יהוה shall be made with leaven, for no leaven or honey may be turned into smoke as an offering by fire to יהוה. ¹²You may bring them to יהוה as an offering of *ʿchoice products;ʿ* but they shall not be offered up on the altar for a pleasing odor. ¹³You shall season your every offering of meal with salt; you shall not omit from your meal offering

the salt of your covenant with God; with all your offerings you must offer salt.

¹⁴If you bring a meal offering of first fruits to יהוה, you shall bring new ears parched with fire, grits of the fresh grain, as your meal offering of first fruits. ¹⁵You shall add oil to it and lay frankincense on it; it is a meal offering. ¹⁶And the priest shall turn a token portion of it into smoke: some of the grits and oil, with all of the frankincense, as an offering by fire to יהוה.

3 If your° offering is a *⁻sacrifice of well-being⁻*—
If you offer of the herd, whether a male or a female, you shall bring before יהוה one without blemish. ²You shall lay a hand upon the head of your offering and slaughter it at the entrance of the Tent of Meeting; and Aaron's sons, the priests, shall dash the blood against all sides of the altar. ³Then present° from the sacrifice of well-being, as an offering by fire to יהוה, the fat that covers the entrails and all the fat that is about the entrails; ⁴the two kidneys and the fat that is on them, that is at the loins; and the protuberance on the liver, which you° shall remove with the kidneys. ⁵Aaron's sons shall turn these into smoke on the altar, with the burnt offering which is upon the wood that is on the fire, as an offering by fire, of pleasing odor to יהוה.

⁶And if your° offering for a sacrifice of well-being to יהוה is from the flock, whether a male or a female, you shall offer one without blemish. ⁷If you present a sheep as your offering, you shall bring it before יהוה ⁸and lay a hand upon the head of your offering. It shall be slaughtered before the Tent of Meeting, and Aaron's sons shall dash its blood against all sides of the altar. ⁹Then present, as an offering by fire to יהוה, the fat from the sacrifice of well-being: the whole broad tail, which you shall remove close to the backbone; the fat that covers the entrails and all the fat that is about the entrails; ¹⁰the two kidneys and the fat that is on them, that is at the loins; and the protuberance on the liver, which you shall remove with the kidneys. ¹¹The priest shall turn these into smoke on the altar as food, an offering by fire to יהוה.

¹²And if your° offering is a goat, you shall bring it before יהוה ¹³and lay a hand upon its head. It shall be slaughtered before the Tent of Meeting, and Aaron's sons shall dash its blood against all

Va-yikra' 159

sides of the altar. ¹⁴Then present° as your offering from it, as an offering by fire to יהוה, the fat that covers the entrails and all the fat that is about the entrails; ¹⁵the two kidneys and the fat that is on them, that is at the loins; and the protuberance on the liver, which you° shall remove with the kidneys. ¹⁶The priest shall turn these into smoke on the altar as food, an offering by fire, of pleasing odor.

All fat is יהוה's. ¹⁷It is a law for all time throughout the ages, in all your settlements: you must not eat any fat or any blood.

4 יהוה spoke to Moses, saying: ²Speak to the Israelite people thus:

When a person unwittingly incurs guilt in regard to any of יהוה's commandments about things not to be done, and does one of them—

³If it is the anointed priest who has incurred guilt, so that blame falls upon the people, he shall offer for the sin of which he is guilty a bull of the herd without blemish as a *⁻sin offering* to יהוה. ⁴He shall bring the bull to the entrance of the Tent of Meeting, before יהוה, and lay a hand upon the head of the bull. The bull shall be slaughtered before יהוה, ⁵and the anointed priest shall take some of the bull's blood and bring it into the Tent of Meeting. ⁶The priest shall dip his finger in the blood, and sprinkle of the blood seven times before יהוה, in front of the curtain of the Shrine. ⁷The priest shall put some of the blood on the horns of the altar of aromatic incense, which is in the Tent of Meeting, before יהוה; and all the rest of the bull's blood he shall pour out at the base of the altar of burnt offering, which is at the entrance of the Tent of Meeting. ⁸He shall remove all the fat from the bull of sin offering: the fat that covers the entrails and all the fat that is about the entrails; ⁹the two kidneys and the fat that is on them, that is at the loins; and the protuberance on the liver, which he shall remove with the kidneys—¹⁰just as it is removed from the ox of the sacrifice of well-being. The priest shall turn them into smoke on the altar of burnt offering. ¹¹But the hide of the bull, and all its flesh, as well as its head and legs, its entrails and its dung—¹²all the rest of the bull—he shall carry to a pure place outside the camp, to the ash heap, and burn it up in a wood fire; it shall be burned on the ash heap.

¹³If it is the °ᐧcommunity leadership°̇ of Israel that has erred and the matter escapes the notice of the congregation, so that they do any of the things which by יהוה's commandments ought not to be done, and they realize guilt—¹⁴when the sin through which they incurred guilt becomes known, the congregation shall offer a bull of the herd as a sin offering, and bring it before the Tent of Meeting. ¹⁵The elders of the community shall lay their hands upon the head of the bull before יהוה, and the bull shall be slaughtered before יהוה. ¹⁶The anointed priest shall bring some of the blood of the bull into the Tent of Meeting, ¹⁷and the priest shall dip his finger in the blood and sprinkle of it seven times before יהוה, in front of the curtain. ¹⁸Some of the blood he shall put on the horns of the altar which is before יהוה in the Tent of Meeting, and all the rest of the blood he shall pour out at the base of the altar of burnt offering, which is at the entrance of the Tent of Meeting. ¹⁹He shall remove all its fat from it and turn it into smoke on the altar. ²⁰He shall do with this bull just as is done with the [priest's] bull of sin offering; he shall do the same with it. The priest shall thus make expiation for them, and they shall be forgiven. ²¹He shall carry the bull outside the camp and burn it as he burned the first bull; it is the sin offering of the congregation.

²²In case it is a chieftain who incurs guilt by doing unwittingly any of the things which by the commandment of his God יהוה ought not to be done, and he realizes guilt—²³or the sin of which he is guilty is made known—he shall bring as his offering a male goat without blemish. ²⁴He shall lay a hand upon the goat's head, and it shall be slaughtered at *ᐧthe spot where the burnt offering is slaughtered·* before יהוה; it is a sin offering. ²⁵The priest shall take with his finger some of the blood of the sin offering and put it on the horns of the altar of burnt offering; and the rest of its blood he shall pour out at the base of the altar of burnt offering. ²⁶All its fat he shall turn into smoke on the altar, like the fat of the sacrifice of well-being. The priest shall thus make expiation on his behalf for his sin, and he shall be forgiven.

²⁷If any person from among the populace* unwittingly incurs guilt by doing any of the things which by יהוה's commandments ought not to be done, and realizes guilt—²⁸or the sin of which one is guilty is made known—that person shall bring a female goat

without blemish as an offering for the sin of which that one is guilty. ²⁹The offerer shall lay a hand upon the head of the sin offering. The sin offering shall be slaughtered at the place of the burnt offering. ³⁰The priest shall take with his finger some of its blood and put it on the horns of the altar of burnt offering; and all the rest of its blood he shall pour out at the base of the altar. ³¹The offerer shall remove all its fat, just as the fat is removed from the sacrifice of well-being; and the priest shall turn it into smoke on the altar, for a pleasing odor to יהוה. The priest shall thus make expiation for that person, who shall be forgiven.

³²If the offering one brings as a sin offering is a sheep, that person shall bring a female without blemish. ³³The offerer shall lay a hand upon the head of the sin offering, and it shall be slaughtered as a sin offering at the spot where the burnt offering is slaughtered. ³⁴The priest shall take with his finger some of the blood of the sin offering and put it on the horns of the altar of burnt offering, and all the rest of its blood he shall pour out at the base of the altar. ³⁵And all its fat the offerer shall remove, just as the fat of the sheep of the sacrifice of well-being is removed; and this the priest shall turn into smoke on the altar, over יהוה's offering by fire. For the sin of which one is guilty, the priest shall thus make expiation on behalf of that person, who shall be forgiven.

5 If a person incurs guilt—
When one has heard a public imprecation* but (although able to testify as having either seen or learned of the matter) has not given information and thus is subject to punishment;

²Or when a person touches any impure thing (be it the carcass of an impure beast or the carcass of impure cattle or the carcass of an impure creeping thing) and the fact has escaped notice, and then, being impure, that person realizes guilt;

³Or when one touches human impurity (any such impurity whereby someone becomes impure) and, though having known about it, the fact has escaped notice, but later that person realizes guilt;

⁴Or when a person utters* an oath to bad or good purpose (whatever a human being may utter in an oath) and, though having known about it, the fact has escaped notice, but later that person realizes guilt in any of these matters—

⁵upon realizing guilt in any of these matters, one shall confess having sinned in that way. ⁶And one shall bring as a penalty to יהוה, for the sin of which one is guilty, a female from the flock, sheep or goat, as a sin offering; and the priest shall make expiation for the sin, on that person's behalf.

⁷But if one's means do not suffice for a sheep, that person shall bring to יהוה, as the penalty for that of which one is guilty, two turtledoves or two pigeons—one for a sin offering and the other for a burnt offering. ⁸The offerer shall bring them to the priest, who shall offer first the bird for the sin offering, pinching its head at the nape without severing it. ⁹He shall sprinkle some of the blood of the sin offering on the side of the altar, and what remains of the blood shall be drained out at the base of the altar; it is a sin offering. ¹⁰And the second bird he shall prepare as a burnt offering, according to regulation. For the sin of which one is guilty, the priest shall thus make expiation on behalf of that person, who shall be forgiven.

¹¹And if one's means do not suffice for two turtledoves or two pigeons, that person shall bring as an offering for that of which one is guilty a tenth of an *ephah* of choice flour for a sin offering; one shall not add oil to it or lay frankincense on it, for it is a sin offering. ¹²The offerer shall bring it to the priest, and the priest shall scoop out of it a handful as a token portion and turn it into smoke on the altar, with יהוה's offerings by fire; it is a sin offering. ¹³For whichever of these sins one is guilty, the priest shall thus make expiation on behalf of that person, who shall be forgiven. It shall belong to the priest, like the meal offering.

¹⁴And יהוה spoke to Moses, saying:
¹⁵When a person commits a trespass, being unwittingly remiss about any of יהוה's sacred things: One shall bring as a penalty to יהוה a ram without blemish from the flock, convertible into payment in silver by the sanctuary weight, as a guilt offering. ¹⁶That person shall make restitution for the remission regarding the sacred things, adding a fifth part to it and giving it to the priest. The priest shall make expiation with the ram of the guilt offering on behalf of that person, who shall be forgiven.

¹⁷And a person who, without knowing it, sins in regard to any of יהוה's commandments about things not to be done, and then

realizes guilt: Such a person shall be subject to punishment. [18]That person shall bring to the priest a ram without blemish from the flock, or *˞the equivalent,˞* as a guilt offering. For the error committed unwittingly, the priest shall make expiation on behalf of that person, who shall be forgiven. [19]It is a guilt offering; guilt has been incurred before יהוה.

[20]*יהוה spoke to Moses, saying: [21]When a person sins and commits a trespass against יהוה—by dealing deceitfully with another in the matter of a deposit or a pledge,* or through robbery, or by defrauding another, [22]or by finding something lost and lying about it; if one swears falsely regarding any one of the various things that someone may do and sin thereby—[23]when one has thus sinned and, realizing guilt, would restore either that which was gotten through robbery or fraud, or the entrusted deposit, or the lost thing that was found, [24]or anything else about which one swore falsely, that person shall repay the principal amount and add a fifth part to it. One shall pay it to its owner upon realizing guilt. [25]Then that person shall bring to the priest, as a penalty to יהוה, a ram without blemish from the flock, or *˞the equivalent,˞* as a guilt offering. [26]The priest shall make expiation before יהוה on behalf of that person, who shall be forgiven for whatever was done to draw blame thereby.

צַו | TSAV

6 יהוה spoke to Moses, saying: [2]Command Aaron and his sons thus:

This is the ritual of the burnt offering: The burnt offering itself shall remain where it is burned upon the altar all night until morning, while the fire on the altar is kept going on it. [3]The priest shall dress in linen raiment, with linen breeches next to his body; and he shall take up the ashes to which the fire has reduced the burnt offering on the altar and place them beside the altar. [4]He shall then take off his vestments and put on other vestments, and carry the ashes outside the camp to a pure place. [5]The fire on the altar shall be kept burning, not to go out: every morning the priest shall feed wood to it, lay out the burnt offering on it, and turn into smoke the fat parts of the offerings of well-being. [6]A perpetual fire shall be kept burning on the altar, not to go out.

⁷And this is the ritual of the meal offering: Aaron's sons shall present it before יהוה, in front of the altar. ⁸A handful of the choice flour and oil of the meal offering shall be taken from it, with all the frankincense that is on the meal offering, and this token portion shall be turned into smoke on the altar as a pleasing odor to יהוה. ⁹What is left of it shall be eaten by Aaron and his sons; it shall be eaten as unleavened cakes, in the sacred precinct; they shall eat it in the enclosure of the Tent of Meeting. ¹⁰It shall not be baked with leaven; I have given it as their portion from My offerings by fire; it is most holy, like the sin offering and the guilt offering. ¹¹Only the males among Aaron's descendants may eat of it, as their due for all time throughout the ages from יהוה's offerings by fire. Anything that touches these shall become holy.

¹²יהוה spoke to Moses, saying: ¹³This is the offering that Aaron and his sons shall offer to יהוה on the occasion of his* anointment: a tenth of an *ephah* of choice flour as a regular meal offering, half of it in the morning and half of it in the evening, ¹⁴shall be prepared with oil on a griddle. You shall bring it well soaked, and offer it as a meal offering of baked slices,* of pleasing odor to יהוה. ¹⁵And so shall the priest, anointed from among his sons to succeed him, prepare it; it is יהוה's—a law for all time—to be turned entirely into smoke. ¹⁶So, too, every meal offering of a priest shall be a whole offering: it shall not be eaten.

¹⁷יהוה spoke to Moses, saying: ¹⁸Speak to Aaron and his sons thus: This is the ritual of the sin offering: the sin offering shall be slaughtered before יהוה, *⁻at the spot⁻* where the burnt offering is slaughtered: it is most holy. ¹⁹The priest who offers it as a sin offering shall eat of it; it shall be eaten in the sacred precinct, in the enclosure of the Tent of Meeting. ²⁰Anything that touches its flesh shall become holy; and if any of its blood is spattered upon a garment, you shall wash the bespattered part in the sacred precinct. ²¹An earthen vessel in which it was boiled shall be broken; if it was boiled in a copper vessel, [the vessel] shall be scoured and rinsed with water. ²²Only the males in the priestly line may eat of it: it is most holy. ²³But no sin offering may be eaten from which any blood is brought into the Tent of Meeting for expiation in the sanctuary; any such shall be consumed in fire.

7 This is the ritual of the guilt offering: it is most holy. ²The guilt offering shall be slaughtered at the spot where the burnt offering is slaughtered, and the blood shall be dashed on all sides of the altar. ³All its fat shall be offered: the broad tail; the fat that covers the entrails; ⁴the two kidneys and the fat that is on them at the loins; and the protuberance on the liver, which shall be removed with the kidneys. ⁵The priest shall turn them into smoke on the altar as an offering by fire to יהוה; it is a guilt offering. ⁶Only the males in the priestly line may eat of it; it shall be eaten in the sacred precinct: it is most holy.

⁷The guilt offering is like the sin offering. The same rule applies to both: it shall belong to the priest who makes expiation thereby. ⁸So, too, the priest who offers a person's burnt offering shall keep the skin of the burnt offering that was offered. ⁹Further, any meal offering that is baked in an oven, and any that is prepared in a pan or on a griddle, shall belong to the priest who offers it. ¹⁰But every other meal offering, with oil mixed in or dry, shall go to the sons of Aaron all alike.

¹¹This is the ritual of the sacrifice of well-being that one may offer to יהוה:

¹²One who offers it for thanksgiving shall offer, together with the sacrifice of thanksgiving, unleavened cakes with oil mixed in—unleavened wafers spread with oil—and cakes of choice flour with oil mixed in, well soaked. ¹³This offering, with cakes of leavened bread added, shall be offered along with one's thanksgiving sacrifice of well-being. ¹⁴Out of this the person shall offer one of each kind* as a gift to יהוה; it shall go to the priest who dashes the blood of the offering of well-being. ¹⁵And the flesh of the thanksgiving sacrifice of well-being shall be eaten on the day that it is offered; none of it shall be set aside until morning.

¹⁶If, however, the sacrifice offered is a votive or a freewill offering, it shall be eaten on the day that one offers the sacrifice, and what is left of it shall be eaten on the morrow. ¹⁷What is then left of the flesh of the sacrifice shall be consumed in fire on the third day. ¹⁸If any of the flesh of the sacrifice of well-being is eaten on the third day, it shall not be acceptable; it shall not count for the

one who offered it. It is an offensive thing, and the person who eats of it shall bear the guilt.

¹⁹Flesh that touches anything impure shall not be eaten; it shall be consumed in fire. As for other flesh, only one who is pure may eat such flesh. ²⁰But the person who, in a state of impurity, eats flesh from יהוה's sacrifices of well-being, that person shall be cut off from kin. ²¹When a person touches anything impure, be it human impurity or an impure animal or any impure creature,* and eats flesh from יהוה's sacrifices of well-being, that person shall be cut off from kin.

²²And יהוה spoke to Moses, saying: ²³Speak to the Israelite people thus: You shall eat no fat* of ox or sheep or goat. ²⁴Fat from animals that died or were torn by beasts may be put to any use, but you must not eat it. ²⁵If anyone eats the fat of animals from which offerings by fire may be made to יהוה, the person who eats it shall be cut off from kin. ²⁶And you must not consume any blood, either of bird or of animal, in any of your settlements. ²⁷Anyone who eats blood shall be cut off from kin.

²⁸And יהוה spoke to Moses, saying: ²⁹Speak to the Israelite people thus: The offering to יהוה from a sacrifice of well-being must be presented by the one who offers that sacrifice of well-being to יהוה: ³⁰one's own hands shall present יהוה's offerings by fire. The offerer shall present the fat with the breast, the breast to be elevated as an elevation offering before יהוה; ³¹the priest shall turn the fat into smoke on the altar, and the breast shall go to Aaron and his sons. ³²And the right thigh from your sacrifices of well-being you shall present to the priest as a gift; ³³he from among Aaron's sons who offers the blood and the fat of the offering of well-being shall get the right thigh as his portion. ³⁴For I have taken the breast of elevation offering and the thigh of gift offering from the Israelites, from their sacrifices of well-being, and given them to Aaron the priest and to his sons as their due from the Israelites for all time.

³⁵Those shall be the perquisites* of Aaron and the perquisites of his sons from יהוה's offerings by fire, once they have been inducted* to serve יהוה as priests; ³⁶these יהוה commanded to be

given them, once they had been anointed, as a due from the Israelites for all time throughout the ages.

³⁷Such are the rituals of the burnt offering, the meal offering,
the sin offering, the guilt offering, the offering of ordination, and
the sacrifice of well-being, ³⁸with which יהוה charged Moses on
Mount Sinai, when commanding that the Israelites present their
offerings to יהוה, in the wilderness of Sinai.

8 יהוה spoke to Moses, saying: ²Take Aaron along with his sons,
and the vestments, the anointing oil, the bull of sin offering,
the two rams, and the basket of unleavened bread; ³and assemble the
°⁻community leadership° at the entrance of the Tent of Meeting.
⁴Moses did as יהוה commanded him. And when the leadership° was
assembled at the entrance of the Tent of Meeting, ⁵Moses said to the
leadership,° "This is what יהוה has commanded to be done."

⁶Then Moses brought Aaron and his sons forward and washed
them with water. ⁷He put the tunic on him, girded him with the
sash, clothed him with the robe, and put the ephod on him, gird-
ing him with the decorated band with which he tied it to him.
⁸He put the breastpiece on him, and put into the breastpiece the
⁻Urim and Thummim. ⁹And he set the headdress on his head;
and on the headdress, in front, he put the gold frontlet, the holy
diadem—as יהוה had commanded Moses.

¹⁰Moses took the anointing oil and anointed the Tabernacle and
all that was in it, thus consecrating them. ¹¹He sprinkled some of
it on the altar seven times, anointing the altar, all its utensils, and
the laver with its stand, to consecrate them. ¹²He poured some of
the anointing oil upon Aaron's head and anointed him, to consecrate him. ¹³Moses then brought Aaron's sons forward, clothed
them in tunics, girded them with sashes, and wound turbans upon
them, as יהוה had commanded Moses.

¹⁴He led forward the bull of sin offering. Aaron and his sons
laid their hands upon the head of the bull of sin offering, ¹⁵and it
was slaughtered. Moses took the blood and with his finger put
some on each of the horns of the altar, purifying the altar; then he
poured out the blood at the base of the altar. Thus he consecrated
it in order to make expiation upon it.

¹⁶Moses then took all the fat that was about the entrails, and the protuberance of the liver, and the two kidneys and their fat, and turned them into smoke on the altar. ¹⁷The rest of the bull, its hide, its flesh, and its dung, he put to the fire outside the camp—as יהוה had commanded Moses.

¹⁸Then he brought forward the ram of burnt offering. Aaron and his sons laid their hands upon the ram's head, ¹⁹and it was slaughtered. Moses dashed the blood against all sides of the altar. ²⁰The ram was cut up into sections and Moses turned the head, the sections, and the suet into smoke on the altar; ²¹Moses washed the entrails and the legs with water and turned all of the ram into smoke. That was a burnt offering for a pleasing odor, an offering by fire to יהוה—as יהוה had commanded Moses.

²²He brought forward the second ram, the ram of ordination. Aaron and his sons laid their hands upon the ram's head, ²³and it was slaughtered. Moses took some of its blood and put it on the ridge* of Aaron's right ear, and on the thumb of his right hand, and on the big toe of his right foot. ²⁴Moses then brought forward the sons of Aaron, and put some of the blood on the ridges of their right ears, and on the thumbs of their right hands, and on the big toes of their right feet; and the rest of the blood Moses dashed against every side of the altar. ²⁵He took the fat—the broad tail, all the fat about the entrails, the protuberance of the liver, and the two kidneys and their fat—and the right thigh. ²⁶From the basket of unleavened bread that was before יהוה, he took one cake of unleavened bread, one cake of oil bread, and one wafer, and placed them on the fat parts and on the right thigh. ²⁷He placed all these on the palms of Aaron and on the palms of his sons, and elevated them as an elevation offering before יהוה. ²⁸Then Moses took them from their hands and turned them into smoke on the altar with the burnt offering. This was an ordination offering for a pleasing odor; it was an offering by fire to יהוה. ²⁹Moses took the breast and elevated it as an elevation offering before יהוה; it was Moses' portion of the ram of ordination—as יהוה had commanded Moses.

³⁰And Moses took some of the anointing oil and some of the blood that was on the altar and sprinkled it upon Aaron and upon his vestments, and also upon his sons and upon their vestments.

Thus he consecrated Aaron and his vestments, and also his sons and their vestments.

³¹Moses said to Aaron and his sons: Boil the flesh at the entrance of the Tent of Meeting and eat it there with the bread that is in the basket of ordination—as *ˑI commanded:ˑ* Aaron and his sons shall eat it; ³²and what is left over of the flesh and the bread you shall consume in fire. ³³You shall not go outside the entrance of the Tent of Meeting for seven days, until the day that your period of ordination is completed. For your ordination will require seven days. ³⁴Everything done today, יהוה has commanded to be done [seven days], to make expiation for you. ³⁵You shall remain at the entrance of the Tent of Meeting day and night for seven days, keeping יהוה's charge—that you may not die—for so I have been commanded.

³⁶And Aaron and his sons did all the things that יהוה had commanded through Moses.

שְׁמִינִי | SHEMINI

9 On the eighth day Moses called Aaron and his sons, and the elders of Israel. ²He said to Aaron: "Take a calf of the herd for a sin offering and a ram for a burnt offering, without blemish, and bring them before יהוה. ³And speak to the Israelites, saying: Take a he-goat for a sin offering; a calf and a lamb, yearlings without blemish, for a burnt offering; ⁴and an ox and a ram for an offering of well-being to sacrifice before יהוה; and a meal offering with oil mixed in. For today יהוה will appear to you."

⁵They brought to the front of the Tent of Meeting the things that Moses had commanded, and the °community leadership° came forward and stood before יהוה. ⁶Moses said: "This is what יהוה has commanded that you do, that the Presence of יהוה may appear to you." ⁷Then Moses said to Aaron: "Come forward to the altar and sacrifice your sin offering and your burnt offering, making expiation for yourself and for the people; and sacrifice the people's offering and make expiation for them, as יהוה has commanded."

⁸Aaron came forward to the altar and slaughtered his calf of sin offering. ⁹Aaron's sons brought the blood to him; he dipped his finger in the blood and put it on the horns of the altar; and he poured out the rest of the blood at the base of the altar. ¹⁰The fat,

the kidneys, and the protuberance of the liver from the sin offering he turned into smoke on the altar—as יהוה had commanded
Moses; ¹¹and the flesh and the skin were consumed in fire outside
the camp. ¹²Then he slaughtered the burnt offering. Aaron's sons
passed the blood to him, and he dashed it against all sides of the
altar. ¹³They passed the burnt offering to him in sections, as well
as the head, and he turned it into smoke on the altar. ¹⁴He washed
the entrails and the legs, and turned them into smoke on the altar
with the burnt offering.

¹⁵Next he brought forward the people's offering. He took the
goat for the people's sin offering, and slaughtered it, and presented
it as a sin offering like the previous one. ¹⁶He brought forward the
burnt offering and sacrificed it according to regulation. ¹⁷He then
brought forward the meal offering and, taking a handful of it, he
turned it into smoke on the altar—in addition to the *⁻burnt offering of the morning.⁻* ¹⁸He slaughtered the ox and the ram, the
people's sacrifice of well-being. Aaron's sons passed the blood to
him—which he dashed against every side of the altar—¹⁹and the
fat parts of the ox and the ram: the broad tail, the covering [fat],
the kidneys, and the protuberances of the livers. ²⁰They laid these
fat parts over the breasts; and Aaron* turned the fat parts into
smoke on the altar, ²¹and elevated the breasts and the right thighs
as an elevation offering before יהוה—as Moses had commanded.

²²Aaron lifted his hands toward the people and blessed them;
and he stepped down after offering the sin offering, the burnt offering, and the offering of well-being. ²³Moses and Aaron then
went inside the Tent of Meeting. When they came out, they blessed
the people; and the Presence of יהוה appeared to all the people.
²⁴Fire came forth from before יהוה and consumed the burnt offering and the fat parts on the altar. And all the people saw, and
shouted, and fell on their faces.

10 Now Aaron's sons Nadab and Abihu each took his fire
pan, put fire in it, and laid incense on it; and they offered
before יהוה alien fire, which had not been enjoined upon them.
²And fire came forth from יהוה and consumed them; thus they
died *⁻at the instance of⁻* יהוה. ³Then Moses said to Aaron, "This
is what יהוה meant by saying:

Through those near to Me I show Myself holy,
And gain glory before all the people."
And Aaron was silent.

⁴Moses called Mishael and Elzaphan, sons of Uzziel the uncle of Aaron, and said to them, "Come forward and carry your kinsmen away from the front of the sanctuary to a place outside the camp." ⁵They came forward and carried them out of the camp by their tunics, as Moses had ordered. ⁶And Moses said to Aaron and to his sons Eleazar and Ithamar, "Do not *-bare your heads-* and do not rend your clothes, lest you die and anger strike the whole community. But your kin,° all the house of Israel, shall bewail the burning that יהוה has wrought. ⁷And so do not go outside the entrance of the Tent of Meeting, lest you die, for יהוה's anointing oil is upon you." And they did as Moses had bidden.

⁸And יהוה spoke to Aaron, saying: ⁹Drink no wine or other intoxicant, you or your sons, when you enter the Tent of Meeting, that you may not die. This is a law for all time throughout the ages, ¹⁰for you must distinguish between the sacred and the profane, and between the impure and the pure; ¹¹and you must teach the Israelites all the laws which יהוה has imparted to them through Moses.

¹²Moses spoke to Aaron and to his remaining sons, Eleazar and Ithamar: Take the meal offering that is left over from יהוה's offerings by fire and eat it unleavened beside the altar, for it is most holy. ¹³You shall eat it in the sacred precinct, inasmuch as it is your due, and that of your sons, from יהוה's offerings by fire; for so I have been commanded. ¹⁴But the breast of elevation offering and the thigh of gift offering you [and your wife], and your sons and daughters with you, may eat in any pure place, for they have been assigned as a due to you and your sons from the Israelites' sacrifices of well-being. ¹⁵Together with the fat of fire offering, they must present the thigh of gift offering and the breast of elevation offering, which are to be elevated as an elevation offering before יהוה, and which are to be your due and that of your sons with you for all time—as יהוה has commanded.

¹⁶Then Moses inquired about the goat of sin offering, and it had already been burned! He was angry with Eleazar and Ithamar,

Aaron's remaining sons, and said, [17]"Why did you not eat the sin offering in the sacred area? For it is most holy, and it is what was given to you to remove the guilt of the community and to make expiation for them before יהוה. [18]Since its blood was not *‑brought inside the sanctuary,* you should certainly have eaten it in the sanctuary, as I commanded." [19]And Aaron spoke to Moses, "See, this day they brought their sin offering and their burnt offering before יהוה, and such things have befallen me! Had I eaten sin offering today, would יהוה have approved?" [20]And when Moses heard this, he approved.

11 יהוה spoke to Moses and Aaron, saying to them: [2]Speak to the Israelite people thus:

These are the creatures that you may eat from among all the land animals: [3]any animal that has true hoofs, with clefts through the hoofs, and that chews* the cud—such you may eat. [4]The following, however, of those that either chew the cud or have true hoofs, you shall not eat: the camel—although it chews the cud, it has no true hoofs: it is impure for you; [5]the daman—although it chews the cud, it has no true hoofs: it is impure for you; [6]the hare—although it chews the cud, it has no true hoofs: it is impure for you; [7]and the swine—although it has true hoofs, with the hoofs cleft through, it does not chew the cud: it is impure for you. [8]You shall not eat of their flesh or touch their carcasses; they are impure for you.

[9]These you may eat of all that live in water: anything in water, whether in the seas or in the streams, that has fins and scales— these you may eat. [10]But anything in the seas or in the streams that has no fins and scales, among all the swarming things of the water and among all the other living creatures that are in the water— they are an abomination for you [11]and an abomination for you they shall remain: you shall not eat of their flesh and you shall abominate their carcasses. [12]Everything in water that has no fins and scales shall be an abomination for you.

[13]The following* you shall abominate among the birds—they shall not be eaten, they are an abomination: the eagle, the vulture, and the black vulture; [14]the kite, falcons of every variety; [15]all varieties of raven; [16]the ostrich, the nighthawk, the sea gull; hawks

of every variety; [17]the little owl, the cormorant, and the great owl; [18]the white owl, the pelican, and the bustard; [19]the stork; herons of every variety; the hoopoe, and the bat.

[20]All winged swarming things that walk on fours shall be an abomination for you. [21]But these you may eat among all the winged swarming things that walk on fours: all that have, above their feet, jointed legs to leap with on the ground—[22]of these you may eat the following: locusts of every variety; all varieties of bald locust; crickets of every variety; and all varieties of grasshopper. [23]But all other winged swarming things that have four legs shall be an abomination for you.

[24]And the following shall make you impure—whoever touches their carcasses shall be impure until evening, [25]and whoever carries the carcasses of any of them shall wash those clothes and be impure until evening—[26]every animal that has true hoofs but without clefts through the hoofs, or that does not chew the cud. They are impure for you; whoever touches them shall be impure. [27]Also all animals that walk on paws, among those that walk on fours, are impure for you; whoever touches their carcasses shall be impure until evening. [28]And anyone who carries their carcasses shall wash those clothes and remain impure until evening. They are impure for you.

[29]The following shall be impure for you from among the things that swarm on the earth: the mole, the mouse, and great lizards of every variety; [30]the gecko, the land crocodile, the lizard, the sand lizard, and the chameleon. [31]Those are for you the impure among all the swarming things; whoever touches them when they are dead shall be impure until evening. [32]And anything on which one of them falls when dead shall be impure: be it any article of wood, or a cloth, or a skin, or a sack—any such article that can be put to use shall be dipped in water, and it shall remain impure until evening; then it shall be pure. [33]And if any of those falls into an earthen vessel, everything inside it shall be impure and [the vessel] itself you shall break. [34]As to any food that may be eaten, it shall become impure *̄if it came in contact with water;⁻* as to any liquid that may be drunk, it shall become impure *̄if it was inside any vessel.⁻* [35]Everything on which the carcass of any of them falls shall be impure: an oven or stove shall be smashed. They are

impure—and impure they shall remain for you. ³⁶However, a spring or cistern in which water is collected shall be pure, but whoever touches such a carcass in it shall be impure. ³⁷If such a carcass falls upon seed grain that is to be sown, it is pure; ³⁸but if water is put on the seed and any part of a carcass falls upon it, it shall be impure for you.

³⁹If an animal that you may eat has died, anyone who touches its carcass shall be impure until evening; ⁴⁰anyone who eats of its carcass shall wash those clothes and remain impure until evening; and anyone who carries its carcass shall wash those clothes and remain impure until evening.

⁴¹All the things that swarm upon the earth are an abomination; they shall not be eaten. ⁴²You shall not eat, among all things that swarm upon the earth, anything that crawls on its belly, or anything that walks on fours, or anything that has many legs; for they are an abomination. ⁴³You shall not draw abomination upon yourselves through anything that swarms; you shall not make yourselves impure therewith and thus become impure. ⁴⁴For I יהוה am your God: you shall sanctify yourselves and be holy, for I am holy. You shall not make yourselves impure through any swarming thing that moves upon the earth. ⁴⁵For I יהוה am the One who brought you up from the land of Egypt to be your God: you shall be holy, for I am holy.

⁴⁶These are the instructions concerning animals, birds, all living creatures that move in water, and all creatures that swarm on earth, ⁴⁷for distinguishing between the impure and the pure, between the living things that may be eaten and the living things that may not be eaten.

תַזְרִיעַ | TAZRIA'

12 יהוה spoke to Moses, saying: ²Speak to the Israelite people thus: When a woman *⁻at childbirth⁻* bears a male, she shall be impure seven days; she shall be impure as at the time of her condition of menstrual separation.—³On the eighth day the flesh of his foreskin shall be circumcised.—⁴She shall remain in a *⁻state of blood purification⁻* for thirty-three days: she shall not touch any consecrated thing, nor enter the sanctuary until her period of purification is completed. ⁵If she bears a female, she shall be impure two weeks as during her menstruation, and she shall remain in a *ˉstate of blood purificationˉ* for sixty-six days.

⁶On the completion of her period of purification, for either son or daughter, she shall bring to the priest, at the entrance of the Tent of Meeting, a lamb in its first year for a burnt offering, and a pigeon or a turtledove for a *ˉsin offering.ˉ* ⁷He shall offer it before יהוה and make expiation on her behalf; she shall then be pure from her flow of blood. Such are the rituals concerning her who bears a child, male or female. ⁸If, however, her means do not suffice for a sheep, she shall take two turtledoves or two pigeons, one for a burnt offering and the other for a sin offering. The priest shall make expiation on her behalf, and she shall be pure.

13 יהוה spoke to Moses and Aaron, saying: ²When a person has on the skin of the body a swelling, a rash, or a discoloration, and it develops into a scaly affection on the skin of the body, *ˉit shall be reportedˉ* to Aaron the priest or to one of his sons, the priests. ³The priest shall examine the affection on the skin of the body: if hair in the affected patch has turned white and the affection appears to be deeper than the skin of the body, it is a leprous* affection; when the priest sees it, he shall pronounce the person impure. ⁴But if it is a white discoloration on the skin of the body which does not appear to be deeper than the skin and the hair in it has not turned white, the priest shall isolate the affected person for seven days. ⁵On the seventh day the priest shall conduct an examination, and if the affection has remained unchanged in color and the disease has not spread on the skin, the priest shall isolate that person for another seven days. ⁶On the seventh day the priest shall again conduct an examination: if the affection has faded and has not spread on the skin, the priest shall pronounce the person pure. It is a rash; after washing those clothes, that person shall be pure. ⁷But if the rash should spread on the skin after the person has been seen by the priest and pronounced pure, that person shall again report to the priest. ⁸And if the priest sees that the rash has spread on the skin, the priest shall pronounce that person impure; it is leprosy.

⁹When a person has a scaly affection, *ˉit shall be reportedˉ* to the priest. ¹⁰If the priest finds on the skin a white swelling which

has turned some hair white, with *⁻a patch of undiscolored flesh⁻* in the swelling, [11]it is chronic leprosy on the skin of the body, and the priest shall pronounce the person impure; being impure, that person need not be isolated. [12]If the eruption spreads out over the skin so that it covers all the skin of the affected person from head to foot, wherever the priest can see—[13]if the priest sees that the eruption has covered the whole body—he shall pronounce as pure the affected person, who is pure from having turned all white. [14]But as soon as undiscolored flesh appears in it, that person shall be impure; [15]when the priest sees the undiscolored flesh, he shall pronounce the person impure. The undiscolored flesh is impure; it is leprosy. [16]But if the undiscolored flesh again turns white, that person shall come to the priest, [17]and the priest shall conduct an examination: if the affection has turned white, the priest shall pronounce as pure the affected person, who is then pure.

[18]When an inflammation appears on the skin of one's body and it heals, [19]and a white swelling or a white discoloration streaked with red develops where the inflammation was, that person shall report to the priest. [20]If the priest finds that it appears lower than the rest of the skin and that the hair in it has turned white, the priest shall pronounce the person impure; it is a leprous affection that has broken out in the inflammation. [21]But if the priest finds that there is no white hair in it and it is not lower than the rest of the skin, and it is faded, the priest shall isolate that person for seven days. [22]If it should spread in the skin, the priest shall pronounce the person impure; it is an affection. [23]But if the discoloration remains stationary, not having spread, it is the scar of the inflammation; the priest shall pronounce that person pure.

[24]When the skin of one's body sustains a burn by fire, and the patch from the burn is a discoloration, either white streaked with red, or white, [25]the priest shall examine it. If some hair has turned white in the discoloration, which itself appears to go deeper than the skin, it is leprosy that has broken out in the burn. The priest shall pronounce the person impure; it is a leprous affection. [26]But if the priest finds that there is no white hair in the discoloration, and that it is not lower than the rest of the skin, and it is faded, the priest shall isolate that person for seven days. [27]On the seventh

day the priest shall conduct an examination: if it has spread in the skin, the priest shall pronounce the person impure; it is a leprous affection. 28But if the discoloration has remained stationary, not having spread on the skin, and it is faded, it is the swelling from the burn. The priest shall pronounce that person pure, for it is the scar of the burn.

29If a man or a woman has an affection on the head or in his beard, 30the priest shall examine the affection. If it appears to go deeper than the skin and there is thin yellow hair in it, the priest shall pronounce the person impure; it is a scall, a scaly eruption in the hair or beard. 31But if the priest finds that the scall affection does not appear to go deeper than the skin, yet there is no black hair in it, the priest shall isolate the person with the scall affection for seven days. 32On the seventh day the priest shall examine the affection. If the scall has not spread and no yellow hair has appeared in it, and the scall does not appear to go deeper than the skin, 33the person with the scall shall shave—but without shaving the scall; the priest shall isolate that person for another seven days. 34On the seventh day the priest shall examine the scall. If the scall has not spread on the skin, and does not appear to go deeper than the skin, the priest shall pronounce the person pure; after washing those clothes, that person shall be pure. 35If, however, the scall should spread on the skin after the person has been pronounced pure, 36the priest shall conduct an examination. If the scall has spread on the skin, the priest need not look for yellow hair: the person is impure. 37But if the scall has remained unchanged in color, and black hair has grown in it, the scall is healed; the person is pure. The priest shall pronounce that person pure.

38If a man or a woman has the skin of the body streaked with white discolorations, 39and the priest sees that the discolorations on the skin of the body are of a dull white, it is a tetter broken out on the skin; that person is pure.

40If a man loses the hair of his head and becomes bald, he is pure. 41If he loses the hair on the front part of his head and becomes bald at the forehead, he is pure. 42But if a white affection streaked with red appears on the bald part in the front or at the back of the head, it is a scaly eruption that is spreading over the bald part in the front or at the back of the head. ⁴³The priest shall examine him: if the swollen affection on the bald part in the front or at the back of his head is white streaked with red, like the leprosy of body skin in appearance, ⁴⁴he is among the leprous; he is impure. The priest shall pronounce him impure; he has the affection on his head.

⁴⁵As for the person with a leprous affection: the clothes shall be rent, the *‑head shall be left bare,‑* and the upper lip shall be covered over; and that person shall call out, "Impure! Impure!" ⁴⁶The person shall be impure as long as the disease is present. Being impure, that person shall dwell apart—in a dwelling outside the camp.

⁴⁷When an eruptive affection occurs in a cloth of wool or linen fabric, ⁴⁸in the warp or in the woof of the linen or the wool, or in a skin or in anything made of skin; ⁴⁹if the affection in the cloth or the skin, in the warp or the woof, or in any article of skin, is streaky green* or red, it is an eruptive affection. It shall be shown to the priest; ⁵⁰and the priest, after examining the affection, shall isolate the affected article for seven days. ⁵¹On the seventh day he shall examine the affection: if the affection has spread in the cloth—whether in the warp or the woof, or in the skin, for whatever purpose the skin may be used—the affection is a malignant eruption; it is impure. ⁵²The cloth—whether warp or woof in wool or linen, or any article of skin—in which the affection is found, shall be burned, for it is a malignant eruption; it shall be consumed in fire. ⁵³But if the priest sees that the affection in the cloth—whether in warp or in woof, or in any article of skin—has not spread, ⁵⁴the priest shall order the affected article washed, and he shall isolate it for another seven days. ⁵⁵And if, after the affected article has been washed, the priest sees that the affection has not changed color and that it has not spread, it is impure. It shall be consumed in fire; it is a fret,* whether on its inner side or on its outer side. ⁵⁶But if the priest sees that the affected part, after it has been washed, is faded, he shall tear it out from the cloth or skin, whether in the warp or in the woof; ⁵⁷and if it occurs again in the cloth—whether in warp or in woof—or in any article of skin, it is a wild growth; the affected article shall be consumed in fire. ⁵⁸If, however, the affection disappears from the

cloth—warp or woof—or from any article of skin that has been washed, it shall be washed again, and it shall be pure.

⁵⁹Such is the procedure for eruptive affections of cloth, woolen or linen, in warp or in woof, or of any article of skin, for pronouncing it pure or impure.

מְצֹרָע | METSORAʻ

14 יהוה spoke to Moses, saying: ²This shall be the ritual for a leper* at the time of being purified.

When *⁻it has been reported⁻* to the priest, ³the priest shall go outside the camp. If the priest sees that the leper has been healed of the scaly affection, ⁴the priest shall order two live pure birds, cedar wood, crimson stuff, and hyssop to be brought for the one to be purified. ⁵The priest shall order one of the birds slaughtered over fresh water in an earthen vessel; ⁶and he shall take the live bird, along with the cedar wood, the crimson stuff, and the hyssop, and dip them together with the live bird in the blood of the bird that was slaughtered over the fresh water. ⁷He shall then sprinkle it seven times on the one to be purified of the eruption and effect the purification; and he shall set the live bird free in the open country. ⁸The one to be purified shall wash those clothes, shave off all hair, and bathe in water—and then shall be pure. After that, the camp may be entered but one must remain outside one's tent seven days. ⁹On the seventh day all hair shall be shaved off—of head, beard [if any], and eyebrows. Having shaved off all hair, the person shall wash those clothes and bathe the body in water—and then shall be pure. ¹⁰On the eighth day that person shall take two male lambs without blemish, one ewe lamb in its first year without blemish, three-tenths of a measure of choice flour with oil mixed in for a meal offering, and one *log* of oil. ¹¹These shall be presented before יהוה, with the person to be purified, at the entrance of the Tent of Meeting, by the priest who performs the purification.

¹²The priest shall take one of the male lambs and offer it with the *log* of oil as a guilt offering, and he shall elevate them as an elevation offering before יהוה. ¹³The lamb shall be slaughtered *⁻at the spot⁻* in the sacred area where the sin offering and the burnt offering are slaughtered. For the guilt offering, like the sin

offering, goes to the priest; it is most holy. ¹⁴The priest shall take some of the blood of the guilt offering, and the priest shall put it on the ridge of the right ear of the one who is being purified, and on the thumb of the right hand, and on the big toe of the right foot. ¹⁵The priest shall then take some of the *log* of oil and pour it into the palm of his own left hand. ¹⁶And the priest shall dip his right finger in the oil that is in the palm of his left hand and sprinkle some of the oil with his finger seven times before יהוה. ¹⁷Some of the oil left in his palm shall be put by the priest on the ridge of the right ear of the one being purified, on the thumb of the right hand, and on the big toe of the right foot—over the blood of the guilt offering. ¹⁸The rest of the oil in his palm the priest shall put on the head of the one being purified. Thus the priest shall make expiation for that person before יהוה. ¹⁹The priest shall then offer the sin offering and make expiation for the one being purified of defilement. Last, the burnt offering shall be slaughtered, ²⁰and the priest shall offer the burnt offering and the meal offering on the altar; the priest shall make expiation for that person, who shall then be pure.

²¹If, however, one is poor and without sufficient means, that person shall take one male lamb for a guilt offering, to be elevated in expiation, one-tenth of a measure of choice flour with oil mixed in for a meal offering, and a *log* of oil; ²²and two turtledoves or two pigeons—depending on that person's means—the one to be the sin offering and the other the burnt offering. ²³On the eighth day of purification, the person shall bring them to the priest at the entrance of the Tent of Meeting, before יהוה. ²⁴The priest shall take the lamb of guilt offering and the *log* of oil, and elevate them as an elevation offering before יהוה. ²⁵When the lamb of guilt offering has been slaughtered, the priest shall take some of the blood of the guilt offering and put it on the ridge of the right ear of the one being purified, on the thumb of the right hand, and on the big toe of the right foot. ²⁶The priest shall then pour some of the oil into the palm of his own left hand, ²⁷and with the finger of his right hand the priest shall sprinkle some of the oil that is in the palm of his left hand seven times before יהוה. ²⁸Some of the oil in his palm shall be put by the priest on the ridge of the right ear of the one being purified, on the thumb of the right hand, and on the

big toe of the right foot, over the same places as the blood of the guilt offering; ²⁹and what is left of the oil in his palm the priest shall put on the head of the one being purified, to make expiation for that person before יהוה. ³⁰That person shall then offer one of the turtledoves or pigeons, depending on the person's means— ³¹whichever that person can afford—the one as a sin offering and the other as a burnt offering, together with the meal offering. Thus the priest shall make expiation before יהוה for the one being puri- fied. ³²Such is the ritual for one who has a scaly affection and whose means for purification are limited.

³³יהוה spoke to Moses and Aaron, saying:

³⁴When you enter the land of Canaan that I give you as a pos- session, and I inflict an eruptive plague upon a house in the land you possess, ³⁵the owner of the house shall come and tell the priest, saying, "Something like a plague has appeared upon my house." ³⁶The priest shall order the house cleared before the priest enters to examine the plague, so that nothing in the house may become impure; after that the priest shall enter to examine the house. ³⁷If, when he examines the plague, the plague in the walls of the house is found to consist of greenish* or reddish streaks* that appear to go deep into the wall, ³⁸the priest shall come out of the house to the entrance of the house, and close up the house for seven days. ³⁹On the seventh day the priest shall return. If he sees that the plague has spread on the walls of the house, ⁴⁰the priest shall order the stones with the plague in them to be pulled out and cast outside the city into an impure place. ⁴¹The house shall be scraped inside all around, and the coating* that is scraped off shall be dumped outside the city in an impure place. ⁴²They shall take other stones and replace those stones with them, and take other coating and plaster the house.

⁴³If the plague again breaks out in the house, after the stones have been pulled out and after the house has been scraped and re- plastered, ⁴⁴the priest shall come to examine: if the plague has spread in the house, it is a malignant eruption in the house; it is impure. ⁴⁵The house shall be torn down—its stones and timber and all the coating on the house—and taken to an impure place outside the city.

⁴⁶Whoever enters the house while it is closed up shall be impure until evening. ⁴⁷Whoever sleeps in the house must wash those clothes, and whoever eats in the house must wash those clothes.

⁴⁸If, however, the priest comes and sees that the plague has not spread in the house after the house was replastered, the priest shall pronounce the house pure, for the plague has healed. ⁴⁹To purge the house, he shall take two birds, cedar wood, crimson stuff, and hyssop. ⁵⁰He shall slaughter the one bird over fresh water in an earthen vessel. ⁵¹He shall take the cedar wood, the hyssop, the crimson stuff, and the live bird, and dip them in the blood of the slaughtered bird and the fresh water, and sprinkle on the house seven times. ⁵²Having purged the house with the blood of the bird, the fresh water, the live bird, the cedar wood, the hyssop, and the crimson stuff, ⁵³he shall set the live bird free outside the city in the open country. Thus he shall make expiation for the house, and it shall be pure.

⁵⁴Such is the ritual for every eruptive affection—for scalls, ⁵⁵for an eruption on a cloth or a house, ⁵⁶for swellings, for rashes, or for discolorations—⁵⁷to determine when they are impure and when they are pure.

Such is the ritual concerning eruptions.

15 יהוה spoke to Moses and Aaron, saying: ²Speak to the Israelite people and say to them:

When any man has a discharge issuing from his member,* he is impure. ³The impurity from his discharge shall mean the following—whether his member runs with the discharge or is stopped up so that there is no discharge, his impurity means this: ⁴Any bedding on which the one with the discharge lies shall be impure, and every object on which he sits shall be impure. ⁵Those° who touch his bedding shall wash their clothes, bathe in water, and remain impure until evening. ⁶All those who sit on an object on which the one with the discharge has sat shall wash their clothes, bathe in water, and remain impure until evening. ⁷Those who touch the body of the one with the discharge shall wash their clothes, bathe in water, and remain impure until evening. ⁸If the one with a discharge spits on someone who is pure, the latter shall wash those clothes, bathe in water, and remain impure until evening. 9Any means for riding that the one with a discharge has mounted shall be impure; 10all those who touch anything that was under him shall be impure until evening; and all those who carry such things shall wash their clothes, bathe in water, and remain impure until evening. 11All those whom the one with a discharge touches, without having rinsed his hands in water, shall wash their clothes, bathe in water, and remain impure until evening. 12An earthen vessel that the one with a discharge touches shall be broken; and any wooden implement shall be rinsed with water.

13When the one with a discharge becomes purified of his discharge, he shall count off seven days for his purification, wash those clothes, and bathe his body in fresh water; then he shall be pure. 14On the eighth day he shall take two turtledoves or two pigeons and come before יהוה at the entrance of the Tent of Meeting and give them to the priest. 15The priest shall offer them, the one as a sin offering and the other as a burnt offering. Thus the priest shall make expiation on his behalf, for his discharge, before יהוה.

16When a man has an emission of semen,° he shall bathe his whole body in water and remain impure until evening. 17All cloth or leather on which semen° falls shall be washed in water and remain impure until evening. 18Likewise for a woman: when a man has carnal relations with her, both shall bathe in water and remain impure until evening.

19When a woman has a discharge, her discharge being blood from her body, she shall remain in her menstrual separation seven days; whoever touches her shall be impure until evening. 20Anything that she lies on during her menstrual separation shall be impure; and anything that she sits on shall be impure. 21°All those° who touch her bedding shall wash their clothes, bathe in water, and remain impure until evening; 22and all those who touch any object on which she has sat shall wash their clothes, bathe in water, and remain impure until evening. 23Be it the bedding or be it the object on which she has sat, on touching it one shall be impure until evening. 24And if a man lies with her, her menstrual separation applies to him; he shall be impure seven days, and any bedding on which he lies shall become impure.

25When a woman has had a discharge of blood for many days, not at the time of her menstrual separation, or when she has a discharge beyond her period of menstrual separation, she shall be impure, as though at the time of her menstrual separation, as long as her discharge lasts. 26Any bedding on which she lies while her discharge lasts shall be for her like bedding during her menstrual separation; and any object on which she sits shall become impure, as it does during her menstrual separation: 27All those who touch them shall be impure—and shall wash their clothes, bathe in water, and remain impure until evening.

28When she becomes purified of her discharge, she shall count off seven days, and after that she shall be pure. 29On the eighth day she shall take two turtledoves or two pigeons, and bring them to the priest at the entrance of the Tent of Meeting. 30The priest shall offer the one as a sin offering and the other as a burnt offering; and the priest shall make expiation on her behalf, for her impure discharge, before יהוה.

31You shall put the Israelites on guard against their impurity, lest they die through their impurity by defiling My Tabernacle which is among them.

32Such is the ritual concerning one who has a discharge: concerning him who has an emission of semen° and becomes impure thereby; 33and concerning her whose condition is that of menstrual separation; and concerning anyone, male or female, who has a discharge; and concerning a man who lies with an impure woman.

אַחֲרֵי מוֹת | 'AHAREI MOT

16 יהוה spoke to Moses after the death of the two sons of Aaron who died when they drew too close to the presence of יהוה. 2יהוה said to Moses:

Tell your brother Aaron that he is not to come *ˉat willˉ* into the Shrine behind the curtain, in front of the cover that is upon the ark, lest he die; for I appear in the cloud over the cover. 3Thus only shall Aaron enter the Shrine: with a bull of the herd for a sin offering and a ram for a burnt offering.—4He shall be dressed in a sacral linen tunic, with linen breeches next to his flesh, and be girt with a linen sash, and he shall wear a linen turban. They are sacral vestments; he shall bathe his body in water and then put them on.—⁵And from the Israelite community he shall take two he-goats for a sin offering and a ram for a burnt offering.

⁶Aaron is to offer his own bull of sin offering, to make expiation for himself and for his household. ⁷Aaron* shall take the two he-goats and let them stand before יהוה at the entrance of the Tent of Meeting; ⁸and he shall place lots upon the two goats, one marked for יהוה and the other marked for Azazel. ⁹Aaron shall bring forward the goat designated by lot for יהוה, which he is to offer as a sin offering; ¹⁰while the goat designated by lot for Azazel shall be left standing alive before יהוה, to make expiation with it and to send it off to the wilderness for Azazel.

¹¹Aaron shall then offer his bull of sin offering, to make expiation for himself and his household. He shall slaughter his bull of sin offering, ¹²and he shall take a panful of glowing coals scooped from the altar before יהוה, and two handfuls of finely ground aromatic incense, and bring this behind the curtain. ¹³He shall put the incense on the fire before יהוה, so that the cloud from the incense screens the cover that is over [the Ark of] the Pact, lest he die. ¹⁴He shall take some of the blood of the bull and sprinkle it with his finger over the cover on the east side; and in front of the cover he shall sprinkle some of the blood with his finger seven times. ¹⁵He shall then slaughter the people's goat of sin offering, bring its blood behind the curtain, and do with its blood as he has done with the blood of the bull: he shall sprinkle it over the cover and in front of the cover.

¹⁶Thus he shall purge the Shrine of the impurity and transgression of the Israelites, whatever their sins; and he shall do the same for the Tent of Meeting, which abides with them in the midst of their impurity. ¹⁷When he goes in to make expiation in the Shrine, nobody else shall be in the Tent of Meeting until he comes out.

When he has made expiation for himself and his household, and for the whole congregation of Israel, ¹⁸he shall go out to the altar that is before יהוה and purge it: he shall take some of the blood of the bull and of the goat and apply it to each of the horns of the altar; ¹⁹and the rest of the blood he shall sprinkle on it with his finger seven times. Thus he shall purify it of the defilement of the Israelites and consecrate it.

²⁰When he has finished purging the Shrine, the Tent of Meeting,

and the altar, the live goat shall be brought forward. ²¹Aaron shall lay both his hands upon the head of the live goat and confess over it all the iniquities and transgressions of the Israelites, whatever their sins, putting them on the head of the goat; and it shall be sent off to the wilderness through a designated* agent.° ²²Thus the goat shall carry on it all their iniquities to an inaccessible region; and the goat shall be set free in the wilderness.

²³And Aaron shall go into the Tent of Meeting, take off the linen vestments that he put on when he entered the Shrine, and leave them there. ²⁴He shall bathe his body in water in the holy precinct and put on his vestments; then he shall come out and offer his burnt offering and the burnt offering of the people, making expiation for himself and for the people. ²⁵The fat of the sin offering he shall turn into smoke on the altar.

²⁶The one who set the Azazel-goat free shall wash those clothes and bathe the body in water—and after that may reenter the camp.

²⁷The bull of sin offering and the goat of sin offering whose blood was brought in to purge the Shrine shall be taken outside the camp; and their hides, flesh, and dung shall be consumed in fire. ²⁸°The one who burned°° them shall wash those clothes and bathe the body in water—and after that may re-enter the camp.

²⁹And this shall be to you a law for all time: In the seventh month, on the tenth day of the month, you shall practice self-denial; and you shall do no manner of work, neither the citizen nor the alien who resides among you. ³⁰For on this day atonement shall be made for you to purify you of all your sins; you shall be pure before יהוה. ³¹It shall be a sabbath of complete rest for you, and you shall practice self-denial; it is a law for all time. ³²The priest who has been anointed and ordained to serve as priest in place of his father shall make expiation. He shall put on the linen vestments, the sacral vestments. ³³He shall purge the innermost Shrine; he shall purge the Tent of Meeting and the altar; and he shall make expiation for the priests and for all the people of the congregation.

³⁴This shall be to you a law for all time: to make atonement for the Israelites for all their sins once a year.

And Moses did as יהוה had commanded him.

17

יהוה spoke to Moses, saying: ²Speak to Aaron and his sons and to all the Israelite people and say to them:

This is what יהוה has commanded: ³if anyone of the house of Israel slaughters an ox or sheep or goat in the camp, or does so outside the camp, ⁴and does not bring it to the entrance of the Tent of Meeting to present it as an offering to יהוה, before יהוה's Tabernacle, bloodguilt shall be imputed to that person: having shed blood, that person shall be cut off from among this people. ⁵This is in order that the Israelites may bring the sacrifices which they have been making in the open—that they may bring them before יהוה, to the priest, at the entrance of the Tent of Meeting, and offer them as sacrifices of well-being to יהוה; ⁶that the priest may dash the blood against the altar of יהוה at the entrance of the Tent of Meeting, and turn the fat into smoke as a pleasing odor to יהוה; ⁷and that they may offer their sacrifices no more to the goat-demons after whom they stray. This shall be to them a law for all time, throughout the ages.

⁸Say to them further: If anyone of the house of Israel or of the strangers who reside among them offers a burnt offering or a sacrifice, ⁹and does not bring it to the entrance of the Tent of Meeting to offer it to יהוה, that person shall be cut off from this people.

¹⁰And if anyone of the house of Israel or of the strangers who reside among them partakes of any blood, I will set My face against the person who partakes of the blood; I will cut that person off from among kin. ¹¹For the life of the flesh is in the blood, and I have assigned it to you for making expiation for your lives upon the altar; it is the blood, as life, that effects expiation. ¹²Therefore I say to the Israelite people: No person among you shall partake of blood, nor shall the stranger who resides among you partake of blood.

¹³And if any Israelite or any stranger who resides among them hunts down an animal or a bird that may be eaten, that person shall pour out its blood and cover it with earth. ¹⁴For the life of all flesh—its blood is its life. Therefore I say to the Israelite people: You shall not partake of the blood of any flesh, for the life of all flesh is its blood. Anyone who partakes of it shall be cut off.

¹⁵Any person, whether citizen or stranger, who eats what has died

or has been torn by beasts shall wash those clothes, bathe in water, remain impure until evening—and shall then be pure. ¹⁶But if the clothes are not washed and the body is not bathed, that person shall bear the guilt.

18

יהוה spoke to Moses, saying: ²Speak to the Israelite people and say to them:

I יהוה am your God. ³You shall not copy the practices of the land of Egypt where you dwelt, or of the land of Canaan to which I am taking you; nor shall you follow their laws. ⁴My rules alone shall you observe, and faithfully follow My laws: I יהוה am your God.

⁵You shall keep My laws and My rules, by the pursuit of which human beings shall live: I am יהוה.

⁶None of you men shall come near anyone of his own flesh to uncover nakedness: I am יהוה.

⁷*⁻Your father's nakedness, that is, the nakedness of your mother, you shall not uncover; she is your mother—you shall not uncover her nakedness.

⁸Do not uncover the nakedness of your father's wife; it is the nakedness of your father.⁻*

⁹The nakedness of your sister—your father's daughter or your mother's, whether born into the household or outside—do not uncover their nakedness.

¹⁰The nakedness of your son's daughter, or of your daughter's daughter—do not uncover their nakedness; for *⁻their nakedness is yours.⁻*

¹¹The nakedness of your father's wife's daughter, who was born into your father's household—she is your sister; do not uncover her nakedness.

¹²Do not uncover the nakedness of your father's sister; she is your father's flesh.

¹³Do not uncover the nakedness of your mother's sister; for she is your mother's flesh.

¹⁴Do not uncover the nakedness of your father's brother: do not approach his wife; she is your aunt.

¹⁵Do not uncover the nakedness of your daughter-in-law: she is your son's wife; you shall not uncover her nakedness.

¹⁶Do not uncover the nakedness of your brother's wife; it is the nakedness of your brother.

¹⁷Do not uncover the nakedness of a woman and her daughter; nor shall you take [into your household as a wife] her son's daughter or her daughter's daughter and uncover her nakedness: they are kindred; it is depravity.

¹⁸Do not take [into your household as a wife] a woman as a rival to her sister and uncover her nakedness in the other's lifetime.

¹⁹Do not come near a woman during her menstrual period of impurity to uncover her nakedness.

²⁰Do not have carnal relations with your neighbor's wife and defile yourself with her.

²¹Do not allow any of your offspring to be offered up to Molech, and do not profane the name of your God: I am יהוה.

²²Do not lie with a male as one lies with a woman; it is an abhorrence.

²³Do not have carnal relations with any beast and defile yourself thereby. Likewise for a woman: she shall not lend herself to a beast to mate with it; it is perversion.

²⁴Do not defile yourselves in any of those ways, for it is by such that the nations that I am casting out before you defiled themselves. ²⁵Thus the land became defiled; and I called it to account for its iniquity, and the land spewed out its inhabitants. ²⁶But you must keep My laws and My rules, and you must not do any of those abhorrent things, neither the citizen nor the stranger who resides among you; ²⁷for all those abhorrent things were done by the people who were in the land before you, and the land became defiled. ²⁸So let not the land spew you out for defiling it, as it spewed out the nation that came before you. ²⁹All who do any of those abhorrent things—such persons shall be cut off from their people. ³⁰You shall keep My charge not to engage in any of the abhorrent practices that were carried on before you, and you shall not defile yourselves through them: I יהוה am your God.

קְדֹשִׁים | KEDOSHIM

19 יהוה spoke to Moses, saying: ²Speak to the whole Israelite community and say to them:

You shall be holy, for I, your God יהוה, am holy.

³You shall each revere your mother and your father, and keep My sabbaths: I יהוה am your God.

⁴Do not turn to idols or make molten gods for yourselves: I יהוה am your God.

⁵When you sacrifice an offering of well-being to יהוה, sacrifice it so that it may be accepted on your behalf. ⁶It shall be eaten on the day you sacrifice it, or on the day following; but what is left by the third day must be consumed in fire. ⁷If it should be eaten on the third day, it is an offensive thing, it will not be acceptable. ⁸And one who eats of it shall bear the guilt for having profaned what is sacred to יהוה; that person shall be cut off from kin.

⁹When you reap the harvest of your land, you shall not reap all the way to the edges of your field, or gather the gleanings of your harvest. ¹⁰You shall not pick your vineyard bare, or gather the fallen fruit of your vineyard; you shall leave them for the poor and the stranger: I יהוה am your God.

¹¹You shall not steal; you shall not deal deceitfully or falsely with one another. ¹²You shall not swear falsely by My name, profaning the name of your God: I am יהוה.

¹³You shall not defraud your fellow [Israelite]. You shall not commit robbery. The wages of a laborer shall not remain with you until morning.

¹⁴You shall not insult the deaf, or place a stumbling block before the blind. You shall fear your God: I am יהוה.

¹⁵You shall not render an unfair decision: do not favor the poor or show deference to the rich; judge your kin fairly. ¹⁶Do not *⁻deal basely with⁻* members of your people. Do not *⁻profit by⁻* the blood of your fellow [Israelite]: I am יהוה.

¹⁷You shall not hate your kinsfolk in your heart. Reprove your kin but* incur no guilt on their account. ¹⁸You shall not take vengeance or bear a grudge against members of your people. Love your fellow [Israelite] as yourself: I am יהוה.

¹⁹You shall observe My laws.

You shall not let your cattle mate with a different kind; you shall not sow your field with two kinds of seed; you shall not put on cloth from a mixture of two kinds of material.

²⁰If a man has carnal relations with a woman who is a slave and has been designated for another man, but has not been redeemed

or given her freedom, there shall be an indemnity; they shall not, however, be put to death, since she has not been freed. ²¹But he must bring to the entrance of the Tent of Meeting, as his guilt offering to יהוה, a ram of guilt offering. ²²With the ram of guilt offering the priest shall make expiation for him before יהוה for the sin that he committed; and the sin that he committed will be forgiven him.

²³When you enter the land and plant any tree for food, you shall regard its fruit as forbidden. Three years it shall be forbidden* for you, not to be eaten. ²⁴In the fourth year all its fruit shall be set aside for jubilation before יהוה; ²⁵and only in the fifth year may you use its fruit—that its yield to you may be increased: I יהוה am your God.

²⁶You shall not eat anything with its blood. You shall not practice divination or soothsaying. ²⁷You [men] shall not round off the side-growth on your head, or destroy the side-growth of your beard. ²⁸You shall not make gashes in your flesh for the dead, or incise any marks on yourselves: I am יהוה.

²⁹Do not degrade your daughter and make her a harlot, lest the land fall into harlotry and the land be filled with depravity. ³⁰You shall keep My sabbaths and venerate My sanctuary: I am יהוה.

³¹Do not turn to ghosts and do not inquire of familiar spirits, to be defiled by them: I יהוה am your God.

³²You shall rise before the aged and show deference to the old; you shall fear your God: I am יהוה.

³³When strangers reside with you in your land, you shall not wrong them. ³⁴The strangers who reside with you shall be to you as your citizens; you shall love each one as yourself, for you were strangers in the land of Egypt: I יהוה am your God.

³⁵You shall not falsify measures of length, weight, or capacity. ³⁶You shall have an honest balance, honest weights, an honest *ephah*, and an honest *hin*.

I יהוה am your God who freed you from the land of Egypt. ³⁷You shall faithfully observe all My laws and all My rules: I am יהוה.

20 And יהוה spoke to Moses: ²Say further to the Israelite people:

Anyone among the Israelites, or among the strangers residing in

Israel, who gives any offspring to Molech, shall be put to death; the people of the land shall pelt the person with stones. ³And I will set My face against that person, whom I will cut off from among the people for having given offspring to Molech and so defiled My sanctuary and profaned My holy name. ⁴And if the people of the land should shut their eyes to that person's giving offspring to Molech, and should not put the person to death, ⁵I Myself will set My face against that person's kin as well; and I will cut off from among their people both that person and all who follow in going astray after Molech. ⁶And if any person turns to ghosts and familiar spirits and goes astray after them, I will set My face against that person, whom I will cut off from among the people.

⁷You shall sanctify yourselves and be holy, for I יהוה am your God. ⁸You shall faithfully observe My laws: I יהוה make you holy.

⁹If anyone insults either father or mother, that person shall be put to death; that person has insulted father and mother—and retains the bloodguilt.

¹⁰If a man commits adultery with another's wife—committing adultery with the wife of his fellow [Israelite]—the adulterer and the adulteress shall be put to death. ¹¹If a man lies with his father's wife, it is the nakedness of his father that he has uncovered; the two shall be put to death—and they retain the bloodguilt. ¹²If a man lies with his daughter-in-law, both of them shall be put to death; they have committed incest—and they retain the bloodguilt. ¹³If a man lies with a male as one lies with a woman, the two of them have done an abhorrent thing; they shall be put to death— and they retain the bloodguilt. ¹⁴If a man takes a woman and her mother [into his household as his wives], it is depravity; both he and they shall be put to the fire, that there be no depravity among you. ¹⁵If a man has carnal relations with a beast, he shall be put to death; and you shall kill the beast. ¹⁶If a woman approaches any beast to mate with it, you shall kill the woman and the beast; they shall be put to death—and they retain the bloodguilt.

¹⁷If a man takes his sister [into his household as a wife], the daughter of either his father or his mother, so that he sees her nakedness and she sees his nakedness, it is a disgrace; they shall be excommunicated* in the sight of their kinsfolk. He has uncovered the nakedness of his sister, he shall bear the guilt. ¹⁸If a man lies

with a woman during her menstrual condition and uncovers her nakedness, he has laid bare her flow and she has exposed her blood flow; both of them shall be cut off from among their people. ¹⁹You [males] shall not uncover the nakedness of your mother's sister or of your father's sister, for that is laying bare one's own flesh; they shall bear their guilt. ²⁰If a man lies with his uncle's wife, it is his uncle's nakedness that he has uncovered. They shall bear their guilt: they shall die childless. ²¹If a man takes the wife of his brother [into his household as a wife], it is indecency. It is the nakedness of his brother that he has uncovered; they shall remain childless.

²²You shall faithfully observe all My laws and all My regulations, lest the land to which I bring you to settle in spew you out. ²³You shall not follow the practices of the nation that I am driving out before you. For it is because they did all these things that I abhorred them ²⁴and said to you: You shall possess their land, for I will give it to you to possess, a land flowing with milk and honey. I יהוה am your God who has set you apart from other peoples. ²⁵So you shall set apart the pure beast from the impure, the impure bird from the pure. You shall not draw abomination upon yourselves through beast or bird or anything with which the ground is alive, which I have set apart for you to treat as impure. ²⁶You shall be holy to Me, for I יהוה am holy, and I have set you apart from other peoples to be Mine.

²⁷A man or a woman who has a ghost or a familiar spirit shall be put to death; they shall be pelted with stones—and they shall retain the bloodguilt.

אמר | 'EMOR

21 יהוה said to Moses: Speak to the priests, the sons of Aaron, and say to them:

None shall defile himself for any [dead] person among his kin, ²except for the relatives that are closest to him: his mother, his father, his son, his daughter, and his brother; ³also for a virgin sister, close to him because she has not become someone's [wife], for her he may defile himself. ⁴But he shall not defile himself *̅for his wife as kin,̅* and so profane himself.

⁵They shall not shave smooth any part of their heads, or cut the

side-growth of their beards, or make gashes in their flesh. ⁶They shall be holy to their God and not profane the name of their God; for they offer יהוה's offerings by fire, the food of their God, and so must be holy.

⁷They shall not take [into their household as their wife] a woman defiled by harlotry, nor shall they take one divorced from her husband. For they are holy to their God ⁸and you must treat them as holy, since they offer the food of your God; they shall be holy to you, for I יהוה who sanctify you am holy.

⁹When the daughter of a priest defiles herself through harlotry, it is her father whom she defiles; she shall be put to the fire.

¹⁰The priest who is exalted above his fellows, on whose head the anointing oil has been poured and who has been ordained to wear the vestments, shall not *¯bare his head¯* or rend his vestments. ¹¹He shall not go in where there is any dead body; he shall not defile himself even for his father or mother. ¹²He shall not go outside the sanctuary and profane the sanctuary of his God, for upon him is the distinction of the anointing oil of his God, Mine יהוה's. ¹³He may take [into his household as his wife] only a woman who is a virgin. ¹⁴A widow, or a divorced woman, or one who is degraded by harlotry—such he may not take. Only a virgin of his own kin may he take as his wife—¹⁵that he may not profane his offspring among his kin, for I יהוה have sanctified him.

¹⁶יהוה spoke further to Moses: ¹⁷Speak to Aaron and say: No man of your offspring throughout the ages who has a defect shall be qualified to offer the food of his God. ¹⁸No one at all who has a defect shall be qualified: no man who is blind, or lame, or *¯has a limb too short or too long;¯* ¹⁹no man who has a broken leg or a broken arm; ²⁰or who is a hunchback, or a dwarf, or who has a growth in his eye, or who has a boil-scar, or scurvy, or crushed testes. ²¹No man among the offspring of Aaron the priest who has a defect shall be qualified to offer יהוה's offering by fire; having a defect, he shall not be qualified to offer the food of his God. ²²He may eat of the food of his God, of the most holy as well as of the holy; ²³but he shall not enter behind the curtain or come near the altar, for he has a defect. He shall not profane these places sacred to Me, for I יהוה have sanctified them.

²⁴Thus Moses spoke to Aaron and his sons and to all the Israelites.

22

יהוה spoke to Moses, saying: [2]Instruct Aaron and his sons to be scrupulous about the sacred donations that the Israelite people consecrate to Me, lest they profane My holy name, Mine יהוה's. [3]Say to them:

Throughout the ages, if any man among your offspring, while in a state of impurity, partakes of any sacred donation that the Israelite people may consecrate to יהוה, that person shall be cut off from before Me: I am יהוה. [4]No man of Aaron's offspring who has an eruption or a discharge* shall eat of the sacred donations until he is pure. If one touches anything made impure by a corpse, or if a man has an emission of semen,° [5]or if a man touches any swarming thing by which he is made impure or any human being by whom he is made impure—whatever his impurity—[6]the person who touches such shall be impure until evening and shall not eat of the sacred donations unless he has washed his body in water. [7]As soon as the sun sets, he shall be pure; and afterward he may eat of the sacred donations, for they are his food. [8]He shall not eat anything that died or was torn by beasts, thereby becoming impure: I am יהוה. [9]They shall keep My charge, lest they incur guilt thereby and die for it, having committed profanation: I יהוה consecrate them.

[10]No lay person shall eat of the sacred donations. No bound or hired laborer of a priest shall eat of the sacred donations; [11]but a person who is a priest's property by purchase may eat of them; and those that are born into his household may eat of his food. [12]If a priest's daughter becomes a layman's [wife], she may not eat of the sacred gifts; [13]but if the priest's daughter is widowed or divorced and without offspring, and is back in her father's house as in her youth, she may eat of her father's food. No lay person may eat of it: [14]but if a person eats of a sacred donation unwittingly, the priest shall be paid for the sacred donation, adding one-fifth of its value. [15]But [the priests] must not allow the Israelites to profane the sacred donations that they set aside for יהוה, [16]or to incur guilt requiring a penalty payment, by eating such sacred donations: for it is I יהוה who make them sacred.

[17]יהוה spoke to Moses, saying: [18]Speak to Aaron and his sons, and to all the Israelite people, and say to them:

When any person of the house of Israel or of the strangers in

Israel presents a burnt offering as the offering for any of the votive or any of the freewill offerings that they offer to יהוה, ¹⁹it must, to be acceptable in your favor, be a male without blemish, from cattle or sheep or goats. ²⁰You shall not offer any that has a defect, for it will not be accepted in your favor.

²¹And when a person offers, from the herd or the flock, a sacrifice of well-being to יהוה for an explicit* vow or as a freewill offering, it must, to be acceptable, be without blemish; there must be no defect in it. ²²Anything blind, or injured, or maimed, or with a wen, boil-scar, or scurvy—such you shall not offer to יהוה; you shall not put any of them on the altar as offerings by fire to יהוה. ²³You may, however, present as a freewill offering an ox or a sheep with a limb extended or contracted; but it will not be accepted for a vow. ²⁴You shall not offer to יהוה anything [with its testes] bruised or crushed or torn or cut. You shall have no such practices* in your own land, ²⁵nor shall you accept such [animals] from a foreigner for offering as food for your God, for they are mutilated, they have a defect; they shall not be accepted in your favor.

²⁶יהוה spoke to Moses, saying: ²⁷When an ox or a sheep or a goat is born, it shall stay seven days with its mother, and from the eighth day on it shall be acceptable as an offering by fire to יהוה. ²⁸However, no animal from the herd or from the flock shall be slaughtered on the same day with its young.

²⁹When you sacrifice a thanksgiving offering to יהוה, sacrifice it so that it may be acceptable in your favor. ³⁰It shall be eaten on the same day; you shall not leave any of it until morning: I am יהוה.

³¹You shall faithfully observe My commandments: I am יהוה. ³²You shall not profane My holy name, that I may be sanctified in the midst of the Israelite people—I יהוה who sanctify you, ³³I who brought you out of the land of Egypt to be your God, I יהוה.

23 יהוה spoke to Moses, saying: ²Speak to the Israelite people and say to them:

These are My fixed times, the fixed times of יהוה, which you shall proclaim as sacred occasions.

³On six days work may be done, but on the seventh day there shall be a sabbath of complete* rest, a sacred occasion.

You shall do no work; it shall be a sabbath of יהוה throughout your settlements.

⁴These are the set times of יהוה, the sacred occasions, which you shall celebrate each at its appointed time: ⁵In the first month, on the fourteenth day of the month, at twilight, there shall be a passover offering to יהוה, ⁶and on the fifteenth day of that month יהוה's Feast of Unleavened Bread. You shall eat unleavened bread for seven days. ⁷On the first day you shall celebrate a sacred occasion: you shall not work at your occupations. ⁸Seven days you shall make offerings by fire to יהוה. The seventh day shall be a sacred occasion: you shall not work at your occupations.

⁹יהוה spoke to Moses, saying: ¹⁰Speak to the Israelite people and say to them:

When you enter the land that I am giving to you and you reap its harvest, you shall bring the first sheaf of your harvest to the priest. ¹¹He shall elevate the sheaf before יהוה for acceptance in your behalf; the priest shall elevate it on the day after the sabbath. ¹²On the day that you elevate the sheaf, you shall offer as a burnt offering to יהוה a lamb of the first year without blemish. ¹³The meal offering with it shall be two-tenths of a measure of choice flour with oil mixed in, an offering by fire of pleasing odor to יהוה; and the libation with it shall be of wine, a quarter of a *hin*. ¹⁴Until that very day, until you have brought the offering of your God, you shall eat *˙no bread or parched grain or fresh ears;* it is a law for all time throughout the ages in all your settlements.

¹⁵And from the day on which you bring the sheaf of elevation offering—the day after the sabbath—you shall count off seven weeks. They must be complete: ¹⁶you must count until the day after the seventh week—fifty days; then you shall bring an offering of new grain to יהוה. ¹⁷You shall bring from your settlements two loaves of bread as an elevation offering; each shall be made of two-tenths of a measure of choice flour, baked after leavening, as first fruits to יהוה. ¹⁸With the bread you shall present, as burnt offerings to יהוה, seven yearling lambs without blemish, one bull of the herd, and two rams, with their meal offerings and libations, an offering by fire of pleasing odor to יהוה. ¹⁹You shall also offer one he-goat as a sin offering and two yearling lambs as a sacrifice of well-being. ²⁰The priest shall elevate these—*˙the two lambs*—

together with the bread of first fruits as an elevation offering before יהוה; they shall be holy to יהוה, for the priest. 21On that same
day you shall hold a celebration; it shall be a sacred occasion for
you; you shall not work at your occupations. This is a law for all
time in all your settlements, throughout the ages.

22And when you reap the harvest of your land, you shall not
reap all the way to the edges of your field, or gather the gleanings
of your harvest; you shall leave them for the poor and the stranger:
I יהוה am your God.

23יהוה spoke to Moses, saying: 24Speak to the Israelite people
thus: In the seventh month, on the first day of the month, you
shall observe complete rest, a sacred occasion commemorated
with loud blasts. 25You shall not work at your occupations; and
you shall bring an offering by fire to יהוה.

26יהוה spoke to Moses, saying: 27Mark, the tenth day of this seventh month is the Day of Atonement. It shall be a sacred occasion
for you: you shall practice self-denial, and you shall bring an offering by fire to יהוה; 28you shall do no work throughout that day. For
it is a Day of Atonement, on which expiation is made on your
behalf before your God יהוה. 29Indeed, any person who does not
practice self-denial throughout that day shall be cut off from kin;
30and whoever does any work throughout that day, I will cause
that person to perish from among the people. 31Do no work whatever; it is a law for all time, throughout the ages in all your settlements. 32It shall be a sabbath of complete rest for you, and you
shall practice self-denial; on the ninth day of the month at evening,
from evening to evening, you shall observe this your sabbath.

33יהוה spoke to Moses, saying: 34Say to the Israelite people:

On the fifteenth day of this seventh month there shall be the
Feast of Booths* to יהוה, [to last] seven days. 35The first day shall
be a sacred occasion: you shall not work at your occupations;
36seven days you shall bring offerings by fire to יהוה. On the
eighth day you shall observe a sacred occasion and bring an offering by fire to יהוה; it is a *-solemn gathering:* you shall not work
at your occupations.

37Those are the set times of יהוה that you shall celebrate as
sacred occasions, bringing offerings by fire to יהוה—burnt offerings, meal offerings, sacrifices, and libations, on each day what is

proper to it—[38]apart from the sabbaths of יהוה, and apart from your gifts and from all your votive offerings and from all your freewill offerings that you give to יהוה.

[39]Mark, on the fifteenth day of the seventh month, when you have gathered in the yield of your land, you shall observe the festival of יהוה [to last] seven days: a complete rest on the first day, and a complete rest on the eighth day. [40]On the first day you shall take the product of *hadar** trees, branches of palm trees, boughs of leafy* trees, and willows of the brook, and you shall rejoice before your God יהוה seven days. [41]You shall observe it as a festival of יהוה for seven days in the year; you shall observe it in the seventh month as a law for all time, throughout the ages. [42]You shall live in booths seven days; all citizens in Israel shall live in booths, [43]in order that future generations may know that I made the Israelite people live in booths when I brought them out of the land of Egypt—I, your God יהוה.

[44]So Moses declared to the Israelites the set times of יהוה.

24 יהוה spoke to Moses, saying: [2]Command the Israelite people to bring you clear oil of beaten olives for lighting, for kindling lamps regularly. [3]Aaron shall set them up in the Tent of Meeting outside the curtain of the Pact [to burn] from evening to morning before יהוה regularly; it is a law for all time throughout the ages. [4]He shall set up the lamps on the pure* lampstand before יהוה [to burn] regularly.

[5]You shall take choice flour and bake of it twelve loaves, two-tenths of a measure for each loaf. [6]Place them on the pure* table before יהוה in two rows, six to a row. [7]With each row you shall place pure frankincense, which is to be a *¬token offering* for the bread, as an offering by fire to יהוה. [8]He shall arrange them before יהוה regularly every sabbath day—it is a commitment for all time on the part of the Israelites. [9]They shall belong to Aaron and his sons, who shall eat them in the sacred precinct; for they are his as most holy things from יהוה's offerings by fire, a due for all time.

[10]There came out among the Israelites a man whose mother was Israelite and whose father was Egyptian. And a fight broke

out in the camp between that half-Israelite* and a certain Israelite. [11]The son of the Israelite woman pronounced the Name in blasphemy, and he was brought to Moses—now his mother's name was Shelomith daughter of Dibri of the tribe of Dan—[12]and he was placed in custody, until the decision of יהוה should be made clear to them.

[13]And יהוה spoke to Moses, saying: [14]Take the blasphemer outside the camp; and let all who were within hearing lay their hands upon his head, and let the °˙community leadership°˙ stone him.

[15]And to the Israelite people speak thus: Anyone who blasphemes God shall bear the guilt; [16]and one who also pronounces the name יהוה shall be put to death. The °˙community leadership°˙ shall stone that person; stranger or citizen—having thus pronounced the Name—shall be put to death.

[17]If anyone kills any human being, that person shall be put to death. [18]One who kills a beast shall make restitution for it: life for life. [19]If anyone maims another [person]: what was done shall be done in return—[20]fracture for fracture, eye for eye, tooth for tooth. The injury inflicted on a human being shall be inflicted in return. [21]One who kills a beast shall make restitution for it; but one who kills a human being shall be put to death. [22]You shall have one standard for stranger and citizen alike: for I יהוה am your God.

[23]Moses spoke thus to the Israelites. And they took the blasphemer outside the camp and pelted him with stones. The Israelites did as יהוה had commanded Moses.

בהר | BE-HAR

25   יהוה spoke to Moses on Mount Sinai: [2]Speak to the Israelite people and say to them:

When you enter the land that I assign to you, the land shall observe a sabbath of יהוה. [3]Six years you may sow your field and six years you may prune your vineyard and gather in the yield. [4]But in the seventh year the land shall have a sabbath of complete rest, a sabbath of יהוה: you shall not sow your field or prune your vineyard. [5]You shall not reap the aftergrowth of your harvest or gather the grapes of your untrimmed vines; it shall be a year of complete rest for the land. [6]But you may eat whatever the land during its sabbath will produce—you, your male and female slaves, the hired and bound laborers who live with you, [7]and your cattle and the beasts in your land may eat all its yield.

[8]You shall count off seven weeks of years—seven times seven years—so that the period of seven weeks of years gives you a total of forty-nine years. [9]Then you shall sound the horn loud; in the seventh month, on the tenth day of the month—the Day of Atonement—you shall have the horn sounded throughout your land [10]and you shall hallow the fiftieth year. You shall proclaim release* throughout the land for all its inhabitants. It shall be a jubilee* for you: each of you shall return to your holding and each of you shall return to your family. [11]That fiftieth year shall be a jubilee for you: you shall not sow, neither shall you reap the aftergrowth or harvest the untrimmed vines, [12]for it is a jubilee. It shall be holy to you: you may only eat the growth direct from the field.

[13]In this year of jubilee, each of you shall return to your holding. [14]When you sell property to your neighbor,* or buy any from your neighbor, you shall not wrong one another. [15]In buying from your neighbor, you shall deduct only for the number of years since the jubilee; and in selling to you, that person shall charge you only for the remaining crop years: [16]the more such years, the higher the price you pay; the fewer such years, the lower the price; for what is being sold to you is a number of harvests. [17]Do not wrong one another, but fear your God; for I יהוה am your God.

[18]You shall observe My laws and faithfully keep My rules, that you may live upon the land in security; [19]the land shall yield its fruit and you shall eat your fill, and you shall live upon it in security. [20]And should you ask, "What are we to eat in the seventh year, if we may neither sow nor gather in our crops?" [21]I will ordain My blessing for you in the sixth year, so that it shall yield a crop sufficient for three years. [22]When you sow in the eighth year, you will still be eating old grain of that crop; you will be eating the old until the ninth year, until its crops come in.

[23]But the land must not be sold beyond reclaim, for the land is Mine; you are but strangers resident with Me. [24]Throughout the land that you hold, you must provide for the redemption of the land.

[25]If one of your kin is in straits and has to sell part of a holding, the nearest redeemer* shall come and redeem what that relative

has sold. 26If a person has no one to be redeemer but prospers and acquires enough to redeem with, 27the years since its sale shall be computed and the difference shall be refunded to the person to whom it was sold, so that the person returns to that holding. 28If that person lacks sufficient means to recover it, what was sold shall remain with the purchaser until the jubilee; in the jubilee year it shall be released, so that the person returns to that holding.

29If someone sells a dwelling house in a walled city, it may be redeemed until a year has elapsed since its sale; the redemption period shall be a year. 30If it is not redeemed before a full year has elapsed, the house in the walled city shall pass to the purchaser beyond reclaim throughout the ages; it shall not be released in the jubilee. 31But houses in villages that have no encircling walls shall be classed as open country: they may be redeemed, and they shall be released through the jubilee. 32As for the cities of Levi, the houses in the cities it holds: Levi shall forever have the right of redemption. 33*Such property as may be redeemed from Levi—houses sold in a city it holds—shall be released through the jubilee; for the houses in the cities of Levi are its holding among the Israelites. 34But the unenclosed land about its cities cannot be sold, for that is its holding for all time.

35If your kin, being in straits, come under your authority, and are held by you as though resident aliens, let them live by your side: 36do not exact *⁻advance or accrued interest,⁻* but fear your God. Let your kin live by your side as such. 37Do not lend your money at advance interest, nor give your food at accrued interest. 38I יהוה am your God, who brought you out of the land of Egypt, to give you the land of Canaan, to be your God.

39If your kin under you continue in straits and must be given over to you, do not subject them to the treatment of a slave. 40Remaining with you as a hired or bound laborer, they shall serve with you only until the jubilee year. 41Then they, along with any children, shall be free of your authority; they shall go back to their family and return to the ancestral holding.—42For they are My servants, whom I freed from the land of Egypt; they may not give themselves over into servitude.—43You shall not rule over them ruthlessly; you shall fear your God. 44Such male and female slaves as you may have—it is from the nations round about you that you may acquire male and female slaves. ⁴⁵You may also buy them from among the children of aliens resident among you, or from their families that are among you, whom they begot in your land. These shall become your property: ⁴⁶you may keep them as a possession for your children after you, for them to inherit as property for all time. Such you may treat as slaves. But as for your Israelite kin, no one shall rule ruthlessly over another.

⁴⁷If a resident alien among you has prospered, and your kin, being in straits, comes under that one's authority and is given over to the resident alien among you, or to an offshoot of an alien's family, ⁴⁸[your kin] shall have the right of redemption even after having been given over. [Typically,] a brother shall do the redeeming, ⁴⁹or an uncle or an uncle's son shall do the redeeming—anyone in the family who is of the same flesh shall do the redeeming; or, having prospered, [your formerly impoverished kin] may do the redeeming. ⁵⁰The total shall be computed with the purchaser as from the year of being given over to the other until the jubilee year; the price of sale shall be applied to the number of years, as though it were for a term as a hired laborer under the other's authority. ⁵¹If many years remain, [your kin] shall pay back for the redemption in proportion to the purchase price; ⁵²and if few years remain until the jubilee year, so shall it be computed: payment shall be made for the redemption according to the years involved. ⁵³One shall be under the other's authority as a laborer hired by the year; the other shall not rule ruthlessly in your sight. ⁵⁴If not redeemed in any of those ways, that person, along with any children, shall go free in the jubilee year. ⁵⁵For it is to Me that the Israelites are servants: they are My servants, whom I freed from the land of Egypt—I, your God יהוה.

26 You shall not make idols for yourselves, or set up for yourselves carved images or pillars, or place figured* stones in your land to worship upon, for I יהוה am your God. ²You shall keep My sabbaths and venerate My sanctuary, Mine, יהוה's.

בחקתי | BE-ḤUKKOTAI

³If you follow My laws and faithfully observe My commandments, ⁴I will grant your rains in their season, so that the earth

shall yield its produce and the trees of the field their fruit. ⁵Your threshing shall overtake the vintage, and your vintage shall overtake the sowing; you shall eat your fill of bread and dwell securely in your land.

⁶I will grant peace in the land, and you shall lie down untroubled by anyone; I will give the land respite from vicious beasts, and no sword shall cross your land. ⁷[Your army] shall give chase to your enemies, and they shall fall before you by the sword. ⁸Five of you shall give chase to a hundred, and a hundred of you shall give chase to ten thousand; your enemies shall fall before you by the sword.

⁹I will look with favor upon you, and make you fertile and multiply you; and I will maintain My covenant with you. ¹⁰You shall eat old grain long stored, and you shall have to clear out the old to make room for the new.

¹¹I will establish My abode in your midst, and I will not spurn you. ¹²I will be ever present in your midst: I will be your God, and you shall be My people. ¹³I יהוה am your God who brought you out from the land of the Egyptians to be their slaves no more, who broke the bars of your yoke and made you walk erect.

¹⁴But if you do not obey Me and do not observe all these commandments, ¹⁵if you reject My laws and spurn My rules, so that you do not observe all My commandments and you break My covenant, ¹⁶I in turn will do this to you: I will wreak misery upon you—*consumption and fever,* which cause the eyes to pine and the body to languish; you shall sow your seed to no purpose, for your enemies shall eat it. ¹⁷I will set My face against you: you shall be routed by your enemies, and your foes shall dominate you. You shall flee though none pursues.

¹⁸And if, for all that, you do not obey Me, I will go on to discipline you sevenfold for your sins, ¹⁹and I will break your proud glory. I will make your skies like iron and your earth like copper, ²⁰so that your strength shall be spent to no purpose. Your land shall not yield its produce, nor shall the trees of the land yield their fruit.

²¹And if you remain hostile toward Me and refuse to obey Me, I will go on smiting you sevenfold for your sins. ²²I will loose wild

beasts against you, and they shall bereave you of your children and wipe out your cattle. They shall decimate you, and your roads shall be deserted.

23And if these things fail to discipline you for Me, and you remain hostile to Me, 24I too will remain hostile to you: I in turn will smite you sevenfold for your sins. 25I will bring a sword against you to wreak vengeance for the covenant; and if you withdraw into your cities, I will send pestilence among you, and you shall be delivered into enemy hands. 26When I break your staff of bread, ten women shall bake your bread in a single oven; they shall dole out your bread by weight, and though you eat, you shall not be satisfied.

27But if, despite this, you disobey Me and remain hostile to Me, 28I will act against you in wrathful hostility; I, for My part, will discipline you sevenfold for your sins. 29You shall eat the flesh of your sons and the flesh of your daughters. 30I will destroy your cult places and cut down your incense stands, and I will heap your carcasses upon your lifeless fetishes.

I will spurn you. 31I will lay your cities in ruin and make your sanctuaries desolate, and I will not savor your pleasing odors. 32I will make the land desolate, so that your enemies who settle in it shall be appalled by it. 33And you I will scatter among the nations, and I will unsheath the sword against you. Your land shall become a desolation and your cities a ruin.

34Then shall the land make up for its sabbath years throughout the time that it is desolate and you are in the land of your enemies; then shall the land rest and make up for its sabbath years. 35Throughout the time that it is desolate, it shall observe the rest that it did not observe in your sabbath years while you were dwelling upon it. 36As for those of you who survive, I will cast a faintness into their hearts in the land of their enemies. The sound of a driven leaf shall put them to flight. Fleeing as though from the sword, they shall fall though none pursues. 37With no one pursuing, they shall stumble over one another as before the sword. You shall not be able to stand your ground before your enemies, 38but shall perish among the nations; and the land of your enemies shall consume you.

39Those of you who survive shall be heartsick over their iniquity

         Be-ḥukkotai

in the land of your enemies; more, they shall be heartsick over the iniquities of their forebears; ⁴⁰and they shall confess their iniquity and the iniquity of their forebears, in that they trespassed against Me, yea, were hostile to Me. ⁴¹When I, in turn, have been hostile to them and have removed them into the land of their enemies, then at last shall their obdurate* heart humble itself, and they shall atone for their iniquity. ⁴²Then will I remember My covenant with Jacob; I will remember also My covenant with Isaac, and also My covenant with Abraham; and I will remember the land.

⁴³For the land shall be forsaken of them, making up for its sabbath years by being desolate of them, while they atone for their iniquity; for the abundant reason that they rejected My rules and spurned My laws. ⁴⁴Yet, even then, when they are in the land of their enemies, I will not reject them or spurn them so as to destroy them, annulling My covenant with them: for I יהוה am their God. ⁴⁵I will remember in their favor the covenant with the ancients, whom I freed from the land of Egypt in the sight of the nations to be their God: I, יהוה.

⁴⁶These are the laws, rules, and instructions that יהוה established, through Moses on Mount Sinai, with the Israelite people.

27 יהוה spoke to Moses, saying: ²Speak to the Israelite people and say to them: When anyone explicitly* vows to יהוה the equivalent for a human being, ³the following scale shall apply: If it is a male from twenty to sixty years of age, the equivalent is fifty shekels of silver by the sanctuary weight; ⁴if it is a female, the equivalent is thirty shekels. ⁵If the age is from five years to twenty years, the equivalent is twenty shekels for a male and ten shekels for a female. ⁶If the age is from one month to five years, the equivalent for a male is five shekels of silver, and the equivalent for a female is three shekels of silver. ⁷If the age is sixty years or over, the equivalent is fifteen shekels in the case of a male and ten shekels for a female. ⁸But if one cannot afford the equivalent, that person shall be presented before the priest, and the priest shall make an assessment; the priest shall make the assessment according to what the vower can afford.

Be-ḥukkotai

⁹If [the vow concerns] any animal that may be brought as an offering to יהוה, any such that may be given to יהוה shall be holy. ¹⁰One may not exchange or substitute another for it, either good for bad, or bad for good; if one does substitute one animal for another, the thing vowed and its substitute shall both be holy. ¹¹If [the vow concerns] any impure animal that may not be brought as an offering to יהוה, the animal shall be presented before the priest, ¹²and the priest shall assess it. Whether high or low, whatever assessment is set by the priest shall stand; ¹³and if one wishes to redeem it, one-fifth must be added to its assessment.

¹⁴If anyone consecrates a house to יהוה, the priest shall assess it. Whether *high or low,* as the priest assesses it, so it shall stand; ¹⁵and if the one who has consecrated the house wishes to redeem it, one-fifth must be added to the sum at which it was assessed, and then it shall be returned.

¹⁶If anyone consecrates to יהוה any land-holding, its assessment shall be in accordance with its seed requirement: fifty shekels of silver to a *chomer* of barley seed. ¹⁷If the land is consecrated as of the jubilee year, its assessment stands. ¹⁸But if the land is consecrated after the jubilee, the priest shall compute the price according to the years that are left until the jubilee year, and its assessment shall be so reduced; ¹⁹and if the one who consecrated the land wishes to redeem it, one-fifth must be added to the sum at which it was assessed, and it shall be passed back. ²⁰But if the one [who consecrated it] does not redeem the land, and the land is sold to another, it shall no longer be redeemable: ²¹when it is released in the jubilee, the land shall be holy to יהוה, as land proscribed; it becomes the priest's holding.

²²If one consecrates to יהוה land that was purchased, which is not one's land-holding, ²³the priest shall compute the proportionate assessment up to the jubilee year, and the assessment shall be paid as of that day, a sacred donation to יהוה. ²⁴In the jubilee year the land shall revert to the one from whom it was bought, whose holding the land is. ²⁵All assessments shall be by the sanctuary weight, the shekel being twenty *gerah*s.

²⁶A firstling of animals, however, which—as a firstling—is יהוה's, cannot be consecrated by anybody; whether ox or sheep, it is יהוה's. ²⁷But if it is of impure animals, it may be ransomed as its

assessment, with one-fifth added; if it is not redeemed, it shall be sold at its assessment.

²⁸But of all that anyone owns, be it human or beast or land-holding, nothing that has been proscribed for יהוה may be sold or redeemed; every proscribed thing is totally consecrated to יהוה. ²⁹No human being who has been proscribed can be ransomed: that person shall be put to death.

³⁰All tithes from the land, whether seed from the ground or fruit from the tree, are יהוה's; they are holy to יהוה. ³¹If anyone wishes to redeem any tithes, one-fifth must be added to them. ³²All tithes of the herd or flock—of all that passes under the shepherd's staff, every tenth one—shall be holy to יהוה. ³³One must not look out for good as against bad, or make substitution for it. If one does make substitution for it, then it and its substitute shall both be holy: it cannot be redeemed.

³⁴These are the commandments that יהוה gave Moses for the Israelite people on Mount Sinai.

חזק

במדבר

NUMBERS

1 On the first day of the second month, in the second year following the exodus from the land of Egypt, יהוה spoke to Moses in the wilderness of Sinai, in the Tent of Meeting, saying: ²Take a census of the whole Israelite °company [of fighters]⁻° by the clans of *⁻its ancestral houses,⁻* listing the names, every male, head by head. ³You and Aaron shall record them by their groups, from the age of twenty years up, all those in Israel who are able to bear arms. ⁴Associated with you shall be a representative° of each tribe, each one the head of his ancestral house.

⁵These are the names of the representatives° who shall assist you:

From Reuben, Elizur son of Shedeur.

⁶From Simeon, Shelumiel son of Zurishaddai.

⁷From Judah, Nahshon son of Amminadab.

⁸From Issachar, Nethanel son of Zuar.

⁹From Zebulun, Eliab son of Helon.

¹⁰From the sons of Joseph:

from Ephraim, Elishama son of Ammihud;

from Manasseh, Gamaliel son of Pedahzur.

¹¹From Benjamin, Abidan son of Gideoni.

¹²From Dan, Ahiezer son of Ammishaddai.

¹³From Asher, Pagiel son of Ochran.

¹⁴From Gad, Eliasaph son of Deuel.

¹⁵From Naphtali, Ahira son of Enan.

¹⁶Those are the elected of the assembly, the chieftains of their ancestral tribes: they are the heads of the contingents of Israel.

¹⁷So Moses and Aaron took those representatives,° who were designated by name, ¹⁸and on the first day of the second month they convoked the whole °company [of fighters],⁻° who were registered by the clans of their ancestral houses—the names of those aged twenty years and over being listed head by head. ¹⁹As יהוה had commanded Moses, so he recorded them in the wilderness of Sinai.

Be-midbar

²⁰They totaled as follows:

The descendants of Reuben, Israel's first-born, the registration of the clans of their ancestral house, as listed by name, head by head, all males aged twenty years and over, all who were able to bear arms—²¹those enrolled from the tribe of Reuben: 46,500.

²²Of the descendants of Simeon, the registration of the clans of their ancestral house, their enrollment as listed by name, head by head, all males aged twenty years and over, all who were able to bear arms—²³those enrolled from the tribe of Simeon: 59,300.

²⁴Of the descendants of Gad, the registration of the clans of their ancestral house, as listed by name, aged twenty years and over, all who were able to bear arms—²⁵those enrolled from the tribe of Gad: 45,650.

²⁶Of the descendants of Judah, the registration of the clans of their ancestral house, as listed by name, aged twenty years and over, all who were able to bear arms—²⁷those enrolled from the tribe of Judah: 74,600.

²⁸Of the descendants of Issachar, the registration of the clans of their ancestral house, as listed by name, aged twenty years and over, all who were able to bear arms—²⁹those enrolled from the tribe of Issachar: 54,400.

³⁰Of the descendants of Zebulun, the registration of the clans of their ancestral house, as listed by name, aged twenty years and over, all who were able to bear arms—³¹those enrolled from the tribe of Zebulun: 57,400.

³²Of the descendants of Joseph:

Of the descendants of Ephraim, the registration of the clans of their ancestral house, as listed by name, aged twenty years and over, all who were able to bear arms—³³those enrolled from the tribe of Ephraim: 40,500.

³⁴Of the descendants of Manasseh, the registration of the clans of their ancestral house, as listed by name, aged twenty years and over, all who were able to bear arms—³⁵those enrolled from the tribe of Manasseh: 32,200.

³⁶Of the descendants of Benjamin, the registration of the clans of their ancestral house, as listed by name, aged twenty years and over, all who were able to bear arms—³⁷those enrolled from the tribe of Benjamin: 35,400.

³⁸Of the descendants of Dan, the registration of the clans of their ancestral house, as listed by name, aged twenty years and over, all who were able to bear arms—³⁹those enrolled from the tribe of Dan: 62,700.

⁴⁰Of the descendants of Asher, the registration of the clans of their ancestral house, as listed by name, aged twenty years and over, all who were able to bear arms—⁴¹those enrolled from the tribe of Asher: 41,500.

⁴²[Of] the descendants of Naphtali, the registration of the clans of their ancestral house as listed by name, aged twenty years and over, all who were able to bear arms—⁴³those enrolled from the tribe of Naphtali: 53,400.

⁴⁴Those are the enrollments recorded by Moses and Aaron and by the chieftains of Israel, who were twelve in number, one representative° of each ancestral house. ⁴⁵All the Israelite males, aged twenty years and over, enrolled by ancestral houses, all those in Israel who were able to bear arms—⁴⁶all who were enrolled came to 603,550.

⁴⁷The Levites, however, were not recorded among them by their ancestral tribe. ⁴⁸For יהוה had spoken to Moses, saying: ⁴⁹Do not on any account enroll the tribe of Levi or take a census of them with the Israelites. ⁵⁰You shall put the Levites in charge of the Tabernacle of the Pact, all its furnishings, and everything that pertains to it: they shall carry the Tabernacle and all its furnishings, and they shall tend it; and they shall camp around the Tabernacle. ⁵¹When the Tabernacle is to set out, the Levites shall take it down, and when the Tabernacle is to be pitched, the Levites shall set it up; any outsider who encroaches shall be put to death. ⁵²The Israelites shall encamp troop by troop, °each man with his division and each under his standard.° ⁵³The Levites, however, shall camp around the Tabernacle of the Pact, that wrath may not strike the Israelite community; the Levites shall stand guard around the Tabernacle of the Pact.

⁵⁴The Israelites did accordingly; just as יהוה had commanded Moses, so they did.

2 יהוה spoke to Moses and Aaron, saying: ²The Israelites shall camp °each man with his standard,° under the banners of their ancestral house; they shall camp around the Tent of Meeting at a distance.

3Camped on the front, or east side: the standard of the division of Judah, troop by troop.

Chieftain of the Judites: Nahshon son of Amminadab. 4His troop, as enrolled: 74,600.

5Camping next to it:

The tribe of Issachar.

Chieftain of the Issacharites: Nethanel son of Zuar. 6His troop, as enrolled: 54,400.

7The tribe of Zebulun.

Chieftain of the Zebulunites: Eliab son of Helon. 8His troop, as enrolled: 57,400.

9The total enrolled in the division of Judah: 186,400, for all troops. These shall march first.

10On the south: the standard of the division of Reuben, troop by troop.

Chieftain of the Reubenites: Elizur son of Shedeur. 11His troop, as enrolled: 46,500.

12Camping next to it:

The tribe of Simeon.

Chieftain of the Simeonites: Shelumiel son of Zurishaddai. 13His troop, as enrolled: 59,300.

14And the tribe of Gad.

Chieftain of the Gadites: Eliasaph son of Reuel. 15His troop, as enrolled: 45,650.

16The total enrolled in the division of Reuben: 151,450, for all troops. These shall march second.

17Then, midway between the divisions, the Tent of Meeting, the division of the Levites, shall move. As they camp, so they shall march, each in position, by their standards.

18On the west: the standard of the division of Ephraim, troop by troop.

Chieftain of the Ephraimites: Elishama son of Ammihud. 19His troop, as enrolled: 40,500.

20Next to it:

The tribe of Manasseh.

Chieftain of the Manassites: Gamaliel son of Pedahzur. ²¹His troop, as enrolled: 32,200.

²²And the tribe of Benjamin.

Chieftain of the Benjaminites: Abidan son of Gideoni. ²³His troop, as enrolled: 35,400.

²⁴The total enrolled in the division of Ephraim: 108,100 for all troops. These shall march third.

²⁵On the north: the standard of the division of Dan, troop by troop.

Chieftain of the Danites: Ahiezer son of Ammishaddai. ²⁶His troop, as enrolled: 62,700.

²⁷Camping next to it:

The tribe of Asher.

Chieftain of the Asherites: Pagiel son of Ochran. ²⁸His troop, as enrolled: 41,500.

²⁹And the tribe of Naphtali.

Chieftain of the Naphtalites: Ahira son of Enan. ³⁰His troop, as enrolled: 53,400.

³¹The total enrolled in the division of Dan: 157,600. These shall march last, by their standards.

³²Those are the enrollments of the Israelites by ancestral houses. The total enrolled in the divisions, for all troops: 603,550. ³³The Levites, however, were not recorded among the Israelites, as יהוה had commanded Moses.

³⁴The Israelites did accordingly; just as יהוה had commanded Moses, so they camped by their standards, and so they marched, °each man with his clan according to his ancestral house.°

3 This is the line of Aaron and Moses at the time that יהוה spoke with Moses on Mount Sinai. ²These were the names of Aaron's sons: Nadab, the first-born, and Abihu, Eleazar and Ithamar; ³those were the names of Aaron's sons, the anointed priests who were ordained for priesthood. ⁴But Nadab and Abihu died *ᵇby the will of* יהוה, when they offered alien fire before יהוה in the wilderness of Sinai; and they left no sons. So it was Eleazar and Ithamar who served as priests in the lifetime of their father Aaron.

⁵יהוה spoke to Moses, saying: ⁶Advance the tribe of Levi and place [its men]° in attendance upon Aaron the priest to serve him. ⁷They shall perform duties for him and for the whole community before the Tent of Meeting, doing the work of the Tabernacle. ⁸They shall take charge of all the furnishings of the Tent of Meeting—a duty on behalf of the Israelites—doing the work of the Tabernacle. ⁹You shall assign the Levites to Aaron and to his sons: they are formally assigned to him from among the Israelites. ¹⁰You shall make Aaron and his sons responsible for observing their priestly duties; and any outsider who encroaches shall be put to death.

¹¹יהוה spoke to Moses, saying: ¹²I hereby take the Levites from among the Israelites in place of all the male first-born, the first issue of the womb among the Israelites: the Levites shall be Mine. ¹³For every male first-born is Mine: at the time that I smote every [male] first-born in the land of Egypt, I consecrated every male first-born in Israel, human and beast, to Myself, to be Mine, יהוה's.

¹⁴יהוה spoke to Moses in the wilderness of Sinai, saying: ¹⁵Record the descendants of Levi by ancestral house and by clan; record every male among them from the age of one month up. ¹⁶So Moses recorded them at the command of יהוה, as he was bidden. ¹⁷These were the sons of Levi by name: Gershon, Kohath, and Merari. ¹⁸These were the names of the sons of Gershon by clan: Libni and Shimei. ¹⁹The sons of Kohath by clan: Amram and Izhar, Hebron and Uzziel. ²⁰The sons of Merari by clan: Mahli and Mushi.

These were the clans of the Levites within their ancestral houses:

²¹To Gershon belonged the clan of the Libnites and the clan of the Shimeites; those were the clans of the Gershonites. ²²The recorded entries of all their males from the age of one month up, as recorded, came to 7,500. ²³The clans of the Gershonites were to camp behind the Tabernacle, to the west. ²⁴The chieftain of the ancestral house of the Gershonites was Eliasaph son of Lael. ²⁵The duties of the Gershonites in the Tent of Meeting comprised: the tabernacle,* the tent, its covering, and the screen for the entrance of the Tent of Meeting; ²⁶the hangings of the enclosure, the screen for the entrance of the enclosure which surrounds

the Tabernacle, the cords thereof, and the altar—all the service connected with these.

²⁷To Kohath belonged the clan of the Amramites, the clan of the Izharites, the clan of the Hebronites, and the clan of the Uzzielites; those were the clans of the Kohathites. ²⁸All the listed males from the age of one month up came to 8,600, attending to the duties of the sanctuary. ²⁹The clans of the Kohathites were to camp along the south side of the Tabernacle. ³⁰The chieftain of the ancestral house of the Kohathite clans was Elizaphan son of Uzziel. ³¹Their duties comprised: the ark, the table, the lampstand, the altars, and the sacred utensils that were used with them, and the screen*—all the service connected with these. ³²The head chieftain of the Levites was Eleazar son of Aaron the priest, in charge of those attending to the duties of the sanctuary.

³³To Merari belonged the clan of the Mahlites and the clan of the Mushites; those were the clans of Merari. ³⁴The recorded entries of all their males from the age of one month up came to 6,200. ³⁵The chieftain of the ancestral house of the clans of Merari was Zuriel son of Abihail. They were to camp along the north side of the Tabernacle. ³⁶The assigned duties of the Merarites comprised: the planks of the Tabernacle, its bars, posts, and sockets, and all its furnishings—all the service connected with these; ³⁷also the posts around the enclosure and their sockets, pegs, and cords.

³⁸Those who were to camp before the Tabernacle, in front—before the Tent of Meeting, on the east—were Moses and Aaron and his sons, attending to the duties of the sanctuary, as a duty on behalf of the Israelites; and any outsider who encroached was to be put to death. ³⁹All the Levites who were recorded, whom at יהוה's command Moses and Aaron recorded by their clans, all the males from the age of one month up, came to 22,000.

⁴⁰יהוה said to Moses: Record every first-born male of the Israelite people from the age of one month up, and make a list of their names; ⁴¹and take the Levites for Me, יהוה, in place of every male first-born among the Israelite people, and the cattle of the Levites in place of every male first-born among the cattle of the Israelites. ⁴²So Moses recorded all the male first-born among the Israelites, as יהוה had commanded him. ⁴³All the first-born males as listed by name, recorded from the age of one month up, came to 22,273.

Be-midbar

⁴⁴יהוה spoke to Moses, saying: ⁴⁵Take the Levites in place of all the male first-born among the Israelite people, and the cattle of the Levites in place of their cattle; and the Levites shall be Mine, יהוה's. ⁴⁶And as the redemption price of the 273 Israelite male first-born over and above the number of the Levites, ⁴⁷take five shekels per head—take this by the sanctuary weight, twenty *gerah*s to the shekel—⁴⁸and give the money to Aaron and his sons as the redemption price for those who are in excess. ⁴⁹So Moses took the redemption money from those over and above the ones redeemed by the Levites; ⁵⁰he took the money from the male first-born of the Israelites, 1,365 sanctuary shekels. ⁵¹And Moses gave the redemption money to Aaron and his sons at יהוה's bidding, as יהוה had commanded Moses.

4 יהוה spoke to Moses and Aaron, saying: ²Take a [separate] census of the Kohathites among the Levites, by the clans of their ancestral house, ³from the age of thirty years up to the age of fifty, all who are subject to service, to perform tasks for the Tent of Meeting. ⁴This is the responsibility of the Kohathites in the Tent of Meeting: the most sacred objects.

⁵At the breaking of camp, Aaron and his sons shall go in and take down the screening curtain and cover the Ark of the Pact with it. ⁶They shall lay a covering of dolphin* skin over it and spread a cloth of pure blue on top; and they shall put its poles in place.

⁷Over the table of display they shall spread a blue cloth; they shall place upon it the bowls, the ladles, the jars, and the libation jugs; and the regular bread shall rest upon it. ⁸They shall spread over these a crimson cloth which they shall cover with a covering of dolphin skin; and they shall put the poles in place.

⁹Then they shall take a blue cloth and cover the lampstand for lighting, with its lamps, its tongs, and its fire pans, as well as all the oil vessels that are used in its service. ¹⁰They shall put it and all its furnishings into a covering of dolphin skin, which they shall then place on a carrying frame.

¹¹Next they shall spread a blue cloth over the altar of gold and cover it with a covering of dolphin skin; and they shall put its poles in place. ¹²They shall take all the service vessels with which

the service in the sanctuary is performed, put them into a blue cloth and cover them with a covering of dolphin skin, which they shall then place on a carrying frame. ¹³They shall remove the ashes from the [copper] altar and spread a purple cloth over it. ¹⁴Upon it they shall place all the vessels that are used in its service: the fire pans, the flesh hooks, the scrapers, and the basins—all the vessels of the altar—and over it they shall spread a covering of dolphin skin; and they shall put its poles in place.

¹⁵When Aaron and his sons have finished covering the sacred objects and all the furnishings of the sacred objects at the breaking of camp, only then shall the Kohathites come and lift them, so that they do not come in contact with the sacred objects and die. These things in the Tent of Meeting shall be the porterage of the Kohathites.

¹⁶Responsibility shall rest with Eleazar son of Aaron the priest for the lighting oil, the aromatic incense, the regular meal offering, and the anointing oil—responsibility for the whole Tabernacle and for everything consecrated that is in it or in its vessels.

¹⁷יהוה spoke to Moses and Aaron, saying: ¹⁸Do not let the group of Kohathite clans be cut off from the Levites. ¹⁹Do this with them, that they may live and not die when they approach the most sacred objects: let Aaron and his sons go in and assign each of them to his duties and to his porterage. ²⁰But let not [the Kohathites] go inside and *⁻witness the dismantling of the sanctuary,⁻* lest they die.

נָשֹׂא | NASO'

²¹יהוה spoke to Moses: ²²Take a census of the Gershonites also, by their ancestral house and by their clans. ²³Record them from the age of thirty years up to the age of fifty, all who are subject to service in the performance of tasks for the Tent of Meeting. ²⁴These are the duties of the Gershonite clans as to labor and porterage: ²⁵they shall carry the cloths of the Tabernacle, the Tent of Meeting with its covering, the covering of dolphin skin that is on top of it, and the screen for the entrance of the Tent of Meeting; ²⁶the hangings of the enclosure, the screen at the entrance of the gate of the enclosure that surrounds the Tabernacle, the cords thereof, and the altar, and all their service equipment and all their

accessories; and they shall perform the service. [27]All the duties of the Gershonites, all their porterage and all their service, shall be performed on orders from Aaron and his sons; you shall make them responsible for attending to all their porterage. [28]Those are the duties of the Gershonite clans for the Tent of Meeting; they shall attend to them under the direction of Ithamar son of Aaron the priest.

[29]As for the Merarites, you shall record them by the clans of their ancestral house; [30]you shall record them from the age of thirty years up to the age of fifty, all who are subject to service in the performance of the duties for the Tent of Meeting. [31]These are their porterage tasks in connection with their various duties for the Tent of Meeting: the planks, the bars, the posts, and the sockets of the Tabernacle; [32]the posts around the enclosure and their sockets, pegs, and cords—all these furnishings and their service: you shall list by name the objects that are their porterage tasks. [33]Those are the duties of the Merarite clans, pertaining to their various duties in the Tent of Meeting under the direction of Ithamar son of Aaron the priest.

[34]So Moses, Aaron, and the chieftains of the community recorded the Kohathites by the clans of their ancestral house, [35]from the age of thirty years up to the age of fifty, all who were subject to service for work relating to the Tent of Meeting. [36]Those recorded by their clans came to 2,750. [37]That was the enrollment of the Kohathite clans, all those who performed duties relating to the Tent of Meeting, whom Moses and Aaron recorded at the command of יהוה through Moses.

[38]The Gershonites who were recorded by the clans of their ancestral house, [39]from the age of thirty years up to the age of fifty, all who were subject to service for work relating to the Tent of Meeting—[40]those recorded by the clans of their ancestral house came to 2,630. [41]That was the enrollment of the Gershonite clans, all those performing duties relating to the Tent of Meeting whom Moses and Aaron recorded at the command of יהוה.

[42]The enrollment of the Merarite clans by the clans of their ancestral house, [43]from the age of thirty years up to the age of fifty, all who were subject to service for work relating to the Tent of Meeting—[44]those recorded by their clans came to 3,200. [45]That

was the enrollment of the Merarite clans which Moses and Aaron recorded at the command of יהוה through Moses.

⁴⁶All the Levites whom Moses, Aaron, and the chieftains of Israel recorded by the clans of their ancestral houses, ⁴⁷from the age of thirty years up to the age of fifty, all who were subject to duties of service and porterage relating to the Tent of Meeting—⁴⁸those recorded came to 8,580. ⁴⁹Each one was given responsibility for his service and porterage at the command of יהוה through Moses, and each was recorded as יהוה had commanded Moses.

5 יהוה spoke to Moses, saying: ²Instruct the Israelites to remove from camp anyone with an *⁻eruption or a discharge⁻* and anyone defiled by a corpse. ³Remove male and female alike; put them outside the camp so that they do not defile the camp of those in whose midst I dwell.

⁴The Israelites did so, putting them outside the camp; as יהוה had spoken to Moses, so the Israelites did.

⁵יהוה spoke to Moses, saying: ⁶Speak to the Israelites: When men or women individually commit any wrong toward a fellow human being, thus breaking faith with יהוה, and they realize their guilt, ⁷they shall confess the wrong that they have done. They shall make restitution in the principal amount and add one-fifth to it, giving it to the one who was wronged. ⁸If the person [is deceased and] has no kin* to whom restitution can be made, the amount repaid shall go to יהוה for the priest—*⁻in addition to the ram of expiation with which expiation is made on their behalf.⁻* ⁹So, too, any gift among the sacred donations that the Israelites offer shall be the priest's. ¹⁰And each shall retain his sacred donations: each priest shall keep what is given to him.

¹¹יהוה spoke to Moses, saying: ¹²Speak to the Israelite people and say to them:

If any wife has gone astray and broken faith with her husband, ¹³in that a man has had carnal relations with her unbeknown to her husband, and she keeps secret the fact that she has defiled herself without being forced, and there is no witness against her—¹⁴but a fit of jealousy comes over him and he is wrought up about the wife who has defiled herself; or if a fit of jealousy comes over one and he is wrought up about his wife although she has not defiled herself—¹⁵the husband shall bring his wife to the priest. And he shall bring as an offering for her one-tenth of an *ephah* of barley flour. No oil shall be poured upon it and no frankincense shall be laid on it, for it is a meal offering of jealousy, a meal offering of remembrance which recalls wrongdoing.

¹⁶The priest shall bring her forward and have her stand before יהוה. ¹⁷The priest shall take sacral water in an earthen vessel and, taking some of the earth that is on the floor of the Tabernacle, the priest shall put it into the water. ¹⁸After he has made the wife stand before יהוה, the priest shall *⁻bare the wife's head⁻* and place upon her hands the meal offering of remembrance, which is a meal offering of jealousy. And in the priest's hands shall be the water of bitterness *⁻that induces the spell.* ¹⁹The priest shall adjure the wife, saying to her, "If no man has lain with you, if you have not gone astray in defilement while °living in your husband's household,° be immune to harm from this water of bitterness that induces the spell. ²⁰But if you have gone astray while °living in your husband's household⁻° and have defiled yourself, if a man other than your husband has had carnal relations with you"— ²¹here the priest shall administer the curse of adjuration to the wife, as the priest goes on to say to the wife—"may יהוה make you a curse and an imprecation among your people, as יהוה causes your thigh to sag and your belly to distend; ²²may this water that induces the spell enter your body, causing the belly to distend and the thigh to sag." And the wife shall say, "Amen, amen!"

²³The priest shall put these curses down in writing and rub it off into the water of bitterness. ²⁴He is to make the wife drink the water of bitterness that induces the spell, so that the spell-inducing water may enter into her to bring on bitterness. ²⁵Then the priest shall take from the wife's hand the meal offering of jealousy, elevate the meal offering before יהוה, and present it on the altar. ²⁶The priest shall scoop out of the meal offering a token part of it and turn it into smoke on the altar. Last, he shall make the wife drink the water.

²⁷Once he has made her drink the water—if she has defiled herself by breaking faith with her husband, the spell-inducing water

shall enter into her to bring on bitterness, so that her belly shall distend and her thigh shall sag; and the wife shall become a curse among her people. 28But if the wife has not defiled herself and is pure, she shall be unharmed and able to retain seed.

29This is the ritual in cases of jealousy, when a wife goes astray while °living in her husband's household,° and defiles herself, 30or when a fit of jealousy comes over a husband and he is wrought up over his wife: the wife shall be made to stand before יהוה and the priest shall carry out all this ritual with her. 31The husband shall be clear of guilt; but that wife shall suffer for her guilt.

6 יהוה spoke to Moses, saying: 2Speak to the Israelites and say to them: If any °men or women° explicitly* utter a nazirite's vow, to set themselves apart for יהוה, 3they shall abstain from wine and any other intoxicant; they shall not drink vinegar of wine or of any other intoxicant, neither shall they drink anything in which grapes have been steeped, nor eat grapes fresh or dried. 4Throughout their term as nazirite, they may not eat anything that is obtained from the grapevine, even *‑seeds or skin.‑*

5Throughout the term of their vow as nazirite, no razor shall touch their head; it shall remain consecrated until the completion of their term as nazirite of יהוה, the hair of their head being left to grow untrimmed. 6Throughout the term that they have set apart for יהוה, they shall not go in where there is a dead person. 7Even if their father or mother, or their brother or sister should die, they must not become defiled for any of them, since *‑hair set apart for their God‑* is upon their head: 8throughout their term as nazirite they are consecrated to יהוה.

9If someone dies suddenly nearby,* defiling the consecrated hair, the person shall shave the head at the time of becoming pure, shaving it on the seventh day. 10On the eighth day the person shall bring two turtledoves or two pigeons to the priest, at the entrance of the Tent of Meeting. 11The priest shall offer one as a *‑sin offering‑* and the other as a burnt offering, and make expiation on the person's behalf for the guilt incurred through the corpse. That same day the head shall be reconsecrated; 12and the person shall rededicate to יהוה the term as nazirite, bringing a lamb in its first year as a penalty offering. The previous period shall be void, since the consecrated hair was defiled.

¹³This is the ritual for the nazirite: On the day that the term as nazirite is completed, *⁻the person⁻* shall be brought to the entrance of the Tent of Meeting. ¹⁴As an offering to יהוה the person shall present: one male lamb in its first year, without blemish, for a burnt offering; one ewe lamb in its first year, without blemish, for a sin offering; one ram without blemish for an offering of well-being; ¹⁵a basket of unleavened cakes of choice flour with oil mixed in, and unleavened wafers spread with oil; and the proper meal offerings and libations.

¹⁶The priest shall present them before יהוה and offer the sin offering and the burnt offering. ¹⁷He shall offer the ram as a sacrifice of well-being to יהוה, together with the basket of unleavened cakes; the priest shall also offer the meal offerings and the libations. ¹⁸The nazirite shall then shave the consecrated hair, at the entrance of the Tent of Meeting, and take those locks of consecrated hair and put them on the fire that is under the sacrifice of well-being.

¹⁹The priest shall take the shoulder of the ram when it has been boiled, one unleavened cake from the basket, and one unleavened wafer, and place them on the hands of the nazirite after the consecrated hair has been shaved. ²⁰The priest shall elevate them as an elevation offering before יהוה; and this shall be a sacred donation for the priest, in addition to the breast of the elevation offering and the thigh of gift offering. After that the nazirite may drink wine.

²¹Such is the obligation of a nazirite; except that those who vow an offering to יהוה of what they can afford, beyond their nazirite requirements, must do exactly according to the vow that they have made beyond their obligation as nazirites.

²²יהוה spoke to Moses: ²³Speak to Aaron and his sons: Thus shall you bless the people of Israel. Say to them:

²⁴יהוה bless you and protect you!

²⁵יהוה *⁻deal kindly and graciously with you!⁻*

²⁶יהוה *⁻bestow [divine] favor⁻* upon you and grant you peace!*

²⁷Thus they shall link My name with the people of Israel, and I will bless them.

7 On the day that Moses finished setting up the Tabernacle, he anointed and consecrated it and all its furnishings, as well as the altar and its utensils. When he had anointed and consecrated them, ²the chieftains of Israel, the heads of ancestral houses, namely, the chieftains of the tribes, those who were in charge of enrollment, *⁻drew near⁻* ³and brought their offering before יהוה: six draught carts and twelve oxen, a cart for every two chieftains and an ox for each one.

When they had brought them before the Tabernacle, ⁴יהוה said to Moses: ⁵Accept these from them for use in the service of the Tent of Meeting, and give them to the Levites according to their respective services.

⁶Moses took the carts and the oxen and gave them to the Levites. ⁷Two carts and four oxen he gave to the Gershonites, as required for their service, ⁸and four carts and eight oxen he gave to the Merarites, as required for their service—under the direction of Ithamar son of Aaron the priest. ⁹But to the Kohathites he did not give any; since theirs was the service of the [most] sacred objects, their porterage was by shoulder.

¹⁰The chieftains also brought the dedication offering for the altar upon its being anointed. As the chieftains were presenting their offerings before the altar, ¹¹יהוה said to Moses: Let them present their offerings for the dedication of the altar, one chieftain each day.

¹²The one who presented his offering on the first day was Nahshon son of Amminadab of the tribe of Judah. ¹³His offering: one silver bowl weighing 130 shekels and one silver basin of 70 shekels by the sanctuary weight, both filled with choice flour with oil mixed in, for a meal offering; ¹⁴one gold ladle of 10 shekels, filled with incense; ¹⁵one bull of the herd, one ram, and one lamb in its first year, for a burnt offering; ¹⁶one goat for a sin offering; ¹⁷and for his sacrifice of well-being: two oxen, five rams, five he-goats, and five yearling lambs. That was the offering of Nahshon son of Amminadab.

¹⁸On the second day, Nethanel son of Zuar, chieftain of Issachar, made his offering. ¹⁹He presented as his offering: one silver bowl weighing 130 shekels and one silver basin of 70 shekels by the sanctuary weight, both filled with choice flour with oil mixed in, for a meal offering; ²⁰one gold ladle of 10 shekels, filled with

incense; ²¹one bull of the herd, one ram, and one lamb in its first year, for a burnt offering; ²²one goat for a sin offering; ²³and for his sacrifice of well-being: two oxen, five rams, five he-goats, and five yearling lambs. That was the offering of Nethanel son of Zuar.

²⁴On the third day, it was the chieftain of the Zebulunites, Eliab son of Helon. ²⁵His offering: one silver bowl weighing 130 shekels and one silver basin of 70 shekels by the sanctuary weight, both filled with choice flour with oil mixed in, for a meal offering; ²⁶one gold ladle of 10 shekels, filled with incense; ²⁷one bull of the herd, one ram, and one lamb in its first year, for a burnt offering; ²⁸one goat for a sin offering; ²⁹and for his sacrifice of well-being: two oxen, five rams, five he-goats, and five yearling lambs. That was the offering of Eliab son of Helon.

³⁰On the fourth day, it was the chieftain of the Reubenites, Elizur son of Shedeur. ³¹His offering: one silver bowl weighing 130 shekels and one silver basin of 70 shekels by the sanctuary weight, both filled with choice flour with oil mixed in, for a meal offering; ³²one gold ladle of 10 shekels, filled with incense; ³³one bull of the herd, one ram, and one lamb in its first year, for a burnt offering; ³⁴one goat for a sin offering; ³⁵and for his sacrifice of well-being: two oxen, five rams, five he-goats, and five yearling lambs. That was the offering of Elizur son of Shedeur.

³⁶On the fifth day, it was the chieftain of the Simeonites, Shelumiel son of Zurishaddai. ³⁷His offering: one silver bowl weighing 130 shekels and one silver basin of 70 shekels by the sanctuary weight, both filled with choice flour with oil mixed in, for a meal offering; ³⁸one gold ladle of 10 shekels, filled with incense; ³⁹one bull of the herd, one ram, and one lamb in its first year, for a burnt offering; ⁴⁰one goat for a sin offering; ⁴¹and for his sacrifice of well-being: two oxen, five rams, five he-goats, and five yearling lambs. That was the offering of Shelumiel son of Zurishaddai.

⁴²On the sixth day, it was the chieftain of the Gadites, Eliasaph son of Deuel. ⁴³His offering: one silver bowl weighing 130 shekels and one silver basin of 70 shekels by the sanctuary weight, both filled with choice flour with oil mixed in, for a meal offering; ⁴⁴one gold ladle of 10 shekels, filled with incense; ⁴⁵one bull of the

herd, one ram, and one lamb in its first year, for a burnt offering; ⁴⁶one goat for a sin offering; ⁴⁷and for his sacrifice of well-being: two oxen, five rams, five he-goats, and five yearling lambs. That was the offering of Eliasaph son of Deuel.

⁴⁸On the seventh day, it was the chieftain of the Ephraimites, Elishama son of Ammihud. ⁴⁹His offering: one silver bowl weighing 130 shekels and one silver basin of 70 shekels by the sanctuary weight, both filled with choice flour with oil mixed in, for a meal offering; ⁵⁰one gold ladle of 10 shekels, filled with incense; ⁵¹one bull of the herd, one ram, and one lamb in its first year, for a burnt offering; ⁵²one goat for a sin offering; ⁵³and for his sacrifice of well-being: two oxen, five rams, five he-goats, and five yearling lambs. That was the offering of Elishama son of Ammihud.

⁵⁴On the eighth day, it was the chieftain of the Manassites, Gamaliel son of Pedahzur. ⁵⁵His offering: one silver bowl weighing 130 shekels and one silver basin of 70 shekels by the sanctuary weight, both filled with choice flour with oil mixed in, for a meal offering; ⁵⁶one gold ladle of 10 shekels, filled with incense; ⁵⁷one bull of the herd, one ram, and one lamb in its first year, for a burnt offering; ⁵⁸one goat for a sin offering; ⁵⁹and for his sacrifice of well-being: two oxen, five rams, five he-goats, and five yearling lambs. That was the offering of Gamaliel son of Pedahzur.

⁶⁰On the ninth day, it was the chieftain of the Benjaminites, Abidan son of Gideoni. ⁶¹His offering: one silver bowl weighing 130 shekels and one silver basin of 70 shekels by the sanctuary weight, both filled with choice flour with oil mixed in, for a meal offering; ⁶²one gold ladle of 10 shekels, filled with incense; ⁶³one bull of the herd, one ram, and one lamb in its first year, for a burnt offering; ⁶⁴one goat for a sin offering; ⁶⁵and for his sacrifice of well-being: two oxen, five rams, five he-goats, and five yearling lambs. That was the offering of Abidan son of Gideoni.

⁶⁶On the tenth day, it was the chieftain of the Danites, Ahiezer son of Ammishaddai. ⁶⁷His offering: one silver bowl weighing 130 shekels and one silver basin of 70 shekels by the sanctuary weight, both filled with choice flour with oil mixed in, for a meal offering; ⁶⁸one gold ladle of 10 shekels, filled with incense; ⁶⁹one bull of the herd, one ram, and one lamb in its first year, for a burnt offering;

[70]one goat for a sin offering; [71]and for his sacrifice of well-being: two oxen, five rams, five he-goats, and five yearling lambs. That was the offering of Ahiezer son of Ammishaddai.

[72]On the eleventh day, it was the chieftain of the Asherites, Pagiel son of Ochran. [73]His offering: one silver bowl weighing 130 shekels and one silver basin of 70 shekels by the sanctuary weight, both filled with choice flour with oil mixed in, for a meal offering; [74]one gold ladle of 10 shekels, filled with incense; [75]one bull of the herd, one ram, and one lamb in its first year, for a burnt offering; [76]one goat for a sin offering; [77]and for his sacrifice of well-being: two oxen, five rams, five he-goats, and five yearling lambs. That was the offering of Pagiel son of Ochran.

[78]On the twelfth day, it was the chieftain of the Naphtalites, Ahira son of Enan. [79]His offering: one silver bowl weighing 130 shekels and one silver basin of 70 shekels by the sanctuary weight, both filled with choice flour with oil mixed in, for a meal offering; [80]one gold ladle of 10 shekels, filled with incense; [81]one bull of the herd, one ram, and one lamb in its first year, for a burnt offering; [82]one goat for a sin offering; [83]and for his sacrifice of well-being: two oxen, five rams, five he-goats, and five yearling lambs. That was the offering of Ahira son of Enan.

[84]This was the dedication offering for the altar from the chieftains of Israel upon its being anointed: silver bowls, 12; silver basins, 12; gold ladles, 12. [85]Silver per bowl, 130; per basin, 70. Total silver of vessels, 2,400 sanctuary shekels. [86]The 12 gold ladles filled with incense—10 sanctuary shekels per ladle—total gold of the ladles, 120.

[87]Total of herd animals for burnt offerings, 12 bulls; of rams, 12; of yearling lambs, 12—with their proper meal offerings; of goats for sin offerings, 12. [88]Total of herd animals for sacrifices of well-being, 24 bulls; of rams, 60; of he-goats, 60; of yearling lambs, 60. That was the dedication offering for the altar after its anointing.

[89]When Moses went into the Tent of Meeting to speak with [God], he would hear the Voice addressing him from above the cover that was on top of the Ark of the Pact between the two cherubim; thus [God] spoke to him.

בְּהַעֲלֹתְךָ | BE-HA'ALOTEKHA

8 יהוה spoke to Moses, saying: ²Speak to Aaron and say to him, "When you mount* the lamps, let the seven lamps give light at the front of the lampstand." ³Aaron did so; he mounted the lamps at the front of the lampstand, as יהוה had commanded Moses.—⁴Now this is how the lampstand was made: it was hammered work of gold, hammered from base to petal. According to the pattern that יהוה had shown Moses, so was the lampstand made.

⁵יהוה spoke to Moses, saying: ⁶Take the Levites from among the Israelites and purify them. ⁷This is what you shall do to them to purify them: sprinkle on them water of purification, and let them go over their whole body with a razor, and wash their clothes; thus they shall be purified. ⁸Let them take a bull of the herd, and with it a meal offering of choice flour with oil mixed in, and you take a second bull of the herd for a sin offering. ⁹You shall bring the Levites forward before the Tent of Meeting. Assemble the °Israelite community leadership;° ¹⁰and bring the Levites forward before יהוה. Let the Israelites lay their hands upon the Levites, ¹¹and let Aaron designate* the Levites before יהוה as an elevation offering from the Israelites, that they may perform the service of יהוה. ¹²The Levites shall now lay their hands upon the heads of the bulls; one shall be offered to יהוה as a sin offering and the other as a burnt offering, to make expiation for the Levites.

¹³You shall place the Levites in attendance upon Aaron and his sons, and designate them as an elevation offering to יהוה. ¹⁴Thus you shall set the Levites apart from the Israelites, and the Levites shall be Mine. ¹⁵Thereafter the Levites shall be qualified for the service of the Tent of Meeting, once you have purified them and designated them as an elevation offering. ¹⁶For they are formally assigned to Me from among the Israelites: I have taken them for Myself in place of all the first issue of the womb, of all the male first-born of the Israelites. ¹⁷For every male first-born among the Israelites, human as well as beast, is Mine; I consecrated them to Myself at the time that I smote every [male] first-born in the land of Egypt. ¹⁸Now I take the Levites instead of every male first-born of the Israelites; ¹⁹and from among the Israelites I formally assign

the Levites to Aaron and his sons, to perform the service for the Israelites in the Tent of Meeting and to make expiation for the Israelites, so that no plague may afflict the Israelites *⁻for coming⁻* too near the sanctuary.

²⁰Moses, Aaron, and the °Israelite community leadership°⁻ did with the Levites accordingly; just as יהוה had commanded Moses in regard to the Levites, so the Israelites did with them. ²¹The Levites purified themselves and washed their clothes; and Aaron designated them as an elevation offering before יהוה, and Aaron made expiation for them to purify them. ²²Thereafter the Levites were qualified to perform their service in the Tent of Meeting, under Aaron and his sons. As יהוה had commanded Moses in regard to the Levites, so they did to them.

²³יהוה spoke to Moses, saying: ²⁴This is the rule for the Levites. From twenty-five years of age up they shall participate in the work force in the service of the Tent of Meeting; ²⁵but at the age of fifty they shall retire from the work force and shall serve no more. ²⁶They may assist their brother Levites at the Tent of Meeting by standing guard, but they shall perform no labor. Thus you shall deal with the Levites in regard to their duties.

9 יהוה spoke to Moses in the wilderness of Sinai, on the first new moon of the second year following the exodus from the land of Egypt, saying: ²Let the Israelite people offer the passover sacrifice at its set time: ³you shall offer it on the fourteenth day of this month, at twilight, at its set time; you shall offer it in accordance with all its rules and rites.

⁴Moses instructed the Israelites to offer the passover sacrifice; ⁵and they offered the passover sacrifice in the first month, on the fourteenth day of the month, at twilight, in the wilderness of Sinai. Just as יהוה had commanded Moses, so the Israelites did.

⁶But there were some householders° who were impure by reason of a corpse and could not offer the passover sacrifice on that day. Appearing that same day before Moses and Aaron, ⁷those householders° said to them,* "Impure though we are by reason of a corpse, why must we be debarred from presenting יהוה's offering at its set time with the rest of the Israelites?" ⁸Moses said to

them, "Stand by, and let me hear what instructions יהוה gives about you."

⁹And יהוה spoke to Moses, saying: ¹⁰Speak to the Israelite people, saying: When any of you or of your posterity who are defiled by a corpse or are on a long journey would offer a passover sacrifice to יהוה—¹¹they shall offer it in the second month, on the fourteenth day of the month, at twilight. They shall eat it with unleavened bread and bitter herbs, ¹²and they shall not leave any of it over until morning. They shall not break a bone of it. They shall offer it in strict accord with the law of the passover sacrifice. ¹³But if a householder° who is pure and not on a journey refrains from offering the passover sacrifice, that person shall be cut off from kin, for יהוה's offering was not presented at its set time; that householder shall bear his guilt.

¹⁴And when a stranger who resides with you would offer a passover sacrifice to יהוה, it must be offered in accordance with the rules and rites of the passover sacrifice. There shall be one law for you, whether stranger or citizen of the country.

¹⁵On the day that the Tabernacle was set up, the cloud covered the Tabernacle, the Tent of the Pact; and in the evening it rested over the Tabernacle in the likeness of fire until morning. ¹⁶It was always so: the cloud covered it, appearing as fire by night. ¹⁷And whenever the cloud lifted from the Tent, the Israelites would set out accordingly; and at the spot where the cloud settled, there the Israelites would make camp. ¹⁸At a command of יהוה the Israelites broke camp, and at a command of יהוה they made camp: they remained encamped as long as the cloud stayed over the Tabernacle. ¹⁹When the cloud lingered over the Tabernacle many days, the Israelites observed יהוה's mandate and did not journey on. ²⁰At such times as the cloud rested over the Tabernacle for but a few days, they remained encamped at a command of יהוה, and broke camp at a command of יהוה. ²¹And at such times as the cloud stayed from evening until morning, they broke camp as soon as the cloud lifted in the morning. Day or night, whenever the cloud lifted, they would break camp. ²²Whether it was two days or a month or a year—however long the cloud lingered over the Tabernacle—the Israelites remained

encamped and did not set out; only when it lifted did they break camp. ²³On a sign from יהוה they made camp and on a sign from יהוה they broke camp; they observed יהוה's mandate at יהוה's bidding through Moses.

10

יהוה spoke to Moses, saying: ²Have two silver trumpets made; make them of hammered work. They shall serve you to summon [military bodies of] the community and to set the divisions in motion. ³When both are blown in *⁻long blasts,⁻* the whole °⁻company [of fighters]⁻° shall assemble before you at the entrance of the Tent of Meeting; ⁴and if only one is blown, the chieftains, heads of Israel's contingents, shall assemble before you. ⁵But when you sound short blasts, the divisions encamped on the east shall move forward; ⁶and when you sound short blasts a second time, those encamped on the south shall move forward. Thus short blasts shall be blown for setting them in motion, ⁷while to convoke [military bodies of] the congregation you shall blow long blasts, not short ones. ⁸The trumpets shall be blown by Aaron's sons, the priests; they shall be for you an institution for all time throughout the ages.

⁹When you are at war in your land against an aggressor who attacks you, you shall sound short blasts on the trumpets, that you may be remembered before your God יהוה and be delivered from your enemies. ¹⁰And on your joyous occasions—your fixed festivals and new moon days—you shall sound the trumpets over your burnt offerings and your sacrifices of well-being. They shall be a reminder of you before your God: I, יהוה, am your God.

¹¹In the second year, on the twentieth day of the second month, the cloud lifted from the Tabernacle of the Pact ¹²and the Israelites set out on their journeys from the wilderness of Sinai. The cloud came to rest in the wilderness of Paran.

¹³When the march was to begin, at יהוה's command through Moses, ¹⁴the first standard to set out, troop by troop, was the division of Judah. In command of its troops was Nahshon son of Amminadab; ¹⁵in command of the tribal troop of Issachar, Nethanel son of Zuar; ¹⁶and in command of the tribal troop of Zebulun, Eliab son of Helon.

¹⁷Then the Tabernacle would be taken apart; and the Gershonites and the Merarites, who carried the Tabernacle, would set out.

¹⁸The next standard to set out, troop by troop, was the division of Reuben. In command of its troop was Elizur son of Shedeur; ¹⁹in command of the tribal troop of Simeon, Shelumiel son of Zurishaddai; ²⁰and in command of the tribal troop of Gad, Eliasaph son of Deuel.

²¹Then the Kohathites, who carried the sacred objects, would set out; and by the time they arrived, the Tabernacle would be set up again.

²²The next standard to set out, troop by troop, was the division of Ephraim. In command of its troop was Elishama son of Ammihud; ²³in command of the tribal troop of Manasseh, Gamaliel son of Pedahzur; ²⁴and in command of the tribal troop of Benjamin, Abidan son of Gideoni.

²⁵Then, as the rear guard of all the divisions, the standard of the division of Dan would set out, troop by troop. In command of its troop was Ahiezer son of Ammishaddai; ²⁶in command of the tribal troop of Asher, Pagiel son of Ochran; ²⁷and in command of the tribal troop of Naphtali, Ahira son of Enan.

²⁸Such was the order of march of the Israelites, as they marched troop by troop.

²⁹Moses said to Hobab son of Reuel the Midianite, Moses' father-in-law, "We are setting out for the place of which יהוה has said, 'I will give it to you.' Come with us and we will be generous with you; for יהוה has promised to be generous to Israel."

³⁰"I will not go," he replied to him, "but will return to my native land." ³¹He said, "Please do not leave us, inasmuch as you know where we should camp in the wilderness and can be our guide.* ³²So if you come with us, we will extend to you the same bounty that יהוה grants us."

³³They marched from the mountain of יהוה a distance of three days. The Ark of the Covenant of יהוה traveled in front of them on that three days' journey to seek out a resting place for them; ³⁴and יהוה's cloud kept above them by day, as they moved on from camp.

³⁵When the Ark was to set out, Moses would say:
Advance, O יהוה!
May Your enemies be scattered,
And may Your foes flee before You!
³⁶And when it halted, he would say:
*ᐨReturn, O יהוה,
You who are Israel's myriads of thousands!ᐨ*

11 The people took to complaining bitterly before יהוה. יהוה heard and was incensed: a fire of יהוה broke out against them, ravaging the outskirts of the camp. ²The people cried out to Moses. Moses prayed to יהוה, and the fire died down. ³That place was named Taberah,* because a fire of יהוה had broken out against them.

⁴The riffraff in their midst felt a gluttonous craving; and then the Israelites wept and said, "If only we had meat to eat! ⁵We remember the fish that we used to eat free in Egypt, the cucumbers, the melons, the leeks, the onions, and the garlic. ⁶Now our gullets are shriveled. There is nothing at all! Nothing but this manna to look to!"

⁷Now the manna was like coriander seed, and in color it was like bdellium. ⁸The people would go about and gather it, grind it between millstones or pound it in a mortar, boil it in a pot, and make it into cakes. It tasted like *ᐨrich cream.ᐨ* ⁹When the dew fell on the camp at night, the manna would fall upon it.

¹⁰Moses heard the people weeping, every clan apart, at the entrance of each tent. יהוה was very angry, and Moses was distressed. ¹¹And Moses said to יהוה, "Why have You dealt ill with Your servant, and why have I not enjoyed Your favor, that You have laid the burden of all this people upon me? ¹²Did I produce all this people, did I engender them, that You should say to me, 'Carry them in your bosom as a caretaker carries an infant,' to the land that You have promised on oath to their fathers? ¹³Where am I to get meat to give to all this people, when they whine before me and say, 'Give us meat to eat!' ¹⁴I cannot carry all this people by myself, for it is too much for me. ¹⁵If You would deal thus with me, kill me rather, I beg You, and let me see no more of my wretchedness!"

16Then יהוה said to Moses, "Gather for Me seventy of Israel's elders of whom you have experience as elders and officers of the people, and bring them to the Tent of Meeting and let them take their place there with you. 17I will come down and speak with you there, and I will draw upon the spirit that is on you and put it upon them; they shall share the burden of the people with you, and you shall not bear it alone. 18And say to the people: *"Purify yourselves"* for tomorrow and you shall eat meat, for you have kept whining before יהוה and saying, 'If only we had meat to eat! Indeed, we were better off in Egypt!' יהוה will give you meat and you shall eat. 19You shall eat not one day, not two, not even five days or ten or twenty, 20but a whole month, until it comes out of your nostrils and becomes loathsome to you. For you have rejected יהוה who is among you, by whining before [God] and saying, 'Oh, why did we ever leave Egypt!'"

21But Moses said, "The people *"who are with me"* number six hundred thousand foot soldiers; yet You say, 'I will give them enough meat to eat for a whole month.' 22Could enough flocks and herds be slaughtered to suffice them? Or could all the fish of the sea be gathered for them to suffice them?" 23And יהוה answered Moses, "*"Is there a limit to יהוה's power?"* You shall soon see whether what I have said happens to you or not!"

24Moses went out and reported the words of יהוה to the people. He gathered seventy of the people's elders and stationed them around the Tent. 25Then, after coming down in a cloud and speaking to him, יהוה drew upon the spirit that was on him and put it upon the seventy representative° elders. And when the spirit rested upon them, they *"spoke in ecstasy,"* but did not continue.

26Two of the elders,° one named Eldad and the other Medad, had remained in camp; yet the spirit rested upon them—they were among those recorded, but they had not gone out to the Tent—and they spoke in ecstasy in the camp. 27An assistant° ran out and told Moses, saying, "Eldad and Medad are acting the prophet in the camp!" 28And Joshua son of Nun, Moses' attendant from his youth, spoke up and said, "My lord Moses, restrain them!" 29But Moses said to him, "Are you wrought up on my account? Would that all יהוה's people were prophets, that יהוה put [the divine] spirit upon them!" ³⁰Moses then reentered the camp together with the elders of Israel.

³¹A wind from יהוה started up, swept quail from the sea and strewed them over the camp, about a day's journey on this side and about a day's journey on that side, all around the camp, and some two cubits deep on the ground. ³²The people set to gathering quail all that day and night and all the next day—even the one who gathered least had ten *chomers*—and they spread them out all around the camp. ³³The meat was still between their teeth, not yet chewed,* when the anger of יהוה blazed forth against the people and יהוה struck the people with a very severe plague. ³⁴That place was named Kibroth-hattaavah,* because the people who had the craving were buried there.

³⁵Then the people set out from Kibroth-hattaavah for Hazeroth. When they were in Hazeroth, **12** ¹Miriam and Aaron spoke against Moses because of the Cushite woman he had taken [into his household as his wife]: "He took a Cushite woman!"

²They said, "Has יהוה spoken only through Moses? Has [God] not spoken through us as well?" יהוה heard it. ³Now Moses was a very humble leader,° more so than any other human being on earth. ⁴Suddenly יהוה called to Moses, Aaron, and Miriam, "Come out, you three, to the Tent of Meeting." So the three of them went out. ⁵יהוה came down in a pillar of cloud, stopped at the entrance of the Tent, and called out, "Aaron and Miriam!" The two of them came forward; ⁶and [God] said, "Hear these My words: *·When prophets of יהוה arise among you, I* make Myself known to them in a vision, I speak with them in a dream. ⁷Not so with My servant Moses; he is trusted throughout My household. ⁸With him I speak mouth to mouth, plainly and not in riddles, and he beholds the likeness of יהוה. How then did you not shrink from speaking against My servant Moses!" ⁹Still incensed with them, יהוה departed.

¹⁰As the cloud withdrew from the Tent, there was Miriam stricken with snow-white scales!* When Aaron turned toward Miriam, he saw that she was stricken with scales. ¹¹And Aaron said to Moses, "O my lord, account not to us the sin which we

committed in our folly. ¹²Let her not be like a stillbirth which emerges from its mother's womb with half its flesh eaten away!" ¹³So Moses cried out to יהוה, saying, "O God, pray heal her!"

¹⁴But יהוה said to Moses, "If her father spat in her face, would she not bear her shame for seven days? Let her be shut out of camp for seven days, and then let her be readmitted." ¹⁵So Miriam was shut out of camp seven days; and the people did not march on until Miriam was readmitted. ¹⁶After that the people set out from Hazeroth and encamped in the wilderness of Paran.

שְׁלַח לְךָ | SHELAH-LEKHA

13 יהוה spoke to Moses, saying, ²"Send emissaries° to scout the land of Canaan, which I am giving to the Israelite people; send one representative° from each of their ancestral tribes, each one a chieftain among them." ³So Moses, by יהוה's command, sent them out from the wilderness of Paran, °all of them being notables,⁻° leaders of the Israelites. ⁴And these were their names:

From the tribe of Reuben, Shammua son of Zaccur.
⁵From the tribe of Simeon, Shaphat son of Hori.
⁶From the tribe of Judah, Caleb son of Jephunneh.
⁷From the tribe of Issachar, Igal son of Joseph.
⁸From the tribe of Ephraim, Hosea* son of Nun.
⁹From the tribe of Benjamin, Palti son of Rafu.
¹⁰From the tribe of Zebulun, Gaddiel son of Sodi.
¹¹From the tribe of Joseph, namely, the tribe of Manasseh, Gaddi son of Susi.
¹²From the tribe of Dan, Ammiel son of Gemalli.
¹³From the tribe of Asher, Sethur son of Michael.
¹⁴From the tribe of Naphtali, Nahbi son of Vophsi.
¹⁵From the tribe of Gad, Geuel son of Machi.

¹⁶Those were the names of the emissaries° whom Moses sent to scout the land; but Moses changed the name of Hosea son of Nun to Joshua.

¹⁷When Moses sent them to scout the land of Canaan, he said to them, "Go up there into the Negeb and on into the hill country, ¹⁸and see what kind of country it is. Are the people who dwell in it strong or weak, few or many? ¹⁹Is the country in which they

Shelaḥ-Lekha

dwell good or bad? Are the towns they live in open or fortified? 20Is the soil rich or poor? Is it wooded or not? And take pains to bring back some of the fruit of the land."—Now it happened to be the season of the first ripe grapes.

21They went up and scouted the land, from the wilderness of Zin to Rehob, at Lebo-hamath.* 22They went up into the Negeb and came to Hebron, where lived Ahiman, Sheshai, and Talmai, the Anakites.—Now Hebron was founded seven years before Zoan of Egypt.—23They reached the wadi Eshcol, and there they cut down a branch with a single cluster of grapes—it had to be borne on a carrying frame by two of them—and some pomegranates and figs. 24That place was named the wadi Eshcol* because of the cluster that the Israelites cut down there.

25At the end of forty days they returned from scouting the land. 26They went straight to Moses and Aaron and the whole Israelite community at Kadesh in the wilderness of Paran, and they made their report to them and to the whole community, as they showed them the fruit of the land. 27This is what they told him: "We came to the land you sent us to; it does indeed flow with milk and honey, and this is its fruit. 28However, the people who inhabit the country are powerful, and the cities are fortified and very large; moreover, we saw the Anakites there. 29Amalekites dwell in the Negeb region; Hittites, Jebusites, and Amorites inhabit the hill country; and Canaanites dwell by the Sea and along the Jordan."

30Caleb hushed the people before Moses and said, "Let us by all means go up, and we shall gain possession of it, for we shall surely overcome it."

31But the emissaries° who had gone up with him said, "We cannot attack that people, for it is stronger than we." 32Thus they spread calumnies among the Israelites about the land they had scouted, saying, "The country that we traversed and scouted is one that devours its settlers. All the people that we saw in it are of great size; 33we saw the Nephilim* there—the Anakites are part of the Nephilim—and we looked like grasshoppers to ourselves, and so we must have looked to them."

14 The whole community broke into loud cries, and the people wept that night. 2All the Israelites railed against Moses and Aaron. "If only we had died in the land of Egypt," the whole community shouted at them, "or if only we might die in this wilderness!" ³"Why is יהוה taking us to that land to fall by the sword?" "Our wives and children will be carried off! It would be better for us to go back to Egypt!" ⁴And they said to one another, "Let us *-head back for-* Egypt."

⁵Then Moses and Aaron fell on their faces before all the assembled congregation of Israelites. ⁶And Joshua son of Nun and Caleb son of Jephunneh, of those who had scouted the land, rent their clothes ⁷and exhorted the whole Israelite community: "The land that we traversed and scouted is an exceedingly good land. ⁸If pleased with us, יהוה will bring us into that land, a land that flows with milk and honey, and give it to us; ⁹only you must not rebel against יהוה. Have no fear then of the people of the country, for they are our prey:* their protection has departed from them, but יהוה is with us. Have no fear of them!" ¹⁰As the whole community threatened to pelt them with stones, the Presence of יהוה appeared in the Tent of Meeting to all the Israelites.

¹¹And יהוה said to Moses, "How long will this people spurn Me, and how long will they have no faith in Me despite all the signs that I have performed in their midst? ¹²I will strike them with pestilence and disown them, and I will make of you a nation far more numerous than they!" ¹³But Moses said to יהוה, "When the Egyptians, from whose midst You brought up this people in Your might, hear the news, ¹⁴they will tell it to the inhabitants of that land. Now they have heard that You, יהוה, are in the midst of this people; that You, יהוה, appear in plain sight when Your cloud rests over them and when You go before them in a pillar of cloud by day and in a pillar of fire by night. ¹⁵If then You slay this people wholesale,° the nations who have heard Your fame will say, ¹⁶'It must be because יהוה was powerless to bring that people into the land promised them on oath that [that god] slaughtered them in the wilderness.' ¹⁷Therefore, I pray, let my lord's forbearance be great, as You have declared, saying,* ¹⁸'יהוה! slow to anger and abounding in kindness; forgiving iniquity and transgression; yet not remitting all punishment, but visiting the iniquity of parents upon children, upon the third and fourth generations.' ¹⁹Pardon, I pray, the iniquity of this people according to Your great kindness, as You have forgiven this people ever since Egypt."

Shelaḥ-Lekha

²⁰And יהוה said, "I pardon, as you have asked. ²¹Nevertheless, as I live and as יהוה's Presence fills the whole world, ²²none of the adults° who have seen My Presence and the signs that I have performed in Egypt and in the wilderness, and who have tried Me these many* times and have disobeyed Me, ²³shall see the land that I promised on oath to their fathers; none of those who spurn Me shall see it. ²⁴But My servant Caleb, because he was imbued with a different spirit and remained loyal to Me—him will I bring into the land that he entered, and his offspring shall hold it as a possession. ²⁵Now the Amalekites and the Canaanites occupy the valleys. Start out, then, tomorrow and march into the wilderness by way of the *⁻Sea of Reeds."⁻*

²⁶יהוה spoke further to Moses and Aaron, ²⁷"How much longer shall that wicked community keep muttering against Me? Very well, I have heeded the incessant muttering of the Israelites against Me. ²⁸Say to them: 'As I live,' says יהוה, 'I will do to you just as you have urged Me. ²⁹In this very wilderness shall your carcasses drop. Of all of you [men]° who were recorded in your various lists from the age of twenty years up, you who have muttered against Me, ³⁰not one shall enter the land in which I swore* to settle you—save Caleb son of Jephunneh and Joshua son of Nun. ³¹Your children who, you said, would be carried off—these will I allow to enter; they shall know the land that you have rejected. ³²But your carcasses shall drop in this wilderness, ³³while your children roam the wilderness for forty years, suffering for your faithlessness, until the last of your carcasses is down in the wilderness. ³⁴You shall bear your punishment for forty years, corresponding to the number of days—forty days—that you scouted the land: a year for each day. Thus you shall know what it means to thwart Me. ³⁵I יהוה have spoken: Thus will I do to all that wicked band that has banded together against Me: in this very wilderness they shall die and so be finished off.'"

³⁶As for the emissaries° whom Moses sent to scout the land, those who came back and caused the whole community to mutter against him by spreading calumnies about the land—³⁷those who spread such calumnies about the land died of plague, by the will of יהוה. ³⁸Of those emissaries° who had gone to scout the land, only Joshua son of Nun and Caleb son of Jephunneh survived.

³⁹When Moses repeated these words to all the Israelites, the people were overcome by grief. ⁴⁰Early next morning [their fighting force] set out toward the crest of the hill country, saying, "We are prepared to go up to the place that יהוה has spoken of, for we were wrong." ⁴¹But Moses said, "Why do you transgress יהוה's command? This will not succeed. ⁴²Do not go up, lest you be routed by your enemies, for יהוה is not in your midst. ⁴³For the Amalekites and the Canaanites will be there to face you, and you will fall by the sword, inasmuch as you have turned from following יהוה and יהוה will not be with you."

⁴⁴Yet defiantly* they marched toward the crest of the hill country, though neither יהוה's Ark of the Covenant nor Moses stirred from the camp. ⁴⁵And the Amalekites and the Canaanites who dwelt in that hill country came down and dealt them a shattering blow at Hormah.

15

יהוה spoke to Moses, saying: ²Speak to the Israelite people and say to them:

When you enter the land that I am giving you to settle in, ³and would present an offering by fire to יהוה from the herd or from the flock, be it burnt offering or sacrifice, in fulfillment of a vow *⁻explicitly uttered,⁻* or as a freewill offering, or at your fixed occasions, producing an odor pleasing to יהוה:

⁴The person who presents the offering to יהוה shall bring as a meal offering: a tenth of a measure of choice flour with a quarter of a *hin* of oil mixed in. ⁵You shall also offer, with the burnt offering or the sacrifice, a quarter of a *hin* of wine as a libation for each sheep.

⁶In the case of a ram, you shall present as a meal offering: two-tenths of a measure of choice flour with a third of a *hin* of oil mixed in; ⁷and a third of a *hin* of wine as a libation—as an offering of pleasing odor to יהוה.

⁸And if it is an animal from the herd that you offer to יהוה as a burnt offering or as a sacrifice, in fulfillment of a vow explicitly uttered or as an offering of well-being, ⁹there shall be offered a meal offering along with the animal: three-tenths of a measure of choice flour with half a *hin* of oil mixed in; ¹⁰and as libation you shall offer half a *hin* of wine—these being offerings by fire of pleasing odor to יהוה.

¹¹Thus shall be done with each ox, with each ram, and with any sheep or goat, ¹²as many as you offer; you shall do thus with each one, as many as there are. ¹³Every citizen, when presenting an offering by fire of pleasing odor to יהוה, shall do so with them.

¹⁴And when, throughout the ages, a stranger who has taken up residence with you, or one who lives among you, would present an offering by fire of pleasing odor to יהוה—as you do, so *⁻shall it be done by ¹⁵the rest of the congregation.⁻* There shall be one law for you and for the resident stranger; it shall be a law for all time throughout the ages. You and the stranger shall be alike before יהוה; ¹⁶the same ritual and the same rule shall apply to you and to the stranger who resides among you.

¹⁷יהוה spoke to Moses, saying: ¹⁸Speak to the Israelite people and say to them:

When you enter the land to which I am taking you ¹⁹and you eat of the bread of the land, you shall set some aside as a gift to יהוה: ²⁰as the first yield of your baking,* you shall set aside a loaf as a gift; you shall set it aside as a gift like the gift from the threshing floor. ²¹You shall make a gift to יהוה from the first yield of your baking, throughout the ages.

²²If you unwittingly fail to observe any one of the commandments that יהוה has declared to Moses—²³anything that יהוה has enjoined upon you through Moses—from the day that יהוה gave the commandment and on through the ages:

²⁴If this was done unwittingly, through the inadvertence of the community, the °community leaders⁻° shall present one bull of the herd as a burnt offering of pleasing odor to יהוה, with its proper meal offering and libation, and one he-goat as a sin offering. ²⁵The priest shall make expiation for the whole Israelite community and they shall be forgiven; for it was an error, and for their error they have brought their offering, an offering by fire to יהוה and their sin offering before יהוה. ²⁶The whole Israelite community and the stranger residing among them shall be forgiven, for it happened to the entire people through error.

²⁷In case it is an individual who has sinned unwittingly, that person shall offer a she-goat in its first year as a sin offering. ²⁸The priest shall make expiation before יהוה on behalf of the person

who erred, for having sinned unwittingly, making such expiation that the person may be forgiven. ²⁹For the citizen among the Israelites and for the stranger who resides among them—you shall have one ritual for anyone who acts in error.

³⁰But the person, whether citizen or stranger, who acts defiantly* reviles יהוה; that person shall be cut off from among the people. ³¹Because it was the word of יהוה that was spurned and [God's] commandment that was violated, that person shall be cut off—and bears the guilt.

³²Once, when the Israelites were in the wilderness, they came upon a man gathering wood on the sabbath day. ³³Those who found him as he was gathering wood brought him before Moses, Aaron, and the community leadership. ³⁴He was placed in custody, for it had not been specified what should be done to him. ³⁵Then יהוה said to Moses, "This fellow shall be put to death: the community leadership shall pelt him with stones outside the camp." ³⁶So the community leadership took him outside the camp and stoned him to death—as יהוה had commanded Moses.

³⁷יהוה said to Moses as follows: ³⁸Speak to the °Israelite people° and instruct them to make for themselves fringes on the corners of their garments throughout the ages; let them attach a cord of blue to the fringe at each corner. ³⁹That shall be your fringe; look at it and recall all the commandments of יהוה and observe them, so that you do not follow your heart and eyes in your lustful urge. ⁴⁰Thus you shall be reminded to observe all My commandments and to be holy to your God. ⁴¹I יהוה am your God, who brought you out of the land of Egypt to be your God: I, your God יהוה.

קֹרַח | KORAH

16 Now Korah, son of Izhar son of Kohath son of Levi, *⁻betook himself,* along with Dathan and Abiram sons of Eliab, *⁻and On son of Peleth—descendants of Reuben*—²to rise up against Moses, together with two hundred and fifty Israelite notables°—chieftains of the community, chosen in the assembly, °⁻with fine reputations.° ³They combined against Moses and Aaron and said to them, "You have gone too far! For all the community are holy, all of them, and יהוה is in their midst. Why then do you raise yourselves above יהוה's congregation?"

[4]When Moses heard this, he *-fell on his face.-* [5]Then he spoke to Korah and all his company, saying, "Come morning, יהוה will make known who is [God's] and who is holy, and will grant him direct access; the one whom [God] has chosen will be granted access. [6]Do this: You, Korah and all your* band, take fire pans, [7]and tomorrow put fire in them and lay incense on them before יהוה. Then the candidate° whom יהוה chooses, he shall be the holy one. You have gone too far, sons of Levi!"

[8]Moses said further to Korah, "Hear me, sons of Levi. [9]Is it not enough for you that the God of Israel has set you apart from the community of Israel and given you direct access, to perform the duties of יהוה's Tabernacle and to minister to the community and serve them? [10]Now that [God] has advanced you and all your fellow Levites with you, do you seek the priesthood too? [11]Truly, it is against יהוה that you and all your company have banded together. For who is Aaron that you should rail against him?"

[12]Moses sent for Dathan and Abiram, sons of Eliab; but they said, "We will not come! [13]Is it not enough that you brought us from a land flowing with milk and honey to have us die in the wilderness, that you would also lord it over us? [14]*-Even if you had-* brought us to a land flowing with milk and honey, and given us possession of fields and vineyards, should you *-gouge out those subordinates' eyes?-* We will not come!" [15]Moses was much aggrieved and he said to יהוה, "Pay no regard to their oblation. I have not taken the ass of any one of them, nor have I wronged any one of them."

[16]And Moses said to Korah, "Tomorrow, you and all your company appear before יהוה, you and they and Aaron. [17]Each of you take his fire pan and lay incense on it, and each of you bring his fire pan before יהוה, two hundred and fifty fire pans; you and Aaron also [bring] your fire pans." [18]Each of them took his fire pan, put fire in it, laid incense on it, and took his place at the entrance of the Tent of Meeting, as did Moses and Aaron. [19]Korah gathered the whole community against them at the entrance of the Tent of Meeting.

Then the Presence of יהוה appeared to the whole community, [20]and יהוה spoke to Moses and Aaron, saying, [21]"Stand back from this community that I may annihilate them in an instant!" [22]But they fell on their faces and said, "O God, Source* of the breath of all flesh! When one member° sins, will You be wrathful with the whole community?"

[23]יהוה spoke to Moses, saying, [24]"Speak to the community and say: Withdraw from about the abodes of Korah, Dathan, and Abiram."

[25]Moses rose and went to Dathan and Abiram, the elders of Israel following him. [26]He addressed the community, saying, "Move away from the tents of these wicked fellows° and touch nothing that belongs to them, lest you be wiped out for all their sins." [27]So they withdrew from about the abodes of Korah, Dathan, and Abiram.

Now Dathan and Abiram had come out and they stood at the entrance of their tents, with their wives, their [grown] children, and their little ones. [28]And Moses said, "By this you shall know that it was יהוה who sent me to do all these things; that they are not of my own devising: [29]if these people's death is that of all humankind, if their lot is humankind's common fate, it was not יהוה who sent me. [30]But if יהוה brings about something unheard-of, so that the ground opens its mouth and swallows them up with all that belongs to them, and they go down alive into Sheol, you shall know that these fellows have spurned יהוה." [31]Scarcely had he finished speaking all these words when the ground under them burst asunder, [32]and the earth opened its mouth and swallowed them up with their households, all Korah's people and all their possessions. [33]They went down alive into Sheol, with all that belonged to them; the earth closed over them and they vanished from the midst of the congregation. [34]All Israel around them fled at their shrieks, for they said, "The earth might swallow us!"

[35]And a fire went forth from יהוה and consumed the two hundred and fifty notables° offering the incense.

17 *יהוה spoke to Moses, saying: [2]Order Eleazar son of Aaron the priest to remove the fire pans—for they have become sacred—from among the charred remains; and scatter the coals abroad. [3]*[Remove] the fire pans of those who have sinned at the cost of their lives, and let them be made into hammered sheets as plating for the altar—for once they have been used for offering to יהוה, they have become sacred—and let them serve as a warning to the people of Israel. ⁴Eleazar the priest took the copper fire pans which had been used for offering by those who died in the fire; and they were hammered into plating for the altar, ⁵as יהוה had ordered him through Moses. It was to be a reminder to the Israelites, so that no outsider—one not of Aaron's offspring—should presume to offer incense before יהוה and suffer the fate of Korah and his band.

⁶Next day the whole Israelite community railed against Moses and Aaron, saying, "You two have brought death upon יהוה's people!" ⁷But as the community gathered against them, Moses and Aaron turned toward the Tent of Meeting; the cloud had covered it and the Presence of יהוה appeared.

⁸When Moses and Aaron reached the Tent of Meeting, ⁹יהוה spoke to Moses, saying, ¹⁰"Remove yourselves from this community, that I may annihilate them in an instant." They fell on their faces. ¹¹Then Moses said to Aaron, "Take the fire pan, and put on it fire from the altar. Add incense and take it quickly to the community and make expiation for them. For wrath has gone forth from יהוה: the plague has begun!" ¹²Aaron took it, as Moses had ordered, and ran to the midst of the congregation, where the plague had begun among the people. He put on the incense and made expiation for the people; ¹³he stood between the dead and the living until the plague was checked. ¹⁴Those who died of the plague came to fourteen thousand and seven hundred, aside from those who died on account of Korah. ¹⁵Aaron then returned to Moses at the entrance of the Tent of Meeting, since the plague was checked.

¹⁶*יהוה spoke to Moses, saying: ¹⁷Speak to the Israelite people and take from them—from the chieftains *˙of their ancestral houses˙*— one staff for each chieftain of an ancestral house: twelve staffs in all. Inscribe each one's name on his staff, ¹⁸there being one staff for each head of an ancestral house; also inscribe Aaron's name on the staff of Levi. ¹⁹Deposit them in the Tent of Meeting before the Pact, where I meet with you. ²⁰The staff of the candidate° whom I choose shall sprout, and *˙I will rid˙* Myself of the incessant mutterings of the Israelites against you.

²¹Moses spoke thus to the Israelites. Their chieftains gave him

a staff for each chieftain of an ancestral house, twelve staffs in all; among these staffs was that of Aaron. ²²Moses deposited the staffs before יהוה, in the Tent of the Pact. ²³The next day Moses entered the Tent of the Pact, and there the staff of Aaron of the house of Levi had sprouted: it had brought forth sprouts, produced blossoms, and borne almonds. ²⁴Moses then brought out all the staffs from before יהוה to all the Israelites; each identified and recovered his staff.

²⁵יהוה said to Moses, "Put Aaron's staff back before the Pact, to be kept as a lesson to rebels, so that their mutterings against Me may cease, lest they die." ²⁶This Moses did; just as יהוה had commanded him, so he did.

²⁷But the Israelites said to Moses, "Lo, we perish! We are lost, all of us lost! ²⁸Everyone who so much as ventures near יהוה's Tabernacle must die. Alas, we are doomed to perish!"

18 יהוה said to Aaron: You and your sons and the ancestral house under your charge shall bear any guilt connected with the sanctuary; you and your sons alone shall bear any guilt connected with your priesthood. ²You shall also associate with yourself your kinsmen the tribe of Levi, your ancestral tribe, to be attached to you and to minister to you, *⁻while you and your sons under your charge are before the Tent of the Pact.⁻* ³They shall discharge their duties to you and to the Tent as a whole, but they must not have any contact with the furnishings of the Shrine or with the altar, lest both they and you die. ⁴They shall be attached to you and discharge the duties of the Tent of Meeting, all the service of the Tent; but no outsider shall intrude upon you ⁵as you discharge the duties connected with the Shrine and the altar, that wrath may not again strike the Israelites.

⁶I hereby take your fellow Levites from among the Israelites; they are assigned to you in dedication to יהוה, to do the work of the Tent of Meeting; ⁷while you and your sons shall be careful to perform your priestly duties in everything pertaining to the altar and to what is behind the curtain. I make your priesthood a service of dedication; any outsider who encroaches shall be put to death.

⁸יהוה spoke further to Aaron: I hereby give you charge of My gifts, all the sacred donations of the Israelites; I grant them to you and to your sons as a perquisite,* a due for all time. ⁹This shall be

yours from the most holy sacrifices, *˞the offerings by fire:˞* every such offering that they render to Me as most holy sacrifices, namely, every meal offering, sin offering, and guilt offering of theirs, shall belong to you and your sons. ¹⁰You shall partake of them as most sacred donations: only males may eat them; *˞you shall treat them as consecrated.˞*

¹¹This, too, shall be yours: the *˞gift offerings˞* of their contributions, all the elevation offerings of the Israelites, I give to you [and your wives], to your sons, and to the daughters that are with you, as a due for all time; everyone of your household who is pure may eat it.

¹²All the best of the new oil, wine, and grain—the choice parts that they present to יהוה—I give to you. ¹³The first fruits of everything in their land, that they bring to יהוה, shall be yours; everyone of your household who is pure may eat them. ¹⁴Everything that has been *˞proscribed in Israel˞* shall be yours. ¹⁵The first [male] issue of the womb of every being, human or beast, that is offered to יהוה, shall be yours; but you shall have the male firstborn of human beings redeemed, and you shall also have the firstling of impure animals redeemed. ¹⁶Take as *˞their redemption price,˞* from the age of one month up, the money equivalent of five shekels by the sanctuary weight, which is twenty *gerah*s. ¹⁷But the firstlings of cattle, sheep, or goats may not be redeemed; they are consecrated. You shall dash their blood against the altar, and turn their fat into smoke as an offering by fire for a pleasing odor to יהוה. ¹⁸But their meat shall be yours: it shall be yours like the breast of elevation offering and like the right thigh.

¹⁹All the sacred gifts that the Israelites set aside for יהוה I give to you, to your sons, and to the daughters that are with you, as a due for all time. It shall be an everlasting *˞covenant of salt˞* before יהוה for you and for your offspring as well. ²⁰And יהוה said to Aaron: You shall, however, have no territorial share among them or own any portion in their midst; I am your portion and your share among the Israelites.

²¹And to the Levites I hereby give all the tithes in Israel as their share in return for the services that they perform, the services of the Tent of Meeting. ²²Henceforth, Israelites shall not trespass on the Tent of Meeting, and thus incur guilt and die: ²³only Levites

Koraḥ

shall perform the services of the Tent of Meeting; others* would incur guilt. It is the law for all time throughout the ages. But they shall have no territorial share among the Israelites; 24for it is the tithes set aside by the Israelites as a gift to יהוה that I give to the Levites as their share. Therefore I have said concerning them: They shall have no territorial share among the Israelites.

25יהוה spoke to Moses, saying: 26Speak to the Levites and say to them: When you receive from the Israelites their tithes, which I have assigned to you as your share, you shall set aside from them one-tenth of the tithe as a gift to יהוה. 27This shall be accounted to you as your gift. As with the new grain from the threshing floor or the flow from the vat, 28so shall you on your part set aside a gift for יהוה from all the tithes that you receive from the Israelites; and from them you shall bring the gift for יהוה to Aaron the priest. 29You shall set aside all gifts due to יהוה from everything that is donated to you, from each thing its best portion, the part thereof that is to be consecrated.

30Say to them further: When you have removed the best part from it, you Levites may consider it the same as the yield of threshing floor or vat. 31You and your households may eat it anywhere, for it is your recompense for your services in the Tent of Meeting. 32You will incur no guilt through it, once you have removed the best part from it; but you must not profane the sacred donations of the Israelites, lest you die.

חֻקַּת | ḤUKKAT

19 יהוה spoke to Moses and Aaron, saying: 2This is the ritual law that יהוה has commanded:

Instruct the Israelite people to bring you a red cow without blemish, in which there is no defect and on which no yoke has been laid. 3You shall give it to Eleazar the priest. It shall be taken outside the camp and slaughtered in his presence. 4Eleazar the priest shall take some of its blood with his finger and sprinkle it seven times toward the front of the Tent of Meeting. 5The cow shall be burned in his sight—its hide, flesh, and blood shall be burned, its dung included—6and the priest shall take cedar wood, hyssop, and crimson stuff, and throw them into the fire consuming the cow. 7The priest shall wash his garments and bathe his body in water; after that the priest may reenter the camp, but he shall be impure until evening. ⁸°He who performed the burning⁻° shall also wash his garments in water, bathe his body in water, and be impure until evening. ⁹A man° who is pure shall gather up the ashes of the cow and deposit them outside the camp in a pure place, to be kept for *⁻water of lustration⁻* for the Israelite community. It is for purgation. ¹⁰He who gathers up the ashes of the cow shall also wash his clothes and be impure until evening.

This shall be a permanent law for the Israelites and for the strangers who reside among you.

¹¹Those° who touch the corpse of any human being shall be impure for seven days. ¹²They shall purify themselves with [the ashes] on the third day and on the seventh day, and then be pure; if they fail to purify themselves on the third and seventh days, they shall not be pure. ¹³Those who touch a corpse, the body of a person who has died, and do not purify themselves, defile יהוה's Tabernacle; those persons shall be cut off from Israel. Since the water of lustration was not dashed on them, they remain impure; their impurity is still upon them.

¹⁴This is the ritual: When a person dies in a tent, whoever enters the tent and whoever is in the tent shall be impure seven days; ¹⁵and every open vessel, with no lid fastened down, shall be impure. ¹⁶And in the open, anyone who touches a person who was killed* or who died naturally, or human bone, or a grave, shall be impure seven days. ¹⁷Some of the ashes* from the fire of purgation shall be taken for the impure person, and fresh water shall be added to them in a vessel. ¹⁸A person° who is pure shall take hyssop, dip it in the water, and sprinkle on the tent and on all the vessels and people who were there, or on the one who touched the bones or the person who was killed or died naturally or the grave. ¹⁹The pure person shall sprinkle it upon the impure person on the third day and on the seventh day, thus purifying that person by the seventh day. [The one being purified] shall then wash those clothes and bathe in water—and at nightfall shall be pure. ²⁰If anyone who has become impure fails to undergo purification, that person shall be cut off from the congregation for having defiled יהוה's sanctuary. The water of lustration was not dashed on that person, who is impure.

²¹That shall be for them a law for all time. Further, the one who sprinkled the water of lustration shall wash those clothes; and whoever touches the water of lustration shall be impure until evening. ²²Whatever that impure person touches shall be impure; and the person who touches the impure one shall be impure until evening.

20 The Israelites arrived in a body at the wilderness of Zin on the *⸗first new moon,⸗* and the people stayed at Kadesh. Miriam died there and was buried there.

²The community was without water, and they joined against Moses and Aaron. ³The people quarreled with Moses, saying, "If only we had perished when our brothers perished at the instance of יהוה! ⁴Why have you brought יהוה's congregation into this wilderness for us and our beasts to die there? ⁵Why did you make us leave Egypt to bring us to this wretched place, a place with no grain or figs or vines or pomegranates? There is not even water to drink!"

⁶Moses and Aaron came away from the congregation to the entrance of the Tent of Meeting, and fell on their faces. The Presence of יהוה appeared to them, ⁷and יהוה spoke to Moses, saying, ⁸"You and your brother Aaron take the rod and assemble the community, and before their very eyes order the rock to yield its water. Thus you shall produce water for them from the rock and provide drink for the congregation and their beasts."

⁹Moses took the rod from before יהוה, as he had been commanded. ¹⁰Moses and Aaron assembled the congregation in front of the rock; and he said to them, "Listen, you rebels, shall we get water for you out of this rock?" ¹¹And Moses raised his hand and struck the rock twice with his rod. Out came copious water, and the community and their beasts drank.

¹²But יהוה said to Moses and Aaron, "Because you did not trust Me enough to affirm My sanctity in the sight of the Israelite people, therefore you shall not lead this congregation into the land that I have given them." ¹³Those are the Waters of Meribah*—meaning that the Israelites quarrelled with יהוה—whose sanctity was affirmed through them.

¹⁴From Kadesh, Moses sent messengers to the king of Edom: "Thus says your brother, Israel: You know all the hardships that

Ḥukkat

have befallen us; ¹⁵that our ancestors went down to Egypt, that we dwelt in Egypt a long time, and that the Egyptians dealt harshly with us and our ancestors. ¹⁶We cried to יהוה who heard our plea, sending a messenger* who freed us from Egypt. Now we are in Kadesh, the town on the border of your territory. ¹⁷Allow us, then, to cross your country. We will not pass through fields or vineyards, and we will not drink water from wells. We will follow the king's highway, turning off neither to the right nor to the left until we have crossed your territory."

¹⁸But Edom answered him, "You shall not pass through us, else we will go out against you with the sword." ¹⁹"We will keep to the beaten track," the Israelites said to them, "and if we or our cattle drink your water, we will pay for it. We ask only for passage on foot—it is but a small matter." ²⁰But they replied, "You shall not pass through!" And Edom went out against them in heavy force, strongly armed. ²¹So Edom would not let Israel cross their territory, and Israel turned away from them.

²²Setting out from Kadesh, the Israelites arrived in a body at Mount Hor. ²³At Mount Hor, on the boundary of the land of Edom, יהוה said to Moses and Aaron, ²⁴"Let Aaron be gathered to his kin: he is not to enter the land that I have assigned to the Israelite people, because you disobeyed my command about the waters of Meribah. ²⁵Take Aaron and his son Eleazar and bring them up on Mount Hor. ²⁶Strip Aaron of his vestments and put them on his son Eleazar. There Aaron shall be gathered *⁻unto the dead."⁻*

²⁷Moses did as יהוה had commanded. They ascended Mount Hor in the sight of the whole community. ²⁸Moses stripped Aaron of his vestments and put them on his son Eleazar, and Aaron died there on the summit of the mountain. When Moses and Eleazar came down from the mountain, ²⁹the whole community knew that Aaron had breathed his last. All the house of Israel bewailed Aaron thirty days.

21 When the Canaanite, king of Arad, who dwelt in the Negeb, learned that Israel was coming by the way of Atharim,* he engaged Israel in battle and took some of them captive. ²Then Israel made a vow to יהוה and said, "If You deliver this people into our hand, we will proscribe* their towns." ³יהוה

heeded Israel's plea and delivered up the Canaanites; and they and their cities were proscribed. So that place was named Hormah.*

⁴They set out from Mount Hor by way of the *⁻Sea of Reeds⁻* to skirt the land of Edom. But the people grew restive on the journey, ⁵and the people spoke against God and against Moses, "Why did you make us leave Egypt to die in the wilderness? There is no bread and no water, and we have come to loathe this miserable food." ⁶יהוה sent *seraph** serpents against the people. They bit the people and many of the Israelites died. ⁷The people came to Moses and said, "We sinned by speaking against יהוה and against you. Intercede with יהוה to take away the serpents from us!" And Moses interceded for the people. ⁸Then יהוה said to Moses, "Make a *seraph** figure and mount it on a standard. And anyone who was bitten who then looks at it shall recover." ⁹Moses made a copper serpent and mounted it on a standard; and when bitten by a serpent, anyone who looked at the copper serpent would recover.

¹⁰The Israelites marched on and encamped at Oboth. ¹¹They set out from Oboth and encamped at Iye-abarim, in the wilderness bordering on Moab to the east. ¹²From there they set out and encamped at the wadi Zered. ¹³From there they set out and encamped beyond the Arnon, that is, in the wilderness that extends from the territory of the Amorites. For the Arnon is the boundary of Moab, between Moab and the Amorites. ¹⁴Therefore the Book of the Wars of יהוה speaks of *"...Waheb in Suphah, and the wadis: the Arnon ¹⁵with its tributary wadis, stretched along the settled country of Ar, hugging the territory of Moab..."

¹⁶And from there to Beer,* which is the well where יהוה said to Moses, "Assemble the people that I may give them water." ¹⁷Then Israel sang this song:

Spring up, O well—sing to it—
¹⁸The well which the chieftains dug,
Which the nobles of the people started
With maces, with their own staffs.

And from Midbar* to Mattanah, ¹⁹and from Mattanah to Nahaliel, and from Nahaliel to Bamoth, ²⁰and from Bamoth to the valley that is in the country of Moab, at the peak of Pisgah, over-looking the wasteland.*

21Israel now sent messengers to Sihon king of the Amorites, say-ing, 22"Let me pass through your country. We will not turn off into fields or vineyards, and we will not drink water from wells. We will follow the king's highway until we have crossed your ter-ritory." 23But Sihon would not let Israel pass through his territory. Sihon gathered all his people and went out against Israel in the wilderness. He came to Jahaz and engaged Israel in battle. 24But Israel put them to the sword, and took possession of their land, from the Arnon to the Jabbok, as far as [Az] of the Ammonites, for Az* marked the boundary of the Ammonites. 25Israel took all those towns. And Israel settled in all the towns of the Amorites, in Heshbon and all its dependencies.

26Now Heshbon was the city of Sihon king of the Amorites, who had fought against a former king of Moab and taken all his land from him as far as the Arnon. 27Therefore the bards would recite:

> *"Come to Heshbon; firmly built
> And well founded is Sihon's city.
> 28For fire went forth from Heshbon,
> Flame from Sihon's city,
> Consuming Ar of Moab,
> The lords of Bamoth* by the Arnon.
> 29Woe to you, O Moab!
> You are undone, O people of Chemosh!
> His sons are rendered fugitive
> And his daughters captive
> By an Amorite king, Sihon."
> 30*Yet we have cast them down utterly,
> Heshbon along with Dibon;
> We have wrought desolation at Nophah,
> Which is hard by Medeba.

31So Israel occupied the land of the Amorites. 32Then Moses sent to spy out Jazer, and they captured its dependencies and dispos-sessed the Amorites who were there.

³³They marched on and went up the road to Bashan, and King Og of Bashan, with all his people, came out to Edrei to engage them in battle. ³⁴But יהוה said to Moses, "Do not fear him, for I give him and all his people and his land into your hand. You shall do to him as you did to Sihon king of the Amorites who dwelt in Heshbon." ³⁵They defeated him and his sons and all his people, until no remnant was left him; and they took possession of his country.

22 ¹The Israelites then marched on and encamped in the steppes of Moab, across the Jordan from Jericho.

בָּלָק | BALAK

²Balak son of Zippor saw all that Israel had done to the Amorites.

³Moab was alarmed because that people was so numerous. Moab dreaded the Israelites, ⁴and Moab said to the elders of Midian, "Now this horde will lick clean all that is about us as an ox licks up the grass of the field."

Balak son of Zippor, who was king of Moab at that time, ⁵sent messengers to Balaam son of Beor in Pethor, which is by the Euphrates,* in the land of his kinsfolk, to invite him, saying, "There is a people that came out of Egypt; it hides the earth from view, and it is settled next to me. ⁶Come then, put a curse upon this people for me, since they are too numerous for me; perhaps I can thus defeat them and drive them out of the land. For I know that he whom you bless is blessed indeed, and he whom you curse is cursed."

⁷The elders of Moab and the elders of Midian, *⁻versed in divination,* set out. They came to Balaam and gave him Balak's message. ⁸He said to them, "Spend the night here, and I shall reply to you as יהוה may instruct me." So the Moabite dignitaries stayed with Balaam.

⁹God came to Balaam and said, "What do these envoys° want of you?" ¹⁰Balaam said to God, "Balak son of Zippor, king of Moab, sent me this message: ¹¹Here is a people that came out from Egypt and hides the earth from view. Come now and curse them for me; perhaps I can engage them in battle and drive them off." ¹²But God said to Balaam, "Do not go with them. You must not curse that people, for they are blessed."

¹³Balaam arose in the morning and said to Balak's dignitaries, "Go back to your own country, for יהוה will not let me go with

you." [14]The Moabite dignitaries left, and they came to Balak and said, "Balaam refused to come with us."

[15]Then Balak sent other dignitaries, more numerous and distinguished than the first. [16]They came to Balaam and said to him, "Thus says Balak son of Zippor: Please do not refuse to come to me. [17]I will reward you richly and I will do anything you ask of me. Only come and damn this people for me." [18]Balaam replied to Balak's officials, "Though Balak were to give me his house full of silver and gold, I could not do anything, big or little, contrary to the command of my God יהוה. [19]So you, too, stay here overnight, and let me find out what else יהוה may say to me." [20]That night God came to Balaam and said to him, "If these envoys° have come to invite you, you may go with them. But whatever I command you, that you shall do."

[21]When he arose in the morning, Balaam saddled his ass and departed with the Moabite dignitaries. [22]But God was incensed at his going; so a messenger of יהוה took a position in his way as an adversary.

He was riding on his she-ass, with his two servants alongside, [23]when the ass caught sight of the messenger of יהוה standing in the way, with his drawn sword in his hand. The ass swerved from the road and went into the fields; and Balaam beat the ass to turn her back onto the road. [24]The messenger of יהוה then stationed himself in a lane between the vineyards, with a fence on either side. [25]The ass, seeing the messenger of יהוה, pressed herself against the wall and squeezed Balaam's foot against the wall; so he beat her again. [26]Once more the messenger of יהוה moved forward and stationed himself on a spot so narrow that there was no room to swerve right or left. [27]When the ass now saw the messenger of יהוה, she lay down under Balaam; and Balaam was furious and beat the ass with his stick.

[28]Then יהוה opened the ass's mouth, and she said to Balaam, "What have I done to you that you have beaten me these three times?" [29]Balaam said to the ass, "You have made a mockery of me! If I had a sword with me, I'd kill you." [30]The ass said to Balaam, "Look, I am the ass that you have been riding all along until this day! Have I been in the habit of doing thus to you?" And he answered, "No."

³¹Then יהוה uncovered Balaam's eyes, and he saw the messenger of יהוה standing in the way, his drawn sword in his hand; thereupon he bowed *⁻right down to the ground.* ³²The messenger of יהוה said to him, "Why have you beaten your ass these three times? It is I who came out as an adversary, for the errand is obnoxious* to me. ³³And when the ass saw me, she shied away because of me those three times. If she had not shied away from me, you are the one I should have killed, while sparing her."

³⁴Balaam said to the messenger of יהוה, "I erred because I did not know that you were standing in my way. If you still disapprove, I will turn back." ³⁵But the messenger of יהוה said to Balaam, "Go with those envoys.° But you must say nothing except what I tell you." So Balaam went on with Balak's dignitaries.

³⁶When Balak heard that Balaam was coming, he went out to meet him at Ir-moab, which is on the Arnon border, at its farthest point. ³⁷Balak said to Balaam, "When I first sent to invite you, why didn't you come to me? Am I really unable to reward you?" ³⁸But Balaam said to Balak, "And now that I have come to you, have I the power to speak freely? I can utter only the word that God puts into my mouth."

³⁹Balaam went with Balak and they came to Kiriath-huzoth.

⁴⁰Balak sacrificed oxen and sheep, and had them served to Balaam and the dignitaries with him. ⁴¹In the morning Balak took Balaam up to Bamoth-baal. From there he could see a portion of the people.

23 Balaam said to Balak, "Build me seven altars here and have seven bulls and seven rams ready here for me." ²Balak did as Balaam directed; and Balak and Balaam offered up a bull and a ram on each altar. ³Then Balaam said to Balak, "Stay here beside your offerings while I am gone. Perhaps יהוה will grant me a manifestation, and whatever is revealed to me I will tell you." And he went off alone.*

⁴God became manifest to Balaam, who stated, "I have set up the seven altars and offered up a bull and a ram on each altar." ⁵And יהוה put a word in Balaam's mouth and said, "Return to Balak and speak thus."

⁶So he returned to him and found him standing beside his offerings, and all the Moabite dignitaries with him. ⁷He took up his theme, and said:

> From Aram has Balak brought me,
> Moab's king from the hills of the East:
> Come, curse me Jacob,
> Come, tell Israel's doom!
> ⁸How can I damn whom God* has not damned,
> How doom when יהוה has not doomed?
> ⁹As I see them from the mountain tops, .
> Gaze on them from the heights,
> There is a people that dwells apart,
> Not reckoned among the nations,
> ¹⁰Who can count the dust* of Jacob,
> Number* the dust-cloud of Israel?
> May I die the death of the upright,*
> May my fate be like theirs!

¹¹Then Balak said to Balaam, "What have you done to me? Here I brought you to damn my enemies, and instead you have blessed them!" ¹²He replied, "I can only repeat faithfully what יהוה puts in my mouth." ¹³Then Balak said to him, "Come with me to another place from which you can see them—you will see only a portion of them; you will not see all of them—and damn them for me from there." ¹⁴With that, he took him to Sedehzophim,* on the summit of Pisgah. He built seven altars and offered a bull and a ram on each altar. ¹⁵And [Balaam] said to Balak, "Stay here beside your offerings, while I seek a manifestation yonder."

¹⁶יהוה became manifest to Balaam and put a word in his mouth, saying, "Return to Balak and speak thus." ¹⁷He went to him and found him standing beside his offerings, and the Moabite dignitaries with him. Balak asked him, "What did יהוה say?" ¹⁸And he took up his theme, and said:

> Up, Balak, attend,
> Give ear unto me, son of Zippor!
> ¹⁹God is not human to be capricious,
> Or mortal to have a change of heart.
> Would [God] speak and not act,
> Promise and not fulfill?
> ²⁰My message was to bless:
> When [God] blesses, I cannot reverse it.

²¹No harm is in sight for Jacob,
No woe in view for Israel.
Their God יהוה is with them,
And their King's° acclaim in their midst.
²²God who freed them from Egypt
Is for them like the horns* of the wild ox.
²³Lo, there is no augury in Jacob,
⁻No divining in Israel:⁻
*⁻Jacob is told at once,
Yea Israel, what God has planned.⁻*
²⁴Lo, a people that rises like a lioness,°
Leaps up like a lion,°
Rests not till it has feasted on prey
And drunk the blood of the slain.

²⁵Thereupon Balak said to Balaam, "Don't curse them and don't bless them!" ²⁶In reply, Balaam said to Balak, "But I told you: Whatever יהוה says, that I must do." ²⁷Then Balak said to Balaam, "Come now, I will take you to another place. Perhaps God will deem it right that you damn them for me there." ²⁸Balak took Balaam to the peak of Peor, which overlooks the wasteland.* ²⁹Balaam said to Balak, "Build me here seven altars, and have seven bulls and seven rams ready for me here." ³⁰Balak did as Balaam said: he offered up a bull and a ram on each altar.

24 Now Balaam, seeing that it pleased יהוה to bless Israel, did not, as on previous occasions, go in search of omens, but turned his face toward the wilderness. ²As Balaam looked up and saw Israel encamped tribe by tribe, the spirit of God came upon him. ³Taking up his theme, he said:

*Word of Balaam son of Beor,
Word of the man° *⁻whose eye is true,⁻*
⁴Word of one who hears God's speech,
Who beholds visions from the Almighty,
Prostrate, but with eyes unveiled:
⁵How fair are your tents, O Jacob,
Your dwellings, O Israel!
⁶Like palm-groves that stretch out,
Like gardens beside a river,

Like aloes planted by יהוה,
Like cedars beside the water;
⁷Their boughs drip with moisture,
‑Their roots‑ have abundant water.
Their ruler shall rise above Agag,
Their sovereignty shall be exalted.
⁸God who freed them from Egypt
Is for them like the horns* of the wild ox.
They shall devour enemy nations,
Crush their bones,
And smash their arrows.
⁹They crouch, they lie down like a lion,
Like a lioness;* who dares rouse them?
Blessed are they who bless you,
Accursed they who curse you!

¹⁰Enraged at Balaam, Balak struck his hands together. "I called you," Balak said to Balaam, "to damn my enemies, and instead you have blessed them these three times! ¹¹Back with you at once to your own place! I was going to reward you richly, but יהוה has denied you the reward." ¹²Balaam replied to Balak, "But I even told the messengers you sent to me, ¹³'Though Balak were to give me his house full of silver and gold, I could not of my own accord do anything good or bad contrary to יהוה's command. What יהוה says, that I must say.' ¹⁴And now, as I go back to my people, let me inform you of what this people will do to your people in days to come." ¹⁵He took up his theme, and said:

Word of Balaam son of Beor,
Word of the man° whose eye is true,
¹⁶Word of one who hears God's speech,
Who obtains knowledge from the Most High,
And beholds visions from the Almighty,
Prostrate, but with eyes unveiled:
¹⁷What I see for them is not yet,
What I behold will not be soon:
A star rises from Jacob,
A scepter comes forth from Israel;
It smashes the brow of Moab,

⁻The foundation of⁻ all children of Seth.
¹⁸Edom becomes a possession,
Yea, Seir a possession of its enemies;
But Israel is triumphant.
¹⁹A victor issues from Jacob
To wipe out what is left of Ir.

²⁰He saw Amalek and, taking up his theme, he said:

A leading nation is Amalek;
But its fate is to perish forever.

²¹He saw the Kenites and, taking up his theme, he said:

Though your abode be secure,
And your nest be set among cliffs,
²²Yet shall Kain* be consumed,
When Asshur takes you captive.

²³He took up his theme and said:

Alas, who can survive except God has willed it!
²⁴Ships come from the quarter of Kittim;
They subject Asshur, subject Eber.
They, too, shall perish forever.

²⁵Then Balaam set out on his journey back home; and Balak also went his way.

25 While Israel was staying at Shittim, the menfolk° *⁻pro-faned themselves by whoring⁻* with the Moabite women, ²who invited the menfolk to the sacrifices for their god. The menfolk partook of them and worshiped that god. ³Thus Israel attached itself to Baal-peor, and יהוה was incensed with Israel. ⁴יהוה said to Moses, "Take all the ringleaders* and have them publicly* impaled before יהוה, so that יהוה's wrath may turn away from Israel." ⁵So Moses said to Israel's officials, "Each of you slay those of his men° who attached themselves to Baal-peor."

⁶Just then one of the Israelite notables° came and brought a Midianite woman over to his companions, in the sight of Moses and of the whole Israelite community who were weeping at the entrance of the Tent of Meeting. ⁷When Phinehas, son of Eleazar son of Aaron the priest, saw this, he left the assembly and, taking

a spear in his hand, ⁸he followed the Israelite notable° into the chamber and stabbed both of them, the Israelite notable° and the woman, through the belly. Then the plague against the Israelites was checked. ⁹Those who died of the plague numbered twenty-four thousand.

פִּינְחָס | PINHAS

¹⁰יהוה spoke to Moses, saying, ¹¹"Phinehas, son of Eleazar son of Aaron the priest, has turned back My wrath from the Israelites by displaying among them his passion for Me, so that I did not wipe out the Israelite people in My passion. ¹²Say, therefore, 'I grant him My pact of friendship. ¹³It shall be for him and his descendants after him a pact of priesthood for all time, because he took impassioned action for his God, thus making expiation for the Israelites.'"

¹⁴The name of the Israelite notable° who was killed, the one who was killed with the Midianite woman, was Zimri son of Salu, chieftain of a Simeonite ancestral house. ¹⁵The name of the Midianite woman who was killed was Cozbi daughter of Zur; he was the tribal head of an ancestral house in Midian.

¹⁶יהוה spoke to Moses, saying, ¹⁷"Assail the Midianites and defeat them—¹⁸for they assailed you by the trickery they practiced against you—because of the affair of Peor and because of the affair of their kinswoman Cozbi, daughter of the Midianite chieftain, who was killed at the time of the plague on account of Peor."

¹⁹When the plague was over, **26** ¹יהוה said to Moses and to Eleazar son of Aaron the priest, ²"Take a census of the whole Israelite °company [of fighters]° from the age of twenty years up, by their ancestral houses, all Israelite males able to bear arms." *³So Moses and Eleazar the priest, on the steppes of Moab, at the Jordan near Jericho, gave instructions about them, namely, ⁴those from twenty years up, as יהוה had commanded Moses.

The [eligible male] descendants of the Israelites who came out of the land of Egypt were:

⁵Reuben, Israel's first-born. Descendants of Reuben: [Of] Enoch,* the clan of the Enochites; of Pallu, the clan of the Pallu-ites; ⁶of Hezron, the clan of the Hezronites; of Carmi, the clan of

the Carmites. ⁷Those are the clans of the Reubenites. The men enrolled came to 43,730.

⁸*⁻Born to⁻* Pallu: Eliab. ⁹The sons of Eliab were Nemuel, and Dathan and Abiram. These are the same Dathan and Abiram, chosen in the assembly, who agitated against Moses and Aaron as part of Korah's band when they agitated against יהוה. ¹⁰Whereupon the earth opened its mouth and swallowed them up with Korah—when that band died, when the fire consumed the two hundred and fifty notables°—and they became an example. ¹¹The sons of Korah, however, did not die.

¹²Descendants of Simeon by their clans: Of Nemuel, the clan of the Nemuelites; of Jamin, the clan of the Jaminites; of Jachin, the clan of the Jachinites; ¹³of Zerah, the clan of the Zerahites; of Saul,* the clan of the Saulites. ¹⁴Those are the clans of the Simeonites; [men enrolled:] 22,200.

¹⁵Descendants of Gad by their clans: Of Zephon, the clan of the Zephonites; of Haggi, the clan of the Haggites; of Shuni, the clan of the Shunites; ¹⁶of Ozni, the clan of the Oznites; of Eri, the clan of the Erites; ¹⁷of Arod, the clan of the Arodites; of Areli, the clan of the Arelites. ¹⁸Those are the clans of Gad's descendants; men enrolled: 40,500.

¹⁹Born to Judah: Er and Onan. Er and Onan died in the land of Canaan.

²⁰Descendants of Judah by their clans: Of Shelah, the clan of the Shelanites; of Perez, the clan of the Perezites; of Zerah, the clan of the Zerahites. ²¹Descendants of Perez: of Hezron, the clan of the Hezronites; of Hamul, the clan of the Hamulites. ²²Those are the clans of Judah; men enrolled: 76,500.

²³Descendants of Issachar by their clans: [Of] Tola, the clan of the Tolaites; of Puvah, the clan of the Punites; ²⁴of Jashub, the clan of the Jashubites; of Shimron, the clan of the Shimronites. ²⁵Those are the clans of Issachar; men enrolled: 64,300.

²⁶Descendants of Zebulun by their clans: Of Sered, the clan of the Seredites; of Elon, the clan of the Elonites; of Jahleel, the clan of the Jahleelites. ²⁷Those are the clans of the Zebulunites; men enrolled: 60,500.

²⁸The sons of Joseph were Manasseh and Ephraim—by their clans.

²⁹Descendants of Manasseh: Of Machir, the clan of the Machirites.—Machir begot Gilead.—Of Gilead, the clan of the Gileadites. ³⁰These were the descendants of Gilead: [Of] Iezer, the clan of the Iezerites; of Helek, the clan of the Helekites; ³¹[of] Asriel, the clan of the Asrielites; [of] Shechem, the clan of the Shechemites; ³²[of] Shemida, the clan of the Shemidaites; [of] Hepher, the clan of the Hepherites.—³³Now Zelophehad son of Hepher had no sons, only daughters. The names of Zelophehad's daughters were Mahlah, Noah, Hoglah, Milcah, and Tirzah.—³⁴Those are the clans of Manasseh; men enrolled: 52,700.

³⁵These are the descendants of Ephraim by their clans: Of Shuthelah, the clan of the Shuthelahites; of Becher, the clan of the Becherites; of Tahan, the clan of the Tahanites. ³⁶These are the descendants of Shuthelah: Of Eran, the clan of the Eranites. ³⁷Those are the clans of Ephraim's descendants; men enrolled: 32,500.

Those are the descendants of Joseph by their clans.

³⁸The descendants of Benjamin by their clans: Of Bela, the clan of the Belaites; of Ashbel, the clan of the Ashbelites; of Ahiram, the clan of the Ahiramites; ³⁹of Shephupham, the clan of the Shuphamites; of Hupham, the clan of the Huphamites. ⁴⁰The sons of Bela were Ard and Naaman: [Of Ard,] the clan of the Ardites; of Naaman, the clan of the Naamanites. ⁴¹Those are the descendants of Benjamin by their clans; men enrolled: 45,600.

*⁴²These are the descendants of Dan by their clans: Of Shuham, the clan of the Shuhamites. Those are the clans of Dan, by their clans. ⁴³All the clans of the Shuhamites; men enrolled: 64,400.

⁴⁴Descendants of Asher by their clans: Of Imnah, the clan of the Imnites; of Ishvi, the clan of the Ishvites; of Beriah, the clan of the Beriites. ⁴⁵Of the descendants of Beriah: Of Heber, the clan of the Heberites; of Malchiel, the clan of the Malchielites.—⁴⁶The name of Asher's daughter was Serah.—⁴⁷These are the clans of Asher's descendants; men enrolled: 53,400.

⁴⁸Descendants of Naphtali by their clans: Of Jahzeel, the clan of the Jahzeelites; of Guni, the clan of the Gunites; ⁴⁹of Jezer, the clan of the Jezerites; of Shillem, the clan of the Shillemites. ⁵⁰Those are the clans of the Naphtalites, clan by clan; men enrolled: 45,400.

⁵¹This is the enrollment of the Israelite men: 601,730.

⁵²יהוה spoke to Moses, saying, ⁵³"Among these shall the land be

apportioned as shares, according to the listed names: ⁵⁴with larger groups increase the share, with smaller groups reduce the share. Each is to be assigned its share according to its enrollment. ⁵⁵The land, moreover, is to be apportioned by lot; and the allotment shall be made according to the listings of their ancestral tribes. ⁵⁶Each portion shall be assigned by lot, whether for larger or smaller groups."

⁵⁷This is the enrollment of the Levites by their clans: Of Gershon, the clan of the Gershonites; of Kohath, the clan of the Kohathites; of Merari, the clan of the Merarites. ⁵⁸These are the clans of Levi: The clan of the Libnites, the clan of the Hebronites, the clan of the Mahlites, the clan of the Mushites, the clan of the Korahites.—Kohath begot Amram. ⁵⁹The name of Amram's wife was Jochebed daughter of Levi, who was born to Levi in Egypt; she bore to Amram Aaron and Moses and their sister Miriam. ⁶⁰To Aaron were born Nadab and Abihu, Eleazar and Ithamar. ⁶¹Nadab and Abihu died when they offered alien fire before יהוה.—⁶²Their enrollment of 23,000 comprised all males from a month up. They were not part of the regular enrollment of the Israelites, since no share was assigned to them among the Israelites.

⁶³These are the males enrolled by Moses and Eleazar the priest who registered the Israelites on the steppes of Moab, at the Jordan near Jericho. ⁶⁴Among these there was not one of those enrolled by Moses and Aaron the priest when they recorded the Israelites in the wilderness of Sinai. ⁶⁵For יהוה had said of them, "They shall die in the wilderness." Not one of them survived, except Caleb son of Jephunneh and Joshua son of Nun.

27 The daughters of Zelophehad, of Manassite family—son of Hepher son of Gilead son of Machir son of Manasseh son of Joseph—came forward. The names of the daughters were Mahlah, Noah, Hoglah, Milcah, and Tirzah. ²They stood before Moses, Eleazar the priest, the chieftains, and the whole assembly, at the entrance of the Tent of Meeting, and they said, ³"Our father died in the wilderness. He was not one of the faction, Korah's faction, which banded together against יהוה, but died for his own sin; and he has left no sons. ⁴Let not our father's name be lost to

his clan just because he had no son! Give us a holding among our father's kinsmen!"

⁵Moses brought their case before יהוה.

⁶And יהוה said to Moses, ⁷"The plea of Zelophehad's daughters is just: you should give them a hereditary holding among their father's kinsmen; transfer their father's share to them.

⁸"Further, speak to the Israelite people as follows: 'If a house-holder° dies without leaving a son, you shall transfer his property to his daughter. ⁹If he has no daughter, you shall assign his property to his brothers. ¹⁰If he has no brothers, you shall assign his property to his father's brothers. ¹¹If his father had no brothers, you shall assign his property to his nearest relative in his own clan, who shall inherit it.' This shall be the law of procedure for the Israelites, in accordance with יהוה's command to Moses."

¹²יהוה said to Moses, "Ascend these heights of Abarim and view the land that I have given to the Israelite people. ¹³When you have seen it, you too shall be gathered to your kin, just as your brother Aaron was. ¹⁴For, in the wilderness of Zin, when the community was contentious, you disobeyed My command to uphold My sanctity in their sight by means of the water." Those are the Waters of Meribath-kadesh,* in the wilderness of Zin.

¹⁵Moses spoke to יהוה, saying, ¹⁶"Let יהוה, Source of the breath of all flesh, appoint a leader° for the community ¹⁷*˙who shall go out before them and come in before them, and who shall take them out and bring them in,* so that יהוה's community may not be like sheep that have no shepherd." ¹⁸And יהוה answered Moses, "Single out Joshua son of Nun, an inspired leader,° and lay your hand upon him. ¹⁹Have him stand before Eleazar the priest and before the whole community, and commission him in their sight. ²⁰Invest him with some of your authority, so that the whole Israelite community may obey. ²¹But he shall present himself to Eleazar the priest, who shall on his behalf seek the decision of the Urim before יהוה. By such instruction they shall go out and by such instruction they shall come in, he and all the Israelite [militia], and the whole community."

²²Moses did as יהוה commanded him. He took Joshua and had him stand before Eleazar the priest and before the whole commu-

nity. 23He laid his hands upon him and commissioned him—as יהוה had spoken through Moses.

28 יהוה spoke to Moses, saying: 2Command the Israelite people and say to them: Be punctilious in presenting to Me at stated times *⁻the offerings of food due Me,⁻* as offerings by fire of pleasing odor to Me.

3Say to them: These are the offerings by fire that you are to present to יהוה:

As a regular burnt offering every day, two yearling lambs without blemish. 4You shall offer one lamb in the morning, and the other lamb you shall offer at twilight. 5And as a meal offering, there shall be a tenth of an *ephah* of choice flour with a quarter of a *hin* of beaten oil mixed in—6*⁻the regular burnt offering instituted at Mount Sinai⁻*—an offering by fire of pleasing odor to יהוה.

7The libation with it shall be a quarter of a *hin* for each lamb, to be poured in the sacred precinct as an offering of *⁻fermented drink⁻* to יהוה. 8The other lamb you shall offer at twilight, preparing the same meal offering and libation as in the morning—an offering by fire of pleasing odor to יהוה.

9On the sabbath day: two yearling lambs without blemish, together with two-tenths *⁻of a measure⁻* of choice flour with oil mixed in as a meal offering, and with the proper libation—10a burnt offering for every sabbath, in addition to the regular burnt offering and its libation.

11On your new moons you shall present a burnt offering to יהוה: two bulls of the herd, one ram, and seven yearling lambs, without blemish. 12As meal offering for each bull: three-tenths of a measure of choice flour with oil mixed in. As meal offering for each ram: two-tenths of a measure of choice flour with oil mixed in. 13As meal offering for each lamb: a tenth of a measure of fine flour with oil mixed in. Such shall be the burnt offering of pleasing odor, an offering by fire to יהוה. 14Their libations shall be: half a *hin* of wine for a bull, a third of a *hin* for a ram, and a quarter of a *hin* for a lamb. That shall be the monthly burnt offering for each new moon of the year. 15And there shall be one goat as a sin offering to יהוה, to be offered in addition to the regular burnt offering and its libation.

Pinḥas

¹⁶In the first month, on the fourteenth day of the month, there shall be a passover sacrifice to יהוה, ¹⁷and on the fifteenth day of that month a festival. Unleavened bread shall be eaten for seven days. ¹⁸The first day shall be a sacred occasion: you shall not work at your occupations. ¹⁹You shall present an offering by fire, a burnt offering, to יהוה: two bulls of the herd, one ram, and seven yearling lambs—*˙see that they are˙* without blemish. ²⁰The meal offering with them shall be of choice flour with oil mixed in: prepare three-tenths of a measure for a bull, two-tenths for a ram; ²¹and for each of the seven lambs prepare one-tenth of a measure. ²²And there shall be one goat for a sin offering, to make expiation in your behalf. ²³You shall present these in addition to the morning portion of the regular burnt offering. ²⁴You shall offer the like daily for seven days as food, an offering by fire of pleasing odor to יהוה; they shall be offered, with their libations, in addition to the regular burnt offering. ²⁵And the seventh day shall be a sacred occasion for you: you shall not work at your occupations.

²⁶On the day of the first fruits, your Feast of Weeks, when you bring an offering of new grain to יהוה, you shall observe a sacred occasion: you shall not work at your occupations. ²⁷You shall present a burnt offering of pleasing odor to יהוה: two bulls of the herd, one ram, seven yearling lambs. ²⁸The meal offering with them shall be of choice flour with oil mixed in, three-tenths of a measure for a bull, two-tenths for a ram, ²⁹and one-tenth for each of the seven lambs. ³⁰And there shall be one goat for expiation in your behalf. ³¹You shall present them—see that they are without blemish—with their libations, in addition to the regular burnt offering and its meal offering.

29 In the seventh month, on the first day of the month, you shall observe a sacred occasion: you shall not work at your occupations. You shall observe it as *˙a day when the horn is sounded.˙* ²You shall present a burnt offering of pleasing odor to יהוה: one bull of the herd, one ram, and seven yearling lambs, without blemish. ³The meal offering with them—choice flour with oil mixed in—shall be: three-tenths of a measure for a bull, two-tenths for a ram, ⁴and one-tenth for each of the seven lambs. ⁵And there shall be one goat for a sin offering, to make expiation in your behalf—⁶in addition to the burnt offering of the new moon with its meal offering and the regular burnt offering with its meal offering, each with its libation as prescribed, offerings by fire of pleasing odor to יהוה.

⁷On the tenth day of the same seventh month you shall observe a sacred occasion when you shall practice self-denial. You shall do no work. ⁸You shall present to יהוה a burnt offering of pleasing odor: one bull of the herd, one ram, seven yearling lambs; *⁻see that they are⁻* without blemish. ⁹The meal offering with them—of choice flour with oil mixed in—shall be: three-tenths of a measure for a bull, two-tenths for the one ram, ¹⁰one-tenth for each of the seven lambs. ¹¹And there shall be one goat for a sin offering, in addition to the sin offering of expiation and the regular burnt offering with its meal offering, each with its libation.

¹²On the fifteenth day of the seventh month, you shall observe a sacred occasion: you shall not work at your occupations.— Seven days you shall observe a festival of יהוה.—¹³You shall present a burnt offering, an offering by fire of pleasing odor to יהוה: Thirteen bulls of the herd, two rams, fourteen yearling lambs; they shall be without blemish. ¹⁴The meal offerings with them— of choice flour with oil mixed in—shall be: three-tenths of a measure for each of the thirteen bulls, two-tenths for each of the two rams, ¹⁵and one-tenth for each of the fourteen lambs. ¹⁶And there shall be one goat for a sin offering—in addition to the regular burnt offering, its meal offering and libation.

¹⁷Second day: Twelve bulls of the herd, two rams, fourteen yearling lambs, without blemish; ¹⁸the meal offerings and libations for the bulls, rams, and lambs, in the quantities prescribed; ¹⁹and one goat for a sin offering—in addition to the regular burnt offering, its meal offering and libations.

²⁰Third day: Eleven bulls, two rams, fourteen yearling lambs, without blemish; ²¹the meal offerings and libations for the bulls, rams, and lambs, in the quantities prescribed; ²²and one goat for a sin offering—in addition to the regular burnt offering, its meal offering and libation.

²³Fourth day: Ten bulls, two rams, fourteen yearling lambs, without blemish; ²⁴the meal offerings and libations for the bulls, rams, and lambs, in the quantities prescribed; ²⁵and one goat for

a sin offering—in addition to the regular burnt offering, its meal offering and libation.

²⁶Fifth day: Nine bulls, two rams, fourteen yearling lambs, without blemish; ²⁷the meal offerings and libations for the bulls, rams, and lambs, in the quantities prescribed; ²⁸and one goat for a sin offering—in addition to the regular burnt offering, its meal offering and libation.

²⁹Sixth day: Eight bulls, two rams, fourteen yearling lambs, without blemish; ³⁰the meal offerings and libations for the bulls, rams, and lambs, in the quantities prescribed; ³¹and one goat for a sin offering—in addition to the regular burnt offering, its meal offering and libations.

³²Seventh day: Seven bulls, two rams, fourteen yearling lambs, without blemish; ³³the meal offerings and libations for the bulls, rams, and lambs, in the quantities prescribed; ³⁴and one goat for a sin offering—in addition to the regular burnt offering, its meal offering and libation.

³⁵On the eighth day you shall hold a *⁻solemn gathering;⁻* you shall not work at your occupations. ³⁶You shall present a burnt offering, an offering by fire of pleasing odor to יהוה; one bull, one ram, seven yearling lambs, without blemish; ³⁷the meal offerings and libations for the bull, the ram, and the lambs, in the quantities prescribed; ³⁸and one goat for a sin offering—in addition to the regular burnt offering, its meal offering and libation.

³⁹All these you shall offer to יהוה at the stated times, in addition to your votive and freewill offerings, be they burnt offerings, meal offerings, libations, or offerings of well-being. **30** ¹*So Moses spoke to the Israelites just as יהוה had commanded Moses.

מטות | MATTOT

²Moses spoke to the heads of the Israelite tribes, saying: This is what יהוה has commanded:

³If a householder° makes a vow to יהוה or takes an oath imposing *⁻an obligation⁻* on himself, he shall not break his pledge; he must carry out all that has *⁻crossed his lips.⁻*

⁴If a woman makes a vow to יהוה or assumes an obligation while still in her father's household by reason of her youth, ⁵and her father learns of her vow or her self-imposed obligation and offers

no objection, all her vows shall stand and every self-imposed obligation shall stand. 6But if her father restrains her on the day he
finds out, none of her vows or self-imposed obligations shall stand;
and יהוה will forgive her, since her father restrained her.

7If she should become someone's [wife] while her vow or the
commitment* to which she bound herself is still in force, 8and her
husband learns of it and offers no objection on the day he finds
out, her vows shall stand and her self-imposed obligations shall
stand. 9But if her husband restrains her on the day that he learns
of it, he thereby annuls her vow which was in force or the commitment to which she bound herself; and יהוה will forgive her.—
10The vow of a widow or of a divorced woman, however, whatever she has imposed on herself, shall be binding upon her.—11So,
too, if, while in her husband's household, she makes a vow or im-
poses an obligation on herself by oath, 12and her husband learns
of it, yet offers no objection—thus failing to restrain her—all her
vows shall stand and all her self-imposed obligations shall stand.
13But if her husband does annul them on the day he finds out, then
nothing that has crossed her lips shall stand, whether vows or self-
imposed obligations. Her husband has annulled them, and יהוה
will forgive her. 14Every vow and every sworn obligation of self-
denial may be upheld by her husband or annulled by her husband.
15If her husband offers no objection from that day to the next, he
has upheld all the vows or obligations she has assumed: he has
upheld them by offering no objection on the day he found out.
16But if he annuls them after [the day] he finds out, he shall bear
her guilt.

17Those are the laws that יהוה enjoined upon Moses between a
husband and his wife, and as between a father and his daughter
while in her father's household by reason of her youth.

31 יהוה spoke to Moses, saying, 2"Avenge the Israelite people
on the Midianites; then you shall be gathered to your kin."
3Moses spoke to the militia,° saying, "Let troops° be picked out
from among you for a campaign, and let them fall upon Midian
to wreak יהוה's vengeance on Midian. 4You shall dispatch on the
campaign a thousand from every one of the tribes of Israel."
5So a thousand from each tribe were furnished from the divisions

of Israel, twelve thousand picked for the campaign. ⁶Moses dispatched them on the campaign, a thousand from each tribe, with Phinehas son of Eleazar serving as a priest on the campaign, equipped with the *⁻sacred utensils⁻* and the trumpets for sounding the blasts. ⁷They took the field against Midian, as יהוה had commanded Moses, and slew every male. ⁸Along with their other victims, they slew the kings of Midian: Evi, Rekem, Zur, Hur, and Reba, the five kings of Midian. They also put Balaam son of Beor to the sword.

⁹The Israelites took the women and °⁻other dependents⁻° of the Midianites captive, and seized as booty all their beasts, all their herds, and all their wealth. ¹⁰And they destroyed by fire all the towns in which they were settled, and their encampments. ¹¹They gathered all the spoil and all the booty, human and beast, ¹²and they brought the captives, the booty, and the spoil to Moses, Eleazar the priest, and the Israelite community leadership, at the camp in the steppes of Moab, at the Jordan near Jericho.

¹³Moses, Eleazar the priest, and all the chieftains of the community came out to meet them outside the camp. ¹⁴Moses became angry with the commanders of the army, the officers of thousands and the officers of hundreds, who had come back from the military campaign. ¹⁵Moses said to them, "You have spared every female! ¹⁶Yet they are the very ones who, at the bidding of Balaam, induced* the Israelites to trespass against יהוה in the matter of Peor, so that יהוה's community was struck by the plague. ¹⁷Now, therefore, slay every male among the dependents,° and slay also every woman who has known a man carnally; ¹⁸but spare every °⁻female dependent⁻° who has not had carnal relations with a man.

¹⁹"You shall then stay outside the camp seven days; every one among you or among your captives who has slain a person or touched a corpse shall purify himself on the third and seventh days. ²⁰You shall also purify every cloth, every article of skin, everything made of goats' hair, and every object of wood."

²¹Eleazar the priest said to the troops who had taken part in the fighting, "This is the ritual law that יהוה has enjoined upon Moses: ²²Gold and silver, copper, iron, tin, and lead—²³any article that can withstand fire—these you shall pass through fire and they shall be pure, except that they must be purified with water of lus-

tration; and anything that cannot withstand fire you must pass through water. [24]On the seventh day you shall wash your clothes and be pure, and after that you may enter the camp."

[25]יהוה said to Moses: [26]"You and Eleazar the priest and the family heads of the community take an inventory of the booty that was captured, human and beast, [27]and divide the booty equally between the combatants who engaged in the campaign and the rest of the community. [28]You shall exact a levy for יהוה: in the case of the warriors who engaged in the campaign, one item in five hundred, of persons, oxen, asses, and sheep, [29]shall be taken from their half-share and given to Eleazar the priest as a contribution to יהוה; [30]and from the half-share of the other Israelites you shall withhold one in every fifty human beings as well as cattle, asses, and sheep—all the animals—and give them to the Levites, who attend to the duties of יהוה's Tabernacle."

[31]Moses and Eleazar the priest did as יהוה commanded Moses. [32]The amount of booty, other than the spoil that the troops had plundered, came to 675,000 sheep, [33]72,000 head of cattle, [34]61,000 asses, [35]and a total of 32,000 human beings, namely, the females who had not had carnal relations.

[36]Thus, the half-share of those who had engaged in the campaign [was as follows]: The number of sheep was 337,500, [37]and יהוה's levy from the sheep was 675; [38]the cattle came to 36,000, from which יהוה's levy was 72; [39]the asses came to 30,500, from which יהוה's levy was 61. [40]And the number of human beings was 16,000, from which יהוה's levy was 32. [41]Moses gave the contributions levied for יהוה to Eleazar the priest, as יהוה had commanded Moses.

[42]As for the half-share of the other Israelites, which Moses withdrew from the troops who had taken the field, [43]that half-share of the community consisted of 337,500 sheep, [44]36,000 head of cattle, [45]30,500 asses, [46]and 16,000 human beings. [47]From this half-share of the Israelites, Moses withheld one in every fifty humans and animals; and he gave them to the Levites, who attended to the duties of יהוה's Tabernacle, as יהוה had commanded Moses.

[48]The commanders of the troop divisions, the officers of thousands and the officers of hundreds, approached Moses. [49]They

said to Moses, "Your servants have made a check of the warriors in our charge, and not one of us is missing. ⁵⁰So we have brought as an offering to יהוה such articles of gold as each of us came upon: armlets, bracelets, signet rings, earrings, and pendants,* that expiation may be made for our persons before יהוה." ⁵¹Moses and Eleazar the priest accepted the gold from them, all kinds of wrought articles. ⁵²All the gold that was offered by the officers of thousands and the officers of hundreds as a contribution to יהוה came to 16,750 shekels.—⁵³But in the ranks, everyone kept his booty for himself.—⁵⁴So Moses and Eleazar the priest accepted the gold from the officers of thousands and the officers of hundreds and brought it to the Tent of Meeting, as a reminder in behalf of the Israelites before יהוה.

32 The Reubenites and the Gadites owned cattle in very great numbers. Noting that the lands of Jazer and Gilead were a region suitable for cattle, ²the Gadite and Reubenite [leaders] came to Moses, Eleazar the priest, and the chieftains of the community, and said, ³"Ataroth, Dibon, Jazer, Nimrah, Heshbon, Elealeh, Sebam, Nebo, and Beon—⁴the land that יהוה has conquered for the community of Israel—is cattle country, and your servants have cattle. ⁵It would be a favor to us," they continued, "if this land were given to your servants as a holding; do not move us across the Jordan."

⁶Moses replied to the Gadites and the Reubenites, "Are your brothers to go to war while you stay here? ⁷Why will you turn the minds of the Israelites from crossing into the land that יהוה has given them? ⁸That is what your fathers did when I sent them from Kadesh-barnea to survey the land. ⁹After going up to the wadi Eshcol and surveying the land, they turned the minds of the Israelites from invading the land that יהוה had given them. ¹⁰Thereupon יהוה was incensed and swore, ¹¹'None of the men° from twenty years up who came out of Egypt shall see the land that I promised on oath to Abraham, Isaac, and Jacob, for they did not remain loyal to Me—¹²none except Caleb son of Jephunneh the Kenizzite and Joshua son of Nun, for they remained loyal to יהוה.' ¹³יהוה, incensed at Israel, made them wander in the wilderness for forty years, until the whole generation that had provoked יהוה's dis-

pleasure was gone. ¹⁴And now you, a breed of sinful fellows,° have replaced your fathers, to add still further to יהוה's wrath against Israel. ¹⁵If you turn away from [God], who then abandons them once more in the wilderness, you will bring calamity upon all this people."

¹⁶Then they stepped up to him and said, "We will build here sheepfolds for our flocks and towns for our children. ¹⁷And we will hasten* as shock-troops in the van of the Israelites until we have established them in their home, while our children stay in the fortified towns because of the inhabitants of the land. ¹⁸We will not return to our homes until the Israelites—every one of them—are in possession of their portion. ¹⁹But we will not have a share with them in the territory beyond the Jordan, for we have received our share on the east side of the Jordan."

²⁰Moses said to them, "If you do this, if you go to battle as shock-troops, at the instance of יהוה, ²¹and every shock-fighter among you crosses the Jordan, at the instance of יהוה, until [God] has personally dispossessed the enemies, ²²and the land has been subdued, at the instance of יהוה, and then you return—you shall be clear before יהוה and before Israel; and this land shall be your holding under יהוה. ²³But if you do not do so, you will have sinned against יהוה; and know that your sin will overtake you. ²⁴Build towns for your children and sheepfolds for your flocks, but do what you have promised."

²⁵The Gadites and the Reubenites answered Moses, "Your servants will do as my lord commands. ²⁶Our children, our wives, our flocks, and all our other livestock will stay behind* in the towns of Gilead; ²⁷while your servants, all those recruited for war, cross over, at the instance of יהוה, to engage in battle—as my lord orders."

²⁸Then Moses gave instructions concerning them to Eleazar the priest, Joshua son of Nun, and the family heads of the Israelite tribes. ²⁹Moses said to them, "If every shock-fighter among the Gadites and the Reubenites crosses the Jordan with you to do battle, at the instance of יהוה, and the land is subdued before you, you shall give them the land of Gilead as a holding. ³⁰But if they do not cross over with you as shock-troops, they shall receive holdings among you in the land of Canaan."

Mattot

³¹The Gadites and the Reubenites said in reply, "Whatever יהוה has spoken concerning your servants, that we will do. ³²We ourselves will cross over as shock-troops, at the instance of יהוה, into the land of Canaan; and we shall keep our hereditary holding *⁻across the Jordan."⁻*

³³So Moses assigned to them—to the Gadites, the Reubenites, and the half-tribe of Manasseh son of Joseph—the kingdom of Sihon king of the Amorites and the kingdom of King Og of Bashan, the land with its various cities and the territories of their surrounding towns. ³⁴The Gadites rebuilt Dibon, Ataroth, Aroer, ³⁵Atroth-shophan, Jazer, Jogbehah, ³⁶Beth-nimrah, and Beth-haran as fortified towns or as enclosures for flocks. ³⁷The Reubenites rebuilt Heshbon, Elealeh, Kiriathaim, ³⁸Nebo, Baal-meon—some names being changed—and Sibmah; *⁻they gave [their own] names to towns that they rebuilt.⁻* ³⁹The descendants of Machir son of Manasseh went to Gilead and captured it, dispossessing the Amorites who were there; ⁴⁰so Moses gave Gilead to Machir son of Manasseh, and he settled there. ⁴¹Jair son of Manasseh went and captured *⁻their villages,⁻* which he renamed Havvoth-jair.* ⁴²And Nobah went and captured Kenath and its dependencies, renaming it Nobah after himself.

מַסְעֵי | MAS'EI

33 These were the marches of the Israelites who started out from the land of Egypt, troop by troop, in the charge of Moses and Aaron. ²Moses recorded the starting points of their various marches as directed by יהוה. Their marches, by starting points, were as follows:

³They set out from Rameses in the first month, on the fifteenth day of the first month. It was on the morrow of the passover offering that the Israelites started out defiantly,* in plain view of all the Egyptians. ⁴The Egyptians meanwhile were burying those among them whom יהוה had struck down, every [male] first-born—whereby יהוה executed judgment on their gods.

⁵The Israelites set out from Rameses and encamped at Succoth. ⁶They set out from Succoth and encamped at Etham, which is on the edge of the wilderness. ⁷They set out from Etham and turned about toward Pi-hahiroth, which faces Baal-zephon, and they

encamped before Migdol. ⁸They set out from Pene*-hahiroth and passed through the sea into the wilderness; and they made a three-days' journey in the wilderness of Etham and encamped at Marah. ⁹They set out from Marah and came to Elim. There were twelve springs in Elim and seventy palm trees, so they encamped there. ¹⁰They set out from Elim and encamped by the *ˉSea of Reeds.ˉ* ¹¹They set out from the Sea of Reeds and encamped in the wilderness of Sin. ¹²They set out from the wilderness of Sin and encamped at Dophkah. ¹³They set out from Dophkah and encamped at Alush. ¹⁴They set out from Alush and encamped at Rephidim; it was there that the people had no water to drink. ¹⁵They set out from Rephidim and encamped in the wilderness of Sinai. ¹⁶They set out from the wilderness of Sinai and encamped at Kibroth-hattaavah. ¹⁷They set out from Kibroth-hattaavah and encamped at Hazeroth. ¹⁸They set out from Hazeroth and encamped at Rithmah. ¹⁹They set out from Rithmah and encamped at Rimmon-perez. ²⁰They set out from Rimmon-perez and encamped at Libnah. ²¹They set out from Libnah and encamped at Rissah. ²²They set out from Rissah and encamped at Kehelath. ²³They set out from Kehelath and encamped at Mount Shepher. ²⁴They set out from Mount Shepher and encamped at Haradah. ²⁵They set out from Haradah and encamped at Makheloth. ²⁶They set out from Makheloth and encamped at Tahath. ²⁷They set out from Tahath and encamped at Terah. ²⁸They set out from Terah and encamped at Mithkah. ²⁹They set out from Mithkah and encamped at Hashmonah. ³⁰They set out from Hashmonah and encamped at Moseroth. ³¹They set out from Moseroth and encamped at Bene-jaakan. ³²They set out from Bene-jaakan and encamped at Hor-haggidgad. ³³They set out from Hor-haggidgad and encamped at Jotbath. ³⁴They set out from Jotbath and encamped at Abronah. ³⁵They set out from Abronah and encamped at Ezion-geber. ³⁶They set out from Ezion-geber and encamped in the wilderness of Zin, that is, Kadesh. ³⁷They set out from Kadesh and encamped at Mount Hor, on the edge of the land of Edom.

³⁸Aaron the priest ascended Mount Hor at the command of יהוה and died there, in the fortieth year after the Israelites had left the land of Egypt, on the first day of the fifth month. ³⁹Aaron was a hundred and twenty-three years old when he died on Mount

Hor. [40]*And the Canaanite, king of Arad, who dwelt in the Negeb, in the land of Canaan, learned of the coming of the Israelites.

[41]They set out from Mount Hor and encamped at Zalmonah. [42]They set out from Zalmonah and encamped at Punon. [43]They set out from Punon and encamped at Oboth. [44]They set out from Oboth and encamped at Iye-abarim, in the territory of Moab. [45]They set out from Iyim and encamped at Dibon-gad. [46]They set out from Dibon-gad and encamped at Almon-diblathaim. [47]They set out from Almon-diblathaim and encamped in the hills of Abarim, before Nebo. [48]They set out from the hills of Abarim and encamped in the steppes of Moab, at the Jordan near Jericho; [49]they encamped by the Jordan from Beth-jeshimoth as far as Abel-shittim, in the steppes of Moab.

[50]In the steppes of Moab, at the Jordan near Jericho, יהוה spoke to Moses, saying: [51]Speak to the Israelite people and say to them: When you cross the Jordan into the land of Canaan, [52]you shall dispossess all the inhabitants of the land; you shall destroy all their figured* objects; you shall destroy all their molten images, and you shall demolish all their cult places. [53]And you shall take possession of the land and settle in it, for I have assigned the land to you to possess. [54]You shall apportion the land among yourselves by lot, clan by clan: with larger groups increase the share, with smaller groups reduce the share. Wherever the lot falls for it, that shall be its location. You shall have your portions according to your ancestral tribes. [55]But if you do not dispossess the inhabitants of the land, those whom you allow to remain shall be stings in your eyes and thorns in your sides, and they shall harass you in the land in which you live; [56]so that I will do to you what I planned to do to them.

34 יהוה spoke to Moses, saying: [2]Instruct the Israelite people and say to them: When you enter the land of Canaan, this is the land that shall fall to you as your portion, the land of Canaan with its various boundaries:

[3]Your southern sector shall extend from the wilderness of Zin alongside Edom. Your southern boundary shall start on the east from the tip of the Dead Sea. [4]Your boundary shall then turn to pass south of the ascent of Akrabbim and continue to Zin, and its

limits shall be south of Kadesh-barnea, reaching Hazar-addar and continuing to Azmon. ⁵From Azmon the boundary shall turn toward the Wadi of Egypt and terminate at the Sea.*

⁶For the western boundary you shall have the coast of the *‑Great Sea;‑* that shall serve as your western boundary.

⁷This shall be your northern boundary: Draw a line from the Great Sea to Mount Hor; ⁸from Mount Hor draw a line to Lebo-hamath,* and let the boundary reach Zedad. ⁹The boundary shall then run to Ziphron and terminate at Hazar-enan. That shall be your northern boundary.

¹⁰For your eastern boundary you shall draw a line from Hazar-enan to Shepham. ¹¹From Shepham the boundary shall descend to Riblah on the east side of Ain; from there the boundary shall continue downward and abut on the eastern slopes of the *‑Sea of Chinnereth.‑* ¹²The boundary shall then descend along the Jordan and terminate at the Dead Sea.

That shall be your land as defined by its boundaries on all sides.

¹³Moses instructed the Israelites, saying: This is the land you are to receive by lot as your hereditary portion, which יהוה has commanded to be given to the nine and a half tribes. ¹⁴For the Reubenite tribe by its ancestral houses, the Gadite tribe by its ancestral houses, and the half-tribe of Manasseh have already received their portions: ¹⁵those two and a half tribes have received their portions across the Jordan, opposite Jericho, on the east, the orient side.

¹⁶יהוה spoke to Moses, saying: ¹⁷These are the names of the commissioners° through whom the land shall be apportioned for you: Eleazar the priest and Joshua son of Nun. ¹⁸And you shall also take a chieftain from each tribe through whom the land shall be apportioned. ¹⁹These are the names of those commissioners:° from the tribe of Judah: Caleb son of Jephunneh. ²⁰From the Simeonite tribe: Samuel* son of Ammihud. ²¹From the tribe of Benjamin: Elidad son of Chislon. ²²From the Danite tribe: a chieftain, Bukki son of Jogli. ²³For the descendants of Joseph: from the Manassite tribe: a chieftain, Hanniel son of Ephod; ²⁴and from the Ephraimite tribe: a chieftain, Kemuel son of Shiphtan. ²⁵From the Zebulunite tribe: a chieftain, Elizaphan son of Parnach. ²⁶From

Mas'ei

the Issacharite tribe: a chieftain, Paltiel son of Azzan. ²⁷From the
Asherite tribe: a chieftain, Ahihud son of Shelomi. ²⁸From the
Naphtalite tribe: a chieftain, Pedahel son of Ammihud.

²⁹It was these whom יהוה designated to allot portions to the
Israelites in the land of Canaan.

35 יהוה spoke to Moses in the steppes of Moab at the Jordan
near Jericho, saying: ²Instruct the Israelite people to assign, out of the holdings apportioned to them, towns for the
Levites to dwell in; you shall also assign to the Levites pasture
land around their towns. ³The towns shall be theirs to dwell in,
and the pasture shall be for the cattle they own and all their other
beasts. ⁴The town pasture that you are to assign to the Levites
shall extend a thousand cubits outside the town wall all around.
⁵You shall measure off two thousand cubits outside the town on
the east side, two thousand on the south side, two thousand on
the west side, and two thousand on the north side, with the town
in the center. That shall be the pasture for their towns.

⁶The towns that you assign to the Levites shall comprise the six
cities of refuge that you are to designate for a [male]° killer° to flee
to, to which you shall add forty-two towns. ⁷Thus the total of the
towns that you assign to the Levites shall be forty-eight towns,
with their pasture. ⁸In assigning towns from the holdings of the
Israelites, take more from the larger groups and less from the
smaller, so that each assigns towns to the Levites in proportion to
the share it receives.

⁹יהוה spoke further to Moses: ¹⁰Speak to the Israelite people
and say to them: When you cross the Jordan into the land of
Canaan, ¹¹you shall provide yourselves with places to serve you as
cities of refuge to which a [male] killer who has slain a person
unintentionally may flee. ¹²The cities shall serve you as a refuge
from the avenger,* so that the killer may not die unless he has
stood trial before the assembly.

¹³The towns that you thus assign shall be six cities of refuge in
all. ¹⁴Three cities shall be designated beyond the Jordan, and the
other three shall be designated in the land of Canaan: they shall
serve as cities of refuge. ¹⁵These six cities shall serve the Israelites

and the resident aliens among them for refuge, so that any man who slays a person unintentionally may flee there.

16Anyone, however, who strikes another with an iron object so that death results is a murderer; the murderer must be put to death. 17If one struck another with a stone tool* that could cause death, and death resulted, that person is a murderer; the murderer must be put to death. 18Similarly, if one struck another with a wooden tool that could cause death, and death resulted, that person is a murderer; the murderer must be put to death. 19The blood-avenger himself shall put the murderer to death; it is he who shall put that person to death upon encounter. 20So, too, if one pushed another in hate or hurled something at [the victim] on purpose and death resulted, 21or if one struck another with the hand in enmity and death resulted, the assailant shall be put to death; that person is a murderer. The blood-avenger shall put the murderer to death upon encounter.

22But if [a man] pushed without malice aforethought or hurled any object at [the victim] unintentionally, 23or inadvertently* dropped upon [the victim] any deadly object of stone, and death resulted—though not being an enemy and not seeking to harm—24in such cases the assembly shall decide between the slayer and the blood-avenger. 25The assembly shall protect the killer from the blood-avenger, and the assembly shall restore him to the city of refuge to which he fled, and there he shall remain until the death of the high priest who was anointed with the sacred oil. 26But if the killer ever goes outside the limits of the city of refuge to which he has fled, 27and the blood-avenger comes upon him outside the limits of his city of refuge, and the blood-avenger kills the killer, there is no bloodguilt on his account. 28For he must remain inside his city of refuge until the death of the high priest; after the death of the high priest, the killer may return to his land holding.

29Such shall be your law of procedure throughout the ages in all your settlements.

30If anyone slays a person, the killer may be executed only on the evidence of witnesses; the testimony of a single witness against a person shall not suffice for a sentence of death. 31You may not accept a ransom for the life of a murderer who is guilty of a capital crime; [a murderer] must be put to death. ³²Nor may you accept ransom in lieu of flight to a city of refuge, enabling a man to return to live on his land before the death of the priest. ³³You shall not pollute the land in which you live; for blood pollutes the land, and the land can have no expiation for blood that is shed on it, except by the blood of the one who shed it. ³⁴You shall not defile the land in which you live, in which I Myself abide, for I יהוה abide among the Israelite people.

36 The *⁻family heads⁻* in the clan of the descendants of Gilead son of Machir son of Manasseh, one of the Josephite clans, came forward and appealed to Moses and the chieftains, family heads of the Israelites. ²They said, "יהוה commanded my lord to assign the land to the Israelites as shares by lot, and my lord was further commanded by יהוה to assign the share of our kinsman Zelophehad to his daughters. ³Now, if they become the wives of persons from another Israelite tribe, their share will be cut off from our ancestral portion and be added to the portion of the tribe into which they become [wives]; thus our allotted portion will be diminished. ⁴And even when the Israelites observe the jubilee, their share will be added to that of the tribe into which they become [wives], and their share will be cut off from the ancestral portion of our tribe."

⁵So Moses, at יהוה's bidding, instructed the Israelites, saying: "The plea of the Josephite tribe is just. ⁶This is what יהוה has commanded concerning the daughters of Zelophehad: They may become the wives of anyone they wish, provided they become wives within a clan of their father's tribe. ⁷No inheritance of the Israelites may pass over from one tribe to another, but the Israelite [heirs]—each of them—must remain bound to the ancestral portion of their tribe. ⁸Every daughter among the Israelite tribes who inherits a share must become the wife of someone from a clan of her father's tribe, in order that every Israelite [heir] may keep an ancestral share. ⁹Thus no inheritance shall pass over from one tribe to another, but the Israelite tribes shall remain bound each to its portion."

¹⁰The daughters of Zelophehad did as יהוה had commanded Moses: ¹¹Mahlah, Tirzah, Hoglah, Milcah, and Noah, Zelophe-

had's daughters, became the wives of their uncles' sons, [12]becoming wives within clans of descendants of Manasseh son of Joseph; and so their share remained in the tribe of their father's clan.

[13]These are the commandments and regulations that יהוה enjoined upon the Israelites, through Moses, on the steppes of Moab, at the Jordan near Jericho.

חזק

דברים

DEUTERONOMY

1 These are the words that Moses addressed to all Israel on the other side of the Jordan.—*ˉThrough the wilderness, in the Arabah near Suph, between Paran and Tophel, Laban, Hazeroth, and Di-zahab, ²it is eleven days from Horeb to Kadesh-barnea by the Mount Seir route.*—³It was in the fortieth year, on the first day of the eleventh month, that Moses addressed the Israelites in accordance with the instructions that יהוה had given him for them, ⁴after he had defeated Sihon king of the Amorites, who dwelt in Heshbon, and King Og of Bashan, who dwelt at Ashtaroth [and]* Edrei. ⁵On the other side of the Jordan, in the land of Moab, Moses undertook to expound this Teaching. He said:

⁶יהוה our God spoke to us at Horeb, saying: You have stayed long enough at this mountain. ⁷Start out and make your way to the hill country of the Amorites and to all their neighbors in the Arabah, the hill country, the Shephelah,* the Negeb, the seacoast, the *ˉland of the Canaanites,ˉ* and the Lebanon, as far as the Great River, the river Euphrates. ⁸See, I place the land at your disposal. Go, take possession of the land that יהוה swore to your fathers Abraham, Isaac, and Jacob, to assign to them and to their heirs after them.

⁹Thereupon I said to you, "I cannot bear the burden of you by myself. ¹⁰יהוה your God has multiplied you until you are today as numerous as the stars in the sky.—¹¹May יהוה, the God of your ancestors, increase your numbers a thousandfold, and bless you as promised.—¹²How can I bear unaided the trouble of you, and the burden, and the bickering! ¹³Pick from each of your tribes representatives° who are wise, discerning, and experienced, and I will appoint them as your heads." ¹⁴You answered me and said, "What you propose to do is good." ¹⁵So I took your tribal leaders as representatives° who are wise and experienced, and appointed them heads over you: chiefs of thousands, chiefs of hundreds, chiefs of fifties, and chiefs of tens, and officials for your tribes. ¹⁶I charged

your magistrates at that time as follows, "Hear out your fellow Israelites, and decide justly between anyone and a fellow Israelite or a stranger. ¹⁷You shall not be partial in judgment: hear out low and high alike. Fear no one, for judgment is God's. And any matter that is too difficult for you, you shall bring to me and I will hear it." ¹⁸Thus I instructed you, at that time, about the various things that you should do.

¹⁹We set out from Horeb and traveled the great and terrible wilderness that you saw, along the road to the hill country of the Amorites, as our God יהוה had commanded us. When we reached Kadesh-barnea, ²⁰I said to you, "You have come to the hill country of the Amorites which our God יהוה is giving to us. ²¹See, your God יהוה has placed the land at your disposal. Go up, take possession, as יהוה, the God of your fathers, promised you. Fear not and be not dismayed."

²²Then all of you came to me and said, "Let us send emissaries° ahead to reconnoiter the land for us and bring back word on the route we shall follow and the cities we shall come to." ²³I approved of the plan, and so I selected from among you twelve representatives,° one from each tribe. ²⁴They made for the hill country, came to the wadi Eshcol, and spied it out. ²⁵They took some of the fruit of the land with them and brought it down to us. And they gave us this report: "It is a good land that our God יהוה is giving to us."

²⁶Yet you refused to go up, and flouted the command of your God יהוה. ²⁷*·You sulked·* in your tents and said, "It is out of hatred for us that יהוה brought us out of the land of Egypt, to hand us over to the Amorites to wipe us out. ²⁸*·What kind of place·* are we going to? Our brothers have taken the heart out of us, saying, 'We saw there a people stronger and taller than we, large cities with walls sky-high, and even Anakites.'"

²⁹I said to you, "Have no dread or fear of them. ³⁰None other than your God יהוה, who goes before you, will fight for you, just as [God] did for you in Egypt before your very eyes, ³¹and in the wilderness, where you saw how your God יהוה carried you, as a householder° carries his son,° all the way that you traveled until you came to this place. ³²Yet for all that, you have no faith in your God יהוה, ³³who goes before you on your journeys—to scout the

place where you are to encamp—in fire by night and in cloud by day, in order to guide you on the route you are to follow."

34יהוה heard your loud complaint and, becoming angry, vowed: 35Not one of the men [counted in the census], this evil generation, shall see the good land that I swore to give to your fathers— 36none except Caleb son of Jephunneh; he shall see it, and to him and his descendants will I give the land on which he set foot, because he remained loyal to יהוה.—37Because of you יהוה was incensed with me too, saying: You shall not enter it either. 38Joshua son of Nun, who attends you, he shall enter it. Imbue him with strength, for he shall allot it to Israel. 39Moreover, your little ones who you said would be carried off, your children who do not yet know good from bad, they shall enter it; to them will I give it and they shall possess it. 40As for you, turn about and march into the wilderness by the way of the Sea of Reeds.

41You replied to me, saying, "We stand guilty before יהוה. We will go up now and fight, just as our God יהוה commanded us." And [the men among] you each girded yourselves with war gear and recklessly* started for the hill country. 42But יהוה said to me, "Warn them: Do not go up and do not fight, since I am not in your midst; else you will be routed by your enemies." 43I spoke to you, but you would not listen; you flouted יהוה's command and willfully marched into the hill country. 44Then the Amorites who lived in those hills came out against you like so many bees and chased you, and they crushed you at Hormah in Seir. 45Again you wept before יהוה; but יהוה would not heed your cry or give ear to you.

46Thus, after you had remained at Kadesh *⁻all that long time,⁻* 2 1we marched back into the wilderness by the way of the Sea of Reeds, as יהוה had spoken to me, and skirted the hill country of Seir a long time.

2Then יהוה said to me: 3You have been skirting this hill country long enough; now turn north. 4And charge the people as follows: You will be passing through the territory of your kin, the descendants of Esau, who live in Seir. Though they will be afraid of you, be very careful 5not to provoke them. For I will not give you of their land so much as a foot can tread on; I have given the hill country of Seir as a possession to Esau. 6*What food you eat you shall obtain from them for money; even the water you drink you shall procure from them for money. [7]Indeed, your God יהוה has blessed you in all your undertakings. [God] has watched over your wanderings through this great wilderness; your God יהוה has been with you these past forty years: you have lacked nothing.

[8]We then moved on, away from our kin, the descendants of Esau, who live in Seir, away from the road of the Arabah, away from Elath and Ezion-geber; and we marched on in the direction of the wilderness of Moab. [9]And יהוה said to me: Do not harass the Moabites or provoke them to war. For I will not give you any of their land as a possession; I have assigned Ar as a possession to the descendants of Lot.—

> [10]It was formerly inhabited by the Emim, a people great and numerous, and as tall as the Anakites. [11]Like the Anakites, they are counted as Rephaim; but the Moabites call them Emim. [12]Similarly, Seir was formerly inhabited by the Horites; but the descendants of Esau dispossessed them, wiping them out and settling in their place, just as Israel did in the land they were to possess, which יהוה had given to them.—

[13]Up now! Cross the wadi Zered!

So we crossed the wadi Zered. [14]The time that we spent in travel from Kadesh-barnea until we crossed the wadi Zered was thirty-eight years, until that whole generation of warriors had perished from the camp, as יהוה had sworn concerning them. [15]Indeed, the hand of יהוה struck them, to root them out from the camp until they were finished off.

[16]When all the warriors among the people had died off, [17]יהוה spoke to me, saying: [18]You are now passing through the territory of Moab, through Ar. [19]You will then be close to the Ammonites; do not harass them or start a fight with them. For I will not give any part of the land of the Ammonites to you as a possession; I have assigned it as a possession to the descendants of Lot.—

> [20]It, too, is counted as Rephaim country. It was formerly inhabited by Rephaim, whom the Ammonites call Zamzummim, [21]a people great and numerous and as tall as the Anakites. יהוה wiped them out, so that [the Ammonites] dispossessed them and settled in their place, [22]as [God] did for the descendants of Esau who live in Seir, by wiping out the Horites before them, so that they dispossessed them and set-

tled in their place, *⁻as is still the case.⁻* ²³So, too, with the Avvim who dwelt in villages in the vicinity of Gaza: the Caphtorim, who came from Crete,* wiped them out and settled in their place.—

²⁴Up! Set out across the wadi Arnon! See, I give into your power Sihon the Amorite, king of Heshbon, and his land. Begin the occupation: engage him in battle. ²⁵This day I begin to put the dread and fear of you upon the peoples everywhere under heaven, so that they shall tremble and quake because of you whenever they hear you mentioned.

²⁶Then I sent messengers from the wilderness of Kedemoth to King Sihon of Heshbon with an offer of peace, as follows, ²⁷"Let me pass through your country. I will keep strictly to the highway, turning off neither to the right nor to the left. ²⁸What food I eat you will supply for money, and what water I drink you will furnish for money; just let me pass through*—²⁹as the descendants of Esau who dwell in Seir did for me, and the Moabites who dwell in Ar—that I may cross the Jordan into the land that our God יהוה is giving us."

³⁰But King Sihon of Heshbon refused to let us pass through, because יהוה had stiffened his will and hardened his heart in order to deliver him into your power—as is now the case. ³¹And יהוה said to me: See, I begin by placing Sihon and his land at your disposal. Begin the occupation; take possession of his land.

³²Sihon with all his troops took the field against us at Jahaz, ³³and our God יהוה delivered him to us and we defeated him and his sons and all his troops. ³⁴At that time we captured all his towns, and we doomed* every town—°⁻men, women, and children⁻°—leaving no survivor. ³⁵We retained as booty only the cattle and the spoil of the cities that we captured. ³⁶From Aroer on the edge of the Arnon valley, *⁻including the town⁻* in the valley itself, to Gilead, not a city was too mighty for us; our God יהוה delivered everything to us. ³⁷But you did not encroach upon the land of the Ammonites, all along the wadi Jabbok and the towns of the hill country, just as our God יהוה had commanded.

3 We made our way up the road toward Bashan, and King Og of Bashan with all his troops took the field against us at Edrei. ²But יהוה said to me: Do not fear him, for I am delivering him and all his troops and his country into your power, and you will do to him as you did to Sihon king of the Amorites, who lived in Heshbon.

³So our God יהוה also delivered into our power King Og of Bashan, with all his troops, and we dealt them such a blow that no survivor was left. ⁴At that time we captured all his towns; there was not a town that we did not take from them: sixty towns, the whole district of Argob, the kingdom of Og in Bashan—⁵all those towns were fortified with high walls, gates,* and bars—apart from a great number of unwalled towns. ⁶We doomed them as we had done in the case of King Sihon of Heshbon; we doomed every town—men, women, and children—⁷and retained as booty all the cattle and the spoil of the towns.

⁸Thus we seized, at that time, from the two Amorite kings, the country beyond the Jordan, from the wadi Arnon to Mount Hermon—⁹Sidonians called Hermon Sirion, and the Amorites call it Senir—¹⁰all the towns of the Tableland and the whole of Gilead and Bashan as far as Salcah* and Edrei, the towns of Og's kingdom in Bashan. ¹¹Only King Og of Bashan was left of the remaining Rephaim. His bedstead, an iron bedstead, is now in Rabbah of the Ammonites; it is nine cubits long and four cubits wide, by *‐the standard cubit!‐*

¹²*And this is the land which we apportioned at that time: The part from Aroer along the wadi Arnon, with part of the hill country of Gilead and its towns, I assigned to the Reubenites and the Gadites. ¹³The rest of Gilead, and all of Bashan under Og's rule—the whole Argob district, all that part of Bashan which is called Rephaim country—I assigned to the half-tribe of Manasseh. ¹⁴Jair son of Manasseh received the whole Argob district (that is, Bashan) as far as the boundary of the Geshurites and the Maacathites, and named it after himself: Havvoth-jair*—as is still the case. ¹⁵To Machir I assigned Gilead. ¹⁶And to the Reubenites and the Gadites I assigned the part from Gilead down to the wadi Arnon, the middle of the wadi being the boundary, and up to the wadi Jabbok, the boundary of the Ammonites.

¹⁷*[We also seized] the Arabah, from the foot of the slopes of Pisgah on the east, to the edge of the Jordan, and from Chinnereth down to the sea of the Arabah, the Dead Sea.

¹⁸At that time I charged you [men of Reuben, Gad, and Man-asseh], saying, "Your God יהוה has given you this country to pos-sess. You must go as shock-troops, warriors all, at the head of your Israelite kin. ¹⁹Only your wives, children, and livestock—I know that you have much livestock—shall be left in the towns I have assigned to you, ²⁰until יהוה has granted your kin a haven such as you have, and they too have taken possession of the land that your God יהוה is assigning them, beyond the Jordan. Then you may return each to the homestead that I have assigned to him."

²¹I also charged Joshua at that time, saying, "You have seen with your own eyes all that your God יהוה has done to these two kings; so shall יהוה do to all the kingdoms into which you shall cross over. ²²Do not fear them, for it is your God יהוה who will battle for you."

ואתחנן | VA-'ETHANNAN

²³I pleaded with יהוה at that time, saying, ²⁴"O lord יהוה, You who let Your servant see the first works of Your greatness and Your mighty hand, You whose powerful deeds no god in heaven or on earth can equal! ²⁵Let me, I pray, cross over and see the good land on the other side of the Jordan, that good hill country, and the Lebanon." ²⁶But יהוה was wrathful with me on your account and would not listen to me. יהוה said to me, "Enough! Never speak to Me of this matter again! ²⁷Go up to the summit of Pisgah and gaze about, to the west, the north, the south, and the east. Look at it well, for you shall not go across yonder Jordan. ²⁸Give Joshua his instructions, and imbue him with strength and courage, for he shall go across at the head of this people, and he shall allot to them the land that you may only see."

²⁹Meanwhile we stayed on in the valley near Beth-peor.

4 And now, O Israel, give heed to the laws and rules that I am instructing you to observe, so that you may live to enter and occupy the land that יהוה, the God of your fathers, is giving you. ²You shall not add anything to what I command you or take any-thing away from it, but keep the commandments of your God יהוה that I enjoin upon you. ³You saw with your own eyes what יהוה did in the matter of Baal-peor, that your God יהוה wiped out

from among you every person who followed Baal-peor; ⁴while you, who held fast to your God יהוה, are all alive today.

⁵See, I have imparted to you laws and rules, as my God יהוה has commanded me, for you to abide by in the land that you are about to enter and occupy. ⁶Observe them faithfully, for that will be proof of your wisdom and discernment to other peoples, who on hearing of all these laws will say, "Surely, that great nation is a wise and discerning people." ⁷For what great nation is there that has a god so close at hand as is our God יהוה whenever we call? ⁸Or what great nation has laws and rules as perfect as all this Teaching that I set before you this day?

⁹But take utmost care and watch yourselves scrupulously, so that you do not forget the things that you saw with your own eyes and so that they do not fade from your mind as long as you live. And make them known to your children and to your children's children: ¹⁰The day you stood before your God יהוה at Horeb, when יהוה said to Me, "Gather the people to Me that I may let them hear My words, in order that they may learn to revere Me as long as they live on earth, and may so teach their children." ¹¹You came forward and stood at the foot of the mountain. The mountain was ablaze with flames to the very skies, dark with densest clouds. ¹²יהוה spoke to you out of the fire; you heard the sound of words but perceived no shape—nothing but a voice. ¹³[God] declared to you the covenant that you were commanded to observe, the Ten Commandments, inscribing them on two tablets of stone. ¹⁴At the same time יהוה commanded me to impart to you laws and rules for you to observe in the land that you are about to cross into and occupy.

¹⁵For your own sake, therefore, be most careful—since you saw no shape when your God יהוה spoke to you at Horeb out of the fire—¹⁶not to act wickedly and make for yourselves a sculptured image in any likeness whatever: the form of °ˉa man or a woman,ˉ° ¹⁷the form of any beast on earth, the form of any winged bird that flies in the sky, ¹⁸the form of anything that creeps on the ground, the form of any fish that is in the waters below the earth. ¹⁹And when you look up to the sky and behold the sun and the moon and the stars, the whole heavenly host, you must not be lured into bowing down to them or serving them. These your God יהוה

allotted to other peoples everywhere under heaven; 20but you יהוה took and brought out of Egypt, that iron blast furnace, to be God's very own people, as is now the case.

21Now יהוה was angry with me on your account and swore that I should not cross the Jordan and enter the good land that your God יהוה is assigning you as a heritage. 22For I must die in this land; I shall not cross the Jordan. But you will cross and take possession of that good land. 23Take care, then, not to forget the covenant that your God יהוה concluded with you, and not to make for yourselves a sculptured image in any likeness, against which your God יהוה has enjoined you. 24For your God יהוה is a consuming fire, an impassioned God.

25When you have begotten children and children's children and are long established in the land, should you act wickedly and make for yourselves a sculptured image in any likeness, causing your God יהוה displeasure and vexation, 26I call heaven and earth this day to witness against you that you shall soon perish from the land that you are crossing the Jordan to possess; you shall not long endure in it, but shall be utterly wiped out. 27יהוה will scatter you among the peoples, and only a scant few of you shall be left among the nations to which יהוה will drive you. 28There you will serve gods of wood and stone, made by human hands, that cannot see or hear or eat or smell.

29But if you search there, you will find your God יהוה, if only you seek with all your heart and soul—30when you are in distress because all these things have befallen you and, in the end, return to and obey your God יהוה. 31For your God יהוה is a compassionate God, who will not fail you nor let you perish; [God] will not forget the covenant made on oath with your fathers.

32You have but to inquire about bygone ages that came before you, ever since God created humankind on earth, from one end of heaven to the other: has anything as grand as this ever happened, or has its like ever been known? 33Has any people heard the voice of a god speaking out of a fire, as you have, and survived? 34Or has any deity ventured to go and take one nation from the midst of another by prodigious acts, by signs and portents, by war, by a mighty and an outstretched arm and awesome power, as your

Va-'ethannan

293

God יהוה did for you in Egypt before your very eyes? ³⁵*It has been clearly demonstrated to you-* that יהוה alone is God; there is none else. ³⁶From the heavens [God] let you hear the divine voice to discipline you; on earth [God] let you see the great divine fire; and from amidst that fire you heard God's words. ³⁷And having loved your ancestors, [God] chose their heirs after them; *-[God] personally-*—in great, divine might—led you out of Egypt, ³⁸to drive from your path nations greater and more populous than you, to take you into their land and assign it to you as a heritage, as is still the case. ³⁹Know therefore this day and keep in mind that יהוה alone is God in heaven above and on earth below; there is no other. ⁴⁰Observe God's laws and commandments, which I enjoin upon you this day, that it may go well with you and your children after you, and that you may long remain in the land that your God יהוה is assigning to you for all time.

⁴¹Then Moses set aside three cities on the east side of the Jordan ⁴²to which a [male]° killer° could escape, one who unwittingly slew another without having been an enemy in the past; he could flee to one of these cities and live: ⁴³Bezer, in the wilderness in the Tableland, belonging to the Reubenites; Ramoth, in Gilead, belonging to the Gadites; and Golan, in Bashan, belonging to the Manassites.

⁴⁴This is the Teaching that Moses set before the Israelites: ⁴⁵these are the decrees, laws, and rules that Moses addressed to the people of Israel, after they had left Egypt, ⁴⁶beyond the Jordan, in the valley at Beth-peor, in the land of King Sihon of the Amorites, who dwelt in Heshbon, whom Moses and the Israelites defeated after they had left Egypt. ⁴⁷They had taken possession of his country and that of King Og of Bashan—the two kings of the Amorites—which were on the east side of the Jordan ⁴⁸from Aroer on the banks of the wadi Arnon, as far as Mount Sion,* that is, Hermon; ⁴⁹also the whole Arabah on the east side of the Jordan, as far as the Sea of the Arabah, at the foot of the slopes of Pisgah.

5 Moses summoned all the Israelites and said to them: Hear, O Israel, the laws and rules that I proclaim to you this day! Study them and observe them faithfully!

²יהוה our God made a covenant with us at Horeb. ³It was not with our ancestors that יהוה made this covenant, but with us, the living, every one of us who is here today. ⁴Face to face יהוה spoke to you on the mountain out of the fire—⁵I stood between יהוה and you at that time to convey יהוה's words to you, for you were afraid of the fire and did not go up the mountain—saying:

⁶*I יהוה am your God who brought you° out of the land of Egypt, the house of bondage: ⁷You shall have no other gods beside Me.

⁸You shall not make for yourself a sculptured image, any likeness of what is in the heavens above, or on the earth below, or in the waters below the earth. ⁹You shall not bow down to them or serve them. For I your God יהוה am an impassioned God, visiting the guilt of the parents upon the children, upon the third and upon the fourth generations of those who reject Me, ¹⁰but showing kindness to the thousandth generation of those who love Me and keep My commandments.

¹¹You shall not swear falsely by the name of your God יהוה; for יהוה will not clear one who swears falsely by God's name.

¹²Observe the sabbath day and keep it holy, as your God יהוה has commanded you. ¹³Six days you shall labor and do all your work, ¹⁴but the seventh day is a sabbath of your God יהוה; you shall not do any work—you, your son or your daughter, your male or female slave, your ox or your ass, or any of your cattle, or the stranger in your settlements, so that your male and female slave may rest as you do. ¹⁵Remember that you were a slave in the land of Egypt and your God יהוה freed you from there with a mighty hand and an outstretched arm; therefore your God יהוה has commanded you to observe the sabbath day.

¹⁶Honor your father and your mother, as your God יהוה has commanded you, that you may long endure, and that you may fare well, in the land that your God יהוה is assigning to you.

¹⁷You shall not murder. You shall not commit adultery. You shall not steal. You shall not bear false witness against your neighbor.

¹⁸You [men]° shall not covet your neighbor's wife. Likewise, none of you shall crave your neighbor's house, or field, or male or female slave, or ox, or ass, or anything that is your neighbor's.

¹⁹יהוה spoke those words—those and no more—to your whole congregation at the mountain, with a mighty voice out of the fire

Va-'etḥannan

and the dense clouds. [God] inscribed them on two tablets of stone and gave them to me. 20When you heard the voice out of the darkness, while the mountain was ablaze with fire, you came up to me, all your tribal heads and elders, 21and said, "Our God יהוה has just shown us a majestic Presence, and we have heard God's voice out of the fire; we have seen this day that humankind may live though addressed by God. 22Let us not die, then, for this fearsome fire will consume us; if we hear the voice of our God יהוה any longer, we shall die. 23For what mortal ever heard the voice of the living God speak out of the fire, as we did, and lived? 24You go closer and hear all that our God יהוה says, and then you tell us everything that our God יהוה tells you, and we will willingly do it."

25יהוה heard the plea that you made to me, and יהוה said to me, "I have heard the plea that this people made to you; they did well to speak thus. 26May they always be of such mind, to revere Me and follow all My commandments, that it may go well with them and with their children forever! 27Go, say to them, 'Return to your tents.' 28But you remain here with Me, and I will give you the whole Instruction—the laws and the rules—that you shall impart to them, for them to observe in the land that I am giving them to possess."

29Be careful, then, to do as your God יהוה has commanded you. Do not turn aside to the right or to the left: 30follow only the path that your God יהוה has enjoined upon you, so that you may thrive and that it may go well with you, and that you may long endure in the land you are to possess.

6 And this is the Instruction—the laws and the rules—that your God יהוה has commanded [me] to impart to you, to be observed in the land that you are about to cross into and occupy, 2so that you, your children, and your children's children may revere your God יהוה and follow, as long as you live, all the divine laws and commandments that I enjoin upon you, to the end that you may long endure. 3Obey, O Israel, willingly and faithfully, that it may go well with you and that you may increase greatly [in] *ᐨa land flowing with milk and honey,* as יהוה, the God of your ancestors, spoke to you.

4Hear, O Israel! *ᐨיהוה is our God, יהוה alone.* 5You shall love your God יהוה with all your heart, with all your soul, and with all your might. ⁶Take to heart these instructions with which I charge you this day. ⁷Impress them upon your children. Recite them when you stay at home and when you are away, when you lie down and when you get up. ⁸Bind them as a sign on your hand and let them serve as a symbol* *⁻on your forehead;⁻* ⁹inscribe them on the doorposts of your house and on your gates.

¹⁰When your God יהוה brings you into the land that was sworn to your fathers Abraham, Isaac, and Jacob, to be assigned to you—great and flourishing cities that you did not build, ¹¹houses full of all good things that you did not fill, hewn cisterns that you did not hew, vineyards and olive groves that you did not plant—and you eat your fill, ¹²take heed that you do not forget יהוה who freed you from the land of Egypt, the house of bondage. ¹³Revere only your God יהוה and worship [God] alone, and swear only by God's name. ¹⁴Do not follow other gods, any gods of the peoples about you—¹⁵for your God יהוה in your midst is an impassioned God—lest the anger of your God יהוה blaze forth against you, wiping you off the face of the earth.

¹⁶Do not try your God יהוה, *⁻as you did at Massah.⁻* ¹⁷Be sure to keep the commandments, decrees, and laws that your God יהוה has enjoined upon you. ¹⁸Do what is right and good in the sight of יהוה, that it may go well with you and that you may be able to possess the good land that your God יהוה promised on oath to your fathers, ¹⁹and that all your enemies may be driven out before you, as יהוה has spoken.

²⁰When, in time to come, your children ask you, "What mean the decrees, laws, and rules that our God יהוה has enjoined upon you?"* ²¹you shall say to your children, "We were slaves to Pharaoh in Egypt and יהוה freed us from Egypt with a mighty hand. ²²יהוה wrought before our eyes marvelous and destructive signs and portents in Egypt, against Pharaoh and all his household; ²³and us [God] freed from there, in order to take us and give us the land promised on oath to our fathers. ²⁴Then יהוה commanded us to observe all these laws, to revere our God יהוה, for our lasting good and for our survival, as is now the case. ²⁵It will be therefore to our merit before our God יהוה to observe faithfully this whole Instruction, as [God] has commanded us."

7 When your God יהוה brings you to the land that you are about to enter and possess, and [God] dislodges many nations before you—the Hittites, Girgashites, Amorites, Canaanites, Perizzites, Hivites, and Jebusites, seven nations much larger than you—²and your God יהוה delivers them to you and you defeat them, you must doom them to destruction: grant them no terms and give them no quarter. ³You shall not intermarry with them: do not give your daughters to their sons or take their daughters for your sons. ⁴For they will turn your children away from Me to worship other gods, and יהוה's anger will blaze forth against you, promptly wiping you out. ⁵Instead, this is what you shall do to them: you shall tear down their altars, smash their pillars, cut down their sacred posts, and consign their images to the fire.

⁶For you are a people consecrated to your God יהוה: of all the peoples on earth your God יהוה chose you to be God's treasured people. ⁷It is not because you are the most numerous of peoples that יהוה grew attached to you and chose you—indeed, you are the smallest of peoples; ⁸but it was because יהוה favored you and kept the oath made to your fathers that יהוה freed you with a mighty hand and rescued you from the house of bondage, from the power of Pharaoh king of Egypt.

⁹Know, therefore, that only your God יהוה is God, the steadfast God who keeps the divine covenant faithfully to the thousandth generation of those who love [God] and keep the divine commandments, ¹⁰but who instantly requites with destruction those who reject [God]—never slow with those who reject, but requiting them instantly. ¹¹Therefore, observe faithfully the Instruction—the laws and the rules—with which I charge you today.

עֵקֶב | ʾEKEV

¹²And if you do obey these rules and observe them carefully, your God יהוה will maintain faithfully for you the covenant made on oath with your fathers: ¹³[God] will favor you and bless you and multiply you—blessing the issue of your womb and the produce of your soil, your new grain and wine and oil, the calving of your herd and the lambing of your flock, in the land sworn to your fathers to be assigned to you. ¹⁴You shall be blessed above all other peoples: there shall be no sterile male or female among you

or among your livestock. [15]יהוה will ward off from you all sickness; [God] will not bring upon you any of the dreadful diseases of Egypt, about which you know, but will inflict them upon all your enemies.

[16]You shall destroy all the peoples that your God יהוה delivers to you, showing them no pity. And you shall not worship their gods, for that would be a snare to you. [17]Should you say to yourselves, "These nations are more numerous than we; how can we dispossess them?" [18]You need have no fear of them. You have but to bear in mind what your God יהוה did to Pharaoh and all the Egyptians: [19]the wondrous acts that you saw with your own eyes, the signs and the portents, the mighty hand, and the outstretched arm by which your God יהוה liberated you. Thus will your God יהוה do to all the peoples you now fear. [20]יהוה your God will also send a plague* against them, until those who are left in hiding perish before you. [21]Do not stand in dread of them, for your God יהוה is in your midst, a great and awesome God.

[22]יהוה your God will dislodge those peoples before you little by little; you will not be able to put an end to them at once, else the wild beasts would multiply to your hurt. [23]יהוה your God will deliver them up to you, throwing them into utter panic until they are wiped out. [24][God] will deliver their kings into your hand, and you shall obliterate their name from under the heavens; no one shall stand up to you, until you have wiped them out.

[25]You shall consign the images of their gods to the fire; you shall not covet the silver and gold on them and keep it for yourselves, lest you be ensnared thereby; for that is abhorrent to your God יהוה. [26]You must not bring an abhorrent thing into your house, or you will be proscribed like it; you must reject it as abominable and abhorrent, for it is proscribed.

8 You shall faithfully observe all the Instruction that I enjoin upon you today, that you may thrive and increase and be able to possess the land that יהוה promised on oath to your fathers.

[2]Remember the long way that your God יהוה has made you travel in the wilderness these past forty years, in order to test you by hardships to learn what was in your hearts: whether you would keep the divine commandments or not. [3][God] subjected you to

'Ekev

the hardship of hunger and then gave you manna to eat, which neither you nor your ancestors had ever known, in order to teach you that a human being does not live on bread alone, but that one may live on anything that יהוה decrees. 4The clothes upon you did not wear out, nor did your feet swell these forty years. 5Bear in mind that your God יהוה disciplines you just as a householder° disciplines his son. 6Therefore keep the commandments of your God יהוה: walk in God's ways and show reverence.

7For your God יהוה is bringing you into a good land, a land with streams and springs and fountains issuing from plain and hill; 8a land of wheat and barley, of vines, figs, and pomegranates, a land of olive trees and honey; 9a land where you may eat food without stint, where you will lack nothing; a land whose rocks are iron and from whose hills you can mine copper. 10When you have eaten your fill, give thanks to your God יהוה for the good land given to you.

11Take care lest you forget your God יהוה and fail to keep the divine commandments, rules, and laws which I enjoin upon you today. 12When you have eaten your fill, and have built fine houses to live in, 13and your herds and flocks have multiplied, and your silver and gold have increased, and everything you own has prospered, 14[beware] lest* your heart grow haughty and you forget your God יהוה—who freed you from the land of Egypt, the house of bondage; 15who led you through the great and terrible wilderness with its seraph* serpents and scorpions, a parched land with no water in it, who brought forth water for you from the flinty rock; 16who fed you in the wilderness with manna, which your ancestors had never known, in order to test you by hardships only to benefit you in the end—17and you say to yourselves, "My own power and the might of my own hand have won this wealth for me." 18Remember that it is your God יהוה who gives you the power to get wealth, in fulfillment of the covenant made on oath with your fathers, as is still the case.

19If you do forget your God יהוה and follow other gods to serve them or bow down to them, I warn you this day that you shall certainly perish; 20like the nations that יהוה will cause to perish before you, so shall you perish—because you did not heed your God יהוה.

9 Hear, O Israel! You are about to cross the Jordan to go in and dispossess nations greater and more populous than you: great cities with walls sky-high; [2]a people great and tall, the Anakites, of whom you have knowledge; for you have heard it said, "Who can stand up to the children of Anak?" [3]Know then this day that none other than your God יהוה is crossing at your head, a devouring fire; it is [God] who will wipe them out—subduing them before you, that you may quickly dispossess and destroy them, as יהוה promised you. [4]And when your God יהוה has thrust them from your path, say not to yourselves, "יהוה has enabled us to possess this land because of our virtues"; it is rather because of the wickedness of those nations that יהוה is dispossessing them before you. [5]It is not because of your virtues and your rectitude that you will be able to possess their country; but it is because of their wickedness that your God יהוה is dispossessing those nations before you, and in order to fulfill the oath that יהוה made to your fathers Abraham, Isaac, and Jacob.

[6]Know, then, that it is not for any virtue of yours that your God יהוה is giving you this good land to possess; for you are a stiff-necked people. [7]Remember, never forget, how you provoked your God יהוה to anger in the wilderness: from the day that you left the land of Egypt until you reached this place, you have continued defiant toward יהוה.

[8]At Horeb you so provoked יהוה that יהוה was angry enough with you to have destroyed you. [9]I had ascended the mountain to receive the tablets of stone, the Tablets of the Covenant that יהוה had made with you, and I stayed on the mountain forty days and forty nights, eating no bread and drinking no water. [10]And יהוה gave me the two tablets of stone inscribed by the finger of God, with the exact words that יהוה had addressed to you on the mountain out of the fire on the day of the Assembly.

[11]At the end of those forty days and forty nights, יהוה gave me the two tablets of stone, the Tablets of the Covenant. [12]And יהוה said to me, "Hurry, go down from here at once, for the people whom you brought out of Egypt have acted wickedly; they have been quick to stray from the path that I enjoined upon them; they have made themselves a molten image." [13]יהוה further said to me, "I see that this is a stiffnecked people. [14]Let Me alone and I will

destroy them and blot out their name from under heaven, and I will make you a nation far more numerous than they."

¹⁵I started down the mountain, a mountain ablaze with fire, the two Tablets of the Covenant in my two hands. ¹⁶I saw how you had sinned against your God יהוה: you had made yourselves a molten calf; you had been quick to stray from the path that יהוה had enjoined upon you. ¹⁷Thereupon I gripped the two tablets and flung them away with both my hands, smashing them before your eyes. ¹⁸I threw myself down before יהוה—eating no bread and drinking no water forty days and forty nights, as before—because of the great wrong you had committed, doing what displeased and vexed יהוה. ¹⁹For I was in dread of the fierce anger against you which moved יהוה to wipe you out. And that time, too, יהוה gave heed to me.—²⁰Moreover, יהוה was angry enough with Aaron to have destroyed him; so I also interceded for Aaron at that time.—²¹As for that sinful thing you had made, the calf, I took it and put it to the fire; I broke it to bits and ground it thoroughly until it was fine as dust, and I threw its dust into the brook that comes down from the mountain.

²²Again you provoked יהוה at Taberah, and at Massah, and at Kibroth-hattaavah.

²³And when יהוה sent you on from Kadesh-barnea, saying, "Go up and take possession of the land that I am giving you," you flouted the command of your God יהוה—whom you did not put your trust in nor obey.

²⁴As long as I have known you, you have been defiant toward יהוה.

²⁵When I lay prostrate before יהוה *⁻those forty days and forty nights,* because יהוה was determined to destroy you, ²⁶I prayed to יהוה and said, "O lord יהוה, do not annihilate Your very own people, whom You redeemed in Your majesty and whom You freed from Egypt with a mighty hand. ²⁷Give thought to Your servants Abraham, Isaac, and Jacob, and pay no heed to the stubbornness of this people, its wickedness, and its sinfulness. ²⁸Else the country from which You freed us will say, 'It was because יהוה was powerless to bring them into the land promised to them, and because of having rejected them, that [their god] brought

them out to have them die in the wilderness.' ²⁹Yet they are Your very own people, whom You freed with Your great might and Your outstretched arm."

10 Thereupon יהוה said to me, "Carve out two tablets of stone like the first, and come up to Me on the mountain; and make an ark of wood. ²I will inscribe on the tablets the commandments that were on the first tablets that you smashed, and you shall deposit them in the ark."

³I made an ark of acacia wood and carved out two tablets of stone like the first; I took the two tablets with me and went up the mountain. ⁴After inscribing on the tablets the same text as on the first—the Ten Commandments that יהוה addressed to you on the mountain out of the fire on the day of the Assembly—יהוה gave them to me. ⁵Then I left and went down from the mountain, and I deposited the tablets in the ark that I had made, where they still are, as יהוה had commanded me.

⁶From Beeroth-bene-jaakan* the Israelites marched to Moserah. Aaron died there and was buried there; and his son Eleazar became priest in his stead. ⁷From there they marched to *⁻Gudgod,⁻* and from Gudgod to Jotbath, a region of running brooks.

⁸At that time יהוה set apart the tribe of Levi to carry the Ark of יהוה's Covenant, to stand in attendance upon יהוה, and to bless in God's name, as is still the case. ⁹That is why Levi has received no hereditary portion along with its kin: יהוה is its portion, as your God יהוה spoke concerning it.

¹⁰I had stayed on the mountain, as I did the first time, forty days and forty nights; and יהוה heeded me once again: יהוה agreed not to destroy you. ¹¹And יהוה said to me, "Up, resume the march at the head of the people, that they may go in and possess the land that I swore to their fathers to give them."

¹²And now, O Israel, what does your God יהוה demand of you? Only this: to revere your God יהוה, to walk only in divine paths, to love and to serve your God יהוה with all your heart and soul, ¹³keeping יהוה's commandments and laws, which I enjoin upon you today, for your good. ¹⁴Mark, the heavens *⁻to their uttermost reaches⁻* belong to your God יהוה, the earth and all that is on it!

¹⁵Yet it was to your ancestors that יהוה was drawn out of love for them, so that you, their lineal descendants, were chosen from among all peoples—as is now the case. ¹⁶Cut away, therefore, the thickening about your hearts and stiffen your necks no more. ¹⁷For your God יהוה is *⁻God supreme and Lord supreme,⁻* the great, the mighty, and the awesome God, who shows no favor and takes no bribe, ¹⁸but upholds the cause of the fatherless and the widow, and befriends the stranger, providing food and clothing.— ¹⁹You too must befriend the stranger, for you were strangers in the land of Egypt.

²⁰You must revere יהוה: only your God shall you worship, to [God] shall you hold fast, and by God's name shall you swear. ²¹[יהוה] is your glory and your God, who wrought for you those marvelous, awesome deeds that you saw with your own eyes. ²²Your ancestors went down to Egypt seventy persons; and now your God יהוה has made you as numerous as the stars of heaven.

11 Love, therefore, your God יהוה, and always keep God's charge, God's laws, God's rules, and God's commandments.

²*Take thought this day that it was not your children, who neither experienced nor witnessed the lesson of your God יהוה—

God's majesty, mighty hand, and outstretched arm; ³the signs and the deeds that [God] performed in Egypt against Pharaoh king of Egypt and all his land; ⁴what [God] did to Egypt's army, its horses and chariots; how יהוה rolled back upon them the waters of the Sea of Reeds when they were pursuing you, thus destroying them *⁻once and for all;⁻* ⁵what [God] did for you in the wilderness before you arrived in this place; ⁶and what [God] did to Dathan and Abiram, sons of Eliab son of Reuben, when the earth opened her mouth and swallowed them, along with their households, their tents, and every living thing in their train, from amidst all Israel—

⁷but that it was you who saw with your own eyes all the marvelous deeds that יהוה performed.

⁸Keep, therefore, all the Instruction that I enjoin upon you today, so that you may have the strength to enter and take possession of the land that you are about to cross into and possess, ⁹and that you may long endure upon the soil that יהוה swore to your

fathers to assign to them and to their heirs, a land flowing with milk and honey.

¹⁰For the land that you are about to enter and possess is not like the land of Egypt from which you have come. There the grain you sowed had to be watered *˗by your own labors,˗* like a vegetable garden; ¹¹but the land you are about to cross into and possess, a land of hills and valleys, soaks up its water from the rains of heaven. ¹²It is a land which your God יהוה looks after, on which your God יהוה always keeps an eye, from year's beginning to year's end.

¹³If, then, you obey the commandments that I enjoin upon you this day, loving your God יהוה and serving [God] with all your heart and soul, ¹⁴I will grant the rain for your land in season, the early rain and the late. You shall gather in your new grain and wine and oil—¹⁵I* will also provide grass in the fields for your cattle—and thus you shall eat your fill. ¹⁶Take care not to be lured away to serve other gods and bow to them. ¹⁷For יהוה's anger will flare up against you, shutting up the skies so that there will be no rain and the ground will not yield its produce; and you will soon perish from the good land that יהוה is assigning to you.

¹⁸Therefore impress these My words upon your *˗very heart:˗* bind them as a sign on your hand and let them serve as a *˗symbol on your forehead,˗* ¹⁹and teach them to your children—reciting them when you stay at home and when you are away, when you lie down and when you get up; ²⁰and inscribe them on the doorposts of your house and on your gates—²¹to the end that you and your children may endure, in the land that יהוה swore to your fathers to assign to them, as long as there is a heaven over the earth.

²²If, then, you faithfully keep all this Instruction that I command you, loving your God יהוה, walking in all God's ways, and holding fast to [God], ²³יהוה will dislodge before you all these nations: you will dispossess nations greater and more numerous than you. ²⁴Every spot on which your foot treads shall be yours; your territory shall extend from the wilderness to the Lebanon and from the River—the Euphrates—to the Western* Sea. ²⁵No one shall stand up to you: your God יהוה will put the dread and the fear of you over the whole land in which you set foot, as promised.

ראה | RE'EH

26See, this day I set before you blessing and curse: 27blessing, if you obey the commandments of your God יהוה that I enjoin upon you this day; 28and curse, if you do not obey the commandments of your God יהוה, but turn away from the path that I enjoin upon you this day and follow other gods, *⁻whom you have not experienced.⁻* 29When your God יהוה brings you into the land that you are about to enter and possess, you shall pronounce the blessing at Mount Gerizim and the curse at Mount Ebal.—30Both are on the other side of the Jordan, beyond the west road that is in the land of the Canaanites who dwell in the Arabah—near Gilgal, by the terebinths of Moreh.

31For you are about to cross the Jordan to enter and possess the land that your God יהוה is assigning to you. When you have occupied it and are settled in it, 32take care to observe all the laws and rules that I have set before you this day.

12 These are the laws and rules that you must carefully observe in the land that יהוה, God of your ancestors, is giving you to possess, as long as you live on earth.

2You must destroy all the sites at which the nations you are to dispossess worshiped their gods, whether on lofty mountains and on hills or under any luxuriant tree. 3Tear down their altars, smash their pillars, put their sacred posts to the fire, and cut down the images of their gods, obliterating their name from that site.

4Do not worship your God יהוה in like manner, 5but look only to the site that your God יהוה will choose amidst all your tribes as God's habitation, to establish the divine name there. There you are to go, 6and there you are to bring your burnt offerings and other sacrifices, your tithes and contributions,* your votive and freewill offerings, and the firstlings of your herds and flocks. 7°⁻Together with your households,⁻° you shall feast there before your God יהוה, happy in all the undertakings in which your God יהוה has blessed you.

8You shall not act at all as we now act here, each [householder] as he pleases, 9because you have not yet come to the allotted haven that your God יהוה is giving you. 10When you cross the Jordan

Re'eh

and settle in the land that your God יהוה is allotting to you, and [God] grants you safety from all your enemies around you and you live in security, ¹¹then you must bring everything that I command you to the site where your God יהוה will choose to establish the divine name: your burnt offerings and other sacrifices, your tithes and contributions, and all the choice votive offerings that you vow to יהוה. ¹²And you° shall rejoice before your God יהוה with your sons and daughters and with your male and female slaves, along with the [family of the] Levite in your settlements, for he has no territorial allotment among you.

¹³Take care not to sacrifice your burnt offerings in any place you like, ¹⁴but only in the place that יהוה will choose in one of your tribal territories. There you° shall sacrifice your burnt offerings and there you shall observe all that I enjoin upon you. ¹⁵But whenever you desire, you may slaughter and eat meat in any of your settlements, according to the blessing that your God יהוה has granted you. The impure and the pure alike may partake of it, as of the *⁻gazelle and the deer.⁻* ¹⁶But you must not partake of the blood; you shall pour it out on the ground like water.

¹⁷You may not partake in your settlements of the tithes of your new grain or wine or oil, or of the firstlings of your herds and flocks, or of any of the votive offerings that you vow, or of your freewill offerings, or of your contributions. ¹⁸These you must consume before your God יהוה in the place that your God יהוה will choose—you° and your sons and your daughters, your male and female slaves, and the [family of the] Levite in your settlements— happy before your God יהוה in all your undertakings. ¹⁹Be sure not to neglect the [family of the] Levite as long as you live in your land.

²⁰When יהוה enlarges your territory, as promised, and you say, "I shall eat some meat," for you have the urge to eat meat, you may eat meat whenever you wish. ²¹If the place where יהוה has chosen to establish the divine name is too far from you, you may slaughter any of the cattle or sheep that יהוה gives you, as I have instructed you; and you may eat to your heart's content in your settlements. ²²Eat it, however, as the gazelle and the deer are eaten: the impure may eat it together with the pure. ²³But make sure that you do not partake of the blood; for the blood is the life, and you

must not consume the life with the flesh. [24]You must not partake of it; you must pour it out on the ground like water: [25]you must not partake of it, in order that it may go well with you and with your descendants to come, for you will be doing what is right in the sight of יהוה.

[26]But such sacred and votive donations as you may have *⁻shall be taken by you⁻* to the site that יהוה will choose. [27]You° shall offer your burnt offerings, both the flesh and the blood, on the altar of your God יהוה; and of your other sacrifices, the blood shall be poured out on the altar of your God יהוה, and you shall eat the flesh.

[28]Be careful to heed all these commandments that I enjoin upon you; thus it will go well with you and with your descendants after you forever, for you will be doing what is good and right in the sight of your God יהוה.

[29]When your God יהוה has cut down before you the nations that you are about to enter and dispossess, and you have dispossessed them and settled in their land, [30]beware of being lured into their ways after they have been wiped out before you! Do not inquire about their gods, saying, "How did those nations worship their gods? I too will follow those practices." [31]You shall not act thus toward your God יהוה, for they perform for their gods every abhorrent act that יהוה detests; they even offer up their sons and daughters in fire to their gods. **13** [1]*Be careful to observe only that which I enjoin upon you: neither add to it nor take away from it.

[2]If there appears among you a prophet or a dream-diviner, who gives you a sign or a portent, [3]saying, "Let us follow and worship another god"—*⁻whom you have not experienced⁻*— even if the sign or portent named to you comes true, [4]do not heed the words of that prophet or that dream-diviner. For your God יהוה is testing you to see whether you really love your God יהוה with all your heart and soul. [5]It is your God יהוה alone whom you should follow, whom you should revere, whose commandments you should observe, whose orders you should heed, whom you should worship, and to whom you should hold fast. [6]As for

that prophet or dream-diviner, such a one shall be put to death for having urged disloyalty to your God יהוה—who freed you from the land of Egypt and who redeemed you from the house of bondage—to make you stray from the path that your God יהוה commanded you to follow. Thus you will sweep out evil from your midst.

⁷If your brother, *⁻your own mother's son,⁻* or your son or daughter, or the wife of your bosom, or your *⁻closest friend⁻* entices you in secret, saying, "Come let us worship other gods"—whom neither you nor your ancestors have experienced—⁸from among the gods of the peoples around you, either near to you or distant, anywhere from one end of the earth to the other: ⁹do not assent or give heed to any of them. Show no pity or compassion, and do not cover up the matter; ¹⁰but take that person's life. Let your hand be the first to put that person to death, followed by the hand of the rest of the people. ¹¹Stone that person to death for having sought to make you stray from your God יהוה, who brought you out of the land of Egypt, out of the house of bondage. ¹²Thus all Israel will hear and be afraid, and such evil things will not be done again in your midst.

¹³If you hear it said, of one of the towns that your God יהוה is giving you to dwell in, ¹⁴that some scoundrels from among you have gone and subverted the inhabitants of their town, saying, "Come let us worship other gods"—whom you have not experienced—¹⁵you shall investigate and inquire and interrogate thoroughly. If it is true, the fact is established—that abhorrent thing was perpetrated in your midst—¹⁶put the inhabitants of that town to the sword and put its cattle to the sword. Doom it and all that is in it to destruction: ¹⁷gather all its spoil into the open square, and burn the town and all its spoil as a holocaust to your God יהוה. And it shall remain an everlasting ruin, never to be rebuilt. ¹⁸Let nothing that has been doomed stick to your hand, in order that יהוה may turn from a blazing anger and show you compassion, and in compassion increase you as promised on oath to your fathers—¹⁹for you will be heeding your God יהוה, obeying all the divine commandments that I enjoin upon you this day, doing what is right in the sight of your God יהוה.

14 You are children of your God יהוה. You shall not gash yourselves or shave the front of your heads because of the dead. ²For you are a people consecrated to your God יהוה: your God יהוה chose you from among all other peoples on earth to be a treasured people.

³You shall not eat anything abhorrent. ⁴These are the animals that you may eat: the ox, the sheep, and the goat; ⁵*the deer, the gazelle, the roebuck, the wild goat, the ibex, the antelope, the mountain sheep, ⁶and any other animal that has true hoofs which are cleft in two and brings up the cud—such you may eat. ⁷But the following, which do bring up the cud or have true hoofs which are cleft through, you may not eat: the camel, the hare, and the daman—for although they bring up the cud, they have no true hoofs—they are impure for you; ⁸also the swine—for although it has true hoofs, it does not bring up the cud—is impure for you. You shall not eat of their flesh or touch their carcasses.

⁹These you may eat of all that live in water: you may eat anything that has fins and scales. ¹⁰But you may not eat anything that has no fins and scales: it is impure for you.

¹¹You may eat any pure bird. ¹²The following you may not eat: *the eagle, the vulture, and the black vulture; ¹³the kite, the falcon, and the buzzard of any variety; ¹⁴every variety of raven; ¹⁵the ostrich, the nighthawk, the sea gull, and the hawk of any variety; ¹⁶the little owl, the great owl, and the white owl; ¹⁷the pelican, the bustard, and the cormorant; ¹⁸the stork, any variety of heron, the hoopoe, and the bat.

¹⁹All winged swarming things are impure for you: they may not be eaten. ²⁰You may eat only pure winged creatures.

²¹You shall not eat anything that has died a natural death; give it to the stranger in your community to eat, or you may sell it to a foreigner. For you are a people consecrated to your God יהוה.

You shall not boil a kid in its mother's milk.

²²You° shall set aside every year a tenth part of all the yield of your sowing that is brought from the field. ²³You shall consume the tithes of your new grain and wine and oil, and the firstlings of your herds and flocks, in the presence of your God יהוה, in the place where [God] will choose to establish the divine name, so

that you may learn to revere your God יהוה forever. ²⁴Should the distance be too great for you, should you be unable to transport them, because the place where your God יהוה has chosen to establish the divine name is far from you and because your God יהוה *⁻has blessed you,⁻* ²⁵you may convert them into money. Wrap up the money and take it with you to the place that your God יהוה has chosen, ²⁶and spend the money on anything you want—cattle, sheep, wine, or other intoxicant, or anything you may desire. And you shall feast there, in the presence of your God יהוה, and rejoice with your household.

²⁷But do not neglect the [family of the] Levite in your community, for he has no hereditary portion as you have.

²⁸*⁻Every third year⁻* you shall bring out the full tithe of your yield of that year, but leave it within your settlements. ²⁹Then the [family of the] Levite, who has no hereditary portion as you have, and the stranger, the fatherless, and the widow in your settlements shall come and eat their fill, so that your God יהוה may bless you in all the enterprises you undertake.

15 *⁻Every seventh year⁻* you shall practice remission of debts. ²This shall be the nature of the remission: all creditors shall remit the due that they claim from their fellow [Israelites]; they shall not dun their fellow [Israelites] or kin, for the remission proclaimed is of יהוה. ³You may dun the foreigner; but you must remit whatever is due you from your kin.

⁴There shall be no needy among you—since your God יהוה will bless you in the land that your God יהוה is giving you as a hereditary portion—⁵if only you heed your God יהוה and take care to keep all this Instruction that I enjoin upon you this day. ⁶For your God יהוה will bless you as promised: you will extend loans to many nations, but require none yourself; you will dominate many nations, but they will not dominate you.

⁷If, however, there is a needy person among you, one of your kin in any of your settlements in the land that your God יהוה is giving you, do not harden your heart and shut your hand against your needy kin. ⁸Rather, you must open your hand and lend whatever is sufficient to meet the need. ⁹Beware lest you harbor the base thought, "The seventh year, the year of remission, is

approaching," so that you are mean and give nothing to your needy kin—who will cry out to יהוה against you, and you will incur guilt. ¹⁰Give readily and have no regrets when you do so, for in return your God יהוה will bless you in all your efforts and in all your undertakings. ¹¹For there will never cease to be needy ones in your land, which is why I command you: open your hand to the poor and needy kin in your land.

¹²If a fellow Hebrew man—or woman—is sold to you, he shall serve you six years, and in the seventh year you shall set him free. ¹³When you set him free, do not let him go empty-handed: ¹⁴Furnish him out of the flock, threshing floor, and vat, with which your God יהוה has blessed you. ¹⁵Bear in mind that you were slaves in the land of Egypt and your God יהוה redeemed you; therefore I enjoin this commandment upon you today.

¹⁶But should he say to you, "I do not want to leave you"—for he loves you and your household and is happy with you—¹⁷you shall take an awl and put it through his ear into the door, and he shall become your slave in perpetuity. Do the same with your female slave. ¹⁸When you do set either one free, do not feel aggrieved; for in the six years you have been given double the service of a hired worker. Moreover, your God יהוה will bless you in all you do.

¹⁹You° shall consecrate to your God יהוה all male firstlings that are born in your herd and in your flock: you must not work your firstling ox or shear your firstling sheep. ²⁰You and your household shall eat it annually before your God יהוה in the place that יהוה will choose. ²¹But if it has a defect, lameness or blindness, any serious defect, you shall not sacrifice it to your God יהוה. ²²Eat it in your settlements, the impure among you no less than the pure, just like the gazelle and the deer. ²³Only you must not partake of its blood; you shall pour it out on the ground like water.

16 Observe the month* of Abib and offer a passover sacrifice to your God יהוה, for it was in the month of Abib, at night, that your God יהוה freed you from Egypt. ²You shall slaughter the passover sacrifice for your God יהוה, from the flock and the herd, in the place where יהוה will choose to establish the divine name. ³You shall not eat anything leavened with it; for seven days thereafter* you shall eat unleavened bread, bread of distress—for you departed from the land of Egypt hurriedly—so that you may remember the day of your departure from the land of Egypt as long as you live. ⁴For seven days no leaven shall be found with you in all your territory, and none of the flesh of what you slaughter on the evening of the first day shall be left until morning.

⁵You are not permitted to slaughter the passover sacrifice in any of the settlements that your God יהוה is giving you; ⁶but at the place where your God יהוה will choose to establish the divine name, there alone shall you slaughter the passover sacrifice, in the evening, at sundown, the time of day when you departed from Egypt. ⁷You shall cook and eat it at the place that your God יהוה will choose; and in the morning you may start back on your journey home. ⁸After eating unleavened bread six days, you shall hold a *⁻solemn gathering* for your God יהוה on the seventh day: you shall do no work.

⁹You shall count off seven weeks; start to count the seven weeks when the sickle is first put to the standing grain. ¹⁰Then you° shall observe the Feast of Weeks for your God יהוה, offering your free-will contribution according as your God יהוה has blessed you. ¹¹You shall rejoice before your God יהוה with your son and daughter, your male and female slave, the [family of the] Levite in your communities, and the stranger, the fatherless, and the widow in your midst, at the place where your God יהוה will choose to establish the divine name. ¹²Bear in mind that you were slaves in Egypt, and take care to obey these laws.

¹³After the ingathering from your threshing floor and your vat, you shall hold the Feast of Booths for seven days. ¹⁴You shall rejoice in your festival, with your son and daughter, your male and female slave, the [family of the] Levite, the stranger, the fatherless, and the widow in your communities. ¹⁵You° shall hold a festival for your God יהוה seven days, in the place that יהוה will choose; for your God יהוה will bless all* your crops and all your undertakings, and you shall have nothing but joy.

¹⁶Three times a year—on the Feast of Unleavened Bread, on the Feast of Weeks, and on the Feast of Booths—all your males shall

appear before your God יהוה in the place that [God] will choose. They shall not appear before יהוה empty-handed, ¹⁷but each with his own gift, according to the blessing that your God יהוה has bestowed upon you.

שֹׁפְטִים | SHOFETIM

¹⁸You shall appoint magistrates and officials for your tribes, in all the settlements that your God יהוה is giving you, and they shall govern the people with due justice. ¹⁹You shall not judge unfairly: you shall show no partiality; you shall not take bribes, for bribes blind the eyes of the discerning and upset the plea of the just. ²⁰Justice, justice shall you pursue, that you may thrive and occupy the land that your God יהוה is giving you.

²¹You shall not set up a sacred post—any kind of pole beside the altar of your God יהוה that you may make—²²or erect a stone pillar; for such your God יהוה detests.

17 `You shall not sacrifice to your God יהוה an ox or a sheep that has any defect of a serious kind, for that is abhorrent to your God יהוה.

²If there is found among you, in one of the settlements that your God יהוה is giving you, a man or woman who has affronted your God יהוה and transgressed the Covenant—³turning to the worship of other gods and bowing down to them, to the sun or the moon or any of the heavenly host, something I never commanded—⁴and you have been informed or have learned of it, then you shall make a thorough inquiry. If it is true, the fact is established, that abhorrent thing was perpetrated in Israel, ⁵you shall take the man or the woman who did that wicked thing out to the public place, and you shall stone that man or woman to death.—⁶A person shall be put to death only on the testimony of two or more* witnesses; no one shall be put to death on the testimony of a single witness.—⁷Let the hands of the witnesses be the first to put [the condemned] to death, followed by the hands of the rest of the people. Thus you will sweep out evil from your midst.

⁸If a case is too baffling for you to decide, be it a controversy over homicide, civil law, or assault—matters of dispute in your courts—you shall promptly repair to the place that your God יהוה

will have chosen, [9]and appear before the levitical priests, or the magistrate in charge at the time, and present your problem. When they have announced to you the verdict in the case, [10]you shall carry out the verdict that is announced to you from that place that יהוה chose, observing scrupulously all their instructions to you. [11]You shall act in accordance with the instructions given you and the ruling handed down to you; you must not deviate from the verdict that they announce to you either to the right or to the left. [12]Should either party° act presumptuously and disregard the priest charged with serving there your God יהוה, or the magistrate, that party° shall die. Thus you will sweep out evil from Israel: [13]all the people will hear and be afraid and will not act presumptuously again.

[14]If, after you have entered the land that your God יהוה has assigned to you, and taken possession of it and settled in it, you decide, "I will set a king over me, as do all the nations about me," [15]you shall be free to set a king over yourself, one chosen by your God יהוה. Be sure to set as king over yourself one of your own people; you must not set a foreigner over you, one who is not your kin. [16]Moreover, he shall not keep many horses or send people back to Egypt to add to his horses, since יהוה has warned you, "You must not go back that way again." [17]And he shall not have many wives, lest his heart go astray; nor shall he amass silver and gold to excess.

[18]When he is seated on his royal throne, he shall have a copy of this Teaching written for him on a scroll by* the levitical priests. [19]Let it remain with him and let him read in it all his life, so that he may learn to revere his God יהוה, to observe faithfully every word of this Teaching as well as these laws. [20]Thus he will not act haughtily toward his fellows or deviate from the Instruction to the right or to the left, to the end that he and his descendants may reign long in the midst of Israel.

18 The levitical priests, the whole tribe of Levi, shall have no territorial portion with Israel. They shall live only off יהוה's offerings by fire as their* portion, [2]and shall have no portion among their brother tribes: יהוה is their portion, as promised.

[3]This then shall be the priests' due from the people: Everyone who offers a sacrifice, whether an ox or a sheep, must give the

shoulder, the cheeks, and the stomach to the priest. 4You shall also
give him the first fruits of your new grain and wine and oil, and
the first shearing of your sheep. 5For your God יהוה has chosen
him and his descendants, out of all your tribes, to be in attendance
for service in the name of יהוה for all time.

6If a Levite would go, from any of the settlements throughout
Israel where he has been residing, to the place that יהוה has chosen, he may do so whenever he pleases. 7He may serve in the name
of his God יהוה like all his fellow Levites who are there in attendance before יהוה. 8They shall receive equal shares of the dues,
-without regard to personal gifts or patrimonies.-

9When you enter the land that your God יהוה is giving you, you
shall not learn to imitate the abhorrent practices of those nations.
10Let no one be found among you who consigns a son or daughter to the fire, or who is an augur, a soothsayer, a diviner, a sor-
cerer, 11one who casts spells, or one who consults ghosts or familiar spirits, or one who inquires of the dead. 12For anyone who
does such things is abhorrent to יהוה, and it is because of these
abhorrent things that your God יהוה is dispossessing them before
you. 13You must be wholehearted with your God יהוה. 14Those
nations that you are about to dispossess do indeed resort to
soothsayers and augurs; to you, however, your God יהוה has not
assigned the like.

15From among your own people, your God יהוה will raise up
for you a prophet like myself; that is whom you shall heed. 16This
is just what you asked of your God יהוה at Horeb, on the day of
the Assembly, saying, "Let me not hear the voice of my God יהוה
any longer or see this wondrous fire any more, lest I die." 17Where-
upon יהוה said to me, "They have done well in speaking thus. 18I
will raise up for them from among their own people a prophet like
yourself, in whose mouth I will put My words and who will speak
to them all that I command; 19and anybody who fails to heed the
words [the prophet] speaks in My name, I Myself will call to account. 20But any prophet who presumes to speak in My name an
oracle that I did not command to be uttered, or who speaks in the
name of other gods—that prophet shall die." 21And should you

ask yourselves, "How can we know that the oracle was not spoken by יהוה?"—²²if the prophet speaks in the name of יהוה and the oracle does not come true, that oracle was not spoken by יהוה; the prophet has uttered it presumptuously: do not stand in dread of that person.

19 When your God יהוה has cut down the nations whose land your God יהוה is assigning to you, and you have dispossessed them and settled in their towns and homes, ²you shall set aside three cities in the land that your God יהוה is giving you to possess. ³You shall survey the distances, and divide into three parts the territory of the country that your God יהוה has allotted to you, so that any [male]° killer° may have a place to flee to.— ⁴Now this is the case of the killer who may flee there and live: one who has slain another unwittingly, without having been an enemy in the past. ⁵For instance, a man goes with another fellow into a grove to cut wood; as his hand swings the ax to cut down a tree, the ax-head flies off the handle and strikes the other so that he dies. That man shall flee to one of these cities and live.—⁶Otherwise, when the distance is great, the blood-avenger, pursuing the killer in hot anger, may overtake him and strike him down; yet he did not incur the death penalty, since he had never been the other's enemy. ⁷That is why I command you: set aside three cities.

⁸And when your God יהוה enlarges your territory, as was sworn to your fathers, and gives you all the land that was promised to be given to your fathers—⁹if you faithfully observe all this Instruction that I enjoin upon you this day, to love your God יהוה and to walk in God's ways at all times—then you shall add three more towns to those three. ¹⁰Thus blood of the innocent will not be shed, bringing bloodguilt upon you in the land that your God יהוה is allotting to you.

¹¹If, however, a man who is the enemy of another lies in wait and sets upon [the victim] and strikes a fatal blow and then flees to one of these towns, ¹²the elders of his town shall have him brought back from there and shall hand him over to the blood-avenger to be put to death; ¹³you must show him no pity. Thus you will *⁻purge Israel of the blood of the innocent,⁻* and it will go well with you.

¹⁴You shall not move your neighbor's landmarks, set up by previous generations, in the property that will be allotted to you in the land that your God יהוה is giving you to possess.

¹⁵A single witness may not validate against a person any guilt or blame for any offense that may be committed; a case can be valid only on the testimony of two witnesses or more.* ¹⁶If someone appears against another to testify maliciously and gives incriminating yet false testimony, ¹⁷the two parties to the dispute shall appear before יהוה, before the priests or magistrates in authority at the time, ¹⁸and the magistrates shall make a thorough investigation. If the one who testified is a false witness, having testified falsely against a fellow Israelite, ¹⁹you shall do to the one as the one schemed to do to the other. Thus you will sweep out evil from your midst; ²⁰others will hear and be afraid, and such evil things will not again be done in your midst. ²¹Nor must you show pity: life for life, eye for eye, tooth for tooth, hand for hand, foot for foot.

20 When you [an Israelite warrior] take the field against your enemies, and see horses and chariots—forces larger than yours—have no fear of them, for your God יהוה, who brought you from the land of Egypt, is with you. ²Before you join battle, the priest shall come forward and address the troops. ³He shall say to them, "Hear, O Israel! You are about to join battle with your enemy. Let not your courage falter. Do not be in fear, or in panic, or in dread of them. ⁴For it is your God יהוה who marches with you to do battle for you against your enemy, to bring you victory."

⁵Then the officials shall address the troops, as follows: "Is there anyone who has built a new house but has not dedicated it? Let him go back to his home, lest he die in battle and another dedicate it. ⁶Is there anyone who has planted a vineyard but has never harvested it? Let him go back to his home, lest he die in battle and another harvest it. ⁷Is there anyone who has *⁻paid the bride-price for a wife,⁻* but who has not yet taken her [into his household]? Let him go back to his home, lest he die in battle and another take her [into his household as his wife]." ⁸The officials shall go on addressing the troops and say, "Is there anyone afraid and disheartened? Let him go back to his home, lest the courage of his

comrades flag like his." ⁹When the officials have finished addressing the troops, army commanders shall assume command of the
troops.

¹⁰When you approach a town to attack it, you shall *⁻offer it
terms of peace.⁻* ¹¹If it responds peaceably and lets you in, all the
people present there shall serve you at forced labor. ¹²If it does not
surrender to you, but would join battle with you, you shall lay
siege to it; ¹³and when your God יהוה delivers it into your hand,
you shall put all its males to the sword. ¹⁴You may, however, take
as your booty the women, the children, the livestock, and everything in the town—all its spoil—and enjoy the use of the spoil of
your enemy, which your God יהוה gives you.

¹⁵Thus you shall deal with all towns that lie very far from you,
towns that do not belong to nations hereabout. ¹⁶In the towns of
the latter peoples, however, which your God יהוה is giving you as
a heritage, you shall not let a soul remain alive. ¹⁷No, you must
proscribe* them—the Hittites and the Amorites, the Canaanites
and the Perizzites, the Hivites and the Jebusites—as your God
יהוה has commanded you, ¹⁸lest they lead you into doing all the
abhorrent things that they have done for their gods and you stand
guilty before your God יהוה.

¹⁹When in your war against a city you have to besiege it a long
time in order to capture it, you must not destroy its trees, wielding the ax against them. You may eat of them, but you must not
cut them down. Are trees of the field human to withdraw before
you into the besieged city? ²⁰Only trees that you know do not
yield food may be destroyed; you may cut them down for con-
structing siegeworks against the city that is waging war on you,
until it has been reduced.

21 If, in the land that your God יהוה is assigning you to possess, someone slain is found lying in the open, the identity of the slayer not being known, ²your elders and magistrates
shall go out and measure the distances from the corpse to the
nearby towns. ³The elders of the town nearest to the corpse shall
then take a heifer which has never been worked, which has never
pulled in a yoke; ⁴and the elders of that town shall bring the heifer
down to an everflowing wadi, which is not tilled or sown. There,

in the wadi, they shall break the heifer's neck. ⁵The priests, sons of Levi, shall come forward; for your God יהוה has chosen them for divine service and to pronounce blessing in the name of יהוה, and every lawsuit and case of assault* is subject to their ruling. ⁶Then all the elders of the town nearest to the corpse shall wash their hands over the heifer whose neck was broken in the wadi. ⁷And they shall make this declaration: "Our hands did not shed this blood, nor did our eyes see it done. ⁸Absolve, יהוה, Your people Israel whom You redeemed, and do not let guilt for the blood of the innocent remain among Your people Israel." And they will be absolved of bloodguilt. ⁹Thus you will remove from your midst guilt for the blood of the innocent, for you will be doing what is right in the sight of יהוה.

כי תצא | KI TETSE'

¹⁰When you [an Israelite warrior] take the field against your enemies, and your God יהוה delivers them into your power and you take some of them captive, ¹¹and you see among the captives a beautiful woman and you desire her and would take her [into your household] as your wife, ¹²you shall bring her into your household, and she shall trim her hair, pare her nails, ¹³and discard her captive's garb. She shall spend a month's time in your house lamenting her father and mother; after that you may come to her and thus become her husband, and she shall be your wife. ¹⁴Then, should you no longer want her, you must release her outright. You must not sell her for money: since you had your will of her, you must not enslave her.

¹⁵If a householder° has two wives, one loved and the other unloved, and both the loved and the unloved have borne him sons, but the first-born is the son of the unloved one—¹⁶when he wills his property to his sons, he may not treat as first-born the son of the loved one in disregard of the son of the unloved one who is older. ¹⁷Instead, he must accept the first-born, the son of the unloved one, and allot to him a *⁻double portion⁻* of all he possesses; since he is the first fruit of his vigor, the birthright is his due.

¹⁸If a householder° has a wayward and defiant son, who does

not heed his father or mother and does not obey them even after they discipline him, [19]his father and mother shall take hold of him and bring him out to the elders of his town at the public place of his community. [20]They shall say to the elders of his town, "This son of ours is disloyal and defiant; he does not heed us. He is a glutton and a drunkard." [21]Thereupon his °town's council-° shall stone him to death. Thus you will sweep out evil from your midst: all Israel will hear and be afraid.

[22]If someone is guilty of a capital offense and is put to death, and you impale the body on a stake, [23]you must not let the corpse remain on the stake overnight, but must bury it the same day. For an impaled body is an affront to God: you shall not defile the land that your God יהוה is giving you to possess.

22 If you see your fellow Israelite's ox or sheep gone astray, do not ignore it; you must take it back to your peer. [2]If your fellow Israelite does not live near you or you do not know who [the owner] is, you shall bring it home and it shall remain with you until your peer claims it; then you shall give it back. [3]You shall do the same with that person's ass; you shall do the same with that person's garment; and so too shall you do with anything that your fellow Israelite loses and you find: you must not remain indifferent.

[4]If you see your fellow Israelite's ass or ox fallen on the road, do not ignore it; you must raise it together.

[5]A woman must not put on man's apparel, nor shall a man wear woman's clothing; for whoever does these things is abhorrent to your God יהוה.

[6]If, along the road, you chance upon a bird's nest, in any tree or on the ground, with fledglings or eggs and the mother sitting over the fledglings or on the eggs, do not take the mother together with her young. [7]Let the mother go, and take only the young, in order that you may fare well and have a long life.

[8]When you build a new house, you shall make a parapet for your roof, so that you do not bring bloodguilt on your house if anyone should fall from it.

[9]You shall not sow your vineyard with a second kind of seed, else the crop—from the seed you have sown—and the yield of the vineyard may not be used. [10]You shall not plow with an ox and

an ass together. ¹¹You shall not wear cloth combining wool and linen.

¹²You shall make tassels on the four corners of the garment with which you cover yourself.

¹³A householder° takes a woman [as his wife] and cohabits with her. Then he takes an aversion to her ¹⁴and makes up charges against her and defames her, saying, "I took this woman; but when I approached her, I found that she was not a virgin." ¹⁵In such a case, the girl's father and mother shall produce the evidence of the girl's virginity before the elders of the town at the gate. ¹⁶And the girl's father shall say to the elders, "I gave this householder my daughter to wife, but he has taken an aversion to her; ¹⁷so he has made up charges, saying, 'I did not find your daughter a virgin.' But here is the evidence of my daughter's virginity!" And they shall spread out the cloth before the elders of the town. ¹⁸The elders of that town shall then take that householder and flog him, ¹⁹and they shall fine him a hundred [shekels of] silver and give it to the girl's father; for [that householder] has defamed a virgin in Israel. Moreover, she shall remain his wife; he shall never have the right to divorce her.

²⁰But if the charge proves true, the girl was found not to have been a virgin, ²¹then the girl shall be brought out to the entrance of her father's house, and her °town's council-° shall stone her to death; for she did a shameful thing in Israel, committing fornication while under her father's authority. Thus you will sweep away evil from your midst.

²²If a man is found lying with another man's wife, both of them—the man and the woman with whom he lay—shall die. Thus you will sweep away evil from Israel.

²³In the case of a virgin *˙who is engaged to a man˙*—if a man comes upon her in town and lies with her, ²⁴you shall take the two of them out to the gate of that town and stone them to death: the girl because she did not cry for help in the town, and the man because he violated another man's wife. Thus you will sweep away evil from your midst. ²⁵But if the man comes upon the engaged girl in the open country, and the man lies with her by force, only the man who lay with her shall die, ²⁶but you shall do nothing to

the girl. The girl did not incur the death penalty, for this case is like that of one person attacking and murdering another. ²⁷He came upon her in the open; though the engaged girl cried for help, there was no one to save her.

²⁸If a man comes upon a virgin who is not engaged and he seizes her and lies with her, and they are discovered, ²⁹the man who lay with her shall pay the girl's father fifty [shekels of] silver, and she shall be his wife. Because he has violated her, he can never have the right to divorce her.

23

*No householder° shall take his father's former wife [as his own wife], so as to *⁻remove his father's garment.⁻*

²No man whose testes are crushed or whose member is cut off shall be admitted into the congregation° of יהוה.

°³No one misbegotten* shall be admitted into the congregation of יהוה; no descendant of such, even in the tenth generation, shall be admitted into the congregation of יהוה.

⁴No Ammonite or Moabite shall be admitted into the congregation of יהוה; no descendants of such, even in the tenth generation, shall ever be admitted into the congregation of יהוה, ⁵because they did not meet you with food and water on your journey after you left Egypt, and because they hired Balaam son of Beor, from Pethor of Aram-naharaim, to curse you.—⁶But your God יהוה refused to heed Balaam; instead, your God יהוה turned the curse into a blessing for you, for your God יהוה loves you.—⁷You shall never concern yourself with their welfare or benefit as long as you live.

⁸You shall not abhor an Edomite, for such is your kin. You shall not abhor an Egyptian, for you were a stranger in that land. ⁹Children born to them may be admitted into the congregation of יהוה *⁻in the third generation.⁻*

¹⁰When you [men] go out as a troop against your enemies, be on your guard against anything untoward. ¹¹If anyone among you has been rendered impure by a nocturnal emission, he must leave the camp, and he must not reenter the camp. ¹²Toward evening he shall bathe in water, and at sundown he may reenter the camp. ¹³Further, there shall be an area for you outside the camp, where

you may relieve yourself. ¹⁴With your gear you shall have a spike, and when you have squatted you shall dig a hole with it and cover up your excrement. ¹⁵Since your God יהוה moves about in your camp to protect you and to deliver your enemies to you, let your camp be holy; let [God] not find anything unseemly among you and turn away from you.

¹⁶You shall not turn over to the master a slave who seeks refuge with you from that master. ¹⁷Such individuals shall live with you in any place they may choose among the settlements in your midst, wherever they please; you must not ill-treat them.

¹⁸No Israelite woman shall be a prostitute, nor shall any Israelite man be a prostitute. ¹⁹You shall not bring the fee of a whore or the pay of a dog* into the house of your God יהוה in fulfillment of any vow, for both are abhorrent to your God יהוה.

²⁰You shall not deduct interest from loans to your fellow Israelites, whether in money or food or anything else that can be deducted as interest; ²¹but you may deduct interest from loans to foreigners. Do not deduct interest from loans to your fellow Israelites, so that your God יהוה may bless you in all your undertakings in the land that you are about to enter and possess.

²²When you make a vow to your God יהוה, do not put off fulfilling it, for your God יהוה will require it of you, and you will have incurred guilt; ²³whereas you incur no guilt if you refrain from vowing. ²⁴You must fulfill what has crossed your lips and perform what you have voluntarily vowed to your God יהוה, having made the promise with your own mouth.

²⁵When you enter a fellow [Israelite]'s vineyard, you may eat as many grapes as you want, until you are full, but you must not put any in your vessel. ²⁶When you enter a fellow [Israelite]'s field of standing grain, you may pluck ears with your hand; but you must not put a sickle to your neighbor's grain.

24 A householder° takes a woman [as his wife] and becomes her husband. She fails to please him because he finds something obnoxious about her, and he writes her a bill of divorcement, hands it to her, and sends her away from his house; ²she leaves his household and becomes [the wife] of another householder; ³then this latter householder rejects her, writes her a bill of divorcement, hands it to her, and sends her away from his house-

hold; or the householder dies who had last taken her as his wife.
⁴Then the first husband who divorced her shall not take her [into his household] to become his wife again, since she has been de-filed*—for that would be abhorrent to יהוה. You must not bring sin upon the land that your God יהוה is giving you as a heritage.

⁵When a man has newly taken a woman [into his household as his wife], he shall not go out with the army or be assigned to it for any purpose; he shall be exempt one year for the sake of his house-hold, to give happiness to the woman he has taken.

⁶A handmill or an upper millstone shall not be taken in pawn, for that would be taking someone's life in pawn.

⁷If one is found to have kidnapped—and then enslaved or sold—a fellow Israelite, that kidnapper shall die; thus you will sweep out evil from your midst.

⁸In cases of a *⁻skin affection⁻* be most careful to do exactly as the levitical priests instruct you. Take care to do as I have com-manded them. ⁹Remember *⁻what your God יהוה did to Miriam on the journey after you left Egypt.⁻*

¹⁰When you make a loan of any sort to your compatriot, you must not enter the house to seize the pledge. ¹¹You must remain outside, while the householder° to whom you made the loan brings the pledge out to you. ¹²If the person is needy, you shall not go to sleep in that pledge; ¹³you must return the pledge at sundown, that its owner may sleep in the cloth and bless you; and it will be to your merit before your God יהוה.

¹⁴You shall not abuse a needy and destitute laborer, whether a fellow Israelite or a stranger in one of the communities of your land. ¹⁵You must pay out the wages due on the same day, before the sun sets, for the worker is needy and urgently depends on it; else a cry to יהוה will be issued against you and you will incur guilt.

¹⁶Parents shall not be put to death for children, nor children be put to death for parents: one shall be put to death only for one's own crime.

¹⁷You shall not subvert the rights of the stranger or the fatherless; you shall not take a widow's garment in pawn. ¹⁸Remember that you were a slave in Egypt and that your God יהוה redeemed you from there; therefore do I enjoin you to observe this commandment.

¹⁹When you reap the harvest in your field and overlook a sheaf

Ki Tetse'

in the field, do not turn back to get it; it shall go to the stranger, the fatherless, and the widow—in order that your God יהוה may bless you in all your undertakings.

20When you beat down the fruit of your olive trees, do not go over them again; that shall go to the stranger, the fatherless, and the widow. 21When you gather the grapes of your vineyard, do not pick it over again; that shall go to the stranger, the fatherless, and the widow. 22Always remember that you were a slave in the land of Egypt; therefore do I enjoin you to observe this commandment.

25 When there is a dispute between parties° and they go to law, and a decision is rendered declaring the one in the right and the other in the wrong—2if the guilty one is to be flogged, the magistrate shall have the person lie down and shall supervise the giving of lashes, by count, as warranted by the offense. 3The guilty one may be given up to forty lashes, but not more, lest being flogged further, to excess, your peer be degraded before your eyes.

4You shall not muzzle an ox while it is threshing.

5When brothers dwell together and one of them dies and leaves no offspring,° the °wife of the deceased-° shall not become another householder's° [wife], outside the family. Her husband's brother shall unite with her: he shall take her as his wife and perform the levir's duty. 6The first child that she bears shall be accounted to the dead brother, that his name may not be blotted out in Israel. 7But if the [family] representative° does not want to take his brother's widow [to wife], his brother's widow shall appear before the elders in the gate and declare, "My husband's brother refuses to establish a name in Israel for his brother; he will not perform the duty of a levir." 8The elders of his town shall then summon him and talk to him. If he insists, saying, "I do not want to take her," 9his brother's widow shall go up to him in the presence of the elders, pull the sandal off his foot, spit in his face, and make this declaration: Thus shall be done to the [family] representative who will not build up his brother's house! 10And he shall go in Israel by the name of "the family of the unsandaled one."

11If two men get into a fight with each other, and the wife of one comes up to save her husband from his antagonist and puts out her hand and seizes him by his genitals, [12]you shall cut off her hand; show no pity.

[13]You shall not have in your pouch alternate weights, larger and smaller. [14]You shall not have in your house alternate measures, a larger and a smaller. [15]You must have completely honest weights and completely honest measures, if you are to endure long on the soil that your God יהוה is giving you. [16]For everyone who does those things, everyone who deals dishonestly, is abhorrent to your God יהוה.

[17]Remember what Amalek did to you on your journey, after you left Egypt—[18]how, undeterred by fear of God, he surprised you on the march, when you were famished and weary, and cut down all the stragglers in your rear. [19]Therefore, when your God יהוה grants you safety from all your enemies around you, in the land that your God יהוה is giving you as a hereditary portion, you shall blot out the memory of Amalek from under heaven. Do not forget!

כי תבוא | KI TAVO'

26 When you enter the land that your God יהוה is giving you as a heritage, and you possess it and settle in it, [2]you shall take some of every first fruit of the soil, which you harvest from the land that your God יהוה is giving you, put it in a basket and go to the place where your God יהוה will choose to establish the divine name. [3]You shall go to the priest in charge at that time and say to him, "I acknowledge this day before your God יהוה that I have entered the land that יהוה swore to our fathers to assign us."

[4]The priest shall take the basket from your hand and set it down in front of the altar of your God יהוה.

[5]You° shall then recite as follows before your God יהוה: "My father was a fugitive Aramean. He went down to Egypt with meager numbers and sojourned there; but there he became a great and very populous nation. [6]The Egyptians dealt harshly with us and oppressed us; they imposed heavy labor upon us. [7]We cried to יהוה, the God of our ancestors, and יהוה heard our plea and saw our plight, our misery, and our oppression. [8]יהוה freed us from Egypt by a mighty hand, by an outstretched arm and awesome

power, and by signs and portents, ⁹bringing us to this place and giving us this land, a land flowing with milk and honey. ¹⁰Wherefore I now bring the first fruits of the soil which You, יהוה, have given me."

You shall leave it* before your God יהוה and bow low before your God יהוה. ¹¹And you shall enjoy, together with the [family of the] Levite and the stranger in your midst, all the bounty that your God יהוה has bestowed upon you and your household.

¹²When you have set aside in full the tenth part of your yield— *⁻in the third year, the year of the tithe⁻*—and have given it to the [family of the] Levite, the stranger, the fatherless, and the widow, that they may eat their fill in your settlements, ¹³you° shall declare before your God יהוה: "I have cleared out the consecrated portion from the house; and I have given it to the [family of the] Levite, the stranger, the fatherless, and the widow, just as You commanded me; I have neither transgressed nor neglected any of Your commandments: ¹⁴*I have not eaten of it while in mourning, I have not cleared out any of it while I was impure, and I have not *⁻deposited any of it with the dead.* I have obeyed my God יהוה; I have done just as You commanded me. ¹⁵Look down from Your holy abode, from heaven, and bless Your people Israel and the soil You have given us, a land flowing with milk and honey, as You swore to our fathers."

¹⁶יהוה your God commands you this day to observe these laws and rules; observe them faithfully with all your heart and soul. ¹⁷You have affirmed* this day that יהוה is your God, in whose ways you will walk, whose laws and commandments and rules you will observe, and whom you will obey. ¹⁸And יהוה has affirmed this day that you are, as promised, God's treasured people who shall observe all the divine commandments, ¹⁹and that [God] will set you, in fame and renown and glory, high above all the nations that [God] has made; and that you shall be, as promised, a holy people to your God יהוה.

27 Moses and the elders of Israel charged the people, saying: Observe all the Instruction that I enjoin upon you this day. ²*As soon as you have crossed the Jordan into the land that your God יהוה is giving you, you shall set up large stones.

Coat them with plaster ³and inscribe upon them all the words of this Teaching. When you cross over to enter the land that your God יהוה is giving you, a land flowing with milk and honey, as יהוה, the God of your ancestors, promised you—⁴upon crossing the Jordan, you shall set up these stones, about which I charge you this day, on Mount Ebal, and coat them with plaster. ⁵There, too, you shall build an altar to your God יהוה, an altar of stones. Do not wield an iron tool over them; ⁶you must build the altar of your God יהוה of unhewn* stones. You shall offer on it burnt offerings to your God יהוה, ⁷and you shall sacrifice there offerings of well-being and eat them, rejoicing before your God יהוה. ⁸And on those stones you shall inscribe every word of this Teaching most distinctly.

⁹Moses and the levitical priests spoke to all Israel, saying: Silence! Hear, O Israel! Today you have become the people of your God יהוה: ¹⁰Heed your God יהוה and observe the divine commandments and laws, which I enjoin upon you this day.

¹¹Thereupon Moses charged the people, saying: ¹²*After you have crossed the Jordan, the following shall stand on Mount Gerizim when the blessing for the people is spoken: Simeon, Levi, Judah, Issachar, Joseph, and Benjamin. ¹³And for the curse, the following shall stand on Mount Ebal: Reuben, Gad, Asher, Zebulun, Dan, and Naphtali. ¹⁴The Levites shall then proclaim in a loud voice to all the people of Israel:

¹⁵Cursed be anyone who makes a sculptured or molten image, abhorred by יהוה, a craftsman's handiwork, and sets it up in secret.— And all the people shall respond, Amen.

¹⁶Cursed be the one who insults father or mother.—And all the people shall say, Amen.

¹⁷Cursed be the one who moves a neighbor's landmark.—And all the people shall say, Amen.

¹⁸Cursed be the one who misdirects a blind person on the way.— And all the people shall say, Amen.

¹⁹Cursed be the one who subverts the rights of the stranger, the fatherless, and the widow.—And all the people shall say, Amen.

²⁰Cursed be the [man] who lies with his father's wife, for he has *⁻removed his father's garment.*—And all the people shall say, Amen.

²¹Cursed be the one who lies with any beast.—And all the people shall say, Amen.

²²Cursed be the [man] who lies with his sister, whether daughter of his father or of his mother.—And all the people shall say, Amen.

²³Cursed be the [man] who lies with his mother-in-law.—And all the people shall say, Amen.

²⁴Cursed be the one who strikes down a fellow [Israelite] in secret.—And all the people shall say, Amen.

²⁵Cursed be the one who accepts a bribe *⁻in the case of the murder of⁻* an innocent person.—And all the people shall say, Amen.

²⁶Cursed be whoever will not uphold the terms of this Teaching and observe them.—And all the people shall say, Amen.

28 Now, if you obey your God יהוה, to observe faithfully all the divine commandments which I enjoin upon you this day, your God יהוה will set you high above all the nations of the earth. ²All these blessings shall come upon you and take effect, if you will but heed the word of your God יהוה:

³Blessed shall you be in the city and blessed shall you be in the country.

⁴Blessed shall be the issue of your womb, the produce of your soil, and the offspring of your cattle, the calving of your herd and the lambing of your flock.

⁵Blessed shall be your basket and your kneading bowl.

⁶Blessed shall you be in your comings and blessed shall you be in your goings.

⁷יהוה will put to rout before [your army] the enemies who attack you; they will march out against you by a single road, but flee from you by many* roads. ⁸יהוה will ordain blessings for you upon your barns and upon all your undertakings: you will be blessed in the land that your God יהוה is giving you. ⁹יהוה will establish you as God's holy people, as was sworn to you, if you keep the commandments of your God יהוה and walk in God's ways. ¹⁰And all the peoples of the earth shall see that *⁻יהוה's name is proclaimed over you,⁻* and they shall stand in fear of you. ¹¹יהוה will give you abounding prosperity in the issue of your womb, the

offspring of your cattle, and the produce of your soil in the land that יהוה swore to your fathers to assign to you. [12]יהוה will open for you that bounteous store, the heavens, to provide rain for your land in season and to bless all your undertakings. You will be creditor to many nations, but debtor to none.

[13]יהוה will make you the head, not the tail; you will always be at the top and never at the bottom—if only you obey and faithfully observe the commandments of your God יהוה that I enjoin upon you this day, [14]and do not deviate to the right or to the left from any of the commandments that I enjoin upon you this day and turn to the worship of other gods.

[15]But if you do not obey your God יהוה to observe faithfully all the commandments and laws which I enjoin upon you this day, all these curses shall come upon you and take effect:

[16]Cursed shall you be in the city and cursed shall you be in the country.

[17]Cursed shall be your basket and your kneading bowl.

[18]Cursed shall be the issue of your womb and the produce of your soil, the calving of your herd and the lambing of your flock.

[19]Cursed shall you be in your comings and cursed shall you be in your goings.

[20]יהוה will let loose against you calamity, panic, and frustration in all the enterprises you undertake, so that you shall soon be utterly wiped out because of your evildoing in forsaking Me. [21]יהוה will make pestilence cling to you, until putting an end to you in the land that you are entering to possess. [22]יהוה will strike you with consumption, fever, and inflammation,* with scorching heat and drought, with blight and mildew; they shall hound you until you perish. [23]The skies above your head shall be copper and the earth under you iron. [24]יהוה will make the rain of your land dust, and sand shall drop on you from the sky, until you are wiped out.

[25]יהוה will put you to rout before your enemies; you shall march out against them by a single road, but flee from them by many* roads; and you shall become a horror to all the kingdoms of the earth. [26]Your carcasses shall become food for all the birds of the sky and all the beasts of the earth, with none to frighten them off.

²⁷יהוה will strike you with *־the Egyptian inflammation,־* with hemorrhoids, boil-scars, and itch, from which you shall never recover.

²⁸יהוה will strike you with madness, blindness, and dismay.* ²⁹You shall grope at noon as the blind grope in the dark; you shall not prosper in your ventures, but shall be constantly abused and robbed, with none to give help.

³⁰If you [a man] pay the bride-price for a wife, another man shall enjoy her.

If you build a house, you shall not live in it. *If you plant a vineyard, you shall not harvest it. ³¹Your ox shall be slaughtered before your eyes, but you shall not eat of it; your ass shall be seized in front of you, and it shall not be returned to you; your flock shall be delivered to your enemies, with none to help you. ³²Your sons and daughters shall be delivered to another people, while you look on; and your eyes shall strain for them constantly, but you shall be helpless. ³³A people you do not know shall eat up the produce of your soil and all your gains; you shall be abused and downtrodden continually, ³⁴until you are driven mad by what your eyes behold. ³⁵יהוה will afflict you at the knees and thighs with a severe inflammation, from which you shall never recover—from the sole of your foot to the crown of your head.

³⁶יהוה will drive you, and the king you have set over you, to a nation unknown to you or your ancestors, where you shall serve other gods, of wood and stone. ³⁷You shall be a consternation, a proverb, and a byword among all the peoples to which יהוה will drive you.

³⁸Though you take much seed out to the field, you shall gather in little, for the locust shall consume it. ³⁹Though you plant vineyards and till them, you shall have no wine to drink or store, for the worm shall devour them. ⁴⁰Though you have olive trees throughout your territory, you shall have no oil for anointment, for your olives shall drop off. ⁴¹Though you beget sons and daughters, they shall not remain with you, for they shall go into captivity. ⁴²The cricket shall take over all the trees and produce of your land.

⁴³The strangers in your midst shall rise above you higher and higher, while you sink lower and lower: ⁴⁴they shall be your

creditors, but you shall not be theirs; they shall be the head and you the tail.

45All these curses shall befall you; they shall pursue you and overtake you, until you are wiped out, because you did not heed your God יהוה and keep the commandments and laws that were enjoined upon you. 46They shall serve as signs and proofs against you and your offspring for all time. 47Because you would not serve your God יהוה in joy and gladness over the abundance of everything, 48you shall have to serve—in hunger and thirst, naked and lacking everything—the enemies whom יהוה will let loose against you. [God] will put an iron yoke upon your neck until you are wiped out.

49יהוה will bring a nation against you from afar, from the end of the earth, which will swoop down like the eagle—a nation whose language you do not understand, 50a ruthless nation, that will show the influential° no regard and the vulnerable° no mercy. 51It shall devour the offspring of your cattle and the produce of your soil, until you have been wiped out, leaving you nothing of new grain, wine, or oil, of the calving of your herds and the lambing of your flocks, until it has brought you to ruin. 52It shall shut you up in all your towns throughout your land until every mighty, towering wall in which you trust has come down. And when you are shut up in all your towns throughout your land that your God יהוה has assigned to you, 53you shall eat your own issue, the flesh of your sons and daughters that your God יהוה has assigned to you, because of the desperate straits to which your enemy shall reduce you. 54The householder° who is most tender and fastidious among you shall be too mean to his brother and the wife of his bosom and the children he has spared 55to share with any of them the flesh of the children that he eats, because he has nothing else left as a result of the desperate straits to which your enemy shall reduce you in all your towns. 56And she who is most tender and dainty among you, so tender and dainty that she would never venture to set a foot on the ground, shall begrudge the husband of her bosom, and her son and her daughter, 57the afterbirth that issues from between her legs and the babies she bears; she shall eat them secretly, because of utter want, in the desperate straits to which your enemy shall reduce you in your towns.

Ki Tavo'

⁵⁸If you fail to observe faithfully all the terms of this Teaching that are written in this book, to reverence this honored and awesome Name, your God יהוה, ⁵⁹יהוה will inflict extraordinary plagues upon you and your offspring, strange and lasting plagues, malignant and chronic diseases—⁶⁰bringing back upon you all the sicknesses of Egypt that you dreaded so, and they shall cling to you. ⁶¹Moreover, יהוה will bring upon you all the other diseases and plagues that are not mentioned in this book of Teaching, until you are wiped out. ⁶²You shall be left a scant few, after having been as numerous as the stars in the skies, because you did not heed the command of your God יהוה. ⁶³And as יהוה once delighted in making you prosperous and many, so will יהוה now delight in causing you to perish and in wiping you out; you shall be torn from the land that you are about to enter and possess.

⁶⁴יהוה will scatter you among all the peoples from one end of the earth to the other, and there you shall serve other gods, wood and stone, *⁻whom neither you nor your ancestors have experienced.⁻* ⁶⁵Yet even among those nations you shall find no peace, nor shall your foot find a place to rest. יהוה will give you there an anguished heart and eyes that pine and a despondent spirit. ⁶⁶The life you face shall be precarious; you shall be in terror, night and day, with no assurance of survival. ⁶⁷In the morning you shall say, "If only it were evening!" and in the evening you shall say, "If only it were morning!"—because of what your heart shall dread and your eyes shall see. ⁶⁸יהוה will send you back to Egypt in galleys, by a route which I told you you should not see again. There you shall offer yourselves for sale to your enemies as male and female slaves, but none will buy.

⁶⁹*These are the terms of the covenant which יהוה commanded Moses to conclude with the Israelites in the land of Moab, in addition to the covenant which was made with them at Horeb.

29 Moses summoned all Israel and said to them:
You have seen all that יהוה did before your very eyes in the land of Egypt, to Pharaoh and to all his courtiers and to his whole country: ²the wondrous feats that you saw with your own eyes, those prodigious signs and marvels. ³Yet to this day

יהוה has not given you a mind to understand or eyes to see or ears to hear.

⁴I led you through the wilderness forty years; the clothes on your back did not wear out, nor did the sandals on your feet; ⁵you had no bread to eat and no wine or other intoxicant to drink— that you might know that I יהוה am your God.

⁶When you reached this place, King Sihon of Heshbon and King Og of Bashan came out to engage us in battle, but we defeated them. ⁷We took their land and gave it to the Reubenites, the Gadites, and the half-tribe of Manasseh as their heritage. ⁸Therefore observe faithfully all the terms of this covenant, that you may succeed in all that you undertake.

נִצָּבִים | NITSAVIM

⁹You stand this day, all of you, before your God יהוה—you tribal heads, you elders, and you officials, all the men of Israel, ¹⁰you children, you women, even the stranger within your camp, from woodchopper to water drawer—¹¹to enter into the covenant of your God יהוה, which your God יהוה is concluding with you this day, with *⁻its sanctions;⁻* ¹²in order to establish you this day as God's people and in order to be your God, as promised you and as sworn to your fathers Abraham, Isaac, and Jacob. ¹³I make this covenant, with its sanctions, not with you alone, ¹⁴but both with those who are standing here with us this day before our God יהוה and with those who are not with us here this day.

¹⁵Well you know that we dwelt in the land of Egypt and that we passed through the midst of various other nations through which you passed; ¹⁶and you have seen the detestable things and the fetishes of wood and stone, silver and gold, that they keep. ¹⁷Perchance there is among you some man or woman, or some clan or tribe, whose heart is even now turning away from our God יהוה to go and worship the gods of those nations—perchance there is among you a stock sprouting poison weed and wormwood. ¹⁸When hearing the words of these sanctions, such a one may imagine a special immunity, thinking, "I shall be safe, though I follow my own willful heart"—to the utter ruin of *⁻moist and dry alike.⁻* ¹⁹°יהוה will never forgive such individuals. Rather, יהוה's anger and passion will rage against them, till every sanction

recorded in this book comes down upon them, and יהוה blots out their name from under heaven.

²⁰[As for such a clan or tribe,] יהוה will single it out from all the tribes of Israel for misfortune, in accordance with all the sanctions of the covenant recorded in this book of Teaching. ²¹And later generations will ask—the children who succeed you, and foreigners who come from distant lands and see the plagues and diseases that יהוה has inflicted upon that land, ²²all its soil devastated by sulfur and salt, beyond sowing and producing, no grass growing in it, just like the upheaval of Sodom and Gomorrah, Admah and Zeboiim, which יהוה overthrew in fierce anger—²³all nations will ask, "Why did יהוה do thus to this land? Wherefore that awful wrath?" ²⁴They will be told, "Because they forsook the covenant that יהוה, God of their ancestors, made with them upon freeing them from the land of Egypt; ²⁵they turned to the service of other gods and worshiped them, gods *⁻whom they had not experienced⁻* and whom [God] had not allotted* to them. ²⁶So יהוה was incensed at that land and brought upon it all the curses recorded in this book. ²⁷יהוה uprooted them from their soil in anger, fury, and great wrath, and cast them into another land, as is still the case."

²⁸Concealed acts concern our God יהוה; but with overt acts, it is for us and our children ever to apply all the provisions of this Teaching.

30 When all these things befall you—the blessing and the curse that I have set before you—and you take them to heart amidst the various nations to which your God יהוה has banished you, ²and you return to your God יהוה, and you and your children heed God's command with all your heart and soul, just as I enjoin upon you this day, ³then your God יהוה will restore your fortunes* and °take you back in love.° [God] will bring you together again from all the peoples where your God יהוה has scattered you. ⁴Even if your outcasts are at the ends of the world,* from there your God יהוה will gather you, from there [God] will fetch you. ⁵And your God יהוה will bring you to the land that your fathers possessed, and you shall possess it; and [God] will make you more prosperous and more numerous than your ancestors.

⁶Then your God יהוה will *⁻open up⁻* your heart and the hearts of your offspring—to love your God יהוה with all your heart and soul, in order that you may live. ⁷יהוה your God will inflict all those curses upon the enemies and foes who persecuted you. ⁸You, however, will again heed יהוה and obey all the divine commandments that I enjoin upon you this day. ⁹And your God יהוה will grant you abounding prosperity in all your undertakings, in the issue of your womb, the offspring of your cattle, and the produce of your soil. For יהוה will again delight in your well-being as in that of your ancestors, ¹⁰since you will be heeding your God יהוה and keeping the divine commandments and laws that are recorded in this book of the Teaching—once you return to your God יהוה with all your heart and soul.

¹¹Surely, this Instruction which I enjoin upon you this day is not too baffling for you, nor is it beyond reach. ¹²It is not in the heavens, that you should say, "Who among us can go up to the heavens and get it for us and impart it to us, that we may observe it?" ¹³Neither is it beyond the sea, that you should say, "Who among us can cross to the other side of the sea and get it for us and impart it to us, that we may observe it?" ¹⁴No, the thing is very close to you, in your mouth and in your heart, to observe it.

¹⁵See, I set before you this day life and prosperity, death and adversity. ¹⁶For* I command you this day, to love your God יהוה, to walk in God's ways, and to keep God's commandments, God's laws, and God's rules, that you may thrive and increase, and that your God יהוה may bless you in the land that you are about to enter and possess. ¹⁷But if your heart turns away and you give no heed, and are lured into the worship and service of other gods, ¹⁸I declare to you this day that you shall certainly perish; you shall not long endure on the soil that you are crossing the Jordan to enter and possess. ¹⁹I call heaven and earth to witness against you this day: I have put before you life and death, blessing and curse. Choose life—if you and your offspring would live—²⁰by loving your God יהוה, heeding God's commands, and holding fast to [God]. For thereby you shall have life and shall long endure upon the soil that יהוה swore to your fathers Abraham, Isaac, and Jacob, to give to them.

וַיֵּלֶךְ | VA-YELEKH

31 *-Moses went and spoke* these things to all Israel. [2]He said to them:

I am now one hundred and twenty years old, I can no longer *-be active.* Moreover, יהוה has said to me, "You shall not go across yonder Jordan." [3]It is indeed your God יהוה who will cross over before you, and who will wipe out those nations from your path; and you shall dispossess them.—Joshua is the one who shall cross before you, as יהוה has spoken.—[4]יהוה will do to them as was done to Sihon and Og, kings of the Amorites, and to their countries, when [God] wiped them out. [5]יהוה will deliver them up to you, and you shall deal with them in full accordance with the Instruction that I have enjoined upon you. [6]Be strong and resolute, be not in fear or in dread of them; for it is indeed your God יהוה who marches with you: [God] will not fail you or forsake you.

[7]Then Moses called Joshua and said to him in the sight of all Israel: "Be strong and resolute, for it is you who shall go with this people into the land that יהוה swore to their fathers to give them, and it is you who shall apportion it to them. [8]And it is indeed יהוה who will go before you. [God] will be with you—and will not fail you or forsake you. Fear not and be not dismayed!"

[9]Moses wrote down this Teaching and gave it to the priests, sons of Levi, who carried the Ark of יהוה's Covenant, and to all the elders of Israel.

[10]And Moses instructed them as follows: *-Every seventh year,-* the year set for remission, at the Feast of Booths, [11]when all Israel comes to appear before your God יהוה in the place that [God] will choose, you shall read this Teaching aloud in the presence of all Israel. [12]Gather the people—°-men, women, children,-° and the strangers in your communities—that they may hear and so learn to revere your God יהוה and to observe faithfully every word of this Teaching. [13]Their children, too, who have not had the experience, shall hear and learn to revere your God יהוה as long as they live in the land that you are about to cross the Jordan to possess.

[14]יהוה said to Moses: The time is drawing near for you to die. Call Joshua and present yourselves in the Tent of Meeting, that

I may instruct him. Moses and Joshua went and presented themselves in the Tent of Meeting. [15]יהוה appeared in the Tent, in a pillar of cloud, the pillar of cloud having come to rest at the entrance of the tent.

[16]יהוה said to Moses: You are soon to lie with your ancestors. This people will thereupon go astray after the alien gods in their midst, in the land that they are about to enter; they will forsake Me and break My covenant that I made with them. [17]Then My anger will flare up against them, and I will abandon them and hide My countenance from them. They shall be ready prey; and many evils and troubles shall befall them. And they shall say on that day, "Surely it is because our God is not in our midst that these evils have befallen us." [18]Yet I will keep My countenance hidden on that day, because of all the evil they have done in turning to other gods. [19]Therefore, write down this poem and teach it to the people of Israel; put it in their mouths, in order that this poem may be My witness against the people of Israel. [20]When I bring them into the land flowing with milk and honey that I promised on oath to their fathers, and they eat their fill and grow fat and turn to other gods and serve them, spurning Me and breaking My covenant, [21]and the many evils and troubles befall them— then this poem shall confront them as a witness, since it will never be lost from the mouth of their offspring. For I know what plans they are devising even now, before I bring them into the land that I promised on oath.

[22]That day, Moses wrote down this poem and taught it to the Israelites.

[23]And [God] charged Joshua son of Nun: "Be strong and resolute: for you shall bring the Israelites into the land that I promised them on oath, and I will be with you."

[24]When Moses had put down in writing the words of this Teaching to the very end, [25]Moses charged the Levites who carried the Ark of the Covenant of יהוה, saying: [26]Take this book of Teaching and place it beside the Ark of the Covenant of your God יהוה, and let it remain there as a witness against you. [27]Well I know how defiant and stiffnecked you are: even now, while I am still alive in your midst, you have been defiant toward יהוה; how much more, then, when I am dead! [28]Gather to me all the elders of your tribes

and your officials, that I may speak all these words to them and that I may call heaven and earth to witness against them. ²⁹For I know that, when I am dead, you will act wickedly and turn away from the path that I enjoined upon you, and that in time to come misfortune will befall you for having done evil in the sight of יהוה, whom you vexed by your deeds.

³⁰Then Moses recited the words of the following poem to the very end, in the hearing of the whole congregation of Israel.

הַאֲזִינוּ | HA'AZINU

32 Give ear, O heavens, let me speak;
    Let the earth hear the words I utter!
²*May my discourse come down as the rain,
    My speech distill as the dew,
Like showers on young growth,
    Like droplets on the grass.
³For the name of יהוה I proclaim;
    Give glory to our God!
⁴The Rock!—whose deeds are perfect,
    Yea, all God's ways are just;
A faithful God, never false,
    True and upright indeed.

⁵*Unworthy children—
    That crooked, perverse generation—
    Their baseness has played God false.
⁶Do you thus requite יהוה,
    O dull and witless people?
Is not this the Father° who created you—
    Fashioned you and made you endure!

⁷Remember the days of old,
    Consider the years of ages past;
Ask your parent, who will inform you,
    Your elders, who will tell you:
⁸When the Most High gave nations their homes
    And set the divisions of humanity,
[God] fixed the boundaries of peoples
    In relation to Israel's numbers.

⁹For יהוה's portion is this people;
    Jacob, God's own allotment.

¹⁰[God] found them in a desert region,
    In an empty howling waste.
[God] engirded them, watched over them,
    Guarded them as the pupil of God's eye.
¹¹Like an eagle who rouses its nestlings,
    Gliding down to its young,
So did [God] spread wings and take them,
    Bear them along on pinions;
¹²יהוה alone did guide them,
    No alien god alongside.

¹³[God] set them atop the highlands,
    To feast on the yield of the earth;
Nursing them with honey from the crag,
    And oil from the flinty rock,
¹⁴Curd of kine and milk of flocks;
    With the best* of lambs,
    And rams of Bashan, and he-goats;
With the *‑very finest‑* wheat—
    And foaming grape-blood was your drink.

¹⁵So Jeshurun grew fat and kicked—
    You grew fat and gross and coarse*—
They forsook the God who made them
    And spurned the Rock of their support.
¹⁶They incensed [God] with alien things,
    Vexed [God] with abominations.
¹⁷They sacrificed to demons, no-gods,
    Gods they had never known,
New ones, who came but lately,
    ‑Who stirred not your forebears' fears.‑
¹⁸You neglected the Rock who begot you,
    Forgot the God who labored to bring you forth.

¹⁹יהוה saw and was vexed
    And spurned these sons and daughters.
²⁰[God] said: I will hide My countenance from them,

And see how they fare in the end.
For they are a treacherous breed,
    Children with no loyalty in them.
²¹They incensed Me with no-gods,
    Vexed Me with their futilities;*
I'll incense them with a no-folk,
    Vex them with a nation of fools.
²²For a fire has flared in My wrath
    And burned to the bottom of Sheol,
Has consumed the earth and its increase,
    Eaten down to the base of the hills.
²³I will sweep misfortunes on them,
    Use up My arrows on them:
²⁴Wasting famine, ravaging plague,
    Deadly pestilence, and fanged beasts
Will I let loose against them,
    With venomous creepers in dust.
²⁵The sword shall deal death without,
    As shall the terror within,
To youth and maiden alike,
    The suckling as well as the aged.

²⁶*I might have reduced them to naught,*
    Made their memory cease among humankind,
²⁷But for fear of the taunts of the foe,
    Their enemies who might misjudge
And say, "Our own hand has prevailed;
    None of this was wrought by יהוה!"
²⁸*For they are a folk void of sense,
    Lacking in all discernment.
²⁹Were they wise, they would think upon this,
    Gain insight into their future:
³⁰"How could one have routed a thousand,
    Or two put ten thousand to flight,
Unless their Rock had sold them,
    יהוה had given them up?"
³¹For their rock is not like our Rock,
    In our enemies' own estimation.

³²Ah! The vine for them is from Sodom,
    From the vineyards of Gomorrah;
The grapes for them are poison,
    A bitter growth their clusters.
³³Their wine is the venom of asps,
    The pitiless poison of vipers.
³⁴Lo, I have it all put away,
    Sealed up in My storehouses,
³⁵To be My vengeance and recompense,
    At the time that their foot falters.
Yea, their day of disaster is near,
    And destiny rushes upon them.

³⁶For יהוה will vindicate God's people
    ˙And take revenge for˙ God's servants,
Upon seeing that their might is gone,
    And neither bond nor free is left.
³⁷[God] will say: Where are their gods,
    The rock in whom they sought refuge,
³⁸Who ate the fat of their offerings
    And drank their libation wine?
Let them rise up to your help,
    And let them be a shield unto you!
³⁹See, then, that I, I am the One;
    There is no god beside Me.
I deal death and give life;
    I wounded and I will heal:
    None can deliver from My hand.
⁴⁰Lo, I raise My hand to heaven
    And say: As I live forever,
⁴¹When I whet My flashing blade
    And My hand lays hold on judgment,
Vengeance will I wreak on My foes,
    Will I deal to those who reject Me.
⁴²I will make My arrows drunk with blood—
    As My sword devours flesh—
Blood of the slain and the captive
    From the long-haired enemy chiefs.

⁴³O nations, acclaim God's people!
    For He'll avenge the blood of His servants,
Wreak vengeance on His foes,
    ⁻And cleanse His people's land.⁻

⁴⁴Moses came, together with Hosea son of Nun, and recited all the words of this poem in the hearing of the people.

⁴⁵And when Moses finished reciting all these words to all Israel, ⁴⁶he said to them: Take to heart all the words with which I have warned you this day. Enjoin them upon your children, that they may observe faithfully all the terms of this Teaching. ⁴⁷For this is not a trifling thing for you: it is your very life; through it you shall long endure on the land that you are to possess upon crossing the Jordan.

⁴⁸That very day יהוה spoke to Moses: ⁴⁹Ascend these heights of Abarim to Mount Nebo, which is in the land of Moab facing Jericho, and view the land of Canaan, which I am giving the Israelites as their holding. ⁵⁰You shall die on the mountain that you are about to ascend, and shall be gathered to your kin, as your brother Aaron died on Mount Hor and was gathered to his kin; ⁵¹for you both broke faith with Me among the Israelite people, at the waters of Meribath-kadesh in the wilderness of Zin, by failing to uphold My sanctity among the Israelite people. ⁵²You may view the land from a distance, but you shall not enter it—the land that I am giving to the Israelite people.

וֹזֹאת הברכה | VE-ZO'T HA-BERAKHAH

33 This is the blessing with which Moses, God's envoy,° bade the Israelites farewell before he died. ²He said:

יהוה came from Sinai,
And shone upon them from Seir;
[God] appeared from Mount Paran,
And approached from Ribeboth-kodesh*,
⁻Lightning flashing⁻ at them *⁻from [God's] right.⁻*
³*Lover, indeed, of the people,
Their hallowed are all in Your hand.
They followed in Your steps,
Accepting Your pronouncements,

⁴When Moses charged us with the Teaching
As the heritage of the congregation of Jacob.
⁵Then [God] became King° in Jeshurun,
When the heads of the people assembled,
The tribes of Israel together.

⁶May Reuben live and not die,
Though few be his numbers.

⁷And this he said of Judah:
Hear, יהוה, the voice of Judah
And restore him to his people.
⁻Though his own hands strive for him,⁻
Help him against his foes.

⁸And of Levi he said:
Let Your Thummim and Urim
Be with Your faithful one,
Whom You tested at Massah,
Challenged at the waters of Meribah;
⁹Who said of his father and mother,
"I consider them not."
His brothers he disregarded,
Ignored his own children.
Your precepts alone they observed,
And kept Your covenant.
¹⁰They shall teach Your laws to Jacob
And Your instructions to Israel.
⁻They shall offer You incense to savor⁻
And whole-offerings on Your altar.
¹¹Bless, יהוה, his substance,
And favor his undertakings.
Smite the loins of his foes;
Let his enemies rise no more.

¹²Of Benjamin he said:
Beloved of יהוה,
He rests securely beside [God],

Ve-zo't Ha-berakhah

Who protects him always,
-As he rests between God's shoulders.-

13And of Joseph he said:
Blessed of יהוה be his land
-With the bounty of dew from heaven,-
And of the deep that couches below;
14With the bounteous yield of the sun,
And the bounteous crop of the moons;
15With the best from the ancient mountains,
And the bounty of hills immemorial;
16With the bounty of earth and its fullness,
And the favor of the Presence* in the Bush.
May these rest on the head of Joseph,
On the crown of the elect of his brothers.
17Like a firstling bull in his majesty,
He has horns like the horns of the wild-ox;
With them he gores the peoples,
The ends of the earth one and all.
These* are the myriads of Ephraim,
Those* are the thousands of Manasseh.

18And of Zebulun he said:
Rejoice, O Zebulun, on your journeys,
And Issachar, in your tents.
19They invite their kin to the mountain,
Where they offer sacrifices of success.
For they draw from the riches of the sea
And the hidden hoards of the sand.

20And of Gad he said:
Blessed be the One who enlarges Gad!
Poised is he like a lion
To tear off arm and scalp.
21*He chose for himself the best,
For there is the portion of the revered chieftain,
Where the heads of the people come.
He executed יהוה's judgments

And God's decisions for Israel.

22And of Dan he said:
    Dan is a lion's whelp
    That leaps forth from Bashan.

23And of Naphtali he said:
    O Naphtali, sated with favor
    And full of יהוה's blessing,
    Take possession on the west and south.

24And of Asher he said:
    Most blessed of sons be Asher;
    May he be the favorite of his brothers,
    May he dip his foot in oil.
    25May your doorbolts be iron and copper,
    And your security last all your days.

    26O Jeshurun, there is none like God,
    Riding through the heavens to help you,
    Through the skies in His majesty.
    27*The ancient God is a refuge,
    A support are the arms everlasting.
    He drove out the enemy before you
    By His command: Destroy!
    28Thus Israel dwells in safety,
    Untroubled is Jacob's abode,*
    In a land of grain and wine,
    Under heavens dripping dew.
    29O happy Israel! Who is like you,
    A people delivered by יהוה,
    Your protecting Shield, your Sword triumphant!
    Your enemies shall come cringing before you,
    And you shall tread on their backs.

34 Moses went up from the steppes of Moab to Mount Nebo, to the summit of Pisgah, opposite Jericho, and יהוה showed him the whole land: Gilead as far as Dan; 2all Naphtali;

Ve-zo't Ha-berakhah

the land of Ephraim and Manasseh; the whole land of Judah as far as the Western* Sea; ³the Negeb; and the Plain—the Valley of Jericho, the city of palm trees—as far as Zoar. ⁴And יהוה said to him, "This is the land of which I swore to Abraham, Isaac, and Jacob, 'I will assign it to your offspring.' I have let you see it with your own eyes, but you shall not cross there."

⁵So Moses the servant of יהוה died there, in the land of Moab, at the command of יהוה. ⁶[God] buried him in the valley in the land of Moab, near Beth-peor; and no one knows his burial place to this day. ⁷Moses was a hundred and twenty years old when he died; his eyes were undimmed and his vigor unabated. ⁸And the Israelites bewailed Moses in the steppes of Moab for thirty days.

The period of wailing and mourning for Moses came to an end. ⁹Now Joshua son of Nun was filled with the spirit of wisdom because Moses had laid his hands upon him; and the Israelites heeded him, doing as יהוה had commanded Moses.

¹⁰Never again did there arise in Israel a prophet like Moses— whom יהוה singled out, face to face, ¹¹for the various signs and portents that יהוה sent him to display in the land of Egypt, against Pharaoh and all his courtiers and his whole country, ¹²and for all the great might and awesome power that Moses displayed before all Israel.

חזק חזק ונתחזק

Guide to Notes

Notes are those of the NJPS translation committee unless marked by a 🌿 symbol.

GLOSSARY

Akkadian　An ancient Semitic language spoken in Mesopotamia; its chief dialects were Babylonian and Assyrian.

Dictionary　Dictionary of Gender in the Torah, which is located following the Notes at the back of this edition.

Ibn Ezra　Rabbi Abraham ibn Ezra, a Bible commentator and grammarian who lived in Spain in the twelfth century.

Kethib　The way a word, usually unvocalized, is written in the Bible; see *qere*.

Masorah　The text of the Bible as transmitted, with vowel signs and accents.

Qere　The way the Masorah requires a word to be read, especially when it diverges from the *kethib*.

Rashbam　Rabbi Shmuel ben Meir; he lived in France in the twelfth century and commented on the Torah.

Septuagint　The oldest Jewish translation of the Bible, into Greek. The Torah translation dates from the third century B.C.E.

Targum　A Jewish translation of the Bible into Aramaic, a language once widely spoken in Western Asia, including the land of Israel.

Ugaritic　A language of inscriptions found at Ras Shamra, a town on the Syrian coast, in the second millennium B.C.E. Both the language and its literature have shed much light on the Hebrew Bible.

Vulgate　The Latin translation of the Bible made by the Church father Jerome about the year 400 C.E. It became the official Bible of the Roman Catholic Church.

ABBREVIATIONS AND TERMS

Cf.　A reference to another version, cognate language, or another biblical passage, that justifies the translation adopted.

349

Heb.   The Hebrew word or phrase in transliteration. Also used to indicate the literal wording for which a superior rendering was employed.

I.e.   An explanation, to avoid adding words to the text, in order to clarify the translation.

Lit.   For the literal translation of a word or phrase that was given an idiomatic or somewhat free translation in the text.

Meaning of Heb. uncertain   The translation represents the best that the committee could achieve with an elusive or difficult text.

Moved up   Where clarity required the shifting of a word or phrase, either within a verse or from one verse to another.

NJPS   New Jewish Publication Society translation (1962, with revisions in 1967, 1985, 1992, and 1999).

Or   An alternative reading considered to be almost as acceptable as the one adopted for the body of the translation.

Others   A well-known translation, as in the older (1917) JPS version, that the committee found unacceptable even as an alternative reading.

Trad.   Traditionally translated in English, as exemplified by the older (1917) JPS version, by the King James (1611) version, or by NJPS itself if it did not substantially differ from the foregoing versions.

v.; vv.   Verse; verses.

TRANSLITERATION SCHEMA (FOR NOTES ONLY)

ʾ = א	k = כ or ך	sh = שׁ
ʿ = ע	kh = כ or ך	ṣ = צ or ץ
a = X̱ X̲ or X̤	l = ל	t = ת
ai = ʾX̱ or ʾX̤	m = מ or ם	th = ת
b = בּ or ב	n = נ or ן	ṭ = ט
d = דּ or ד	o = וֹ ˙X or X̤	u = וּ or X̤
e = X̤ X̤ X̤ X̱ or ʾX̤	p = פּ	v = ב
g = גּ or ג	ph = פ or ף	w = ו
h = ה	q = ק	y = י
ḥ = ח	r = ר	z = ז
i = X̤	s = ס or שׂ	

Notes

GENESIS

1:1 ***When God began to create*** Others "In the beginning God created."

1:2 ***a wind from*** Others "the spirit of."

1:5 ***a first day*** Others "one day."

2:2 ***ceased*** Or "rested."

2:5 🌿 ***shrub of the field*** I.e., suitable for pasturage.

  🌿 ***grasses of the field*** I.e., cereal grasses, suitable as crops.

2:7 🌿 ***the Human*** I.e., the progenitor of the species and the point of origin for human society. Heb. *ha-'adam*; trad. "man." In the eyes of ancient Israel, the typical initiator of a lineage was male, and so the first human being would also have been imagined as male. See further the Dictionary under *'adam*.

  🌿 ***soil's humus*** Heb. *'afar min ha-'adamah*, rendered to emulate the wordplay with Heb. *ha-'adam* "the Human"; more precisely, "loose dirt from the soil." NJPS "dust of the earth."

2:12 ***lapis lazuli*** Others "onyx"; meaning of Heb. *shoham* uncertain.

2:21 🌿 ***sides*** Heb. *ṣela'ot*, trad. "ribs." Cf. 1 Kings 6:34; Exod. 25:12, 26:20, 26–27, 35; 30:4.

2:23 🌿 ***Woman*** Heb. *'ishshah*; so trad. More precisely in context, "a (female) member of the human species." See next note and the Dictionary under *'ish*.

  🌿 ***a Human*** More precisely, "the (formerly lone) member of the human species." NJPS "man"; trad. "Man." See the Dictionary under *'ish*.

2:24 🌿 ***man*** So trad.; Heb. *'ish*. Contrast the previous verse.

  🌿 ***wife*** So trad.; Heb. *'ishshah* (with possessive suffix). Cf. the previous note and contrast the previous verse.

2:25 ***naked*** Heb. *'arummim,* play on *'arum* "shrewd" in 3:1.

  🌿 ***the Human*** Heb. *ha-'adam*; trad. "the man." See note to v. 7.

3:5 ***divine beings who know*** Others "God, who knows."

3:16 🌿 ***rule over you*** (So NJPS.) I.e., for matters of sexual relations he will have the last word. Heb. *yimshol bakh*; trad. "rule over thee."

3:19   **dust**   Heb. *'afar.* Cf. the second note to 2:7.

3:20   **Eve**   Heb. *ḥawwah.*

          living   Heb. *ḥai.*

4:1   **knew**   Heb. *yada',* often in a sexual sense.

          created   Heb. *qanithi,* connected with "Cain."

          ❦ **person**   More precisely, a member of the human species. NJPS "male child"; trad. "man." See the Dictionary under *'ish.*

          ❦ **with the help of**   Or "as did"; precise force of Heb. *'et* uncertain.

4:7   Meaning of verse uncertain.

4:8   . . .   Ancient versions, including the Targum, read "Come, let us go out into the field."

4:11   **more cursed than the ground**   See 3:17.

4:18   **Mehujael**   Heb. *Meḥiya'el.*

4:25   **provided me with**   Or "established for me"; Heb. *shath,* connected with "Seth."

5:2   ❦ **Humankind**   Heb. *'adam*; NJPS "Man," trad. "Adam."

5:29   **relief**   Connecting Noah with Heb. *niḥam* "to comfort"; cf. 9:20 ff.

6:2   **divine beings**   Others "the sons of God."

6:3   **abide**   Meaning of Heb. uncertain.

NOAḤ

6:9   ❦ **personage**   Trad. "man." See the Dictionary under *'ish.*

6:16   **terminate it . . .**   Meaning of Heb. uncertain.

9:27   **enlarge**   Heb. *yapht,* play on Heb. *yepheth* "Japheth."

10:4   **Dodanim**   Septuagint and 1 Chron. 1:7 "Rodanim."

10:5   **[These are the descendants of Japheth]**   Cf. vv. 20 and 31.

10:10   **and Calneh**   Heb. *we-khalneh,* better vocalized *we-khullanah* "all of them being."

10:14   **Caphtorim**   I.e., the Cretans; moved up for the sake of clarity; cf. Amos 9:7.

10:25   **divided**   Heb. *niphlegah,* play on "Peleg."

11:9   **Babel**   I.e., "Babylon."

11:9   **confounded**   Heb. *balal* "confound," play on "Babel."

11:11   **After the birth of**   Lit. "After he begot," and so through v. 25.

LEKH LEKHA

12:2   **a blessing**   I.e., a standard by which blessing is invoked; cf. v. 3 end.

12:11   *I*   Or "You"; cf. the second-person feminine form *-ti* in Judg. 5:7; Jer. 2:20; Mic. 4:13, etc.

12:20   🌿 *deputies*   Heb. *'anashim*; trad. "men." Cf. Josh. 10:18. See the Dictionary under *'ish*.

13:9   *Let us separate*   Lit. "Please separate from me."

14:3   *Dead Sea*   Heb. "Salt Sea."

14:14   *retainers*   Meaning of Heb. *ḥanikh* uncertain.

14:18   *God Most High*   Heb. *El 'Elyon.*

14:22   *swear*   Lit. "lift up my hand."

14:24   🌿 *notables*   Heb. *'anashim*; trad. "men." See the Dictionary under *'ish*.

15:2   *lord* יהוה   Heb. *'adonai y-h-w-h*, traditionally read aloud as *'adonai 'elohim* (rather than *'adonai* twice). NJPS "Lord GOD." 🌿 See also the Dictionary under "male metaphors for God."

15:2   *and the one in charge . . .*   Meaning of Heb. uncertain.

16:2   *have a child*   Lit. "be built up," play on *ben* "child" and *banah* "build up." 🌿 See the Dictionary under *ben*.

16:11   *Ishmael*   I.e., "God heeds."

16:12   🌿 *person*   Or perhaps "sire" (cf. Josh. 14:15, Gen. 2:22b–4:1, and Phoenician usage). Trad. "man." See the Dictionary under *'adam*.

16:13   *El-roi*   Apparently "God of Seeing."

       Have I not gone on seeing . . .   Meaning of Heb. uncertain.

16:14   *Beer-lahai-roi*   Apparently "the Well of the Living One who sees me."

17:1   *El Shaddai*   Traditionally rendered "God Almighty."

17:5   *Abraham*   Understood as "father of a multitude."

17:15   *Sarah*   I.e., "princess."

17:19   *Isaac*   Heb. *Yiṣḥaq*, from *ṣaḥaq*, "laugh."

17:20   *I have heeded you*   Heb. *shema'tikha,* play on "Ishmael."

VA-YERA'

18:2   🌿 *envoys*   Heb. *'anashim*; trad. "men." In the eyes of the text's original audience, the context evokes the agency sense of this term already at this point in the story. See further the Dictionary under *'ish*.

18:3   *My lords*   Or "My lord," referring either to the delegation's apparent leader or to God.

18:10   *next year*   Heb. *ka-'et ḥayyah*; cf. Gen. 17:21; 2 Kings 4:16–17.

18:11   🌿 *her periods*   Heb. *'orah ka-nashim*, lit. "the way of women"; NJPS "the periods of women." (Perhaps, in light of Akkadian *'arḫu* "month," the lit. meaning is actually "women's menses.")

18:12   🌿 *I've lost the ability*   Precise force of Heb. *veloti* uncertain. NJPS "I am withered," trad. "I am waxed old."

18:16   🌿 *envoys*   See note to 18:2.

19:4   🌿 *town council [and] the militia of Sodom*   Cf. Gen. 34:20, Josh. 7:4–5, and Judg. 20:2. Heb. *we-'anshe ha-'ir 'anshe Sedom*; NJPS "the townspeople, the men of Sodom," trad. "the men of the city, the men of Sodom."

     🌿 *insignificant and influential alike*   NJPS "young and old," trad. "both young and old"; Heb. *mi-na'ar we-'ad zaqen.* See the Dictionary under *na'ar* and "elders."

19:5   🌿 *envoys*   To the original audience, who understands divine agents to be recognizable unless the text states otherwise, the context would evoke the agency sense of Heb. *'anashim.* See the Dictionary under *'ish* and "agent." Contrast trad. "men."

19:6   🌿 *be intimate with*   I.e., humiliate; cf. "against יהוה" in 13:13.

19:8   🌿 *daughters*   I.e., of great value to Lot; cf. Judg. 11:35; 2 Sam. 12:3.

     🌿 *do to them as you please*   That is, I will entrust them to you as hostages if you will trust me meanwhile with the visiting envoys.

     🌿 *these envoys*   Or "God's envoys." Heb. *ha-'anashim ha-'el*; trad. "these men."

19:9   🌿 *against that householder*   Heb. *ba-'ish*; NJPS "against the person [of Lot]," trad. "upon the man." See the Dictionary under *'ish.*

19:11   🌿 *people*   So NJPS; more precisely, "representatives [of Sodom]." Heb. *'anashim*, the same term as used for the (divine) envoys who are standing on the other side of the door; trad. "men."

     🌿 *low and high alike*   NJPS "young and old," trad. "both small and great"; Heb. *mi-katon we-'ad gadol.* Cf. note to v. 4.

19:22   *Zoar*   Connected with *mis'ar* "a little place," v. 20.

19:26   *Lot's*   Lit. "His."

     back   Lit. "behind him."

19:37   *Moab*   As though *me-'ab* "from (my) father."

19:38   *Ben-ammi*   As though "son of my (paternal) kindred." 🌿 See further the Dictionary under *'am.*

20:4   🌿 *lord*   See note to 18:27.

20:7   🌿 *householder*   Trad. "man." See the Dictionary under *'ish.*

20:8   🌿 *officials*   Trad. "men"; Heb. *'anashim.* Cf. Gen. 12:15, 20; 41:8; 1 Kings 10:8; 12:6; 20:5–9. See the Dictionary under *'ish.*

20:16   *vindication*   Lit. "a covering of the eyes"; meaning of latter half of verse uncertain.

21:6   *with*   Lit. "for."

21:12   *continued*   Lit. "called."

21:31   *Beer-sheba*   I.e., "well of seven" or "well of oath."

22:6   *firestone*   Lit. "fire."

22:13   *a*   Reading *'eḥad* with many Heb. mss. and ancient versions; text *'aḥar* "after."

22:14   *Adonai-yireh*   I.e., "יהוה will see"; cf. v. 8.

         On the mount of יהוה there is vision   Heb. *be-har y-h-w-h yera'eh.*

22:24   ◊ See the discussion of this verse in the Preface, pp. xxii–xxiv.

HAYYEI SARAH

23:7   ◊ *landowning citizens*   Heb. *'am ha-'areṣ*; lit. "people of the land." See the Dictionary under *'am*.

23:10   ◊ *the assembly in his town's gate*   Lit. "all who entered the gate of his town." So NJPS, with a note: "I.e., all his fellow townsmen." Cf. 34:20; Prov. 31:23.

24:9   *as bidden*   Lit. "about this matter."

24:13   ◊ *town's householders*   Heb. *'anshe ha-'ir*; NJPS "townsmen," trad. "men of the city." See the Dictionary under *'ish*.

24:16   ◊ *The maiden was very beautiful—[and] a virgin, no man having known her.*   Or "The maiden was very beautiful, a young woman whom no man had known."

24:21   ◊ *emissary*   Trad. "man." Cf. 12:20, 18:1, 32:25; Num. 13:2, 22:9. See the Dictionary under *'ish*.

24:22   *half-shekel*   Heb. *beqaʿ*.

24:25   *straw*   Heb. *teben*, shredded straw, which in the East is mixed with feed; cf. v. 32.

24:32   ◊ *entourage*   Heb. *'anashim*; trad. "men." See Dictionary under *'ish*.

24:55   *some ten days*   Lit. "days or ten."

24:58   ◊ *emissary*   See note to v. 21.

24:63   *walking*   Meaning of Heb. *lasuaḥ* uncertain; others "to meditate."

24:65   ◊ *dignitary*   Trad. "man." See the Dictionary under *'ish*.

25:4   *Enoch*   Or "Hanoch."

25:8   ◊ *kin*   (So NJPS.) See the Dictionary under "predecessors."

TOLEDOT

25:22   *why do I exist?*   Meaning of Heb. uncertain.

25:25   *Esau*   Synonym of "Seir," play on Heb. *seʿar* "hair."

25:26   **Jacob**   Play on Heb. *'aqeb* "heel."

25:27   ❦ **wild sort**   Lit. "expert of the (unbounded) field"; cf. Isa. 56:9; Ps. 104:11. Heb. *'ish sadeh*; NJPS "a man of the outdoors." See the Dictionary under *'ish*.

    ❦ **mild type**   I.e., civilized and subdued. Heb. *'ish tam*; NJPS "a mild man." See the Dictionary under *'ish*.

    ❦ **raising livestock**   Heb. *yoshev 'ohalim*; NJPS "who stayed in camp," lit. "a sitter in tents." The idiom for a pastoralist; cf. 4:20.

25:28   **he had a taste for game**   Lit. "game was in his mouth."

25:30   **Edom**   Play on Heb. *'adom* "red."

26:7   ❦ **local leaders**   *'anshe ha-maqom* NJPS: "the men of the place". Cf., e.g., Gen. 34:20; Judg. 8:15–17. See the Dictionary under *'ish*.

26:10   ❦ **men**   Cf. 1 Sam. 26:15 and contrast the next verse. NJPS "people." See the Dictionary under *'am*.

26:11   ❦ **householder**   Heb. *'ish*; NJPS "man." See the Dictionary under "householder."

26:12   ❦ **householder**   Moved up from the next verse for clarity. On the rendering, see previous note.

26:21   **Esek**   I.e., "contention."

    Sitnah   I.e., "harassment."

26:22   **ample space**   Heb. *hirhib*, connected with "Rehoboth."

26:33   **Shibah**   As though "oath."

27:11   ❦ **type**   NJPS "man." See the Dictionary under *'ish*.

27:15   ❦ **there**   Or "in her charge"; Heb. *'itah*, lit. 'with her.'"

27:36   **supplant**   Heb. *'aqab*, connected with "Jacob."

27:39   **enjoy the fat of the earth / And**   Others "be away from the fat of the earth and from."

28:3   **El Shaddai**   See note at 17:1.

VA-YETSE'

28:12   **stairway**   Or "ramp"; others "ladder." Heb. *sullam*.

28:19   **Bethel**   I.e., "house of God."

29:1   **resumed his journey**   Lit. "lifted up his feet."

29:10   **uncle**   Lit. "his mother's brother."

29:22   ❦ **people of the place**   Or "the local dignitaries," whose presence clearly validated a marriage; Heb. *'anshe ha-maqom*. See the Dictionary under *'ish*.

29:32   **Reuben**   Understood as "See a son."

29:32   *has seen*   Heb. *ra'ah*, connected with the first part of "Reuben."

will love me   Heb. *ye'ehabani*, connected with the end of "Reuben."

29:33   *heard*   Heb. *shama'*, connected with "Simeon."

29:34   *will become attached*   Heb. *yillaweh*, connected with "Levi."

29:35   *I will praise*   Heb. *'odeh*, connected with "Judah."

30:6   *has vindicated me*   Heb. *dananni*, connected with "Dan."

30:8   *A fateful contest I waged*   Heb. *naphtule . . . naphtalti*, connected with "Naphtali." Lit. "A contest of God . . ."

30:11   *What luck!*   Kethib *begad*; the qere reads *ba' gad* "luck has come"; connected with "Gad."

30:13   *What fortune!*   Heb. *be'oshri*, connected with "Asher."

30:18   *my reward*   Heb. *sekhari*, connected with "Issachar."

30:20   *has given me a choice gift*   Heb. *zebadani . . . zebed.*

will exalt me   Heb. *yizbeleni*; others "will dwell with me."

30:23   *has taken away*   Heb. *'asaph.*

30:24   *add*   Heb. *yoseph.*

30:27   *if you will indulge me*   Lit. "If I have found favor in your eyes."

30:38   *goats*   Lit. "flocks."

30:41   *sturdier*   Or "early-breeding."

30:42   *feebler*   Or "late-breeding."

feeble ones   Cf. previous note.

30:43   ❧ *householder*   Heb. *'ish*; trad. "man." Cf. 26:11–13. See the Dictionary under "householder."

31:7   *time and again*   Lit. "ten times."

31:10   *I had a dream in which I saw*   Lit. "I raised my eyes and saw in a dream, behold."

31:20   *kept Laban the Aramean in the dark*   Lit. "stole the mind of Laban the Aramean"; similarly in v. 26.

31:28   ❧ *sons and daughters*   So NJPS; Heb. *levanai we-livnotai*, a stock phrase (see, e.g., 46:15; 1 Sam. 30:6; Neh. 5:5) that means "progeny," thus including grandchildren.

31:40   *Often*   Lit. "I was."

31:41   *time and again*   Lit. "ten times."

31:42   *Fear*   Meaning of Heb. *pahad* uncertain.

31:47   *Yegar-sahadutha*   Aramaic for "the mound (or, stone-heap) of witness."

Gal-ed   Heb. for "the mound (or, stone-heap) of witness," reflecting the name Gilead, v. 23.

31:49   *watch*   Heb. *yiṣeph*, associated with *Mizpah*.

31:50   🌱 *else*   Or "authorized [to intervene]"; see the Dictionary under *'ish*.

31:53   *Fear*   Meaning of Heb. *paḥad* uncertain.

32:1   🌱 *sons and daughters*   See note to 31:28.

32:3   *Mahanaim*   Connected with Heb. *maḥaneh* "camp."

VA-YISHLAH

32:5   ***"Thus shall you say, 'To my lord Esau, thus says your servant Jacob...'"***   Or "Thus you shall say to my lord Esau, 'Thus says your servant Jacob...'"

32:7   🌱 *retinue*   Trad. "men," but the social-gender force is ambiguous. See 33:15; cf. 24:59; contrast Judg. 9:49 with Exod. 32:28. See further the Dictionary under *'ish*.

32:23   🌱 *sons*   NJPS "children" Heb. *yeladim*. See the Preface, p. vii.

32:25   🌱 *figure*   Or "[divine] agent," i.e., in the eyes of the text's original audience, the circumstantial evidence might well have evoked this sense of *'ish* already at this point in the story. Cf. 18:2; see further the Dictionary under *'ish*.

32:29   *striven*   Heb. *saritha*, connected with first part of "Israel."

   beings divine and human   Or "God (*Elohim*, connected with second part of 'Israel') and human beings."

32:31   *Peniel*   Understood as "face of God."

33:1   🌱 *retinue*   See note to 32:7.

   🌱 *children*   Heb. *yeladim*, referring here only to Jacob's sons (see 32:23) in anticipation of their becoming the progenitors of Israel's tribes; and so through v. 14.

33:17   *Succoth*   Meaning "stalls," "huts," "booths."

33:19   *kesitah*s   Heb. *qesitah*, a unit of unknown value.

33:20   *El-elohe-yisrael*   "El, God of Israel."

34:2   🌱 *and disgraced her*   Heb. *wa-y'anneha*, lit. "and violated her." NJPS "by force," but Dinah may have consented; by the norms of the ancient Near East, she was disgraced either way. OJPS "and humbled her."

34:7   🌱 *representatives*   I.e., for contracting marriage; cf. 24:29–31, 50, 55. Heb. *'anashim*; trad. "men." See the Dictionary under *'ish*.

34:20   *public place*   Lit. "gate."

   🌱 *their town council*   Heb. *'anshe 'iram*; NJPS "their fellow townsmen," trad. "the men of their city." Cf. Ruth 3:11. See the Dictionary under *'ish*.

34:21   🕬 *people*   (So NJPS.) More precisely, "representatives [of Jacob's house]"; see v. 7 and its note. Trad. "men."

34:22   🕬 *representatives*   Heb. *'anashim*; trad. "men." Cf. previous note.

34:24   🕬 *all his fellow townsmen*   So the NJPS footnote here; the reading in NJPS itself is literal ("all who went out of the gate of his town"), but women are not in view here. Heb. *kol yoṣe sha'ar 'iro*.

34:30   🕬 *fighters*   Heb. *metim* (in construct form); cf. Deut. 2:34; 3:6; Isa. 3:25. NJPS "men"; trad. "I."

35:7   *El-bethel*   "The God of Bethel."

35:8   *Allon-bacuth*   Understood as "the oak of the weeping."

35:11   *El Shaddai*   Cf. 17:1.

35:18   *Ben-oni*   Understood as "son of my suffering (or, strength)."

       Benjamin   I.e., "son of the right hand," or "son of the south."

35:29   *He*   Lit. "Isaac."

       🕬 *kin*   (So NJPS.) See the Dictionary under "predecessors."

36:2   *Hivite*   Cf. v. 20, "Horite."

36:24   *Aiah*   Heb. "and Aiah."

       hot springs   Meaning of Heb. *yemim* uncertain.

36:26   *Dishon*   Heb. *Dishan;* but cf. vv. 21, 25, 28, and 30, and 1 Chron. 1:41.

36:37   *Saul*   Or "Shaul."

VA-YESHEV

37:3   🕬 *child of old age*   Heb. *ben zequnim*, used here as a category— apparently an idiom for a special, favored status. Cf. 44:20. NJPS rendered the clause as "he was the child of his old age."

       ornamented tunic   Or "a coat of many colors"; meaning of Heb. uncertain.

37:15   🕬 *someone came upon him*   Or "an agent located him," i.e., someone (human or divine) whom the reader is to understand as acting in God's behalf; cf. 16:7; 18:1–2; 24:12–21; 32:25, 31; 37:17; 38:22. See further the Dictionary under *'ish*.

       🕬 *man*   Or "agent"; see previous note.

37:17   🕬 *man*   Or "agent"; see the first note to v. 15.

37:36   *Midianites*   Heb. "Medanites."

       🕬 *chief prefect*   Precise force of Heb. *sar haṭṭabaḥim* uncertain; cf. Jer. 52:12; 2 Kings 25:8ff. and Jer. 39–40; Gen. 39:20, 40:3. Apparently the office was obscure even to the text's original audience (cf. 39:1). NJPS "chief steward," trad. "captain of the guard."

38:1   ❧ *prominent*   Rendering idiomatically via an adjective, like NJPS "certain." Or (rendering more literally, as a noun) "householder"; trad. "man." See further the Dictionary under *'ish*.

38:8   *duty*   Cf. Deut. 25:5.

38:9   *let [his semen] go to waste*   Heb. *shiḥet arṣah*; lit. "spoil [it] on the ground." ❧ NJPS "let it go to waste," with "seed" (rendered here as "offspring") as the antecedent of "it." See the Dictionary under "seed."

38:12   *his period of mourning was over*   Lit. "he was comforted."

38:14   *Enaim*   Cf. Enam, Josh. 15:34. Others "in an open place" or "at the crossroad."

38:21   ❧ *council of that locale*   Heb. *'anshe meqomah*; cf. 26:7, 29:22, 34:20. NJPS "people of that town," trad. "men of . . ." See further the Dictionary under *'ish*.

       ❧ *prostitute*   Or some type of female functionary at a religious site; precise force of Heb. *qedeshah* uncertain. Trad. "harlot." NJPS "cult prostitute," but extrabiblical evidence for the existence of cultic (i.e., religious) prostitution in the ancient Near East is conspicuously lacking.

38:22   ❧ *local council*   *'anshe ha-maqom*; NJPS "the townspeople." See the first note to the previous verse.

38:24   ❧ *out*   I.e., for a hearing in the local court of law. (Judah does not have jurisdiction over someone living in another household, but he can claim to be an aggrieved party.)

38:25   ❧ *dignitary*   Or "householder." These were the only types of person who owned the items in question, which were symbols of stature and authority. Heb. *'ish*, trad. "man." See further the Dictionary under *'ish* and "householder."

38:29   *breach*   Heb. *pereṣ*.

38:30   *Zerah*   I.e., "brightness," perhaps alluding to the crimson thread.

39:1   ❧ *chief prefect*   See note to 37:36.

       ❧ *official*   Cf. 2 Sam. 23:21; 1 Chron. 11:23. Heb. *'ish*; NJPS (rendering idiomatically via an adjective) "certain." Traditionally taken as a generic noun of class, but see the Dictionary under *'ish*.

39:2   ❧ *highly capable*   Lit. "an expert at producing success." Heb. *'ish maṣliaḥ*; NJPS "a successful man," trad. "a prosperous man."

39:14   ❧ *a Hebrew*   (So trad., apparently taking *'ish* as a generic noun of class.) Or "a Hebrew manager," cf. 43:17. Heb. *'ish 'ivri*. See the Dictionary under *'ish*.

39:23   *Joseph's*   Lit. "his."

40:3   ❧ *chief prefect*   See note to 37:36.

40:13   *pardon you*   Lit. "lift up your head."

40:16   *openwork baskets*   Others "baskets with white bread" or "white baskets"; meaning of Heb. *ḥori* uncertain.

40:20   *singled out*   Lit. "lifted the head of."

MIKKETS

41:10   ◊ *chief prefect*   See note to 37:36.

41:33   ◊ *select an official who's discerning and wise*   Cf. v. 38; 2 Kings 10:3. Or "select someone who's discerning and wise." NJPS "let Pharaoh find a man of discernment and wisdom." See the Dictionary under *'ish*.

41:34   *organize*   Others "take a fifth part of"; meaning of Heb. uncertain.

41:38   ◊ *Could we find an existing official like him—one in whom is the spirit of God?*   Lit. "Could we find one like him—a representative in whom is the spirit of God?" NJPS "Could we find another like him, a man in whom is the spirit of God?"

41:40   *be directed*   Others "order themselves" or "pay homage"; meaning of Heb. *yishshaq* uncertain.

41:43   *Abrek*   Others "Bow the knee," as though from Heb. *barakh* "to kneel"; perhaps from an Egyptian word of unknown meaning.

41:45   *Zaphenath-paneah*   Egyptian for "God speaks; he lives," or "creator of life."

41:48   *the seven years that the land of Egypt was enjoying*   Lit. "the seven years that were in the land of Egypt."

41:51   *has made me forget*   Heb. *nashshani,* connected with "Manasseh" *(Menashsheh).*

41:52   *has made me fertile*   Heb. *hiphrani,* connected with "Ephraim."

42:1   *he*   Lit. "Jacob."

42:11   ◊ *members of the same household*   More precisely, "sons of the same householder," i.e., they are on a mission together for the good of that household. Heb. *bene 'ish 'ehad;* NJPS "sons of the same man," trad. "one man's sons."

42:13   ◊ *householder*   Trad. "man." Heb. *'ish;* see the Dictionary under "householder."

42:30   ◊ *official*   Trad. "man." See the Dictionary under *'ish.*

43:3   ◊ *official*   More precisely, "vizier, regent." See also the previous note.

43:3, 5   *Do not let me see your faces*   Lit. "Do not see my face."

43:15   ◊ *emissaries*   Force of Heb. *'anashim* uncertain in this passage

(43:15–44:4, where it occurs ten times). Trad. "men." See the Dictionary under *'ish*.

43:17   🌿 *steward*   Trad. "man." See the Dictionary under *'ish*.

43:21   *in full*   Lit. "by its weight."

43:34   *several*   Lit. "five."

44:15   🌿 *someone in my position*   Heb. *'ish 'asher kamoni*; NJPS "a man like me," trad. "such a man as I." See the Dictionary under *'ish*.

VA-YIGGASH

44:26   *show our faces to the official*   Lit. "see the official's face."

       🌿 *official*   See note to 43:3.

45:1   🌿 *staff*   Cf. 2 Sam. 13:9. NJPS "one" (in "everyone" and "no one," for the two instances in this verse); trad. "man" ("every man" and "no man"). See the Dictionary under *'ish*.

45:8   🌿 *father to Pharaoh*   (So trad.) Or "Pharaoh's chancellor," cf. Isa. 22:15, 20–21. Heb. *'av le-phar'oh*.

45:14   *embraced*   Lit. "fell on."

45:22   *several*   Lit. "five"; cf. 43:34.

46:7   🌿 *daughters*   (So trad.) The plural is part of a standard formula; cf. vv. 15, 23; Num. 26:8; 1 Chron. 2:8.

46:9   *Enoch*   Or "Hanoch."

46:10   *Saul*   Or "Shaul."

46:15   *33*   Including Jacob.

46:23   *son*   Heb. "sons."

46:26   *who came to Egypt*   Not including Joseph and Joseph's two sons.

46:27   *seventy persons*   Including Jacob and Joseph.

46:29   *ordered*   Lit. "hitched."

46:32   🌿 *householders*   Heb. *'anashim*; trad. "men." See the Dictionary under *'ish* and "householder."

47:2   *a few*   Lit. "five."

       🌿 *representatives*   Heb. *'anashim*. NJPS treats the usage as idiomatic and does not render the word directly; but cf. Deut. 1:23; Josh. 4:2; Judg. 6:27; 20:10; 2 Sam. 21:6 (in light of v. 8); Jer. 38:10; and Ruth 4:2; Judg. 18:2. See further the Dictionary under *'ish*.

47:6   🌿 *capable administrators*   Heb. *'anshe ḥayil*; NJPS "capable men." See the Dictionary under *'ish*.

47:9   🌿 *ancestors*   I.e., predecessors in general. Or, with NJPS, "fathers"—taking the "sojourns" to allude specifically to Terah, Abraham, and Isaac as wandering heads of corporate households. Heb. *'avoth*.

47:21   **town by town**   Meaning of Heb. *'otho le'arim* uncertain.

VA-YEHI

47:30   🍃 *ancestors*   Heb. *'avoth*; trad. "fathers." See the Dictionary under "predecessors."

48:6   *instead*   Lit. "under the name."

48:22   *portion*   Meaning of Heb. *shekhem* uncertain; others "mountain slope."

49:6   🍃 *slay a man*   (So trad.) Or, taking this verse as alluding to the events of chapter 34 (the only narrative reference to these brothers' acting in concert): "killed a governor." Or, with JPS, taking *'ish* as a collective: "slay men." See next note and Dictionary under *'ish*.

    🍃 *maim an ox*   Or, with Canaanite literary usage and taking this verse as referring to the events of chapter 34: "overthrew a dignitary." Or, with JPS, taking *'ish* as a collective: "maimed oxen."

49:9   🍃 *lioness*   (So trad.) Taking Heb. *lavi'* as referring to a different sex than *'ari* earlier in the verse, for it is the females who do the hunting for their pride. NJPS "king of beasts," taking *lavi'* as a breed of lion.

49:10   *So that tribute shall come to him*   Meaning of Heb. *shilo* uncertain. It is understood as *shai lo* "tribute to him," following the Midrash; cf. Isa. 18:7. Lit. "Until he comes to Shiloh."

49:12   *His eyes are darker than wine; / His teeth are whiter than milk*   Or "His eyes are dark from wine, / And his teeth are white from milk."

49:22   *Joseph is a wild ass, / A wild ass by a spring / —Wild colts on a hillside*   Others "Joseph is a fruitful bough, / A fruitful bough by a spring, / Its branches run over a wall."

49:24   *his arms*   Heb. "the arms of his hands."

49:26   *The blessings of your father / Surpass the blessings of my ancestors, / To the utmost bounds of the eternal hills*   Meaning of Heb. uncertain.

49:27   *foe*   Meaning of Heb. *'ad* uncertain; others "booty."

49:29   🍃 *ancestors*   Heb. *'avothai*; trad. "fathers." See the Dictionary under "predecessors."

49:33   🍃 *kin*   Cf. Lev. 21:1–3. NJPS "people," an inconsistent rendering perhaps meant for v. 29. See the Dictionary under "predecessors."

50:10   *Goren*   Or "the threshing floor of."

50:11   *Abel-Mizraim*   Interpreted as "the mourning of the Egyptians."

50:21   🍃 *dependents*   NJPS "children," trad. "little ones." See the Dictionary under *taph*.

EXODUS

SHEMOT

1:10   *rise from the ground*   Meaning perhaps from their wretched condition, cf. Hos. 2:2; or "gain ascendancy over the country." Others "get them up out of the land."

1:11   *garrison cities*   Others "store cities."

1:14   *the various labors that they made them perform. Ruthlessly*   Brought up from the end of the verse for clarity.

1:16   *birthstool*   More precisely, the brick or stone supports used by Egyptian women during childbirth.

1:21   *households*   Meaning of Heb. *batim* uncertain.

2:1   ❧ *member*   NJPS "man." See the Dictionary under *'ish*.

2:10   *Moses*   Heb. *Mosheh* from Egyptian for "born of"; here associated with *mashah* "draw out."

2:15   *arrived*   Lit. "sat" or "settled."

2:19   ❧ *Egyptian*   Perhaps "Egyptian notable," Heb. *'ish miṣri*. See the Dictionary under *'ish*.

2:20   ❧ *[Egyptian]*   More precisely, "member [of the Egyptian people]," or perhaps "notable." Trad. "the man." See the Dictionary under *'ish*.

2:21   ❧ *in that household*   More precisely, "in the custody of that householder." Heb. *'et ha-'ish*. See the Dictionary under *'ish*.

2:22   *Gershom*   Associated with *ger sham*, "a stranger there."

3:14   *Ehyeh-Asher-Ehyeh*   Meaning of Heb. uncertain; variously translated: "I Am That I Am"; "I Am Who I Am"; "I Will Be What I Will Be"; etc.

          Ehyeh   Others "I Am" or "I Will Be."

3:16   יהוה   This name (*y-h-w-h*; traditionally read *Adonai* "the LORD") is here associated with the verb *hayah* "to be."

4:6   *scales*   Cf. Lev. 13:2–3.

4:10   ❧ *good with words*   More precisely, "an expert with words." Heb. *'ish devarim*; trad. "a man of words." See the Dictionary under *'ish*.

4:13   *make someone else Your agent*   Lit. "send through whomever You will send."

4:16   *playing the role of God*   Cf. 7:1.

4:18   *Jether*   I.e., Jethro.

          how they are faring   Lit. "whether they are still alive."

4:19   ❧ *authorities*   Heb. *'anashim*; trad. "men." See the Dictionary under *'ish*.

4:25–26 Meaning of verses uncertain.

5:5 ***The people of the land are already so numerous*** Samaritan "Even now they are more numerous than the people of the land," i.e., than the native population (cf. Gen. 23:7).

from their labors See 1:5–11.

5:9 ֍ ***laborers*** More precisely, "subordinates." Heb. *'anashim;* trad. "men." See the Dictionary under *'ish.*

VA-'ERA'

6:8 ***swore*** Lit. "raised My hand."

6:12 ֍ ***who gets tongue-tied*** Lit. "uncircumcised of lips"; cf. Lev. 19:23; Jer. 6:10. Heb. *'aral sephatayim;* NJPS "a man of impeded speech."

6:14 ***Enoch*** Or "Hanoch"; cf. note to Gen. 46:9.

6:15 ***Saul*** Or "Shaul"; cf. note to Gen. 46:10.

6:30 ֍ ***get tongue-tied*** See note to v. 12.

7:1 ***prophet*** Cf. 4:16.

7:26 This verse constitutes 8:1 in some editions.

8:17 ***swarms of insects*** Others "wild beasts."

8:19 ***distinction*** Meaning of *peduth* uncertain.

9:17 ***thwart*** Others "exalt yourself over."

9:32 ***emmer*** A kind of wheat.

BO'

10:7 ֍ ***notables*** Heb. *'anashim;* trad. "men." See the Dictionary under *'ish.*

10:9 ֍ ***regardless of social station*** Heb. *bi-n'areinu u-vi-ziqneinu,* taking *na'ar* and *zaqen* as terms of socioeconomic status—lit. "with our underlings and with our elders." NJPS "young and old," trad. "with our young and with our old." See the Dictionary under *na'ar* and "elders."

10:19 ***Sea of Reeds*** Traditionally, but incorrectly, "Red Sea."

11:3 ֍ ***their leader*** NJPS "himself," trad. "the man." See the Dictionary under *'ish.*

11:7 ***snarl*** Others "move (or whet) his tongue."

12:3 ֍ ***whole community of Israel*** So NJPS; more precisely, the (male) heads of corporate households who are also known as elders (v. 21) and have the social authority to ensure that God's instructions are carried out. Heb. *kol 'adat yisra'el.* See further the Dictionary under *'edah.*

12:3   *lamb*   Or "kid." Heb. *seh* means either "sheep" or "goat"; cf. v. 5.

12:11   *passover offering*   Or "protective offering"; Heb. *pesaḥ.*

12:23   *pass over*   Or "protect"; cf. note to v. 11.

12:44   ◖ *householder's*   NJPS "a man [has bought]"; trad. "man's." See the Dictionary under *'ish.*

13:4   *in the month*   Or "on the new moon."

13:9   *on your forehead*   Lit. "between your eyes"; cf. Deut. 6:8.

13:16   *symbol*   Others "frontlet."

BE-SHALLAH
.

13:18   *armed*   Meaning of Heb. *ḥamushim* uncertain.

14:6   *ordered*   See note to Gen. 46:29.

14:7   *officers*   Heb. *shalish;* originally "third man on royal chariot"; hence "adjutant," "officer."

14:8   *defiantly*   Lit. "with upraised hand"; cf. Num. 33:3.

14:20   *and it cast a spell upon*   From root *'-r-r,* "cast a spell" or "curse." Others "and it lit up."

14:25   *locked*   From root *'-s-r,* with several ancient versions. Others "took off."

15:1   ◖ *He*   The poetic figure in vv. 1–4 takes ancient Near Eastern gender roles as a given: the (male) role of expert warrior represented salvation from military threats. See the Dictionary under "male metaphors for God."

15:2   יהוה   Heb. *Yah.*

         might   Others "song."

         enshrine   Others "glorify."

15:11   *celestials*   Others "mighty."

15:20   ◖ *hand-drum*   Trad. "timbrel," which incorrectly suggests a tambourine. (As drummers, women set the tempo at public celebrations.)

15:21   ◖ *He*   See note to 15:1.

15:23   *Marah*   I.e., "bitter."

16:7   *Presence*   Others "glory."

16:15   *"What is it?"*   Heb. *man hu;* others "It is manna."

16:20   ◖ *some of them*   So trad.; lit. "representative members." Heb. *'anashim.* See the Dictionary under *'ish.*

16:31   *manna*   Heb. *man.*

         wafers   Meaning of Heb. *ṣappiḥith* uncertain.

16:34   *Pact*   Others "Testimony."

17:7   *Massah*   I.e., "Trial."

          Meribah   I.e., "Quarrel."

17:9   ❦ *some troops*   More precisely, "representatives." Heb. *'anashim*;
          NJPS "some men," trad. "men." See the Dictionary under *'ish*.

17:13   *the people of Amalek*   Lit. "Amalek and his people."

17:15   *Adonai-nissi*   I.e., "יהוה is my banner."

17:16   *throne*   Meaning of Heb. *kes* uncertain.

YITRO

18:3   *stranger*   Heb. *ger*.

18:4   *Eliezer*   Lit. "(My) God is help."

18:11   *yes, by the result of their very schemes against* [*the people*]   Meaning
          of Heb. uncertain.

18:14   *act*   Lit. "sit" as magistrate; cf. v. 13.

18:21, 25 ❦ *individuals*   Heb. *'anashim* (in construct form); trad. "men."
          See the Dictionary under *'ish*.

18:21   ❦ *ones*   See previous note.

19:10   *pure*   Cf. v. 15.

19:13   *sounds a long blast*   Meaning of Heb. uncertain.

19:15   [*the men among*]   See the Dictionary under "you."

19:18   *the whole mountain*   Some Hebrew manuscripts and the Greek
          read "all the people"; cf. v. 16.

20:1   *words*   Tradition varies as to the division of the Commandments
          in vv. 2–14, and as to the numbering of the verses from 13 on. Cf.
          note to Deut. 5:6.

20:3   ❦ *You*   The Decalogue is couched both in the second-person mas-
          culine singular and in terms of a household—the basic social and
          economic unit. Such a format addresses the legal provisions to
          whichever responsible party they apply—most typically the (male)
          householder, or he and his (primary) wife as household adminis-
          trators, or every man, or every adult member of the community.
          Cf. note to Deut. 12:7. See further the Dictionary under "house,"
          "householder," and "you."

20:7   *swear falsely by*   Others "take in vain."

20:14   ❦ *house*   I.e., the corporate household, both persons and posses-
          sions. (Cf. Deut. 5:18.) Heb. *bayith*, in construct form (*beth*). See
          the Dictionary under "house."

          ❦ *wife*   This clause takes ancient Israel's gender roles for granted.
          Typically a man was in a position to take a woman (even more than

one) into the household as a wife; but typically a woman was not in a symmetrical position—which explains why "husband" is not listed here. See also note to v. 3.

20:21   *sacrifices of well-being*   Others "peace-offering." Meaning of Heb. *shelamim* uncertain.

MISHPATIM

21:6   *before God*   Others "to the judges."

21:7   🌿 *parent*   More precisely, "householder," typically but not necessarily male; cf. 2 Kings 4:1. Trad. "man." See the Dictionary under *'ish*.

21:10   *conjugal rights*   Or "ointments."

21:13   🌿 [*a male killer*]   Like all ancient Near Eastern law collections, the Torah here is illustrative rather than comprehensive. Its asylum schema does not appear to treat the case of a female killer, which would have been more complicated.

21:17   *insults*   Or "reviles."

21:20   *there and then*   Lit. "under his hand."

21:22   *the one responsible*   Heb. "he."

          on reckoning   Others "as the judges determine."

21:37   This verse constitutes 22:1 in some editions.

22:1   *tunneling*   I.e., under a wall for housebreaking.

22:4   *impairment*   Lit. "excellence."

22:5   *growing*   Lit. "field."

22:7   *before God*   See note to 21:6.

22:15   *paid*   So that she is unmarried; cf. Deut. 20:7; 22:23 ff.

22:17   *tolerate*   Lit. "let live."

22:19   *proscribed*   See Lev. 27:29.

22:21   [*communal leaders*]   In ancient Israel (and the Near East), assisting and protecting widows and the fatherless was understood to be the responsibility of local householders, elders, priests, and the king. See, e.g., Zech. 7:10, Ezek. 22:6–7, Isa. 1:23, Jer. 22:3.

22:28   *put off the skimming of the first yield of your vats*   Meaning of Heb. uncertain.

22:29   *it*   I.e., the male first-born.

23:2   *mighty*   Others "multitude."

23:5   *raising*   For this use of the verb *'zb*, cf. Neh. 3:8, 34. For the whole verse see Deut. 22:4.

23:15   *in the month*   See note to 13:4.

23:27   *tail*   Lit. "back."

23:28   *plague*   Others "hornet"; meaning of Heb. *ṣirʿah* uncertain. Cf.
Deut. 7:20.

24:5   ◊ *some assistants*   Heb. *naʿarim* (in construct); NJPS "some
young men." See the Dictionary under *naʿar*.

24:7   *we will faithfully do*   Lit. "we will do and obey."

24:11   *leaders*   Meaning of Heb. *ʾaṣilim* uncertain.

TERUMAH

25:5   *tanned ram skins*   Others "rams' skins dyed red."

   dolphin   Or "dugong"; meaning of Hebrew *taḥash* uncertain.

25:7   *lapis lazuli*   Cf. Gen. 2:12 and note.

26:1   *tabernacle*   Heb. *mishkan* refers here specifically to the lowest of
the covers of the Tabernacle, and so its rendering is not capitalized.

26:17   *parallel*   Meaning of Heb. *meshullaboth* uncertain.

26:18   *south*   Heb. uses two terms for "south."

26:24   *They shall match ... inside one ring*   Meaning of Heb. uncertain.

26:9   *south side*   Cf. note to 26:18.

27:19   *Tabernacle*   I.e., of the Tabernacle enclosure. (The furnishings inside were of gold.)

TETSAVVEH

28:3   *skillful, whom I have endowed with the gift of skill*   Lit. "wise of
heart, whom I have filled with a spirit of wisdom."

28:4   *fringed*   Others "checkered."

28:15   *decision*   See v. 30 below; others "judgment."

28:17–20   *carnelian, chrysolite, and emerald ...*   The identity of several
of these twelve stones is uncertain.

28:30   *Urim ... Thummim*   Meaning of these two words uncertain. They
designate a kind of oracle; cf. Num. 27:21.

28:31   *of pure blue*   Others "all of blue."

28:41   *and ordain them*   Lit. "and fill their hands."

29:14   *sin offering*   So throughout this translation and traditionally;
more precisely, "offering of purgation."

29:19   *ridge*   Or "lobe."

30:4   *opposite*   Lit. "its two."

KI TISSA'

30:23   *solidified*   Others "flowing."

31:8   *pure lampstand*   Or "lampstand of pure gold."

31:10   *service*   Others "plaited."

32:1   🌿 *leader*   Trad. "man." See the Dictionary under *'ish*.

32:4   *cast in a mold*   Cf. Zech. 11:13 (*beth hayyoṣer*, "foundry"); others "fashioned it with a graving tool."

        This is your god   Others "These are your gods."

32:25   *a menace*   Others "an object of derision."

32:29   *dedicate yourselves*   Lit. "fill your hands."

32:35   *for what they did with the calf that Aaron made*   Meaning of Heb. uncertain.

33:11   🌿 *[serving as] deputy*   Trad. "a youth." See Dictionary under *na'ar*.

33:14   *I will go in the lead and will*   Lit. "My face will go and I will."

33:19   *and the grace that I grant and the compassion that I show*   Lit. "and I will grant the grace that I will grant and show the compassion that I will show."

34:6   *and proclaimed: "יהוה! יהוה!*   Or "and יהוה proclaimed: יהוה! a God compassionate," etc.; cf. Num. 14:17–18.

34:10   *who are with you*   Lit. "in whose midst you are."

34:18   *of the month*   See note to 13:4.

34:19   *male*   Heb. *tizzakhar*, form uncertain.

VA-YAKHEL

35:6   See 25:4 ff. and the notes there.

35:22   *pendants*   Meaning of Heb. *kumaz* uncertain; cf. Num. 31:50.

35:32   *inspiring him*   Moved up from v. 34 for clarity.

36:13   *units*   Lit. "strip of cloth," here used collectively.

36:22   *parallel*   See note to 26:17.

36:23   *south side*   See note to 26:18.

36:29   *They matched at the bottom, but terminated as one at the top into one ring*   See note to 26:24.

38:8   *women who performed tasks*   Precise nuance of Heb. *ṣove'ot 'asher ṣave'u* uncertain.

38:9   *south*   Cf. note to 26:18.

38:15   *enclosure*   Which accounts for the remaining 20 cubits; cf. v. 18.

38:18   *Its height—or width—was five cubits, like that of*   Meaning of Heb. uncertain.

PEKUDEI

38:24   *talents*   A talent here equals 3,000 shekels.

38:26   *half-shekel*   Heb. *beqa'*.

39:1   *also*   See 36:8.

39:2   *made*   Here and elsewhere in this chapter the singular active verb (lit. "he made") is used impersonally.

39:10   *carnelian, chrysolite, and emerald...*   See note to 28:17.

39:22   *of pure blue*   See note to 28:31.

39:37   *pure lampstand*   See note to 31:8.

40:38   *in it*   I.e., in the cloud.

LEVITICUS

VA-YIKRA'

1:3   ◖ *your*   Lit. "his," referring to the grammatically masculine yet socially generic noun *'adam* (lit. "human being"; NJPS "any") in 1:2.

1:10, 14   ◖ *your*   See note to 1:3.

1:16   *contents*   Others "feathers."

2:12   *choice products*   Exact meaning of Heb. *re'shith* uncertain.

3:1   ◖ *your*   See note to 1:3.

   sacrifice of well-being   Others "peace offering." Exact meaning of Heb. *shelamim* uncertain.

3:3   ◖ *present*   Lit. "he shall present"; cf. note to 1:3.

3:4   ◖ *you*   Lit. "he"; cf. note to 1:3.

3:6, 12   ◖ *your*   See note to 1:3.

3:14   ◖ *present*   Lit. "he shall present"; cf. note to 1:3.

3:15   ◖ *you*   Lit. "he"; cf. note to 1:3.

4:3   *sin offering*   So throughout this translation and traditionally; more precisely, "offering of purgation."

4:13   ◖ *community leadership*   Heb. *kol 'adat yisra'el*, lit. "whole congregation of Israel." See the Dictionary under *'edah*.

4:24   *the spot where the burnt offering is slaughtered*   Cf. 1:11.

4:27   *populace*   Lit. "people of the country."

5:1   *imprecation*   Namely, against one who withholds testimony.

5:4   *utters*   Lit. "utters with his lips."

5:18   *the equivalent*   I.e., in currency; cf. v. 15.

371

5:20   This verse constitutes 6:1 in some editions.

5:21   *pledge*   Meaning of Heb. *tesumeth yad* uncertain.

5:25   *the equivalent*   I.e., in currency; cf. v. 15.

TSAV

6:13   *his*   Or "their."

6:14   *slices*   Meaning of Heb. *tuphine* uncertain.

6:18   *at the spot*   Cf. 1:11.

7:14   *kind*   Lit. "offering."

7:21   *creature*   Heb. *sheqeṣ*, lit. "abomination"; several mss. and ancient versions read *shereṣ* "swarming things."

7:23   *fat*   I.e., hard, coarse fat (suet); cf. 3:3–5.

7:35   *perquisites*   Lit. "anointment," i.e., accruing from anointment.

        inducted   Lit. "brought forward."

8:3   ❧ *community leadership*   Heb. *kol ha-'edah*, lit. "whole congregation." See the Dictionary under *'edah*.

8:4, 5 ❧ *leadership*   Heb. *ha-'edah*, lit. "congregation." See the Dictionary under *'edah*.

8:8   *Urim . . . Thummim*   See note to Exod. 28:30.

8:23   *ridge*   Or "lobe."

8:31   *I commanded*   Or, vocalizing *ṣuwwethi*, "I have been commanded"; cf. below, v. 35 and 10:13.

SHEMINI

9:5   ❧ *community leadership*   See note to 8:3.

9:17   *burnt offering of the morning*   See Exod. 29:38–46.

9:20   *Aaron*   This word moved up from v. 21 for clarity.

10:2   *at the instance of*   Others "before."

10:6   *bare your heads*   Or "dishevel your hair"; cf. Num. 5:18.

        ❧ *kin*   Lit. "brothers." Heb. *aḥim*. See discussion of this verse in the Preface, p. xv.

10:18   *brought inside the sanctuary*   As is done in the case of the most solemn offerings; see 4:3–21; 16:11–17.

11:3   *chews*   Lit. "brings up."

11:13   *following*   A number of these cannot be identified with certainty.

11:34   *if it came in contact with water*   That is, if the food then came in contact with the carcass of any animal named in vv. 29–30.

11:34   *if it was inside any vessel*   That is, any vessel contaminated via contact with a carcass as in vv. 32–33.

TAZRIAʿ

12:2   *at childbirth*   Heb. *tazriaʿ*, lit. "brings forth seed."

12:4, 5   *state of blood purification*   Meaning of Heb. *deme tohorah* uncertain.

12:6   *sin offering*   See note to 4:3.

13:2   *it shall be reported*   Or "[the person] shall be brought."

13:3   *leprous*   Heb. *saraʿath* is used for a variety of diseases. Where a human being is declared unclean by reason of *saraʿath*, the traditional translation "leprosy" has been retained without regard to modern medical terminology.

13:9   *it shall be reported*   See note to 13:2.

13:10   *a patch of undiscolored flesh*   Others "quick raw flesh."

13:45   *head shall be left bare*   Or "hair shall be disheveled"; cf. 10:6.

13:49   *green*   Or "yellow."

13:55   *fret*   Meaning of Heb. *pehetheth* uncertain.

METSORAʿ

14:1   *leper*   Heb. *mesoraʿ*, a person afflicted with *saraʿath*; see note to 13:3.

14:2   *it has been reported*   Cf. note to 13:2.

14:13   *at the spot*   See 1:11; 4:24.

14:37   *greenish*   Or "yellowish."

   streaks   Meaning of Heb. *sheqaʿaruroth* uncertain.

14:41   *coating*   Lit. "dust," "mud."

15:2   *member*   Lit. "flesh."

15:5   ❧ *Those*   Heb. sing. collective, rendered as plural; so too in vv. 6, 7, 10, 11, below.

15:16, 17   ❧ *semen*   Heb. *shikhvath zeraʿ*, an elliptical expression: "a laying down of [what can lead to] seed (i.e., offspring)." Cf. 18:20, 20:15.

15:21   ❧ *All those*   See note to v. 5; so too in vv. 22, 27, below.

15:32   ❧ *semen*   See note to 15:16.

ʾAHAREI MOT

16:2   *at will*   Lit. "at any time."

16:7   **Aaron**   Moved up from v. 8 for clarity.

16:21   **designated**   Meaning of Heb. *'itti* uncertain.

          ☙ **agent**   Trad. "man." See the Dictionary under *'ish*.

16:28   ☙ **The one who burned**   Social-gender force of Heb. *hassoref* uncertain.

18:7–8   **Your father's nakedness . . . the nakedness of your father**   A man and his wife are one flesh (Gen. 2:24), even if he should die or divorce her.

18:10   **their nakedness is yours**   Meaning uncertain.

KEDOSHIM

19:16   **deal basely with**   Others "go about as a talebearer among"; meaning of Heb. idiom *halakh rakhil be-* uncertain.

          profit by   Lit. "stand upon"; precise meaning of Heb. idiom *'amad 'al* uncertain.

19:17   **but**   Exact force of *we-* uncertain.

19:23   **forbidden**   Heb. root *'-r-l*, commonly "to be uncircumcised."

20:17   **excommunicated**   Lit. "cut off."

'EMOR

21:4   **for his wife as kin**   Lit. "as a husband among his kin"; meaning uncertain. NJPS "as a kinsman by marriage."

21:10   **bare his head**   See note to 10:6.

21:18   **has a limb too short or too long**   Or "mutilated or has a limb too long."

22:4   **discharge**   See chapters 13 and 15.

          ☙ **semen**   See note to 15:16.

22:21   **explicit**   Or "unspecified" or "extraordinary"; meaning of Heb. *lephalle* uncertain.

22:24   **practices**   I.e., mutilations.

23:14   **no bread or parched grain or fresh ears**   That is, of the new crop.

23:20   **the two lambs**   Force of Heb. construction uncertain.

23:34   **Booths**   Others "Tabernacles."

23:36   **solemn gathering**   Precise meaning of Heb. *'asereth* uncertain. Cf. Num. 29:35; Deut. 16:8.

23:40   **hadar**   Others "goodly"; exact meaning of Heb. *hadar* uncertain. Traditionally the product is understood as "citron."

          leafy   Meaning of Heb. *'aboth* uncertain.

24:4, 6   **pure**   See note to Exod. 31:8.

24:7   *token offering*   See Lev. 2:2.

24:10   *half-Israelite*   Lit. "the son of an Israelite woman."

24:14, 16 ◍ *community leadership*   Heb. *kol ha-ʿedah*, lit. "whole con-
          gregation." See the Dictionary under *ʿedah*.

BE-HAR

25:10   *release*   Others "liberty."

          jubilee   Heb. *yobel*, "ram" or "ram's horn."

25:14   *neighbor*   I.e., fellow Israelite; see v. 46.

25:25   *redeemer*   I.e., the closest relative able to redeem the land.

25:33   Meaning of first half of verse uncertain.

25:36   *advance or accrued interest*   I.e., interest deducted in advance, or
          interest added at the time of repayment.

26:1   *figured*   Meaning of Heb. *maskith* uncertain; cf. Num. 33:52.

BE-ḤUKKOTAI

26:16   *consumption and fever*   Precise nature of these ills is uncertain.

26:41   *obdurate*   Others "uncircumcised"; lit. "blocked."

27:2   *explicitly*   Cf. note to Lev. 22:21.

27:14   *high or low*   Lit. "good or bad."

NUMBERS

BE-MIDBAR

1:2   ◍ *company [of fighters]*   NJPS "community," trad. "congrega-
          tion." See the Dictionary under *ʿedah*.

          its ancestral houses   I.e., of its tribes.

1:4   ◍ *representative*   Trad. "man." See the Dictionary under *'ish*.

1:5, 17   ◍ *representatives*   Heb. *'anashim*; trad. "men." See the Dictionary
          under *'ish*.

1:18   ◍ *company [of fighters]*   See note to v. 2.

1:44   ◍ *representative*   See note to v. 4.

1:52   ◍ *each man with his division and each under his standard*   Or
          "each [household] with its division and each under its standard."

2:2   ◍ *each man with his standard*   Or "each [household] with its
          standard."

2:34   ◍ *each man with his clan according to his ancestral house*   Or
          "each [household] with its clan according to its ancestral house."

3:4 *by the will of* Others "before."

3:6 ◊ [*its men*] Lit. "it"; cf. 3:15.

3:25 *tabernacle* Here (set in lower case) the lowest of the covers of the Tabernacle; cf. Exod. 26:1.

3:31 *screen* I.e., the screening curtain; cf. 4:5.

4:6 *dolphin* Or "dugong"; meaning of Hebrew *taḥash* uncertain.

4:20 *witness the dismantling of the sanctuary* Others "look at the sacred objects even for a moment."

NASO'

5:2 *eruption...discharge* See Lev. chapters 13 and 15.

5:8 *kin* Lit. "redeemer."

in addition to...on their behalf Cf. Lev. 5:15 f.

5:18 *bare the wife's head* Or "dishevel the wife's hair"; cf. Lev. 10:6.

that induces the spell Meaning of Heb. *ha-me'arerim* uncertain..

5:19, 20 ◊ *living in your husband's household* Heb. *taḥat 'ishekh*; lit. "under the jurisdiction of your householder," NJPS "while married to your husband." See the Dictionary under "householder" and "marriage."

5:29 ◊ *living in her husband's household* Cf. note to v. 19.

6:2 ◊ *men or women* Heb. sing. collectives, rendered as plural.

explicitly See note to Lev. 22:21.

6:4 *seeds...skin* Meaning of Heb. *ḥarṣannim* and *zag* uncertain.

6:7 *hair set apart for their God* Lit. "...for his God." Others "his consecration unto God."

6:9 *nearby* Cf. Num. 19:14–16.

6:11 *sin offering* So traditionally; more precisely, "offering of purgation."

6:13 *the person* Or "it," i.e., the consecrated hair; cf. v. 19.

6:25 *deal kindly and graciously with you* Others "make His face to shine upon thee and be gracious to thee."

6:26 *bestow [divine] favor* Others "lift up His countenance."

peace Or "friendship."

7:2 *drew near* Cf. Exod. 14:10.

BE-HA'ALOTEKHA

8:2 *mount* Cf. Exod. 25:37.

8:9 ◊ *Israelite community leadership* Heb. *kol 'adat bene yisra'el*;

NJPS "whole Israelite community," trad. "whole congregation of the children of Israel." See the Dictionary under *'edah*.

8:11 **designate** Lit. "elevate."

8:19 **for coming** Lit. "when the Israelites come."

8:20 ◊ **Israelite community leadership** See note to v. 9.

9:6, 7 ◊ **householders** Or "people"; the precise social-gender force is uncertain.

9:7 **them** Lit. "him."

9:13 ◊ **householder** See note to v. 6.

10:3 **long blasts** Meaning of Heb. *teru'a* uncertain.

◊ **company** [*of fighters*] See note to 1:2.

10:31 **guide** Lit. "eyes."

10:36 **Return, O יהוה ... thousands** Others "Return, O יהוה, unto the / ten thousands of the families of Israel!"

11:3 **Taberah** From the root *b-'-r*, "to burn."

11:8 **rich cream** Lit. "cream of oil (or, fat)."

11:18 **Purify yourselves** I.e., as for a sacrificial meal.

11:21 **who are with me** Lit. "in whose midst I am."

11:23 **Is there a limit to יהוה's power?** Lit. "Is יהוה's hand too short?"

11:25 ◊ **representative** Trad. understood as "members of (the elders)" and not directly translated. See the Dictionary under *'ish*.

spoke in ecstasy Others "prophesied."

11:26 ◊ **elders** More precisely, "representatives." Heb. *'anashim*; trad. "men." See the Dictionary under *'ish*.

11:27 ◊ **assistant** NJPS "youth," trad. "young man." See the Dictionary under *na'ar*.

11:33 **chewed** Meaning of Heb. *yikkareth* uncertain.

11:34 **Kibroth-hattaavah** I.e., "the graves of craving."

12:3 **leader** Trad. "man." See the Dictionary under *'ish*.

12:6 **When prophets of יהוה arise among you, I** Meaning of Heb. uncertain. Lit. "If there will be your (pl.) prophet, יהוה"; others "If there be a prophet among you, I יהוה."

12:10 **scales** Cf. Lev. 13:2–3.

SHELAḤ-LEKHA

13:2 ◊ **emissaries** Heb. *'anashim*; trad. "men." See the Dictionary under *'ish*.

◊ **representative** Trad. "man." See the Dictionary under *'ish*.

13:3   🕯 *all of them being notables*   Heb. *kullam 'anashim*; NJPS "all the men," trad. "all of them men." See the Dictionary under *'ish*.

13:8   *Hosea*   Or "Hoshea."

13:16, 31   🕯 *emissaries*   See note to v. 2.

13:21   *Lebo-hamath*   Others "the entrance to Hamath."

13:24   *Eshcol*   I.e., "cluster."

13:33   *Nephilim*   See Gen. 6:4.

14:4   *head back for*   Lit. "set the head and return to"; cf. Neh. 9:17. Others "make a captain and return to."

14:9   *prey*   Lit. "food (or, bread)."

14:15   🕯 *wholesale*   Or "every last one." Heb. *ke-'ish 'ehad*; NJPS "to a man," trad. "as one man." See the Dictionary under *'ish*.

14:17   *saying*   Cf. Exod. 34:6–7.

14:22   🕯 *adults*   Heb. *'anashim*; trad. "men." See the Dictionary under *'ish*.

        many   Lit. "ten"; cf. note to Gen. 31:41.

14:25   *Sea of Reeds*   See note to Exod. 10:19.

14:29   🕯 *[men]*   I.e., the whole adult population will die in the wilderness; however, only the men had been counted in the census (1:2–3).

14:30   *swore*   Lit. "raised My hand."

14:36, 38   🕯 *emissaries*   See note to 13:2.

14:44   *defiantly*   Meaning of Heb. *wa-ya'pilu* uncertain.

15:3   *explicitly uttered*   See note to Lev. 22:21.

15:14–15   *shall it be done by the rest of the congregation*   Precise force of Heb. *ya'aseh ha-qahal* uncertain.

15:20   *baking*   Meaning of Heb. *'arisah* uncertain.

15:24   🕯 *community leaders*   Heb. *kol ha-'edah*; cf. note to 8:9.

15:30   *defiantly*   Lit. "with upraised hand."

15:38   🕯 *Israelite people*   Social-gender force here of Heb. *bene yisra'el* uncertain.

KORAH

16:1   *betook himself*   Lit. "took"; nuance of Heb. uncertain.

        and On son of Peleth—descendants of Reuben   According to Num. 26:5, 8–9, Eliab was son of Pallu, son of Reuben.

16:2   🕯 *notables*   Heb. *'anashim*; trad. "men." See the Dictionary under *'ish*.

16:2   ◑ *with fine reputations*   Heb. *'anshe shem*; NJPS "men of re-pute," trad. "men of renown." See the Dictionary under *'ish*.

16:4   *fell on his face*   Perhaps in the sense of "his face fell."

16:6   *your*   Lit. "his."

16:7   ◑ *candidate*   Heb. *'ish*; trad. "man." See the Dictionary under *'ish*.

16:14   *Even if you had*   Lit. "You have not even."

       gouge out those subordinates' eyes   "Those subordinates'" (Heb. *ha-'anashim ha-hem*; NJPS "those men's," trad. "of these men") is a euphemism for "our"; cf. 1 Sam 29:4. Gouging out the eyes was punishment for runaway slaves and rebellious vassals; cf. 2 Kings 25:4–7; Jer. 39:4–7, 52:7–11. On *anashim*, see the Dictionary under *'ish*.

16:22   *Source*   Lit. "God."

       ◑ *member*   Trad. "man." See the Dictionary under *'ish*.

16:26   ◑ *fellows*   I.e., members of the community. Heb. *'anashim*; trad. "men." See the Dictionary under *'ish*.

16:35   ◑ *notables*   See note to v. 2.

17:1   In some editions, the following passage is counted as the continua-tion of chapter 16; see note to v. 16, below.

17:3   Meaning of parts of verse uncertain.

17:16   This verse constitutes 17:1 in some editions.

17:17   *of their ancestral houses*   I.e., of their tribes.

17:20   ◑ *candidate*   See note to 16:7.

       I will rid   Meaning of Heb. *wa-hashikkothi* uncertain.

18:2   *while you and your sons . . . Tent of the Pact*   Force of Heb. uncer-tain.

18:8   *perquisite*   See first note to Lev. 7:35.

18:9   *the offerings by fire*   Force of Heb. *min ha-'esh* uncertain; lit. "from the fire."

18:10   *you shall treat them as consecrated*   Or "they are consecrated for your use."

18:11   *gift offerings*   Cf. Lev. 7:29 ff.

18:14   *proscribed in Israel*   See Lev. 27:28.

18:16   *their redemption price*   I.e., for human first-born; cf. Num. 3:44 ff. For animals see Exod. 34:19–20.

18:19   *covenant of salt*   See Lev. 2:13.

18:23   *others*   Lit. "they."

HUKKAT

19:8　❦ *He who performed the burning*　Social-gender force of Heb. *ha-soref* uncertain.

19:9　❦ *man*　Social-gender force of Heb. uncertain. See the Dictionary under *'ish*.

　　　water of lustration　Lit. "water for impurity."

19:11　❦ *Those*　Heb. impersonal sing., taken as a collective and rendered in the plural.

19:16　*killed*　Lit. "slain by the sword."

19:17　*ashes*　Lit. "earth" or "dust."

19:18　*person*　See note to 19:9.

20:1　*first new moon*　Of the fortieth year; cf. Num. 33:36–38.

20:13　*Meribah*　I.e., "Quarrel"; cf. Exod. 17:7 and the second note there.

20:16　*messenger*　Or angel, that is, "[divine] messenger."

20:26　*unto the dead*　Lit. "and die."

21:1　*Atharim*　Meaning of Heb. *ha-'atharim* uncertain. Targum and other ancient versions render "the way [taken by] the scouts."

21:2　*proscribe*　I.e., utterly destroy, reserving no booty except what is deposited in the Sanctuary; see Josh. 6:24.

21:3　*Hormah*　Connected with *heherim* "to proscribe."

21:4　*Sea of Reeds*　Traditionally, but incorrectly, "Red Sea."

21:6, 8　*seraph*　Cf. Isa. 14:29; 30:6. Others "fiery"; exact meaning of Heb. *saraph* uncertain. Cf. Deut. 8:15.

21:14–15　The quotation that follows is a fragment; its text and meaning are uncertain.

21:16　*Beer*　Lit. "well."

21:18　*Midbar*　Septuagint "the well" (= Beer); cf. v. 16.

21:20　*wasteland*　Or "Jeshimon."

21:24　*Az*　Septuagint "Jazer," cf. v. 32. Others "for the boundary of the Ammonites was strong."

21:27–30　The meaning of several parts of this ancient poem is no longer certain.

21:28　*Bamoth*　Cf. vv. 19 and 20 and Num. 22:21.

21:30　Meaning of verse uncertain. Alternatively: "Their dominion is at an end / From Heshbon to Dibon / And from Nashim to Nophah, / Which is hard by Medeba."

BALAK

22:5   *Euphrates*   Lit. "the River."

22:7   *versed in divination*   Lit. "with divination in their power (hand)."

22:9   ۅ *envoys*   Heb. *'anashim*; NJPS "people," trad. "men." See the Dictionary under *'ish*.

22:20   ۅ *envoys*   Heb. *'anashim*; trad. "men." Cf. previous note.

22:31   *right down to the ground*   Lit. "and prostrated himself to his nostrils."

22:32   *obnoxious*   Precise meaning of Heb. *yarat* uncertain.

22:35   ۅ *envoys*   See note to v. 20.

23:3   *alone*   Others "to a bare height"; exact meaning of Heb. *shephi* uncertain.

23:8   *God*   Heb. *El,* as often in these poems.

23:10   *dust*   Cf. Gen. 13:16.

        Number   Lit. "and the number of."

        upright   Heb. *yesharim*, a play on *yeshurun* ("Jeshurun" in Deut. 32:15), a name for Israel.

23:14   *Sedehzophim*   Or "Lookout Point."

23:21   ۅ *King's*   A poetic figure; in the ancient Near East, the role of "king" represented protection and caring help.

23:22   *horns*   Lit. "eminences," used figuratively.

23:23   *No divining in Israel*   Cf. Deut. 18:10–15.

        Jacob is told at once . . . what God has planned   Or, "Else would it be told to Jacob, / Yea to Israel, what God has planned."

23:24   ۅ *lioness*   So traditionally; NJPS "lion." Precise meaning of Heb. *lavi'* uncertain; see next note.

        ۅ *lion*   So traditionally; NJPS "king of beasts," as English lacks another term for "lion." Heb. *'ari.* Cf. previous note; the two Heb. terms seem to refer either to different sexes or to different breeds.

23:28   *wasteland*   Cf. note to 21:20.

24:3 ff.   Some of the poetic portions of this chapter are unclear.

24:3   ۅ *man*   More precisely, "individual." Heb. *gever.*

        whose eye is true   Others "whose eye is (or, eyes are) open"; meaning of Heb. uncertain.

24:7   *Their roots*   Lit. "and its seed."

24:8   *horns*   See note to 23:22.

24:9   *lioness*   Heb. *lavi'*; NJPS "king of beasts," as English lacks another term for "lion." Cf. notes to 23:24.

24:15   🌿 *man*   See note to v. 3.

24:17   *The foundation of*   Samaritan "the pate of," cf. Jer. 48:45; others "breaks down."

24:22   *Kain*   I.e., the Kenites.

25:1   🌿 *menfolk*   Heb. *'am*, lit. "kinfolk, people"; cf. Exod. 14:6, Num. 21:33; see Num. 31:15–18.

        profaned themselves by whoring   Others "began to commit harlotry."

25:4   *ringleaders*   Lit. "heads of the people."

        publicly   Others "in face of the sun."

25:5   *men*   More precisely, "troops," i.e., those under each official's command when the militia is mustered. Heb. *'anashim*. See the Dictionary under *'ish*.

25:6   🌿 *notables*   See note to 16:2.

25:8   🌿 *notable*   See note to 16:2.

PINḤAS

25:14   🌿 *notable*   See note to 16:2.

26:2   🌿 *company* [*of fighters*]   See note to 1:2.

26:3   Meaning of parts of vv. 3 and 4 uncertain.

26:5   *Enoch*   Or "Hanoch."

26:8   *Born to*   Or "descendants of."

26:10   🌿 *notables*   See note to 16:2.

26:13   *Saul*   Or "Shaul."

26:42–43   Meaning of parts of these verses uncertain.

27:8   🌿 *householder*   Trad. "man." See the Dictionary under *'ish*.

27:14   *Meribath-kadesh*   See note to 20:13.

27:16   🌿 *leader*   NJPS "someone," trad. "man." See the Dictionary under *'ish*.

27:17   *who shall go out . . . and bring them in*   I.e., who shall lead them in all matters and whom they shall follow in all matters.

27:18   🌿 *leader*   Trad. "man." Cf. note to v. 16.

28:2   *the offerings of food due Me*   Lit. "My offering, My food."

28:6   *the regular burnt offering instituted at Mount Sinai*   See Exod. 29:38–41.

28:7   *fermented drink*   I.e., wine.

28:9   *of a measure*   I.e., of an *ephah*.

28:19   *see that they are*   Lit. "they shall be to you."

29:1   *a day when the horn is sounded*   Or "a day of festivity."

29:8   *see that they are*   See note to 28:19.

29:35   *solemn gathering*   Precise meaning of Heb. *'aṣereth* uncertain. Cf. Lev. 23:36; Deut. 16:8.

30:1   This verse constitutes 29:40 in some editions.

MATTOT

30:3   ⚘ *householder*   I.e., vows made by dependent men within his household, like those by his wife or daughter, are implicitly subject to his review. Force of Heb. *'ish* (trad. "man") uncertain; possibly "anyone."

     an obligation   Or "a prohibition."

     crossed his lips   Lit. "come out of his mouth."

30:7   *commitment*   Lit. "utterance of her lips."

31:3   ⚘ *militia*   Heb. *'am*; trad. "people." Cf. note to 25:1.

     ⚘ *troops*   Heb. *'anashim*; trad. "men." See the Dictionary under *'ish*.

31:6   *sacred utensils*   Perhaps the Urim; cf. 27:21.

31:9   ⚘ *other dependents*   Heb. *ṭaf*, including male noncombatants; NJPS "children," trad. "little ones." See the Dictionary under "dependents."

31:12   ⚘ *Israelite community leadership*   Heb. *'adat bene yisra'el*; NJPS "whole Israelite community." Cf. note to 8:9.

31:16   *induced*   Meaning of Heb. *hayu . . . limsor* uncertain.

31:17   ⚘ *dependents*   See note at v. 9.

31:18   ⚘ *female dependent*   Heb. *ha-ṭaf ba-nashim*; NJPS "young woman"; trad. "women children."

31:50   *pendants*   Meaning of Heb. *kumaz* uncertain; cf. Exod. 35:22.

32:11   ⚘ *men*   Measuring the decree in terms of those had been counted during the military muster.

32:14   ⚘ *fellows*   See note to 16:26.

32:17   *hasten*   Meaning of Heb. *hushim* uncertain.

32:26   *behind*   Lit. "there."

32:32   *across the Jordan*   I.e., in Transjordan.

32:38   *they gave [their own] names to towns that they rebuilt*   Cf. vv. 41, 42.

32:41   *their villages*   Or "the villages of Ham"; cf. Gen. 14:5.

     Havvoth-jair   I.e., "the villages of Jair."

MAS'EI

33:3   *defiantly*   Lit. "with upraised hand"; cf. Exod. 14:8.

33:8   *Pene*   Many Hebrew manuscripts and ancient versions read "Pi"; cf. v. 7.

33:10   *Sea of Reeds*   Traditionally, but incorrectly, "Red Sea."

33:40   See 21:1–3.

33:52   *figured*   Meaning of Heb. *maskith* uncertain; cf. Lev. 26:1.

34:5   *Sea*   I.e., the Mediterranean Sea.

34:6   *Great Sea*   I.e., the Mediterranean Sea.

34:8   *Lebo-hamath*   See note to 13:21.

34:11   *Sea of Chinnereth*   I.e., the Sea (or Lake) of Galilee.

34:17, 19   🌿 *commissioners*   Heb. *'anashim*; trad. "men." See the Dictionary under *'ish*.

34:20   *Samuel*   Or "Shemuel."

35:6   🌿 [*male*]   Like all ancient Near Eastern law collections, the Torah's is illustrative rather than comprehensive. The text does not appear to treat the case of a female killer, which would have been more complicated.

🌿 *killer*   Heb. *roṣeaḥ*, a term used regardless either of intent to kill or of the victim's gender; trad. "manslayer."

35:12   *avenger*   Lit. "redeemer," i.e., (male) next of kin; cf. note to Lev. 25:25.

35:17   *tool*   Lit. "of the hand."

32:23   *inadvertently*   Lit. "without seeing."

36:1   *family heads*   I.e., tribal heads.

DEUTERONOMY

DEVARIM

1:1–2   *Through the wilderness . . . by the Mount Seir route*   This passage is unclear; cf. v. 19 and Num. 33:16–36.

1:4   [*and*]   Cf. Josh. 12:4; 13:12, 31.

1:7   *Shephelah*   Others "Lowland."

land of the Canaanites   I.e., Phoenicia.

1:13, 15   🌿 *representatives*   Heb. *'anashim*, trad. "men." See the Dictionary under *'ish*.

1:22   🌿 *emissaries*   Heb. *'anashim*, trad. "men." See the Dictionary under *'ish*.

1:23   *representatives*   See note to v. 13.

1:27   *You sulked*   Precise meaning of Heb. *watteragnu* uncertain.

1:28   *What kind of place*   Lit. "Where."

1:31   *householder*   Taking the image as being of a (quintessentially male) householder, for whom a main responsibility is the corporate household's continuity, represented by his son. For God as house-holder, see Deut. 28:10 (see note there), Num. 12:7, Exod. 4:22; cf. Deut. 32:6. (Alternatively, "parent"—taking *'ish* in its generic sense—cf. Gen. 21:14.) Trad. "man"; cf. Exod. 21:7, Deut. 8:5, and see the Dictionary under *'ish*.

    son   I.e., his heir. (For solicitous care also of a daughter, see, e.g., 2 Sam. 12:3.) So trad.; Heb. *ben*.

1:41   *recklessly*   Meaning of Heb. *wattahinu* uncertain.

1:46   *all that long time*   Lit. "many days, like the days that you re-mained."

2:6   Or "You may obtain food from them to eat for money; and you may also procure water from them to drink for money."

2:22   *as is still the case*   Lit. "until this day."

2:23   *Crete*   Heb. "Caphtor."

2:28   *through*   Lit. "with my feet."

2:34   *doomed*   I.e., placed under *herem*, which meant the annihilation of the population. Cf. note to Num. 21:2; Josh. 6:24.

    men, women, and children   (So NJPS.) Or "combatants, women, and other dependents." Cf. Gen. 34:30; Num. 31:9–18.

2:36   *including the town*   Force of Heb. *we-ha'ir* uncertain.

3:5   *gates*   I.e., two-leaf doors.

3:10   *Salcah*   Others "Salecah" or "Salchah."

3:11   *the standard cubit*   Heb. *'ammat 'ish*; lit. "a representative fore-arm," trad. "the cubit of a man." *See the Dictionary under *'ish*.

3:12   Verses 12–13 proceed from south to north; vv. 14–16 from north to south.

3:14   *Havvoth-jair*   I.e., "villages of Jair."

3:17   Continuing vv. 8–10; cf. 4:47–49.

VA-'ETHANNAN

4:16   *a man or a woman*   More precisely, "male or female."

4:35   *It has been clearly demonstrated to you*   Lit. "You have been shown to know."

4:37   *[God] personally*   Lit. "With His face (or Presence)"; cf. note to Exod. 33:14.

4:42   🌿 *[male]*   Like all ancient Near Eastern law collections, the Torah here is illustrative rather than comprehensive. The text does not appear to treat the case of a female killer, which would have been more complicated.

🌿 *killer*   Heb. *roṣeaḥ*, a homicide regardless either of intent to kill or of the victim's gender; trad. "manslayer."

4:48   *Sion*   Cf. "Sirion," 3:9.

5:6   Tradition varies as to the divisions of the Commandments in vv. 6–18 and the numbering of the verses. Cf. note to Exod. 20:1.

🌿 *you*   The Decalogue is couched both in the second-person masculine singular and in terms of a household—the basic social and economic unit. Such a format addresses the Decalogue's provisions to whichever responsible party they apply—most typically the (male) householder, or he and his (primary) wife as household administrators, or every man, or every adult member of the community. Cf. note to 12:7. See further the Dictionary under "house," "householder," and "you."

5:18   🌿 *[men]*   This clause takes ancient Israel's gender roles for granted. It does not address women because typically they were not in a position take a man into their household. However, typically a man was in a position to take a woman (even more than one) into the household as a wife. See also the previous note.

6:3   *a land flowing with milk and honey*   According to Ibn Ezra this phrase connects with the end of v. 1.

6:4   יהוה *is our God,* יהוה *alone*   Cf. Rashbam and Ibn Ezra; see Zech. 14:9. Others "The LORD our God, the LORD is one."

6:8   *symbol*   Others "frontlet"; cf. Exod. 13:16.

on your forehead   Lit. "between your eyes"; cf. Exod. 13:9.

6:16   *as you did at Massah*   Cf. Exod. 17:1–7.

6:20   *you*   Septuagint and rabbinic quotations read "us."

'EKEV

7:20   *plague*   Others "hornet"; meaning of Heb. *ṣirʿah* uncertain. Cf. Exod. 23:28.

8:5   🌿 *householder*   See note to 1:31.

🌿 *son*   See note to 1:31.

8:14   *lest*   Heb. *pen*; moved down from v. 12 for clarity.

8:15   *seraph*   Cf. Isa. 14:29; 30:6. Others "fiery"; exact meaning of Heb. *saraph* uncertain. Cf. Num. 21:6–8.

9:25   *those forty days and forty nights*   Lit. "the forty days and forty nights that I lay prostrate."

10:6   *Beeroth-bene-jaakan*   Lit. "wells of Bene-jaakan"; cf. Num. 33:31–32.

10:7   *Gudgod*   "Hor-haggidgad" in Num. 33:32–33.

10:14   *to their uttermost reaches*   Lit. "and the heaven of heavens."

10:17   *God supreme and Lord supreme*   Lit. "the God of gods and the
         Lord of lords."   ◊ Heb. *'adon* ("lord") refers to a man in a posi-
         tion of authority. Here it is used metaphorically, taking the ancient
         Near Eastern status and gender hierarchy as a given: God is above
         even the male authority figures.

11:2–7   Syntax of Heb. uncertain.

11:4   *once and for all*   Lit. "to this day."

11:10   *by your own labors*   Lit. "by your foot."

11:15   *I*   That is, יהוה; Samaritan reads "He."

11:18   *very heart*   Lit. "heart and self."

         symbol on your forehead   See notes on 6:8.

11:24   *Western*   I.e., Mediterranean; cf. 34:2.

RE'EH

11:28   *whom you have not experienced*   I.e., who have not proved them-
         selves to you; cf. Hos. 13:4.

12:6   *contributions*   Lit. "the contribution(s) of your hands."

12:7   ◊ *Together with your households*   Moses couches both the cele-
         bration and allocation of harvests in terms of a household—the
         basic social and economic unit. The phrasing of vv. 12, 18 conspic-
         uously omits mention of the householder's (primary) wife. This
         means that she is authorized to carry out such activity in case her
         husband is unavailable. Implicitly, the wording also includes the
         less common case of a woman (typically a widow) whose household
         is not headed by a man. Cf. 5:14 and note to 5:6; see further the
         Dictionary under "house."

12:12, 14, 18   ◊ *you*   See note to v. 7.

12:15   *gazelle . . . deer*   I.e., animals that may be eaten (cf. 14:5; Lev. 11:1
         ff.), but not specified (Lev. 1:1 ff.).

12:26   *shall be taken by you*   Lit. "you shall pick up and come."

12:27   ◊ *you*   See note to v. 7.

13:1   This verse constitutes 12:32 in some editions, so that chapter 13
         starts with the next verse.

13:3   *whom you have not experienced*   See note to 11:28.

13:7   *your own mother's son*   Samaritan reads, "the son of your father
         or the son of your mother."

         closest friend   Lit. "friend who is as yourself."

14:5   A number of these creatures cannot be identified with certainty.

14:12–18   A number of these creatures cannot be identified with certainty.

14:22   🔥 *you*   See note to 12:7.

14:24   *has blessed you*   I.e., with abundant crops.

14:28   *Every third year*   Lit. "After a period of three years"; cf. Deut. 26:12.

15:1   *Every seventh year*   Lit. "After a period of seven years"; cf. 14:28.

15:19   🔥 *you*   See note to 12:7.

16:1   *month*   Cf. Exod. 13:4; 23:15; 34:18.

16:3   *thereafter*   Lit. "upon it."

16:8   *solemn gathering*   Precise meaning of Heb. 'aṣereth uncertain. Cf. Lev. 23:36; Num. 29:35.

16:10, 15   🔥 *you*   See note to 12:7.

16:15   *all*   Lit. "you in all."

SHOFETIM

17:6   *more*   Lit. "three."

17:12   🔥 *party*   I.e., to the dispute. Trad. "man." Cf. NJPS in 19:17; see the Dictionary under 'ish.

17:18   *by*   Nuance of Heb. milliphne uncertain.

18:1   *their*   Lit. "its," i.e., the tribe's.

18:8   *without regard to personal gifts or patrimonies*   Meaning of Heb. uncertain.

19:3   🔥 [*male*]   See note to 4:42.

         🔥 *killer*   See note to 4:42.

19:13   *purge Israel of the blood of the innocent*   Cf. Num. 35:33–34.

19:15   *more*   See note to 17:6.

20:7   *paid the bride-price for a wife*   Thereby making her his wife legally, even though she has not yet moved into his household.

20:10   *offer it terms of peace*   Or "call on it to surrender."

20:17   *proscribe*   See Lev. 27:29.

21:5   *assault*   Cf. 17:8. Or "skin affection"; cf. 24:8.

KI TETSE'

21:15   🔥 *householder*   Trad. "man." See the Dictionary under 'ish.

21:17   *double portion*   Lit. two-thirds.

21:18   🔥 *householder*   See note to v. 15.

21:21   **❦ town's council**   Taking Heb. *'anshe ha-'ir* as a technical term; NJPS "men of the town," trad. "men of the city." See the Dictionary under *'ish*.

22:13   **❦ householder**   So also in vv. 16, 18. See note to 21:15.

22:21   **❦ town's council**   See note to 21:21.

22:23   **who is engaged to a man**   I.e., for whom a bride-price has been paid; see 20:7.

23:1   This verse constitutes 22:30 in some editions, so that chapter 23 starts with the next verse.

      ❦ householder   See note to 21:15.

      remove his father's garment   I.e., lay claim to what his father had possessed. Cf. Lev. 18:8, 20:11; Ezek. 16:8; Ruth 3:9.

23:2   **❦ congregation**   Social-gender force of Heb. *qahal* uncertain, here and in vv. 3–9; cf. Deut. 5:19, 31:30; Josh. 8:35.

23:3–9   **❦** Social-gender force of national ("gentilic") terms uncertain.

23:3   **misbegotten**   Meaning of Heb. *mamzer* uncertain; in Jewish law, the offspring of adultery or incest between Jews. **❦** Social-gender force uncertain.

23:9   **in the third generation**   I.e., of residence in Israel's territory.

23:19   **dog**   I.e., a male prostitute.

24:1   **❦ householder**   See note to 21:15.

24:4   **defiled**   I.e., disqualified for him.

24:8   **skin affection**   Cf. Lev. 13:1 ff.

24:9   **what . . . God did to Miriam . . . after you left Egypt**   See Num. 12:10 ff.

24:11   **❦ householder**   See note to 21:15.

25:1   **❦ parties**   Heb. *'anashim*; trad. "men." Cf. 17:12 and NJPS in 19:17. See the Dictionary under *'ish*.

25:5   **❦ offspring**   Lit. "son"; cf. Num. 27:1–11.

      ❦ wife of the deceased   Heb. *'eshet ha-met*, apparently a status term that refers to the type of widow whose late husband had a share in the patrimony of his lineage, and whose access to support from that patrimony is now stymied by the lack of offspring; cf. Ruth 4:5.

      ❦ householder's   See note to 21:15.

25:7   **❦ representative**   Trad. "men." See the Dictionary under *'ish*.

KI TAVO'

26:5   **❦ you**   See note to 12:7.

26:10   *it*   I.e., the basket of v. 4.

26:12   *in the third year, the year of the tithe*   See Deut. 14:28–29.

26:13   ◟ *you*   See note to 12:7.

26:14   Meaning of first part of verse uncertain.

        deposited any of it with the dead   No part of the tithe may be left as food for the dead.

26:17   *affirmed*   Exact nuance of Heb. *he'emarta* uncertain.

27:2–4   Construction of these verses is uncertain.

27:6   *unhewn*   Lit. "whole."

27:12–13   Construction of these verses is uncertain.

27:20   *removed his father's garment*   See note to 23:1.

27:25   *in the case of the murder of*   I.e., to acquit the murderer of; others "to slay."

28:7   *many*   Lit. "seven."

28:10   יהוה*'s name is proclaimed over you*   I.e., God provides protection as does a householder after having formally established that some-one is part of his house (corporate household); cf. Isa. 4:1; Jer. 14:9; 2 Sam. 12:28. Cf. note to Deut. 1:31.

28:22   *consumption, fever, and inflammation*   Exact nature of these afflic-tions uncertain.

28:25   *many*   Lit. "seven."

28:27   *the Egyptian inflammation*   See Exod. 9:9–10.

28:29   *dismay*   Lit. "numbness of heart."

28:30   *If you plant a vineyard . . .*   Cf. 20:6.

28:50   ◟ *influential*   Taking Heb. *zaqen* as a term of socioeconomic status; trad. "old." See the Dictionary under "elder."

        ◟ *vulnerable*   Taking the Heb. term as referring to socioeconomic status; trad. "young." See previous note and the Dictionary under *na'ar*.

28:54   ◟ *householder*   See note to 21:15.

28:64   *whom neither you nor your ancestors have experienced*   See note to 11:28.

28:69   This verse constitutes 29:1 in some editions.

NITSAVIM

29:11   *its sanctions*   I.e., the curses that covenant violations will entail.

29:18   *moist and dry alike*   I.e., everything.

29:19   ◟ Grammatically masculine singular language with gender-inclusive force (cf. v. 17) is rendered here in the plural.

29:25   *whom they had not experienced* See note to 11:28.

          allotted See 4:19–20.

30:3   *fortunes* Others "captivity."

          ◖ *take you back in love* More precisely, "take you in; restore your standing." The idiom is of a (typically male) householder, who has the authority to determine the standing of the household's members, especially as heirs. Cf. Hos. 1:6, 2:6, 2:25; 14:4; Isa. 54:8; Ps. 103:13. See the Dictionary under "householder."

30:4   *world* Lit. "sky."

30:6   *open up* Others "circumcise."

30:16   *For* Septuagint reads "If you obey the commandments of יהוה your God, which."

VA-YELEKH

31:1   *Moses went and spoke* An ancient Heb. ms. and the Septuagint read: "When Moses had finished speaking..."; cf. 29:1.

31:2   *be active* Lit. "come and go."

31:10   *Every seventh year* See note to 15:1.

31:12   ◖ *men, women, children* Or "householders, wives, [other] dependents." Heb. *ha-'anashim we-ha-nashim we-ha-ṭaph*; cf. 2:34, 3:6. See the Dictionary under "householder" and *ṭaph*.

HA'AZINU

32:2   I.e., may my words be received eagerly; cf. Job 29:22–23.

32:5   Meaning of verse uncertain.

32:6   ◖ *Father* A poetic figure, taking the ancient Near Eastern status and gender hierarchy as a given: a promise of legitimacy, protection, and sustenance in return for obedience. See further the Dictionary under "father."

32:14   *best* Lit. "fat."

          very finest "kidney fat of."

32:15   *coarse* Meaning of Heb. *kasitha* uncertain.

32:17   *Who stirred not your forebears' fears* Meaning of Heb. uncertain; Arabic *sha'ara* suggests the rendering "Whom your forebears did not know."

32:21   *futilities* I.e., idols.

32:26   *I might have reduced them to naught* Lit. "I said, I will reduce..."; meaning of Heb. *'aph'ehem* uncertain.

32:28   Here, apparently, Moses is the speaker; God resumes in v. 32.

32:31   *In our enemies' own estimation*   I.e., as everyone must admit. For Heb. *pelilim* ("own estimation") see Exod. 21:22; cf. Gen. 48:11.

32:36   *And take revenge for*   Cf. Isa. 1:24. Others "and repent Himself concerning."

32:43   *And cleanse His people's land*   Cf. Num. 35:33. Meaning of Heb. uncertain; Ugaritic *'udm't* "tears" suggests the rendering "And wipe away His people's tears." Cf. Isa. 25:8.

VE-ZO'T HA-BERAKHAH

33:1   🔥 *envoy*   Trad. "man"; cf. Exod. 3:10; Num. 12:6–8, 20:16. See the Dictionary under *'ish*.

33:2   *Ribeboth-kodesh*   Cf. Meribath-kadesh, 32:51.

        Lightning flashing . . . from [God's] right   Meaning of Heb. *mi-ymino 'esh dath* uncertain, perhaps a place name.

33:3–5 The meaning of vv. 3–5 is uncertain. An alternative rendering, with v. 3 apostrophizing Moses, is: "³Then were, O lover of the people, / All [God's] worshipers in your care; / They followed your lead, / Accepted your precepts. / ⁴Moses charged us with the Teaching / As the heritage of the congregation of Jacob. / ⁵Thus was he king in Jeshurun . . ."

33:5   🔥 *King*   I.e., one who provides protection and caring help. (This poetic figure takes the ancient Near Eastern status and gender hierarchy as a given.) See further the Dictionary under "king."

33:7   *Though his own hands strive for him*   Better (vocalizing *rab* with *pathaḥ*) "Make his hands strong for him." Cf. *rabbeh*, Judg. 9:29.

33:10   *They shall offer You incense to savor*   Lit. "They shall place incense in Your nostril."

33:12   *As he rests between God's shoulders*   Or "He dwells amid God's slopes."

33:13   *With the bounty of dew from heaven*   Targum Onkelos and two Hebrew manuscripts: "With the bounty of heaven above," reading *me'al* ("above") for *miṭṭal* (lit., "from dew"), cf. Gen. 49:25.

33:16   *Presence*   Lit. "Dweller"; cf. Exod. 3:1 ff.

33:17   *These*   I.e., one of the wild-ox's horns.

        Those   I.e., the other horn.

33:21   Meaning of verse uncertain; cf. vv. 3–5 (with note there), and *saphun* "esteemed" in post-biblical Heb.

33:27   Meaning of verse uncertain.

33:28   *abode*   Others "fountain."

34:2   *Western*   I.e., Mediterranean; cf. 11:24.

Dictionary of Gender in the Torah

THE FOLLOWING ENTRIES on selected topics encapsulate the revising editor's assumptions and conclusions. (Entries for Hebrew terms are relatively technical.) Space permits neither the development of arguments in light of competing views nor full citation of sources. Nonetheless, we hope that this Dictionary orients the reader by explaining the import of, and the reasons for, the renderings in the present translation.

✹ 'adam

The grammatically masculine noun *'adam* is normally a collective common-gender noun. It is regularly employed when gender is *not* germane, signaling to the audience *not* to infer social gender (e.g., Lev. 1:2). Outside of the thirty instances of *'adam* in Genesis 2–3 and two references elsewhere to that first *'adam* (1 Chron. 1:1, Job 31:33)—that is, the other 530 occurrences of *'adam*—none refers to a particular individual. Rather, *'adam* has an indefinite referent (i.e., it is unidentified or generic: "humankind, a human being, a person"), which means that the corresponding language is masculine only for the sake of grammatical concord, implying nothing about the referent's gender.

The lack of an article (*'adam* versus *ha-'adam*) is ambiguous—either way, the referent may be definite or indefinite. The presence of an article is likewise ambiguous. The sense depends upon the context.

That a certain male character has the name Adam does not contradict the gender-inclusive nature of the common noun. Rather, the name Adam is symbolic, like the names Cain, Abel, and many other biblical names.

The meaning of *'adam* in Eden (in particular, in Gen. 2:7–3:30) warrants particular attention because of the unique situation there. The Torah's composer(s) would reasonably have expected its original audience to construe a story about the first human being in terms of their existing views of lineage: individuals cannot be envisioned apart from a patrilineage that situates them in the social structure (*see* Genealogy). Thus the original audience would have reliably read the story of *'adam* in Eden as an etiology not of human biology but rather of lineage—that is, of society. And as the progenitor of the species and originator of all patrilineages, this particular *'adam* could have been conceived of only as male.

Hence the present translation understands *'adam* in Gen. 2:7–3:30 as having a special sense in context: "the first human being (whom it goes without saying was a male)." Such a special sense explains several features of the story that would otherwise be anomalous: how *ha-'adam* refers to a particular individual in the presence of another individual (2:25, 3:12, 20); why Adam is never formally named; and why he continues to be called *ha-'adam* (3:20) even after he is referred to by name (3:17).

❦ *'ish*

The present translation takes as the primary sense of *'ish* (and its effective plural, *'anashim*) "a representative member of a group: a member who serves as a typical or characteristic example." Thus this term exemplifies the group-oriented thinking found throughout the ancient Near East. That primary sense can be seen, for example, in Num. 16:22 ("When one *member* sins, will you be wrathful with the whole community?"). The term *'ish* presumes an inseparability from a larger entity.

In the many situations where a group's members are interchangeable and the grammatical construction is impersonal or distributive, the word *'ish* means "someone, anyone, each one, every one." Furthermore, biblical Hebrew often uses *'ish* in another, related sense of the English word "representative," that of "standing in or acting for another person or group." Where the context indicates that its referent is playing such a role, conspicuous usage of the word *'ish* (sometimes also with grammatical clues such as a construct chain, apposition, or plural form) evokes its sense as a group's *exemplary specimen* or *representative functionary*—e.g., leader, dignitary, expert, householder (*see entry*), agent (*see entry*), warrior, or subordinate.

Various medieval rabbinic grammarians and exegetes perceived the foregoing senses of *'ish* in a wide range of biblical contexts. And as the pioneering lexicographer R. Jonah ibn Janah held nearly a thousand years ago, maleness is not intrinsic to the meaning of *'ish* in biblical Hebrew. Rather, the word *'ish* gains its social-gender sense from context—most fundamentally from the nature of the

Dictionary of Gender in the Torah

group to which it alludes. (Typically the referent's social gender, if not previously stated, simply goes without saying.)

Thus the maleness of the word *'ish* is a grammatical feature rather than a semantic one. Although it does not have a feminine form, in practice the Bible treats the noun *'ishshah* as a functional counterpart. (The two terms are related only by assonance, not by etymology.) The text employs *'ish* for grammatically masculine referents (whether human, animal, or inanimate) or socially gender-neutral (human) referents, while *'ishshah* is for referents marked as either grammatically or socially feminine.

See also the Preface, pp. xxiv–xxv.

🌱 *'am* ("people" and more)

The grammatically masculine collective noun *'am* has a wide semantic range. Its primary meaning in Semitic languages appears to have been "kin." In the Torah it appears once—and only implicitly—in the restricted sense "paternal kin" (Gen. 19:38). More often, the term refers to a wider circle of kin or clan relations (particularly those no longer living; *see* Predecessors)—and by extension, to one's retinue not necessarily related by blood (e.g., Gen. 32:8), or to a local council of householders (*'am ha-'aretz,* e.g., Gen. 23:12), to members of the militia (e.g., Num. 31:32), or to an ethnic populace (e.g., Exod. 36:6, Deut. 31:12). In other words, a social-gender sense was neither inherent nor in practice fixed.

Thus, in each instance the social-gender sense of *'am* must be gleaned from the context. This is often not easy to do. The gender sense can change from one verse to another in the same passage (e.g., Exod. 14:5–6). Further, contextual clues as to gender are often vague if not lacking.

🌱 *'edah* ("community" and more)

Grammatically, the noun *'edah* is a feminine collective; however, its verbs and possessive pronouns are usually inflected in the masculine plural (e.g., Num. 1:2). It is a key term in the book of Numbers, being intensively used there (83 out of its 110 occurrences in the Torah).

NJPS generally rendered *'edah* (after its 1967 revision) as "community." The term refers often to the entire nation (men, women, and and children) but sometimes to a subset that is best considered to consist of men, such as the adult fighting force (as in Num. 1:2) or the leadership—acting on behalf of the whole community (as in Exod. 12:3; Lev. 24:14–15; Num. 1:16, 8:9). The smaller bodies represent the larger groups of which they are a part. In other words, the social-gender sense of *'edah* is not fixed and must be gleaned from the context.

In English, the (gender-inclusive) word "community" is misleading when the context suggests a male-only sense. A more precise rendering is warranted. See the Preface, pp. xviii–xix.

❧ Agent

The workings of agency in ancient Israel are vital to understanding the usage of the gender-related nouns *'ish* (*see entry*) and *mal'akh* (*see* Messenger). In the ancient Near East, the dispatching of agents such as couriers was an ordinary occurrence in all aspects of society: commerce, diplomacy, family relations, the military, and more. Agency was the main means of communicating over a distance, and it was often carried out by professionals.

Certain protocols applied to agents or messengers. With respect to the mission, the sender and the emissary were practically identical. Thus the agent spoke in the sender's stead, in the first person. This explains why the speech of biblical messengers and their senders often are portrayed as interchangeable (e.g., Gen. 22:11–12). Another convention is that recipients responded to, and treated, agents just as one would have treated their principals if the latter were present. This applied to the greeting, to the extension of hospitality, and to how the agents were sent home. This protocol also explains why biblical characters are sometimes portrayed as replying to envoys as if speaking directly to their sender (e.g., Judg. 11:13). A show of disrespect toward an agent was an offense to the sender (e.g., 2 Sam. 10).

The role of agent was not gender marked per se. In Mesopotamia, not only men but also women served in those capacities, both as professionals and as part of other roles such as a servant. (The evidence for women is attested rarely yet consistently across the region and over more than a thousand years—throughout the biblical period.) It appears that men tended to send male agents, while women tended to send female agents, but this appearance of gender differentiation may be due to limitations of the extant evidence. Such gender differentiation, if it existed, did not extend to the recipient; in carrying out their assigned tasks, female messengers regularly confronted men.

There is good reason to think that the Torah text's original audience would have been familiar with female agents (cf. 2 Sam. 17:17; Prov. 9:2–3; Isa. 40:9). Therefore grammatically indefinite references to an agent, as well as definite plural references, take their social-gender sense from the context.

🌿 *Ben* (pl. *banim*) "son"

It is a commonplace that the grammatically masculine relational noun *ben* means "son" (or "son of") in the Bible. Yet when referring to an indefinite subject, *ben* is not sufficient to indicate maleness. Rather, it is unmarked for gender; it refers more generally to offspring, taking its social-gender sense from the context (cf. Jer. 20:15)—like kinship terms in general. Where lineage is at stake, *ben* can connote a male given the society's patrilineal norm (e.g., Gen. 17:16). In other cases, the circumstances argue for a gender-inclusive sense (e.g., Exod. 10:2, 32:27–29).

🌿 Dependents — *See ṭaph*

🌿 Elders (*zeqenim*)

As used in the Torah, the plural noun *zeqenim* almost always refers to a body of peers that has certain functions; that is, it is a social status term, only loosely related to age. (The exception is Gen. 18:11, where it refers to old age, as does the singular form in some Genesis passages.) The Bible does not specify how one became an "elder."

The Bible mentions different yet overlapping types of elders. Variously they were the senior staff members of a *household* (Gen. 24:2, 50:7); or leading members of the more prominent lineages, who represented their community on a *national* level (e.g., Exod. 3:16, 18:12; Lev. 4:15; Num. 11:16; Deut. 29:9); or the *local* village or town leaders who had a number of overlapping functions—including adjudicating conflicts, serving as notarizing witnesses of transactions and agreements, and arranging cooperative projects for the common good. Even locally the referent of "elders" seems fluid: local householders, the leaders of a lineage, or the leaders of a locale—groups that usually were overlapping and in some cases identical. In practice, then, *zeqenim* means "the relevant elders" for the particular function or type of decision at hand. Although this term literally means "bearded ones," by being a masculine plural it is grammatically unmarked for gender. The reader must infer the social-gender sense of *zeqenim* using knowledge of Israelite social structure and from any particular functions mentioned in context. Given that men typically headed both households (*see* House) and lineages (NJPS "clans"), *zeqenim* probably connotes men.

That being said, the possibility of some women serving among the elders cannot be excluded. Indeed, the book of Samuel depicts an *'ishshah* of special status (NJPS "clever woman"; *see 'ish*) who claimed, and acted with, the authority to represent her town in emergency negotiations with a hostile general (2 Sam. 20:15–22). Although that account does not designate her as an elder, if she wasn't one then that would make elders conspicuous in that story by their highly unusual absence.

🌿 Father (*'av*)

The noun *'av* in the Torah means something rather different from what its typical translation, "father," means to most readers of the Bible in English translation. In the ancient social structure, the role of father was a more key position, due to the fundamental nature of the corporate household (*see* House). Typically the head of a corporate household (*see* Householder) was designated the "father" of the household's members, even those who were not literally his kin. He bestowed standing in the household and determined who was to receive what portion of the estate as heirs.

The "father" role in ancient Israel is highlighted best in situations when he was absent. Both the Bible and the literature of nearby Levantine cultures designated persons without a "father" by a special term—even while the mother was still alive (*yatom* "fatherless, orphan"; Exod. 22:23, Ps. 109:8, Lam. 5:3). Throughout the Bible, children who lacked a "father" were exemplars of vulnerable persons in need of special communal protection.

Beyond the household, the term "father" usually refers to *patronage*—that is, to a patron who provides economic support and intercession in return for a client's service and loyalty.

See also Male metaphors for God; and the Preface, p. xiv. On the plural *'avoth*, see the Preface, pp. vi and viii.

🌿 Father's house — *See* House

🌿 Gender

Of the characteristics that vary from one human being to another, each society recognizes certain features as meaningful and important: only certain differences make a difference. Such differential weightings underlie the social system, which by its nature is a structure of inequality. Society allocates prestige, power, and privilege according to an individual's fit into the recognized categories. Those in each category are encouraged to access certain aspects of human expression and development, while being discouraged from attending to other aspects. The structure of inequality both opens up and constrains one's ways to be human.

Among each society's categories are those that divide people according to *gender*—that is, "masculine" and "feminine" categories that are loosely based on biological male and female sex characteristics and procreative functions. Like all conceptual categories, gender consists of an image of the ideal "man" and "woman" as well as a set of attributes that typify the category. Physical characteristics as well as social roles and expectations are defined by what society chooses to notice and to value. Therefore, "sex" is as much socially constructed as the rest of the gender categorization. Thus in this book "gender" refers not only to roles such as mothering but also to anatomical characteristics and to what the society makes of sexual functions such as pregnancy.

Ancient Israelite society did not construct gender precisely the way that contemporary American society does. For example, the spontaneous expression of emotion via tears was part of what defined a real and authentic man in the former case, but not in the latter. Or nowadays a man might be especially valued for being "good with his hands," but in ancient Israel manual dexterity was more central in defining a "real woman." To some extent, when the Torah uses language that is customarily rendered as "men" and "women," it is not necessarily referring to what we mean today by those gender terms.

Although ancient Israelite society was highly gendered, the lives of its members, and the functioning of society as a whole, were determined by more than gender alone. Other categories were at least as significant, which means that viewing Israelite society only through the lens of gender yields a distorted picture. For example, in a corporate household, the prestige, power, and privilege of (male) householders differed dramatically from those of its subordinate men, while those of the principal wife differed dramatically from those of its other women.

Men and women were socially and economically interdependent; their roles were not hierarchical so much as complementary.

Dictionary of Gender in the Torah   399

The ancient Israelite construction of gender with its inequalities was not something established and enforced by men "over" women. Rather, women and men were equally responsible for the ongoing realization of the social system, which allocated opportunities and constraints differentially to each gender.

❧ Gender roles

As throughout the ancient Near East, typically it was men who occupied the formal public leadership and military roles mentioned in the Torah text. The present translation employs "priest" and "Levite" as male terms. Readers should likewise understand nouns like "magistrate" and "warrior" as probably referring to men. Yet women cannot be excluded from such roles with certainty. The Bible is not explicit in this regard, while it does give rare examples, as were found occasionally in nearby societies, of women holding high-profile offices or military posts. (*See* Elders.)

Indefinite references to positions of authority that did not arise directly out of the corporate-household social structure (*see* House), such as "prophet" or "master (of a slave)," should be understood to have generic referents unless the context suggests otherwise.

Many occupational activities were not restricted to one gender. Thus, for example, mention of an otherwise undefined group of shepherds might well have some girls or women in view. Occasionally, women had professional lives—as singers, dancers, musicians, poets, prophets, midwives, perfumers, lamenters, spiritual mediums, and prostitutes, and possibly as scribes and as messengers. Yet most women, like most men, were engaged in agriculture. In ancient Israel, some aspects of "working the land"—such as clearing rocks, building terraces, and plowing—were understood as men's work. Other vital aspects of field and orchard agriculture, horticulture, and viticulture (namely, sowing, weeding, and harvesting) were shared by both men and women: all available hands. And women were the experts in food preservation and processing—activities without which the agricultural enterprise was unsustainable.

Furthermore, women typically cultivated the household's vegetable gardens; fed and milked animals (sheep, goats, cows, oxen); made most clothing, starting with fiber preparation; probably fabricated many of the household's utensils (pots, baskets); and socialized, educated, and trained young children.

In agricultural societies such as that of ancient Israel, even typically gender-marked roles may occasionally be played by the other gender. Thus every once in a while the Bible portrays men as preparing food or caring for young children, and women acting in military capacities.

❧ Genealogy

The Torah's genealogies use the idiom of kinship to express relationships of various kinds—familial, ethnic, social, and political. Genealogically encoded relationships regulated all aspects of daily life. People related to others hierarchically on the basis of the relationships signaled in the genealogies, with persons or groups on the same genealogical level being considered social equals.

Biblical genealogies rarely mention women. However, comparison with the practices of similarly organized cultures suggests that the male-focused way of marking relationships presumes and reinforces the practice of endogamy—marriage within the lineage. Meanwhile, because endogamy results in kin being related to each other in multiple ways, a patrilineage is a shorthand reckoning. It also allows for flexibility in expression as group alignments change over time. In short, genealogies in male terms should not be taken as signaling women's lack of value in Israelite society.

See also Social order; and the Preface, pp. xxii–xxiv.

❧ House (*beth 'av*; "father's house"; corporate household)

Ancient Israelite society was overwhelmingly rural and agricultural. Daily life centered on one's corporate household ("father's house"), which was self-sufficient for most basic needs. Typically it consisted of about a dozen persons, spanning three generations. Forming its core were a primary spousal pair, their married sons and those sons' children, and unmarried sons and daughters. The household often included more distant kin displaced from less stable households, plus transients, foreign slaves, or indentured servants. All lived in a cluster of two or three houses that shared a common courtyard, which was an integral part of the living space. The corporate household also included a garden, fields, orchards, livestock, tools, and equipment. (The typical household was situated in a village of fewer than three hundred people. Even in the half-dozen large "cities" during the monarchy that boasted populations of maybe two thousand, many residents were farmers.)

The majority of Israelites spent most of their time within their corporate household's boundaries. Generally when women married they moved to the corporate household of their husband—who typically was part of the same lineage, so that the bride was still among her kin. Occasionally, a groom moved to his wife's household. At any rate, members of the household specialized in particular aspects of labor—according to age, position in the household, and gender (*see* Gender roles).

The corporate household was the basic social and economic unit in ancient Israel. Individuals gained their sense of identity from their household, subsuming personal interests under its interests. Their sense of honor came largely from their household's prestige. Their ability to thrive depended on its well-being. (Even if reduced via debt to servitude, their household-of-origin continued to protect them.) Their deity was the household's deity, which the Torah typically refers to as the "father's God." The corporate household served as nursery school, day school, place of employment, retirement home, final resting place, and the key to peace in the afterlife. It was an organic entity, persisting across lifetimes. Through hard work and honorable behavior—and with divine favor—its living members aspired for it to grow more stable and prosperous and to gain in reputation and influence.

Not every Israelite lived in a multi-generation corporate household, nor one headed by a male, but such was the social norm. Given that the Torah's audience was oriented in that way, it's not surprising that the text often discusses its concerns in those terms. This also explains much of the Torah's apparently male-centered language (*see* Householder).

In Hebrew the corporate household is referred to as *bayith* or as *beth 'av*. Where *bayith* refers to both persons and property (as an ongoing entity), the present translation—like NJPS—renders in terms of "house"; where *bayith* refers only to the resident persons, it is rendered as "household."

🌿 Householder (and his primary wife)

Ancient Israelite society raised certain of its men to function as the head of its corporate households (*see* House). Such persons were supposed to know the agricultural practices that best suited the local ecology. They would also possess the authority and responsibility for their household's overall health. They decided whom the household comprised, and who would inherit its assets (*see* Father). In comparison to present-day social roles, the Israelite householder was less like today's typical father or husband, and more like the CEO of a family business with several employees.

Because a corporate household typically comprised several nuclear families, one "father's house" could be nested inside a larger one. Who was then viewed as "head of the household" varied depending upon one's perspective and the topic at hand.

The householder's primary wife was responsible for managing the tasks of those junior to her, including the men in the household besides her husband. She functioned as the household's COO (chief operating officer), and as the acting CEO in the householder's absence or incapacity.

The Torah often addresses itself to whichever party has the particular societal authority and responsibility in question (*see* You; Elders). Typically this would have been the (male) head of the household. The Torah's wording and concern sometimes imply that the apparently male addressee actually includes the primary wife (e.g., Exod. 20:10; Lev. 10:14; Num. 18:11; Deut. 5:14; 12:12). At the same time, that male language is *not* addressed to most men, who—like most women—were subordinate members in their "father's house."

Rarely were women householders themselves. Widows in some cases seem to have functioned as householders, at least temporarily (although most did not have that opportunity). Divorcees may occasionally have been of independent means (although most probably found a place in their household-of-origin, as did unhappy or abused wives; cf. Lev. 22:13; Judg. 19:2–3). One indication of the existence of women householders is the occasional appearance of women's names in Israelite genealogies—names that tend to match known place names, suggesting a woman's local prominence.

The present adapted translation sometimes uses the word "householder" where others typically read "man." Biblical Hebrew did not have a unique term for "householder" but rather relied almost always on the more general noun *'ish*. The text's conspicuous usage of *'ish* in the context of control of a corporate household would have reliably evoked in the original audience's minds the sense of *'ish* as "one who has the authority to decide or act on behalf of the group." (*See 'ish*; Elders.) In some biblical instances where *'ishshah* (lit. "woman") is employed conspicuously as a definite noun, it may be the functional equivalent to *'ish* in its sense as "householder" (e.g., 2 Sam. 20:15–22).

❧ Inheritance

Israelite society was *patrilineal*; normally it was a householder's son who inherited the corporate household—including the patrimonial land-holding—and carried on the family line. The society was also *patrilocal*—a female first-born (like daughters in general) tended to leave the homestead upon marriage. But this does not mean that daughters were inherently excluded from inheriting all or part of the family's estate.

All across the ancient Near East, the familial drive was strong to preserve the corporate household with its patrimony into the next generation. By the time that the Torah came together as a normative document, the text's audience would have been familiar with stratagems that enabled a female to be an heir and even to transmit her father's lineage to her son, so as to preserve the household as an entity. The Bible presumes the occasional resort to daughter inheritance without disclosing the exact legal mechanisms, which probably were varied. Such arrangements had long been known across the ancient Near East, including in rural Western Semitic nations: everyone preferred that a daughter inherit in the absence of sons. Apparently such practice was a sort of open secret, for despite extant evidence of its longstanding practice, the only extant supporting law or explicit statement of principles in the entire ancient Near East appears in Num. 27:8–11.

❧ Male metaphors for God

The Torah expressed certain aspects of God's being, and of Israel's relationship with its patron deity, via metaphors that initially applied to human males. The Torah, however, reserves that male God-language for personal address and for poetry. Such metaphors appear to point toward the roles that God plays, rather than making a statement about God's gender.

When a character addresses God as "lord" (e.g., Gen. 18:27, Exod. 5:22), the maleness of the imagery is germane. In Israelite society, someone addressed as "lord" was someone who had autonomous authority. This is how ancient Near Eastern slaves would have addressed their male householders, and how royal ministers would have addressed their king. Thus someone who calls God "lord" is acknowledging divine authority—not making a statement about God's gender. (*See* Social order.)

Similarly, in the ancient Near East, kinship terms were regularly used metaphorically and without gender being at issue (*see* Preface, p. xiv). When Phoenician regents described themselves as "father" to their subjects, clearly they were not referring to their own gender, because they also called themselves the people's "mother." And given what fatherhood represented (*see* Father), it was only natural for the Torah to apply such language to God. The meaning is evident from the context: God vivifies, sustains, nurtures, protects, and guides the nation (Deut. 32:6, 18). The terminology is *not* a reflection on God's gender, which is not at issue.

Gender is probably also not at issue with regard to the poetic styling of God as king (e.g., Exod. 15:18). In the ancient Near East, women occasionally ruled dominions (cf. 1 Kings 10). This does not mean that women rulers were considered men; rather, royal authority was expressed via the male term and masculine symbols. In other words, for the Torah to call God "King" in poetry most likely points to the significance of that office, as can be gleaned from the context: the metaphor expresses divine protection and caring, not maleness.

Similarly, where poetry styles God as a warrior or depicts the Deity as handling quintessentially male weapons (Exod. 15:1–4; Deut. 32:41–42), gender is not at issue. Deliverance is what the context emphasizes, not divine maleness. This distinction holds even when God is called *'ish milḥamah* (Exod. 15:3). In such a construction, *'ish* means "expert in . . ." (*see 'ish*) and the male connotation derives from the association with battle.

In any case, these male metaphors not show that God is imagined as male outside of the poetic figures or forms of address.

⚘ Marriage

The Bible neither defines marriage nor even has a word for it. Yet clearly it was a basic societal institution in ancient Israel. A woman's transfer of from one corporate household (*see* House) to another greatly affected the daily life and the economy of both—particularly if she was becoming the primary wife in her new household. Because it was such an important transaction, it was negotiated by the heads of the two households (*see* Householder).

A man's acquiring a wife was not the same as purchasing property. It was more like a modern sports team acquiring a player who's currently under contract to another franchise in the league: the other team needs to be compensated for its loss. The exchange also helped to strengthen the alliance between the two families. The society had legally binding expectations that regulated marriage even in the absence of a written contract between the parties.

The Torah calls marriage "taking a wife," which in almost every case meant that the bride moved into the groom's household—i.e., he took her into the household in which he lived. Unlike NJPS, the present adaptation uses only that terminology—rather than the word "marry"—in order to underscore marriage's gender-marked spatial relocation.

❧ Menstruation

The Hebrew term *niddah* refers to menstruation (e.g., Lev. 12:2, 15:19) and falls within the scope of a gender-focused study because of what its rendering conveys about the valence with which women were viewed. NJPS rendered *niddah* as "impurity," following a plausible view that this word means "something to be shunned." According to other opinions, the terms are more neutrally about avoiding contact, for the text does not imply that this type of impurity is to be "shunned" more than other. And still other scholars point to a different root and state that *niddah* refers to the flow of blood itself. The present adaptation favored the second view (which yields the basic rendering as "separation") while incorporating the third sense as an overtone.

❧ Messenger

The present translation uses the word "messenger" to render the Hebrew term *mal'akh* regardless of whether the latter refers to a human or a divine agent. (Like *mal'akh*, "messenger" designates not only one who bears a message but also one who does any kind of errand.) Ancient Near Eastern usage did not distinguish between such agents. Thus the Septuagint—the ancient Jewish translation of the Hebrew Bible into Greek—similarly used the same term (*angelos*) either for a human or a divine messenger. In contrast, whenever the context suggests a divine being, NJPS—like many other English translations—rendered *mal'akh* as "angel." In the Torah, the NJPS approach seems inapt, for it misleadingly conjures an image of a white-robed winged figure. But in the eyes of the Torah's original audience, the biblical terminology would have evoked an emissary who happens to be from God but is expected to follow the protocols observed with human emissaries (*see* Agent).

In the ancient Near East, messengers not only delivered messages but also escorted individuals on behalf of the principal (cf., e.g., Gen. 12:20; 24:7) and confronted those with whom the principal wished to settle a score (cf., e.g., 2 Kings 6:32; Gen. 32:25).

One term that the Bible often uses for messenger is *'ish* (*see entry*). The present translation sometimes uses words such as "emissary" or "envoy" where NJPS and others typically read "man." This is because the text's conspicuous usage of *'ish* in the context of agency would have reliably evoked in the original audience's minds the sense of *'ish* as "representative functionary" (*see 'ish*; Agent). This nuance of *'ish* would have significantly affected that audience's interpretation of several passages in Genesis, particularly chapters 18–19.

Regarding the gender of divine messengers ("angels"): In the ancient Near East, the tendency was for men to appoint male agents, while women appointed female agents. To the extent that the Torah presented its God as *beyond* gender—and quite apart from other contextual indications of social gender—it might well have portrayed that God either as an "equal opportunity employer" of messengers, or as dispatching non-gendered divine agents.

✋ Na'ar

The common noun *na'ar* discloses not only gender but also social status. Its social-gender sense is clearly male in definite usage—which would typically go without saying.

The term *na'ar* affects the contextual social-gender sense of *'anashim* in Sodom (Gen. 19:4). Also, NJPS once renders the plural *na'arim* as "some young men" in a nonspecific context where gender does not seem to be at issue (Exod. 24:5). After I revisited the meaning of *na'ar* in those passages, I reviewed its rendering throughout NJPS's *The Torah*, for the sake of consistency.

The term *na'ar* most fundamentally denotes subordination, which is expressed in various ways. One of the most common tasks performed by *na'arim* in the Bible is communicating information to their superiors, e.g., Num. 11:27. Where the context suggests that social status is at issue, I have rendered accordingly. Hence, for example, Exod. 24:5 now reads "some assistants."

✋ Names

In the Bible and in extrabiblical Israelite texts, men typically have received names that are grammatically masculine (technically, the names are *unmarked* for gender), while women's given names are usually grammatically feminine. However, some women have names that are unmarked or even masculine (e.g., Hodesh, Jael, Merab, Rahab, Tamar), whereas some men have feminine names (e.g., Becorath, Goliath, Hirah, Judah, Shammah, Uzzah). In terms of their form, the names Abimelech (a man) and Abigail (a woman) are identical, as are Eliezer (a man) and Elisheba (a woman). Most tellingly, Gomer, Micaiah, and Shelomith are biblical names for both genders. In short, in Hebrew the name alone is not a wholly reliable indicator of a character's gender.

Israelites generally identified themselves and their family property by the "father's" name only. Comparison with the practices of other cultures suggests that this naming practice indicated endogamy, rather than signaling the mothers' lack of importance.

✹ Predecessors

The Torah often mentions predecessors when it speaks of death, employing idioms such as "going to one's *'avoth* (ancestors)," e.g., Gen. 15:15, or "being gathered to one's *'ammim* (kinfolk)," e.g., Gen. 35:29. Likewise, one of the Torah's commonly cited penalties for violation of covenantal precepts is to be "cut off from one's *'ammim* (kinfolk)," e.g., Exod 30:33. Circumstantial evidence suggests that the text's original audience would have understood these references to predecessors as gender-inclusive. Archeology has shown that both men and women were buried in ancient Israel's family tombs. Given the norm of endogamy (marrying within one's lineage), one's predecessors—regardless of gender—typically were buried nearby, within the area of one's own village or that of the next village. That family tomb represented the larger entity of deceased ancestors, who remained in communion with the living (in a manner that is unclear to us today). One's corporate household (*see* House) included one's predecessors.

Biblical evidence is consistent with a gender-inclusive view of predeceased kin (Lev. 21:1–3, 5; Deut. 21:13). Foremothers counted as national ancestors (e.g., Gen. 35:20; 1 Sam. 10:2; Jer. 31:15–17). And just as the Bible portrays mothers as possessing offspring (*see* Seed), so too it would seem that offspring perceived themselves as descended from female ancestors (Judg. 9:1).

Furthermore, some ancient Near Eastern texts imply that the ancients imagined that gender relations continued relatively unimpeded after death, in the netherworld. This implies that the kinship relations were also preserved (including the respect and authority commanded by mothers). In Mesopotamia, both male and female ghosts received offerings from their living descendants; many scholars leave open the possibility that the ancient Israelites also served their ancestors in a similar way.

Therefore the present translation renders inclusively references to *'avot* and *'ammim* as predecessors (typically as "ancestors" and "kin," respectively).

℘ Sacrificial offerings

Leviticus opens its extensive discussion of sacrificial offerings with the conspicuous use of common-gender nouns (*'adam* and *nefesh*) that refer to the worshiper who brings such offerings (e.g., Lev. 1:2; 2:1) and thus is subject to the need for ritual purity (e.g., Lev. 7:20–21). Leviticus thus signals that its schema of offerings is open to, and required for, both men and women.

A person could participate in a sacrificial offering as the technician who literally executed the sacrifice. In ancient Israel—a rural society—nearly everyone worked and literally lived with livestock. Each corporate household slaughtered and dressed its own animals. The text of Leviticus thus presumed that most Israelites would perform their own slaughter at the sanctuary (cf. 1 Sam. 1:25). Although the Bible mentions women's involvement only in profane slaughter (1 Sam. 28:24–25), ancient Near Eastern texts and pictures portray sacrificial slaughter by women as well as men. Thus the Torah probably had both genders in view when mentioning sacrificial slaughter.

A second way of participating in a sacrificial offering was as the representative of the corporate household that brought offerings on certain occasions. That person would lay hands on the designated animal, present it to the priest, and (after the meat was cooked) distribute portions of the meal.

The third way of participating in the offering was simply to eat the meal in communion with those present, including God. This was actually the operative step; without it, what had gone on beforehand was rendered meaningless. Deuteronomy insists that both men and women take part in this step (e.g., 12:18, 16:14).

℘ Seed (*zera'*)

The grammatically masculine noun *zera'* literally means "seed." Where the term refers to human beings, NJPS typically renders *zera'* as "offspring." Calling human progeny "seed" is analogous to calling agricultural produce "seed" (e.g., Lev. 27:30). (However, the Bible employs the term *zera'* to designate progeny six times more often than to designate plant grains or produce!) The significance of this trope is underscored by the fact that the Bible knows at least seven synonyms for referring to offspring in addition to *zera'*—yet the latter term is by far the most common.

The Bible neither clearly confirms nor denies the mother's biological contribution of "life-essence" to her offspring. The usage of *zera'* does not appear to be relevant to that question. "Seed" is not about biology; rather, it is a social category. Thus female characters have "seed" (Gen. 3:15, 16:10, 24:60; Lev. 22:13; Isaiah 54:3) and yield "seed" (Lev. 12:2), but that does not reflect on the social-gender construction of procreation.

The noun *zera'* by itself neither denotes nor connotes semen. The Bible employs the cognate verb (*zara'* "to sow") forty-two times and not once does it mean inseminating a woman. The noun alone—when applied to humans—never refers to the male's contribution to procreation. In the construct expression *shikhvat zera'* (which occurs with slight variations eight times in the Torah; lit. "a laying down of seed"), *zera'* refers elliptically to the outcome: "the laying down of [what will become] seed (i.e., offspring)." (Compare the wording in Lev. 18:20, and contrast the reference to semen in 20:15—where *zera'* is not mentioned presumably because offspring are not possible.)

Both in ancient Israel and in the Bible, generating both produce and progeny is ultimately the responsibility of the householder (*see entry*). For that reason, the Torah typically attributes the family's "seed" (offspring) to men rather than to women.

☙ Social order

Social order in ancient Israel (even under monarchy or imperial governor) was maintained mainly by a "balanced opposition" between groups, each of which was typically headed by a man.

Speaking schematically, the nation of Israel comprised several (nominally twelve) *tribes*, each of which in turn included several *lineages* (which NJPS usually calls "clans"), each of which in turn consisted of several *corporate households* (*see* House), each of which was made up of several nuclear families. When individuals interacted, they desired to elevate the social position of their own group relative to other such groups. To the extent that two individuals each identified with parallel groups, their interests were viewed as *opposing* each other. (Hence the social-science term "balanced opposition.") The overall societal arrangement is illustrated by two sayings from the present-day Middle East: "I against my brother, I and my brother against my cousins, I and my cousins against the world"; and "We are brothers, yet when we evaluate the inventory, we are enemies."

In practically any social situation, all parties were expected to affirm where they stood, societally speaking; but where one stood partly depended upon the particulars of the situation—assessment always being relative to another person or group. As everyone jockeyed for relative standing, the social and political alignments between groups could shift—which would be conveyed by a corresponding change in genealogy.

Encounters between individuals from different groups began with a habitual statement of relative social position, with the inferior or more compliant party showing deference (by prostration and by referring to the other party as "my lord" and to oneself as "your servant" or the like). A prime opportunity to re-align group allegiances was the contracting of a marriage (*see entry*).

❧ *ṭaph* ("child, dependent")

This is a collective noun, unmarked for gender. It refers to a variable category of a community's members and takes its precise meaning—and thus its social-gender sense—from the context. It is not strictly an age grade, although in Num. 14:31 it refers to persons up to age twenty (cf. v. 29).

When counterposed in the text with *gevarim* ("men") or with the collective term *zakhar* ("combatants"), *ṭaph* is a technical term that refers to everyone else—that is, women, children, and infirm or disabled men (Exod. 10:10, 12:37; Num. 31:9, 17, 18).

❧ You (second-person address)

The Torah often addresses its reader, or the Israelite people, in the second person. The implied gender(s) of the audience must be gleaned from the immediate context, understanding that the referent of "you" shifts fluidly as relevant. The speaker (e.g., God or Moses) may momentarily single out a portion of the audience—for example, only parents (Deut. 6:20); certain sub-groups of men (Deut. 1:41, 3:18, 20:1); householders and their wives (Deut. 5:14, 12:7; *see* Householder); or everyone except priests and

Levites (who are referred to as "them" rather than "you"). Yet all of these addressees remain inseparable parts of the Israelites as a whole. This is like a contemporary conductor who, while the orchestra performs a piece, gestures to a section of musicians without neglecting the rest of the ensemble.

In other words, grammatically masculine address does not in itself restrict the social gender of the addressee to men, as certain expressions make clear (Deut. 7:13; 28:4, 68).